D1571309

AIRCRAFT CARRIERS

AIRCRAFT CARRIERS

The World's Greatest Carriers of the last 100 Years

DAVID ROSS

This Amber edition published in 2022

Reprinted in 2023

First published as *The World's Greatest Aircraft Carriers* in 2017

Published by Amber Books Ltd
United House
North Road
London
N7 9DP
United Kingdom
www.amberbooks.co.uk
Instagram: amberbooksltd
Facebook: amberbooks
Twitter: @amberbooks
Pinterest: amberbooksltd

ISBN: 978-1-83886-158-2

Project Editor: Michael Spilling
Picture Research: Terry Forshaw
Design: Andrew Easton

Printed in China

PICTURE CREDITS:
Alamy: 79 (PJF Military Collection), 143, (PJF Military Collection),174 (Dino Fracchia), 175 & 195 (Charles Polidano), 198 (Reuters), 211 (Jim Gibson), 218 & 219 (Reuters/Sivaram V)
Art-Tech: 13, 17, 24, 41, 53, 109, 130, 151
Cody Images: 8, 21, 29, 32, 33, 37, 45, 48, 56, 57, 61, 68, 69, 73, 77, 84, 89, 93, 97, 101, 112, 119, 122, 123, 126, 159, 163
Dreamstime: 187 (Drew Rawcliffe), 202 & 203 (Colin Moore)
Getty Images: 129 (Gamma-Rapho/Eric Bouvet), 199 (Visual China Group), 206 & 207 (The Ashahi Shinbun)
Huntington Ingalls: 214, 215
Royal Navy: 210
U.S. Department of Defense: 7, 92, 105, 113, 114, 134, 135, 147 both, 154, 155, 166, 167, 170, 171, 179, 183, 190, 191

Artworks:
All artworks Art-Tech except for the following:
Huntington Ingalls: 212/213
Military Visualizations, Inc.: 148–151 all, 184–194 all
Patrick Mulrey © Amber Books: 120/121, 196–209 all, 216/217

Contents

Introduction

The aircraft carrier was the most revolutionary naval vessel of the twentieth century. Other types of warship, even the submarine, had a development history going back into the previous century.

There was nothing new about ships with manned aerial devices for military use: air balloons had been launched from naval craft for observational or even bomb-dropping purposes from the late eighteenth century. Two things made the carrier different. One was the powered aeroplane, which from 1903 opened the way to new opportunities for warfare. The other was the design of the vessel. Throughout history, ships had been designed and built on the basis of a centreline, with each side being like a mirror-image of the other. The very first carriers tried to replicate this, but it was soon realized that a different approach was needed: they could launch a plane but not land it again. This led to the 'flat top', a ship with all superstructure, even the funnel, squeezed between a full-length flight deck that was raised above the normal main deck, giving the carrier its characteristic hull profile.

USS *Lexington* (CVN-2) in 1931 with Martin VT-1B T4M torpedo bombers being readied for take-off.

As a solution this did not make for ease of navigation or flight control, and the 'island' superstructure was devised, normally on the starboard side or sponsoned out from it.

Air support

The value of air support for naval ships was first realized in the scouting and reconnaissance function, and thought was very quickly given to carrying planes on shipboard. The first military plane was delivered to the US Navy in June 1909, and on 14 November 1910 Eugene Burton Ely was the first man to take off in a powered aircraft from a ship, USS *Birmingham*. His Curtiss Pusher biplane used a downwards sloping ramp fitted over the bow and momentarily touched the water before gaining height. On 18 January 1911, he was first to make a shipboard landing on a specially-rigged 36.5m (120ft) platform with primitive 'arrester' gear of sandbags and ropes, mounted on USS *Pennsylvania*.

On 9 May 1912, the first take-off from a moving ship was made from HMS *Hibernia* as it steamed into the wind

USS *Nimitz* (CVN-68) in the Gulf of Oman, 22 May 2007, in the course of a maritime operations security and stability patrol.

at 10.5 knots (19.4km/h; 12mph). Enthusiastic officers in other navies were also pressing for attention to be given to this new dimension of action. There was a great deal to be learned, mostly by trial and error, although new scientific equipment, such as wind tunnels, was also employed, and simulated carrier decks were laid out at ground bases.

The concept of the flat-topped ship to launch and land wheeled aircraft was accepted with remarkable speed in Britain's traditionally conservative naval circles, helped by three factors: firstly, from August 1914 World War I was being fought, and innovative ideas that promised a tactical or strategic advantage were at a premium; secondly, aircraft overflying the sea were both immune to submarines and well placed to spot them and either report their presence – by 1916 spotter seaplanes were able to send radio messages back to their tenders – or attack them; and thirdly, the admirals in charge of the Grand Fleet were pressing strongly for more effective air cover.

Numerous British battleships and cruisers were equipped with short fly-off platforms mounted on main gun turrets, the turrets chosen because they could swivel to face the wind without the ship altering direction, and large warships routinely carried aircraft until the end of World War II. The first warship to fly off an aircraft by the use of a catapult was USS *North Carolina*, test-launching a Curtiss AB-2 plane on 5 November 1915. But these developments did nothing to hinder the concept of the dedicated carrier. In 1917, starting with HMS *Furious*, the official designation of 'aircraft carrier' as a ship type was introduced.

Treaty boost

By the end of the war the concept of the carrier was firmly established. The post-war Washington Naval Treaty of 1922 gave it a further unintended push forward. Most navies had very large cruisers or battleships still under construction from the war period, but the building of new capital ships was limited by the Treaty, and also most of these vessels were beyond the requirements of a peacetime fleet. Some were simply scrapped, but numerous hulls were converted into carriers, saving the cost of building complete new ships. In a remarkably short time, a little over a decade, the aircraft carrier had gone from non-existence to a position of prominence and growing strategic importance in every navy.

N-6454

Carriers of the World Wars

The outbreak of war in August 1914 and the consequent build-up of naval forces had a strong effect on the development of a naval air arm. The British Navy, then the world's largest, led the way in the introduction of the aircraft carrier, although this did not come until the late stages of World War I and had little impact on the actual conflict. Its effect on post-war naval policy was substantial. The US and Japanese navies were also quick to seize on the carrier concept. There was no unity of design, and in the 1920s a variety of battleship and cruiser conversions appeared, including ships with two- and even three-level flight decks. It was not until the 1930s that purpose-built carriers began to be planned, and until 1936 construction of new ships was restricted by the tonnage limits imposed by the Washington Naval Treaty of 1922.

A Sopwith Camel plane (introduced in 1917) being craned up to the flight deck of HMS *Furious*, 1918.

HMS Furious (1917)

Originally intended as a cruiser, *Furious* became the first warship in regular use as an aircraft carrier, undergoing successive conversions from partial to full flight deck. With HMS *Argus* it was one of only two ships to serve as a carrier in both World Wars.

One of three sister ships planned as heavy-gun cruisers for coastal bombardment in the Baltic Sea, all of which ended up as carriers, *Furious* was laid down at Armstrong Whitworth's Elswick Yard on the Tyne on 8 June 1915. In 1917 the design was modified to allow for a short flight deck with a small hangar and lift instead of a forward gun turret, and later the aft turret was removed to provide a further short flight deck. Ramps were fitted on each side of the superstructure to enable the movement of planes from end to end. Although Squadron Commander E.H. Dunning made the first successful landing on a carrier steaming into the wind in a Sopwith Pup on *Furious* on 2 August 1917, he was killed in his second attempt. *Furious* at that time had no arrester gear, and deck landings were abandoned as too risky. Incoming planes had to be ditched or find a land site. In this form, the ship mounted

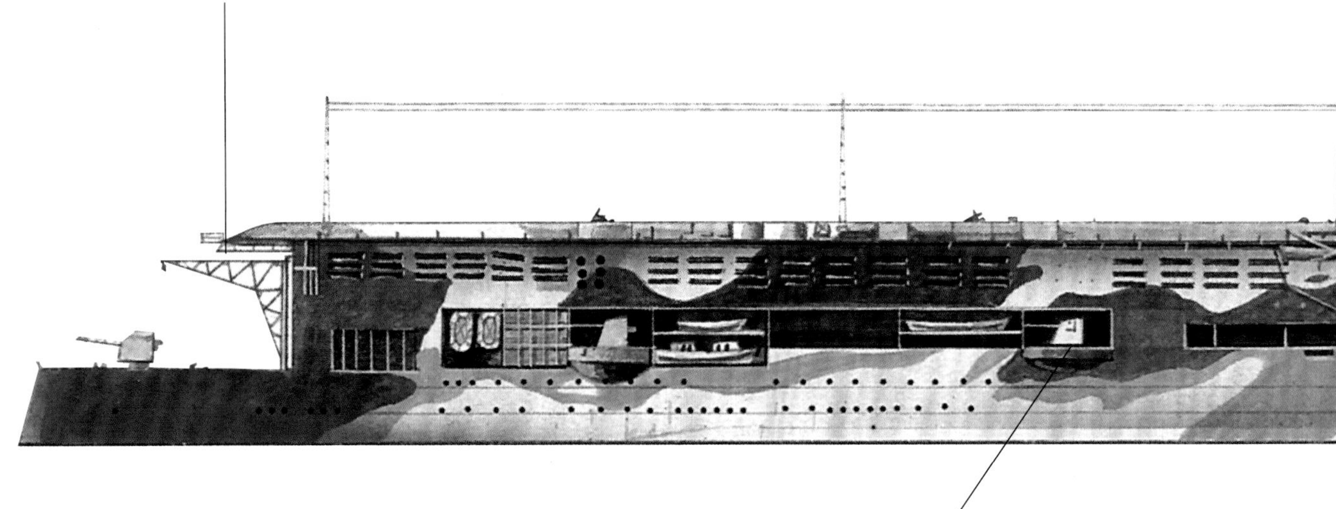

the first carrier-borne hostile operation, a successful raid on the Zeppelin base at Tondern, Schleswig-Holstein, on 19 July 1918, when its seven Sopwith Camel 2F.1 planes destroyed two Zeppelins and their sheds.

Conversion

The vessel's design was not, however, considered adequate to the action required, and *Furious* underwent further alteration between 1921 and 1925 to become a full flush-deck carrier, although at first the flush deck was used only for landings and a short lower-level launch deck was retained over the bow (removed in 1932). The bridge structure and funnel, which had caused problems for pilots because of eddying air currents, were removed, with all control centres situated beneath the flight deck, and exhaust gases ducted to the stern on the model of HMS *Argus*. *Furious* was also the first carrier to have the after edge of the flight deck rounded down rather than presenting a sharp edge, which smoothed airflow as it steamed into the wind; the first on which different arrester wire methods were tested, although at first the systems were longitudinal, intended more to keep planes from

HMS *Furious* in camouflage paintwork. This form of visual deception, developed in World War I, was employed throughout World War II.

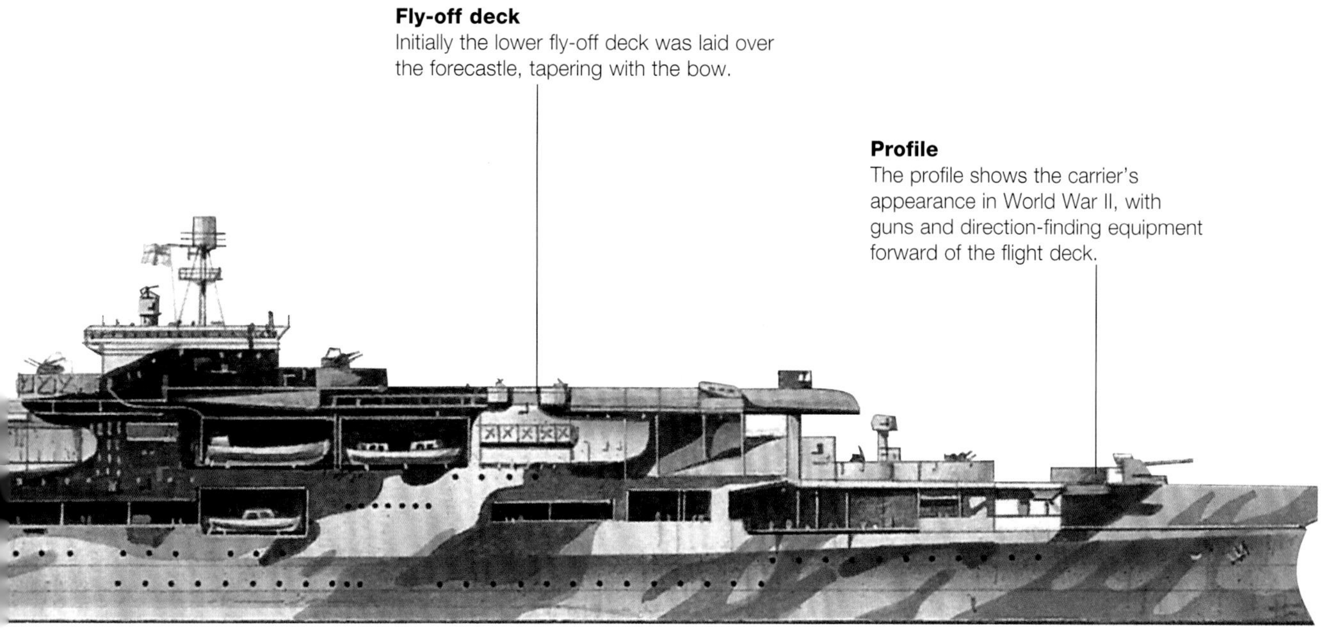

Fly-off deck
Initially the lower fly-off deck was laid over the forecastle, tapering with the bow.

Profile
The profile shows the carrier's appearance in World War II, with guns and direction-finding equipment forward of the flight deck.

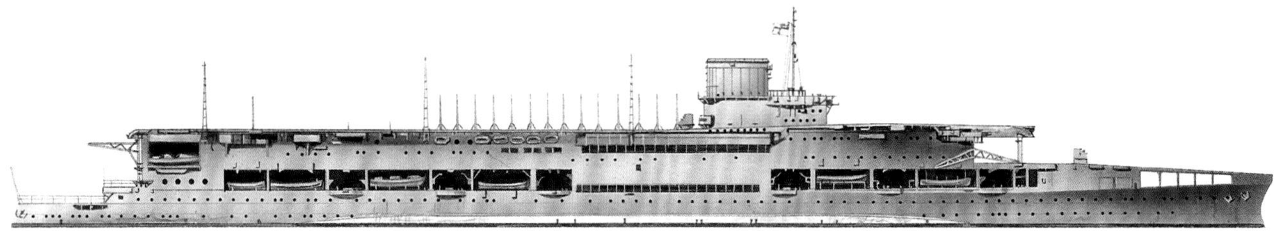

HMS *Courageous*, though built on an identical hull, had a different design as a carrier to *Furious*. The best form of the carrier was still being explored.

veering off the deck than to slow them down, which was hardly necessary with the slow speeds of the time. At this time the sister ships *Courageous* and *Glorious* were also being converted to carriers.

More changes were made to *Furious* in 1931–32, when the stern was built up to the level of the flight deck, and in 1939 when a small island was added on the starboard side, and it was equipped for anti-aircraft defence with six twin 102mm (4in) guns and two gunnery directors, supplemented by three 8-barrelled 2-pdr pom-pom guns. The main propulsion was provided by four Brown-Curtis geared turbines, powered by 18 Yarrow small-tube boilers and driving four screws. The hull was partially armoured with 51–76mm (2–3in) plate to give protection to the engines and steering gear, and anti-torpedo blisters were applied.

The Sopwith Camels first carried on *Furious* were not designed for carriers. In the 1920s a few types adapted for naval use appeared, including the Avro Bison and Blackburn R-1 Blackburn spotter planes, the Blackburn Dart torpedo bomber, the Westland Walrus reconnaissance plane and the Gloster Mars X Nightjar and Fairey Flycatcher, both fighters. In 1940 *Furious* was carrying Fairey Swordfish and Gloster Sea Gladiators.

In World War II *Furious* had a busy and peripatetic career, transporting 28 aircraft squadrons to various destinations apart from its own participation in carrier-borne air strikes. It was with the Home Fleet in the North-western Approaches in September 1939 and took part in hunts for the battleship *Scharnhorst* and cruiser *Köln* in October and November, carrying 18 Fairey Swordfish planes. Continuing in Atlantic convoy duty (on one of which it transported £18,000,000 of gold bullion to Canada for safety) and ocean patrols until April 1940, it then gave support to destroyers in the Battle of Narvik.

Specification

Dimensions:	Length: 224.1m (735ft 2in); Beam: 26.8m (88ft); Draught: 8.3m (27ft 3in)
Displacement:	22,900 tonnes (22,500 tons); 26,900 tonnes (26,500 tons) deep load
Propulsion:	18 Yarrow boilers, 4 Brown-Curtis geared turbines, four shafts; 67,113kW (90,000shp)
Speed:	30 knots (56km/h; 34.5mph)
Range:	7480nm (13,850km; 8610 miles) at 10 knots (18.5km/h; 11.5mph)
Armament:	10 BL 140mm (5.5in) Mk 1 guns, 6 QF 102mm (4in) AA guns
Aircraft:	36
Complement:	795

Lone survivor

After *Glorious* was sunk by *Scharnhorst* it was the only operational carrier in the Norwegian battle zone. On 22 September 1940 it launched 11 Swordfish torpedo bombers, with air cover from six Skua fighters, against German positions around Trondheim, losing five of the Swordfish and one Skua. From December 1940 to July 1941 it was involved with aircraft transport to West Africa and Malta, and troop transport to Gibraltar, apart from a short refit spell at Harland & Wolff's Belfast yard, where it was struck by a bomb on 8 May without serious damage. It then escorted a convoy to Archangel in Northern Russia, made two further plane-ferry trips to Gibraltar and carried planes to Jamaica before undergoing a more substantial refit at the US Navy Yard in Philadelphia, including provision of enhanced Type 285 fire control radar.

Fully operational again from July 1942, *Furious* joined in the much-attacked aircraft supply chain to beat the siege of Malta, then continued to serve in the Mediterranean, surviving at least two attempts by Italian submarines to sink it, and gaining Type 286 radar for air and surface warning. During Operation Torch, the North African landings, it flew its aircraft in sorties against Vichy French airfields in Algeria. By February 1943 it was back with the Home Fleet, serving both in the Western Approaches and on convoy escort duty to Russia. From August to December 1943 it underwent a refit. It was frequently back in Norwegian waters in early 1944, participating in the series of airborne attacks made to sink or immobilize the battleship *Tirpitz*, moored in Kaa Fjord. In October that year it was withdrawn from active service and used for aircrew training. *Furious* was decommissioned in March 1945 and placed on the reserve list. On 23 January 1948 it was sold for breaking.

Profile redesign

HMS *Courageous*, with a hull identical to that of *Furious* but converted later, and commissioned as a carrier in February 1928, displayed a very different profile, with a large vertical funnel set on a small starboard island that held the navigation bridge and flying control station. The profile shows the lower, downwards-tilted forward flight deck, removed in the early 1930s. Experience with *Furious* and improvements in carriers' internal design enabled *Courageous* to carry 48 aircraft compared to *Furious's* 36. Only lightly armoured, it was sunk off Ireland by two torpedoes from U-boat Type VIIA U-29 on 17 September 1939, the first carrier casualty of World War II.

HMS *Courageous* showing the bow flight deck. Note the cranes to port and starboard. In 1931 this became the first British carrier to mount transverse arrester wires to make landings more secure.

HMS Argus (1918)

Commenced as a passenger liner in 1914, it became the first carrier with a full-length flight deck but was commissioned too late for action in World War I. It was first a plane ferry, then for a time a fighting carrier in World War II.

The Glasgow shipbuilder William Beardmore took an early interest in naval aviation and had actually proposed a flat-deck carrier to the Admiralty in 1912. It may have been more than a coincidence that a ship on Beardmore's stocks, laid down at Dalmuir on the Clyde in 1914 as *Conte Rosso* for the Italian Lloyd Subuado company, was acquired by the Admiralty in September 1916. As HMS *Argus* it was launched on 2 December 1917.

Lessons were learned from *Argus*'s top-heavy tendency to roll, as originally converted. Its flat top and pointed bow gained it the nickname 'Flat Iron'.

Flight deck
Only 17.7m (58ft) wide until 1938, the flight deck was barely wider than the aircraft carried, and three planes were blown off by wind on the ship's first cruise.

Cranes
Two seaplane cranes were fitted on the quarterdeck.

Commissioned on 16 September 1918, it was the first carrier in the world to be fitted with a full-length flight deck, enabling wheeled aircraft to land on board, and earning the nickname 'flat iron'. The hull was that of a merchant ship, and armour was applied only as a 50mm (2in) box round the after magazine and torpedo room, while the forward magazine was protected only by a 50mm (2in) deck above it.

Unique appearance

Lessons learned from the conversion of HMS *Furious* to a carrier with only a partial flight deck at first were applied in the design, which initially had provided for island units both to starboard and port, with a bridge deck between them, literally bridging a passageway for planes from one end to the other. This was partly to accommodate two funnels, one on each side. The final fitting-out cost £1.3 million and resulted in a ship of unique appearance. In the end a flush-deck design won the day. A small retractable pilot house was placed behind the forecastle, for use when there were no launchings planned. Exhaust smoke and fumes from the boilers were trunked to the stern through tubes set between the flight deck and the roof of the hangar deck, with some of the heat dissipated by electric fans. Two cranes were mounted on the quarterdeck below the stern end of the flight deck. Two centreline lifts were fitted, one well forward, for the first time on a carrier.

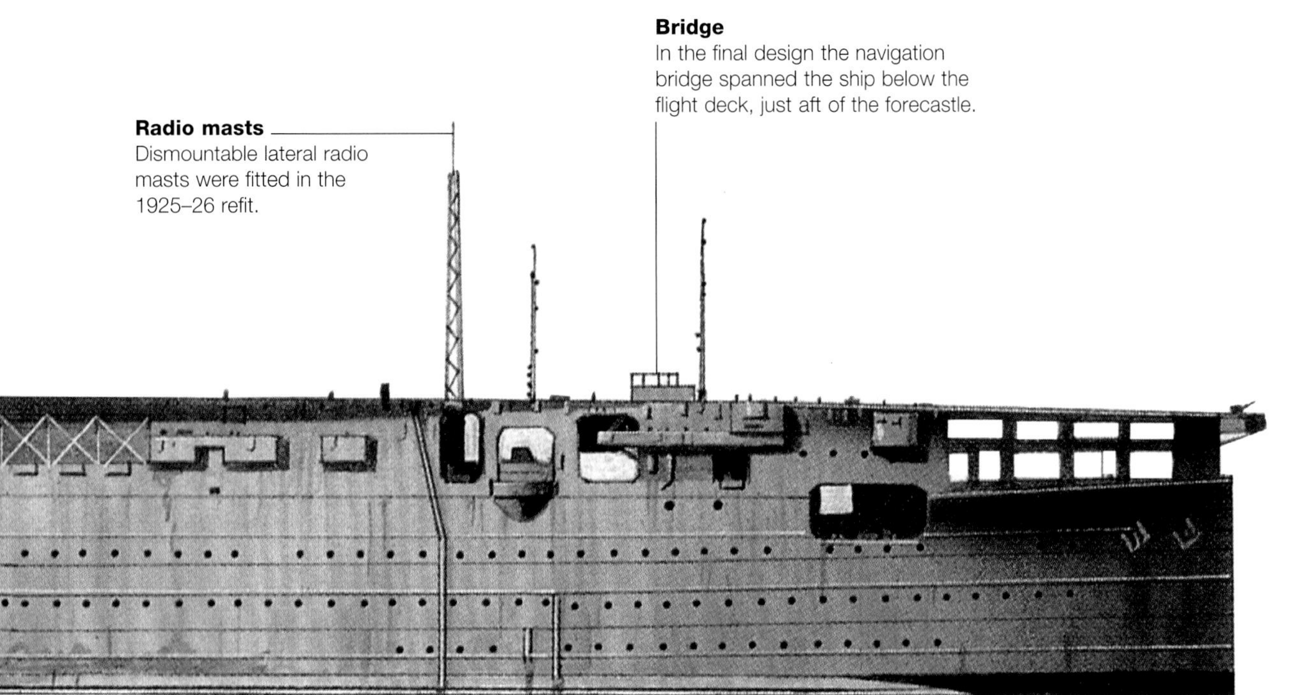

HMS Argus

A Blackburn Skua Mk 2 dive-bomber of 806 Squadron. The Fleet Air Arm's first monoplane, the Skua was a carrier-based dive-bomber introduced in November 1938. Its slow speed led to its withdrawal from front-line service in 1941.

By the time it was commissioned, the war was almost at an end, and *Argus*'s primary role in the 1920s was to be as a testing and training ship to develop the functions of a carrier to steadily greater efficiency. A substantial refit was carried out in 1925, which saw the installation of tanks for aviation fuel, previously carried in 9-litre (two-gallon) cans. The weight of the flight deck on the long narrow hull had resulted in a top-heavy design that affected the ship's stability, and a bulge was fitted along the waterline level in the refit, also offering some protection against torpedoes.

Powered by 12 cylindrical Scotch fire-tube boilers, and four Parsons steam turbines driving four screws, it had only a moderate turn of speed, 20 knots (37km/h; 23mph) maximum, something that would be improved in later carriers. *Argus* turned out to be an easily manoeuvrable ship at high speed, although carrier navigators had to learn to cope with high winds blowing against the high blank sides of the ship and exerting a powerful influence on how it made its way. Four low-angle 102mm (4in) guns were mounted on the forecastle and stern decks, and four 102mm AA guns were mounted laterally on sponsons. *Argus* could carry up to 18 aircraft, at first a squadron of 12 Sopwith Cuckoo torpedo planes and six Sopwith Camel fighters. On a cruise with the Atlantic Fleet in January 1920 it carried Sopwith Strutters, Camels, two Airco DH.9A bombers and two Fairey floatplanes. At other times in the 1920s it carried such planes of the period as Parnall Panthers, Gloster Nightjar and Bristol fighters. Later World War II aircraft carried included Fairey Swordfish and Skuas.

Argus was initially painted in camouflage style before assuming peacetime naval grey. Initially, arrester gear transferred from HMS *Furious* was installed, although later it too would try out various forms. Its first plane landing was on 1 October 1918. In September 1922 it was deployed to the Dardanelles to give air cover to a British naval squadron during the Chanak Crisis when a war between Britain and Turkey seemed possible, and served at Hong Kong on the China Station in the winter of 1927–28. From 1928 to 1936 it was on reserve. In 1936–38 it was refitted as an auxiliary tender for target-towing aircraft, with guns removed, new engines and

Specification

Dimensions:	Length: 172.2m (565ft); Beam: 20.7m (68ft); Draught: 7m (23ft 2in)
Displacement:	14,935 tonnes (14,700 tons); 16,028 tonnes (15,775 tons) deep load
Propulsion:	12 Scotch boilers, 4 Parsons turbines, 2 shafts; 15,000kW (20,000shp)
Speed:	20 knots (37km/h; 23mph)
Range:	3563nm (6598km; 4100 miles)
Armament:	4 102mm (4in) guns, 4 102mm (4in) AA guns
Aircraft:	48
Complement:	495

Argus as it appeared in 1938, with the bow plated up to flight-deck level, though large apertures allowed the mooring deck to be used.

The 'smallest aircraft carrier'

At the same time as *Argus* the Royal Navy produced the H-class 'Seaplane lighter', a barge fitted with a 18.3m (60ft) tilted ramp. In total 35 were built. At first it carried a light biplane flying boat, but a test flight of a Sopwith Pup biplane armed with a machine gun on 21 July 1918 showed that wheeled aircraft could also be launched from the minimal flight deck. With the barge towed by a motor boat into a headwind at a speed of around 20 knots (37km/h; 23mph), the plane's engine was started and revved to full power while held by chocks and ties. With these pulled away, the plane was launched.
On 10 August 1918 a Pup launched from H21 attacked and destroyed Zeppelin L53. This 'smallest aircraft carrier' served its purpose in deterring further Zeppelin raids. A restored H-class boat is preserved at the Fleet Air Arm Museum at Yeovilton, England.

the flight deck widened by 3m (10ft); it was also used in flight training. AA protection was restored in early 1940, with two 102mm (4in) anti-aircraft guns and three Vickers quadruple machine-gun mountings. All that was available at the time, these were later replaced by Oerlikon 20mm AA guns.

Training ship

In the early years of World War II, carrying No. 767 naval air squadron flying Fairey Swordfish planes, it was engaged in convoy escort and aircraft-ferrying duties to Iceland, Malta, the Gold Coast (Ghana), Gibraltar and Murmansk. In June 1942 *Argus* provided air protection for a Malta-bound convoy in Operation Harpoon, and in November it supported the North African landings and sustained a bomb hit, which killed four of the crew and required a return to the UK for repairs. It was reclassified as an escort carrier in May 1943, but by this time more up-to-date ships were becoming available, and it continued to be used for pilot training. *Argus* last saw service with aircraft on 27 September 1944, and was then used at Chatham Dockyard as an accommodation ship from January to August 1945. Sold for scrapping in December 1946, it was broken up in 1947.

HMS Eagle (1924)

Like all the first-generation carriers, *Eagle* was not originally intended for the role, and retained much of its battleship appearance even after conversion to an aircraft carrier.

The Chilean Navy ordered the dreadnought-type battleship *Almirante Cochrane* from Armstrong Whitworth's yard on the Tyne in July 1912, and it was laid down on 20 February 1913, but work ceased with the outbreak of war in August 1914. On 13 February 1918 the British Admiralty completed purchase of the unfinished hull for conversion into a seaplane carrier, subsequently amended to be a standard aircraft carrier, and was first commissioned as HMS *Eagle* at Devonport on 6 April 1920. Intensive trials ensued, with the focus on deck landings, the trickiest aspect of naval aviation then and now, and further work went on at Portsmouth Dockyard, including extension of the island and the fitting of anti-torpedo bulges. It was recommissioned on 26 February 1924, at which time it was the largest aircraft carrier in the world.

The dreadnought-type hull was very evident, with the hangar decks built up over it, and a full-length armoured flight deck. A substantial island structure was mounted to starboard.

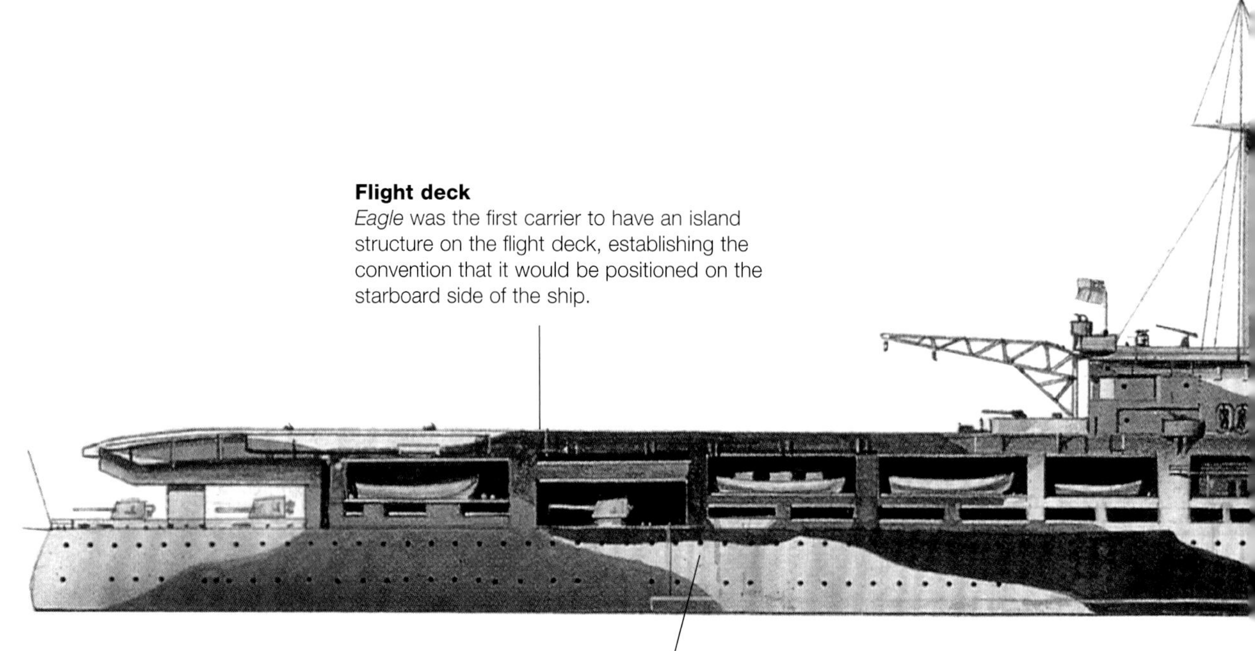

Flight deck
Eagle was the first carrier to have an island structure on the flight deck, establishing the convention that it would be positioned on the starboard side of the ship.

Engine room
The engine room instruments were ordered prior to purchase by the British, and uniquely for a British warship were calibrated in metric units and labelled in Spanish.

This location was chosen after wind tunnel tests showed that it created least smoke interference and turbulence from hot funnel exhaust for planes coming in to land at the stern. Stern landings, with the ship steaming into the wind, were greatly preferable to help with speed reduction.

Eagle had two masts and two funnels – the only Royal Navy carrier so fitted. As part of the conversion the fuel supply was changed from part-coal and part-oil to oil alone. The bunkers held 3088 tonnes (3040 tons) of fuel oil for the ship's own engines, and 14,000 litres (3083 gals) of aviation fuel. Power came from 32 Yarrow water-tube boilers, with four Parsons geared steam turbines and four screws. Nine 152mm (6in) guns were mounted on the main deck. Armour consisted of a 114mm belt (4.5in), deck armour of 25–38mm (1–1.5in) and 102mm (4in) transverse bulkheads. Two aircraft lifts were fitted, one just forward of the island, the other at the stern. *Eagle*'s battleship-type hull restricted it to carry a maximum of 24 aircraft, usually only 20–21. On its final mission it was carrying 20 Sea Hurricanes, although at earlier stages in World War II it also flew Fairey Swordfish, Fairey Flycatchers, Gloster Sea Gladiators and Fairey Fulmars.

For most of the later 1920s *Eagle* was with the Mediterranean Fleet, introducing full carrier-based activity as part of that fleet's operations for the first time, with the Maltese Hal Far airfield as a land base. It returned to Britain for a refit in 1931–33, which included new boilers and the fitting of transverse arrester wires, and then deployed to the Far East, serving on the China Station from 1933–35 and 1937–39. On the outbreak of World War II in September 1939 it was undergoing a further refit at the Singapore naval base. With a destroyer escort it undertook wartime patrols in the Indian Ocean. An accidental bomb explosion off the Nicobar Islands on 14 March 1940 killed 14 crewmen,

Camouflage
The profile shows *Eagle* in 1942 camouflage paint.

Torpedo blisters
Eagle was fitted with torpedo blisters intended to be capable of absorbing a charge of 52kg/cm² (750psi).

Eagle was the ship that confirmed the starboard placing of the island, though its island, with a huge tripod mast, was larger than most.

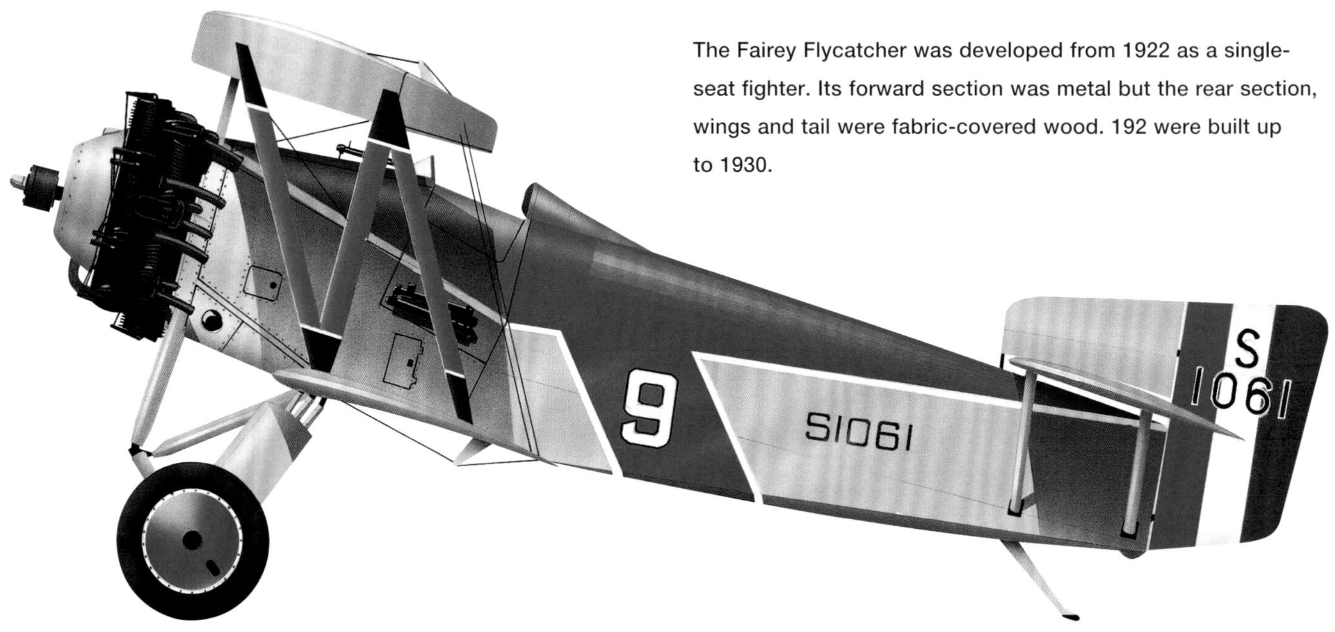

The Fairey Flycatcher was developed from 1922 as a single-seat fighter. Its forward section was metal but the rear section, wings and tail were fabric-covered wood. 192 were built up to 1930.

damaged many of its aircraft and forced it to return to Singapore for repairs. Once repaired, *Eagle* was sent to join the Mediterranean Fleet, and although it had too few planes and was too slow to be considered a fleet carrier, for a time it was the only Royal Navy carrier in the fleet until the arrival of the new and faster HMS *Illustrious*.

Libyan raid

On 9 July its aircraft raided Italian-held Libya, sinking the destroyer *Zeffiro*. Intensive action continued with the sinking of the destroyer *Leone Pancaldo* at Augusta, Sicily, on 10 July, and aerial battles against Italian bomber flights. Its Sea Gladiators also operated as reconnaissance craft for British capital ships in the brief and inconclusive Battle of Calabria on 9 July, and it flew Fairey Swordfish torpedo bombers against Italian ships without making any hits. Attacked by Italian SM79 bombers on 12 October, *Eagle* was damaged by near misses that caused its fuel pipes to spring leaks, and it underwent repairs at the British naval base at Alexandria. As a result it did not participate directly in the naval aircraft attack on the Italian fleet at Taranto on 11 November, but five of its Swordfish, flying off HMS *Illustrious*, were involved. It stayed in the Mediterranean until April 1941, when it was ordered to undertake long-range patrols first in the Indian Ocean, then rounding the Cape of Good Hope to Simonstown, South Africa, into the South Atlantic, hunting German surface raiders, sinking the blockade-runner *Elbe* on 6 June. On 20 September 1941 fire broke out on board, damaging many of the Swordfish torpedo bombers.

Back in Britain in October 1941 it was docked at Birkenhead, where the AA armament was improved with 12 20mm (0.787in) Oerlikon AA guns replacing its quadruple .50 calibre machine guns, and was equipped with Type 290 air warning radar and Type 285 gunnery radar. In February 1942 *Eagle* was again in the

Specification

Dimensions:	Length: 203.5m (667ft 6in); Beam: 35.1m (115ft); Draught (max.): 8.1m (26ft 8in)
Displacement:	(standard): 22,200 tonnes (21,850 tons)
Propulsion:	32 Yarrow boilers, 4 geared turbines, 37,000kW (50,000shp)
Speed:	24 knots (44km/h; 28mph)
Range:	4800nm (8900km; 5500 miles) at 16 knots (29.6km/h; 18.4mph)
Armament:	9 152mm (6in) guns, 5 102mm (4in) AA guns
Aircraft:	24
Complement:	791

Eagle in the 1930s. While the forward end of the flight deck conformed to the hull shape, at the stern it was canted out to provide a broader landing area.

Operation Pedestal

Malta, strategically placed in the centre of the Mediterranean Sea, was a vital point in Allied supply lines to the Middle East, North Africa and the Far East via the Suez Canal, but it had to be kept supplied with arms and ammunition. Operation Pedestal was the most crucial and desperately needed of the many convoys that had to be escorted to Malta in the course of 1942 against relentless attack by air, surface ships and submarines. In August 1942 the stocks of aviation fuel on the island were at danger level and 14 merchant vessels, including the American oil tanker *Ohio*, formed Convoy WS215, with a total escort of 41 warships, including three other carriers as well as *Eagle*. Despite the extent of protection, only five of the merchant ships got through, of which *Ohio* was one.

Mediterranean Sea, replacing *Ark Royal*, giving air support to Force H from 813 and 824 Squadrons, of Swordfish and Sea Hurricanes, and supplying Spitfires to the British garrison on Malta in February and March.

After a return to Gibraltar in April for repairs to the steering gear, the carrier was back on duty between Gibraltar and Malta, delivering aircraft and giving convoy support, surviving a further attack by Italian SM79s on 17 May. In this activity, as part of Operation Pedestal, it was hit on 11 August 1942 by four torpedoes fired by a Type VIIB U-boat, U-73, while steaming 130km (81 miles) south of Majorca. Massively holed below the waterline, *Eagle* capsized and sank in less than eight minutes. Of its crew, 131 were killed and 929 were picked up by escort ships.

Akagi (1927)

Flagship of Japan's Pearl Harbor attack fleet, and flagship again at the start of the Battle of Midway, *Akagi* participated in every major action in the early stages of the Pacific War.

Akagi, the name of a Japanese mountain in Gunma Prefecture, has become the best known of all of Japan's aircraft carriers. Laid down as a battlecruiser at Kure Naval Yard on 6 December 1920, it was finally launched as an aircraft carrier at a construction cost of 53 million yen. It was intended to be one of two such conversions, but its sister vessel *Amagi* was wrecked on the stocks in the Great Kanto earthquake of 1 September 1923 and replaced by *Kaga*, which, despite many similarities in the original design, could not be regarded as a sister ship. It was

Hangar decks
The hangar decks were fully enclosed, a feature that contributed to the ship's destruction when accumulated gas and vapour exploded in the unventilated space.

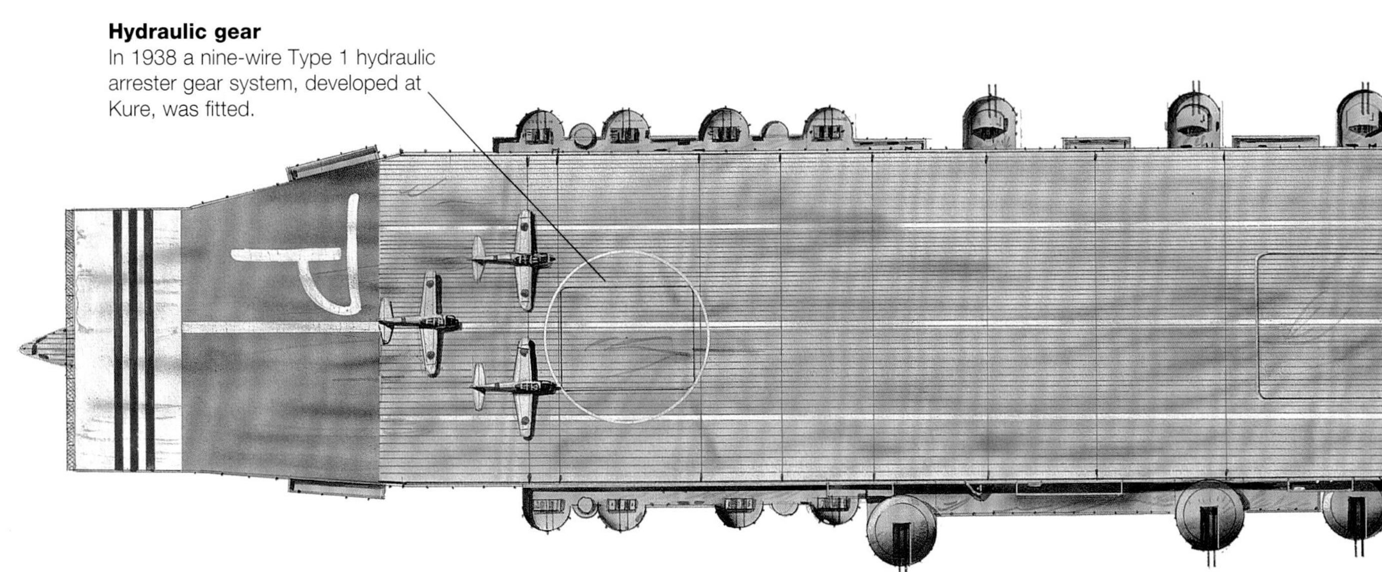

Hydraulic gear
In 1938 a nine-wire Type 1 hydraulic arrester gear system, developed at Kure, was fitted.

Three views showing *Akagi* after the 1935 refit that gave the ship a full-length flight deck, setting the pattern for further carriers of the Imperial Navy, though the port-side island was repeated only on *Hiryú.*

Island
The position of the island was on the port side to keep it away from smoke and gases from the engine exhausts. This was also done on *Hiryū,* but not repeated on subsequent carriers. It is shown here with external protective wrapping against shells and fragments.

Flight deck
From 1938 the flight deck was 249.2m (817ft 6in) long. The flight decks of Japanese carriers were wood-laid, with the planks running longitudinally rather than transversely as in US carriers.

Funnel
The funnel had a large vent on the starboard side. Water could be sprayed into the smoke as it left the funnel, making it heavier so that it would not roll up and over the flight deck and interfere with flight operations.

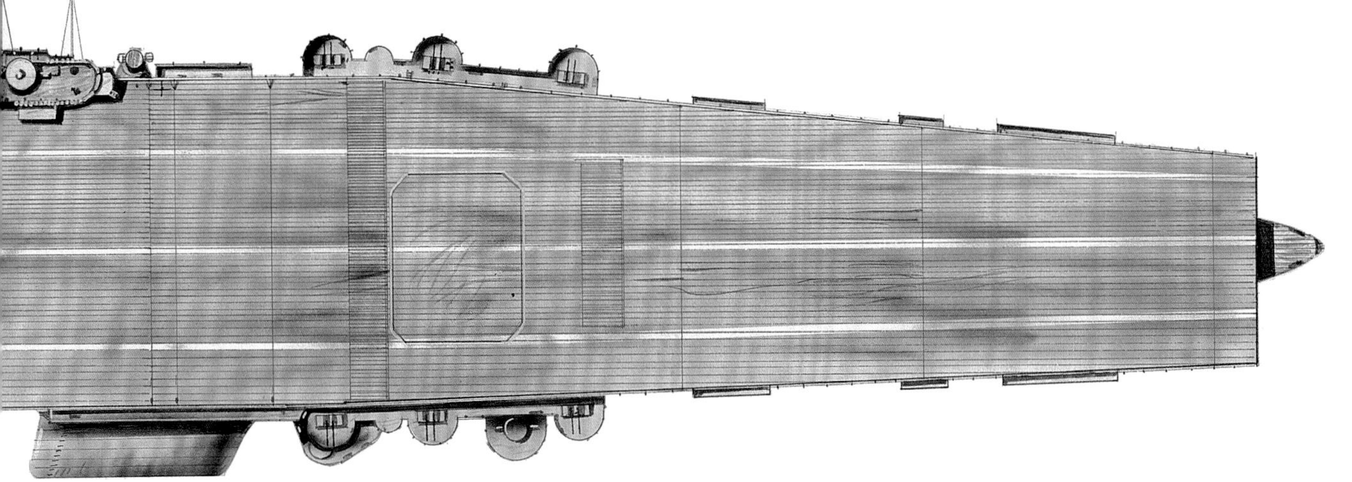

Akagi in its original form with three flight decks, circa 1930. Small-boat drill seems to be going on in the foreground.

Specification (post-1938)

Dimensions:	Length: 260.6m (855ft); Beam: 31.4m (103ft); Draught: 8.8m (29ft)
Displacement:	37,084 tonnes (36,500 tons); 41,961 tonnes (41,300 tons) full load
Propulsion:	19 Kampon boilers, 4 turbines, 4 shafts, 41,013kW (55,000shp)
Speed:	31 knots (57.3km/h; 35.6mph)
Range:	10,000nm (18,520km; 11,510 miles) at 14 knots (25.9km/h; 16.1mph)
Armament:	6 354mm (8in) guns, 12 120mm (4.7in) guns, 14 twin 25mm AA guns
Aircraft:	91
Complement:	1630

commissioned on 25 March 1927. By this time Japan was forming one of the world's three prime carrier fleets, along with the British and US Navies.

There were few useful precedents for carrier construction, and much about *Akagi* was provisional and experimental. Following British practice, it had a double hangar deck, giving the ship a very high freeboard. If the Imperial Navy had watched the British *Furious* class closely, it also added many features of its own. The uppermost or main flight deck was 192m (624ft) long and slightly humped amidships; the middle flight deck, leading directly from the upper hangar, was only 18m (60ft) long and was to be used by the lightest planes; and the lower flight deck opened from the lower hangar and its 49m (160ft) length was considered sufficient in 1927 for torpedo bombers to take off from. A third small hangar was used for storage of disassembled aircraft, towards the aft end of the ship.

The flat-top upper deck, with two elevators, was for landing and aircraft storage, although deck parking was never a standard IJN practice. The armour belt was lowered and thinned from the original battlecruiser specifications and the torpedo bulges changed to enhance stability. As originally constructed, *Akagi* was a 'flush-decker' with no structures on the flight deck.

It was not yet fully appreciated that its own planes were a carrier's best means of defence, and as with other early carriers, gun turrets were mounted, in *Akagi's* case six 203mm (8in) guns, although with a restricted field of fire. The IJN also realized that high speed was a requisite for an aircraft carrier as a form of anti-submarine protection and to provide a headwind for take-offs and landings.

The machinery was Gihon (Gijutsu Honbu: Army Technical Department) geared turbines, powered by 19 Kampon boilers and driving four screws. Exhaust was expelled via two different funnels, one a seaward-pointing vent, the other a smaller vertical funnel, which was combined into the larger one when in 1935–38 a large-scale refit was done at Sasebo Naval Arsenal. This also removed the lower flight decks, closing off the hangar fronts, and added a third lift. An island was placed amidships on the port side, replacing the navigation bridge below the flight deck. Aircraft capacity was increased from 61 to 91.

US appraisal

After August 1945 American officers were able to inspect the machinery as well as other aspects of Japanese ships. They concluded that the standard Kampon (Navy Office) water-tube design of boiler as used in carriers and capital ships was significantly inferior to those of Allied vessels. A three-drum express design dating back to 1914, it lacked many of the detail improvements made in Western navies, with only half the heat release rate of a 1940-type Babcock & Wilcox boiler. Consuming oil at a maximum rate of 7.25 tonnes (7 tons) per hour, it generated steam at a pressure of 30kg/cm^2 (426psi) and a temperature of 350°C (662°F), compared to 40kg/cm^2 (565psi) and 450°C (842°F) on the American boiler. On the other hand, Gihon geared turbines were considered at least as efficient as American and British models. Their ability to deliver up to 29,828kW (40,000shp) compared favourably with the American *Essex* class.

Battle of Midway

Akagi's first captain was Isoroku Yamamoto, future Supreme Commander of the Imperial Combined Fleet. In the early 1930s the ship saw service supporting Japanese military campaigns in Manchuria. In April 1941 the First Air Fleet was formed: the world's first single tactical naval air group, mustering a total of 474 aircraft, which would show its power in December that year. *Akagi* was flagship of Vice Admiral Chuichi Nagumo's Mobile Striking Force, *Kido Butai*, in the attack launched on the American base at Pearl Harbor just before war was formally declared. Six carriers were the central core of the fleet of 30 ships.

On 7 December *Akagi* launched two waves of aircraft, the first including 15 dive-bombers, 12 torpedo planes and ten fighter planes; the second formed of eight dive-bombers and nine fighters. The Japanese carriers lost 29 aircraft in the attack, while apart from the loss of five battleships and damage to numerous other warships, the US lost 239 aircraft in simultaneous raids on the airfields. *Akagi*'s torpedo bombers were responsible for the destruction of USS *Oklahoma* and *West Virginia*. It was a shattering display of naval air power.

In January 1942 *Akagi* and other carriers launched sea-to-ground attacks at Rabaul, New Guinea, in support of troop landings, and at Darwin, Australia, on 19 February. It also joined in the attacks on Colombo and Trincomalee on 5 and 9 April. It again flew Nagumo's flag in the attack on Midway Island that began on 4 June. Intended as a surprise assault, it was in fact known to American intelligence, and the carriers *Enterprise*, *Hornet* and *Yorktown* were sent against *Akagi*, *Sōryū* and *Hiryū*.

A 15-plane torpedo-bomber attack from *Hornet* was a disastrous failure but it forced the Japanese fighters down to low level, leaving their carriers vulnerable to high-flying dive-bombers launched from *Enterprise* and *Yorktown*. A series of direct hits put all three Japanese carriers out of action.

Akagi took two hits and a near miss that jammed its rudder, leaving it unsteerable on a circular course. Nagumo transferred his flag to the light cruiser *Nagara*, and from 13.50 the surviving crew – over 270 were lost – abandoned the burning hulk. It was finally sunk by torpedoes from Japanese destroyers at 02.00 on the 5th, on the orders of its one-time captain Admiral Yamamoto.

USS Lexington (1927)

Laid down first as a battlecruiser, *Lexington* was redesigned as a carrier and taught the US Navy much about sea flying in the 1930s. In 1942 it played a key part in the Battle of the Coral Sea before succumbing to fire after heavy attacks.

Construction of two planned battlecruisers was suspended on 8 February 1922 in the wake of the 1921–22 Washington Naval Treaty, but reactivated in July that year as carrier conversions. Originally to be named USS *Constitution*, *Lexington* was laid down at the Fore River shipbuilding yard at Quincy, Massachusetts, on 8 January 1921, launched on 3 October 1925 and commissioned on 14 December 1927, designated CV-2. CV-1 was USS *Langley*, a 12,192-tonne

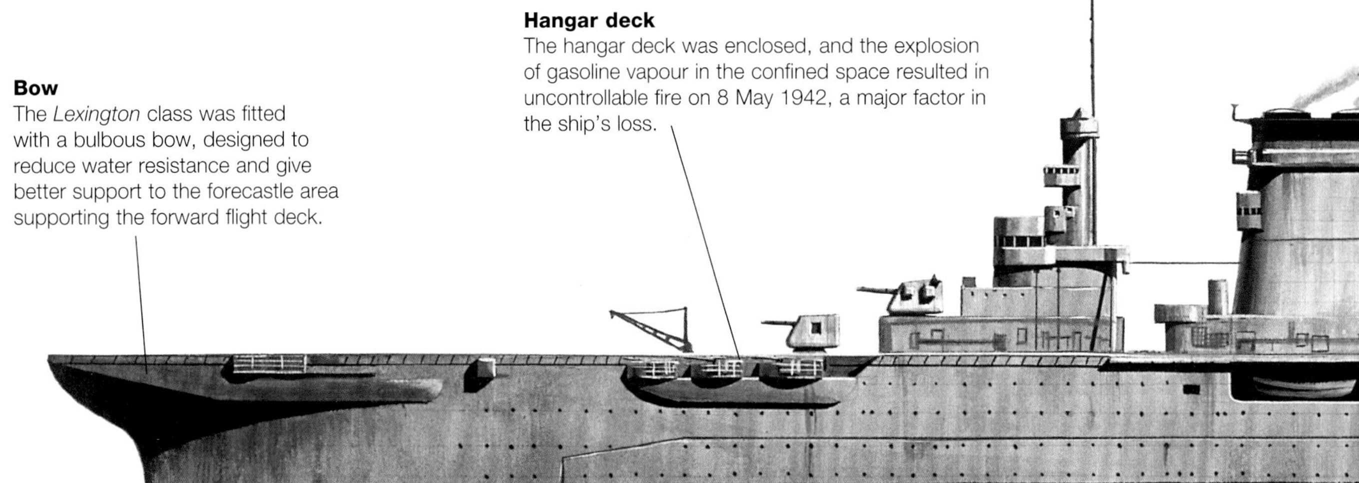

Bow
The *Lexington* class was fitted with a bulbous bow, designed to reduce water resistance and give better support to the forecastle area supporting the forward flight deck.

Hangar deck
The hangar deck was enclosed, and the explosion of gasoline vapour in the confined space resulted in uncontrollable fire on 8 May 1942, a major factor in the ship's loss.

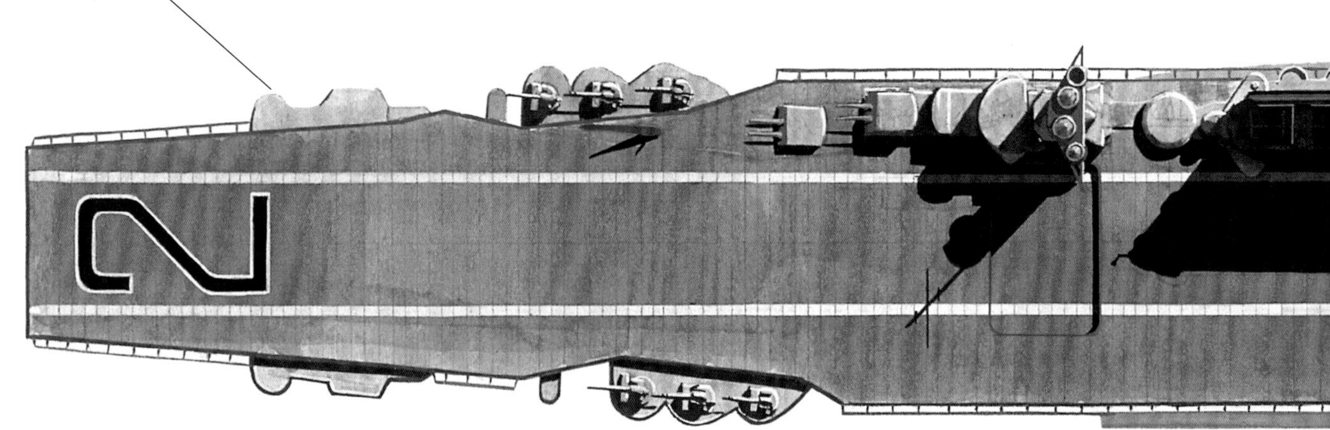

Catapult
Until 1936 the ship carried a flywheel-powered F Mk II catapult on the starboard bow, intended to launch seaplanes.

(12,000-ton) ship converted from the collier *Jupiter* and commissioned in 1922, but *Lexington* and *Saratoga* (CV-3) were much larger, and really the USN's first fleet carriers. *Saratoga* was launched on 7 April 1925 and *Lexington* followed on 3 October. It was commissioned on 14 December 1927. At that time they replaced the British *Eagle* as the world's largest carriers.

Large funnel

As a carrier *Lexington*'s most distinctive feature was the massive funnel dominating the island, supporting observation and signalling platforms and machine-gun positions. The island itself was a tall tower-like structure, topped by a broad platform carrying communications and, later, radar equipment, supporting a pole mast whose arms carried flag signal halyards as well as aerials. As a result of its battlecruiser beginning, *Lexington* carried more armour than the carriers converted from merchant vessels, with belt armour from 127mm to 178mm (5–7in), 76mm (3in) on the main armoured deck and from 76mm to 110mm (3–4.5in) round the steering gear. The flight deck was 268.2m (880ft) long and 27.4m (90ft) wide. An important new development

Largest in the world when commissioned, *Lexington* initiated a pattern for US Navy carriers that has been followed through into the twenty-first century.

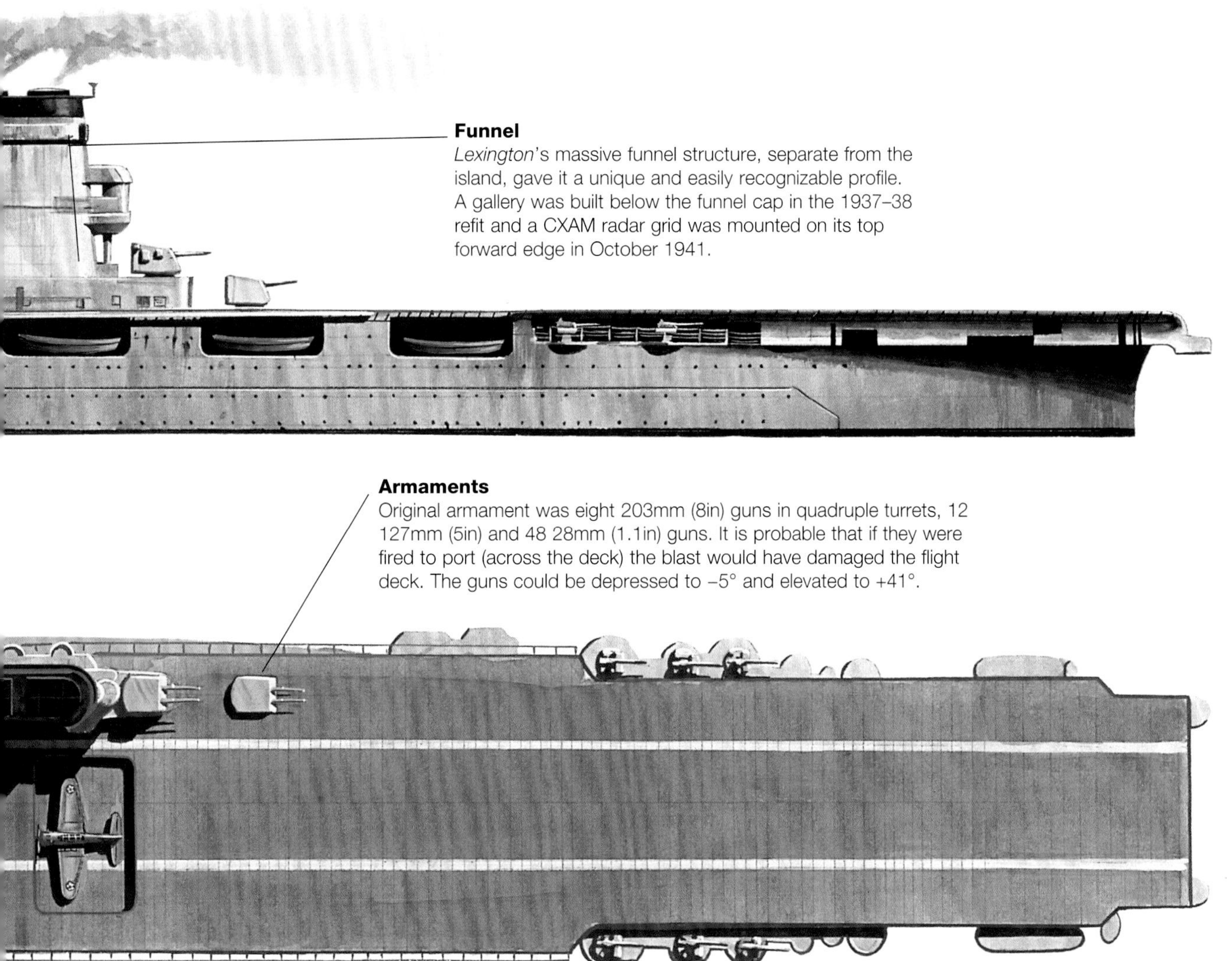

The Grumman SF-1 was a two-seater scout version of the FF-1 fighter plane that had been introduced in 1933. It was the first carrier-borne aircraft to have retractable landing gear.

was the fitting of a transverse arrester wire system at the stern, and a transverse flywheel-worked catapult was mounted forward. Two centreline elevators served the two-level hangar decks. Collapsible cranes to handle cargo loading and hoist seaplanes were fitted.

The machinery was turbo-electric, first tried on *Langley*. In total, 16 Yarrow water-tube boilers supplied steam to the turbines, which in turn provided power to eight electric motors, two to each shaft, giving the ship a maximum speed of over 33 knots (61.1km/h; 37.9mph). One of the features of this system was that it could drive the ship backwards almost at the same speed as forwards. The original armament was four 203mm (8in) 55 calibre twin mounting guns, set in pairs forward and aft of the island and funnel, adding considerable weight on the starboard side that had to be compensated for in the ship's design, and 12 127mm (5in) single-mount AA guns. The heavier guns reflected the assumption that the carrier might have to defend itself against cruisers with similar armament.

Specification

Dimensions:	Length: 270.66m (888ft); Beam: 32.12m (105ft 5in); Draught: 10.15m (33ft 4in)
Displacement:	38,284 tonnes (37,681 tons), 43.744 tonnes (43,055 tons) full load
Propulsion:	16 water-tube boilers, turbo-electric drive, four shafts; 134,226kW (180,000shp)
Speed:	33.25 knots (61.5km/h; 38mph)
Range:	10,500nm (19,456km; 12,075 miles) at 15 knots (27.7km/h; 17.2mph)
Armament:	8 203mm (8in), 12 127mm (5in) guns
Aircraft:	63
Complement:	2791

After a wartime refitting at Pearl Harbor in March–April 1942 *Lexington* lost the 203mm guns and four of the 127mm guns. Dual-purpose twin 127mm/38 twin mounts were to replace the big guns, but had not been installed at the time of *Lexington*'s sinking. It did acquire six 28mm AA guns in quadruple mountings, and 30 20mm Oerlikon AA guns, reflecting the realization that the main threat to the ship would come from the air rather than the surface. In October 1941 during a refit at Hunter's Point naval yard it was one of the first Navy ships to be equipped with the first seagoing radar, RCA CXAM-1. *Lexington* could carry up to 78 aircraft. In 1941–42 its air wing included F2A-1 and F4F-3 fighters, SBD scout bombers and TBD-1 torpedo bombers.

Assigned to the Pacific Fleet at San Pedro, California, *Lexington* and *Saratoga* were just able to fit the Panama Canal locks. They took part in exercises for the first time in January 1929, *Lexington* carrying Curtiss F6C fighters and Martin T3M torpedo bombers. In December 1929 *Lexington*'s turbo-electric machinery was used to supply electric power to Tacoma, Washington, when the city's powerplant failed. In 1935 it underwent a refit at Puget Sound Naval Base, where two sponsons were fitted both fore and aft to mount additional AA guns, and further

USS *Lexington* with other American warships at Hawaii, 1930. There had been a naval station at Pearl Harbor since 1908, but it was much enlarged in the 1930s.

modifications were made in 1936–37 when the forward flight deck was widened.

Pacific War

In the late 1930s the ship went to and fro between the Pacific and Atlantic, but was back in the Pacific by 1941, transporting aircraft to support the garrison on Wake Island at the time of Pearl Harbor. By chance all three Pacific Fleet carriers were away at the time of the Japanese surprise attack, to the chagrin of the Japanese who had hoped to deal a fatal blow to US air power in the Pacific. *Lexington* sent aircraft in search of the Japanese fleet, but without success. In January 1942 it was named flagship of Task Force 11, deployed to the Coral Sea to stem the Japanese advance on the north Australian coast, and on 20 February its aircraft shot down 17 out of a Japanese attack group of 18 Mitsubishi G4M 'Betty' bombers.

Back at Pearl Harbor for the second half of April, *Lexington* left again for the Coral Sea theatre on 1 May in company with *Yorktown* (CV-5), whose planes sank the escort carrier *Shoho* on 7 May. On the following day came the first battle between two carrier forces, both launching their aircraft at each other, and the first sea battle in which the opposing ships, some 322km (200 miles) apart, never saw one another. The Japanese force included the heavy carriers *Shokaku* and *Zuikaku*. A plane from *Lexington* scored a hit on *Shokaku*, but the American ship itself suffered heavy attack. It was hit by two aerial torpedoes on the port side near the bow as well as three bombs, and it caught fire. At first the fires appeared to have been extinguished, but leaking vapour from ruptured fuel tanks built up and exploded at 12.47, causing a series of further explosions. The ship developed a heavy list to port, and its captain gave the order to abandon at 17.00. There were 216 fatalities and 2770 survivors, and its orphan aircraft were redeployed to *Yorktown*. *Lexington* was sunk shortly afterwards by two torpedoes fired from US destroyer *Phelps*. Sister ship *Saratoga* survived World War II and was used as a target craft in the Bikini Atoll A-bomb tests of 1946.

Arresting system

***Lexington* was the first carrier to be fitted with an effective transverse-wire arresting system to allow faster and heavier planes to land. The original Mark 1 system combined lateral wires, to prevent aircraft going over the side, with transverse wires. In August 1931 this was replaced by a hydraulically powered transverse-only system of greater power and elasticity in operation. Further improvements were made in 1934, and modifications made in 1936 including the fitting of a four-wire arrester system on the forward end of the flight deck in case damage should impede the normal stern landings.**

Kaga (1928)

Planned as a battleship, *Kaga* was part of the Japanese fleet that attacked Pearl Harbor. It went on to engage in other operations in the Pacific before being sunk in the Battle of Midway in 1941.

The profile shows the ship in post-1934 modernized form, with the lower flight decks removed. The small island, essentially a conning tower, was added at that time.

Guns
The 200mm (7.9in) guns were mounted so low, below main deck level, as to be of little use except in calm conditions.

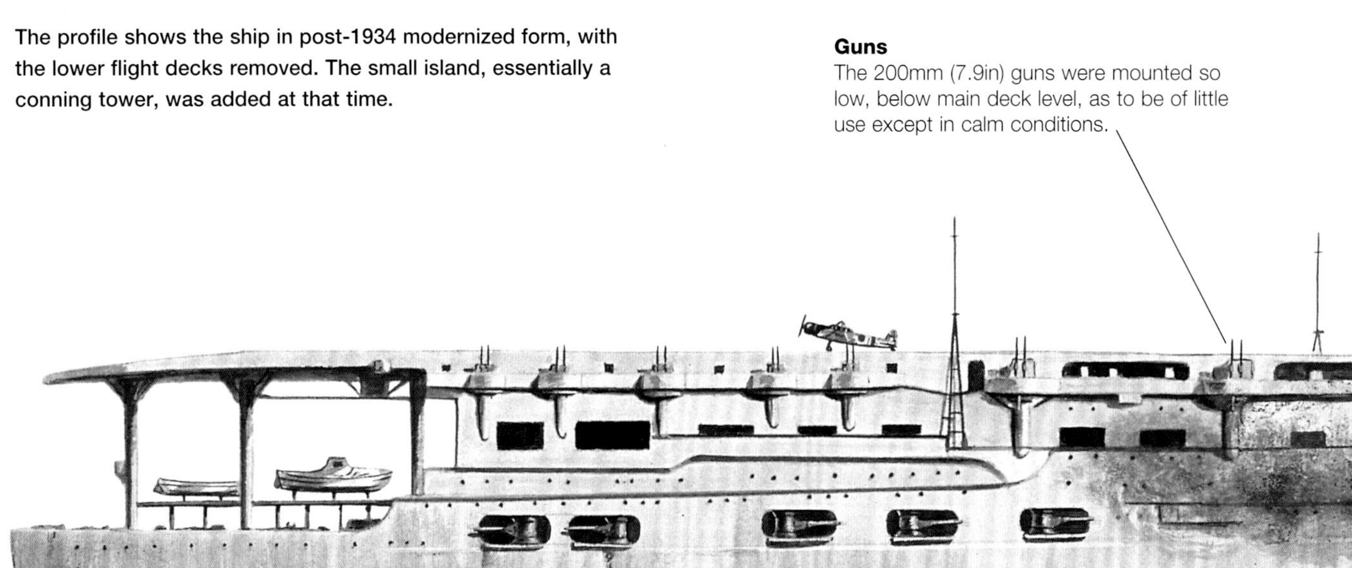

Arrester wires
Japanese carriers could have six arrester wires. Where only three were fitted, hooking on to the second wire was the ideal, and pilots who achieved this were given a pay bonus of 5 yen.

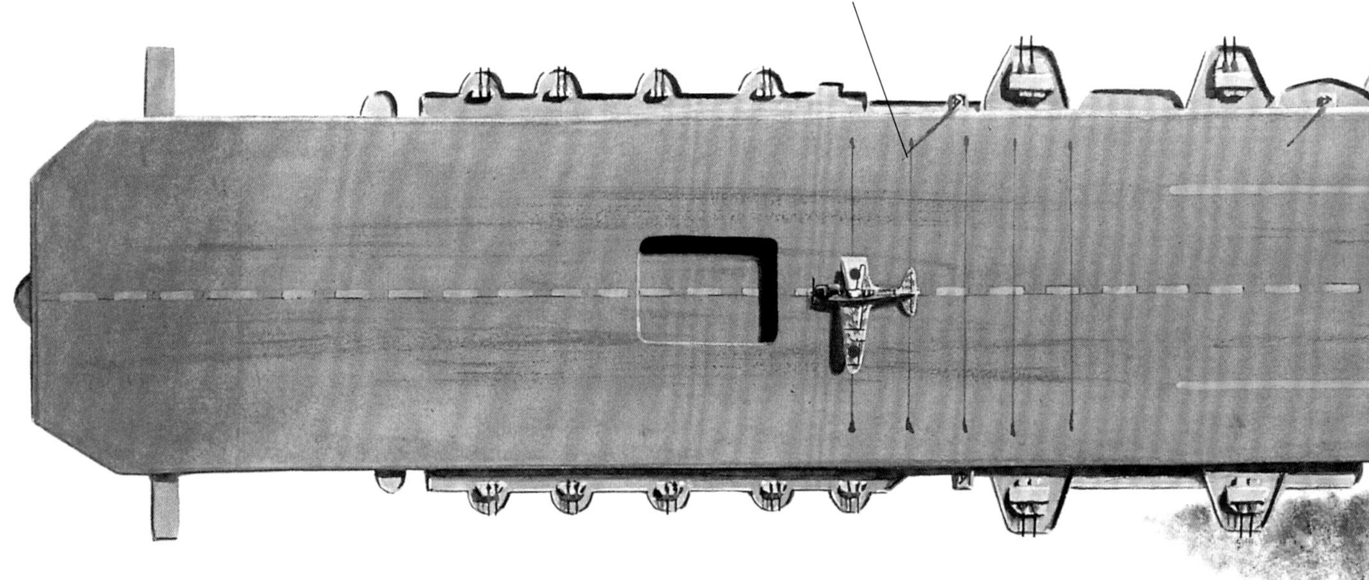

The Washington Naval Treaty of 1922 led to the cancellation of many large warships and to the conversion of some into aircraft carriers. Two selected for conversion, comparable to USS *Saratoga* and *Lexington*, were the battlecruisers *Amagi* and *Akagi*. When the hull of *Amagi*, still in the shipyard, was distorted beyond usability in the Great Kanto earthquake of 1 September 1923, the plan to convert it to a carrier was switched to the new *Tosa*-class fast battleship *Kaga*, laid down at the Kawasaki Shipyard, Kobe, on 19 July 1920 and launched in 1922.

Conversion work began at Yokosuka Naval Dockyard in 1923 and was completed on 31 March 1928 at a cost of 53 million yen. *Kaga*'s size and speed made it highly suitable for transformation into Japan's first fleet carrier.

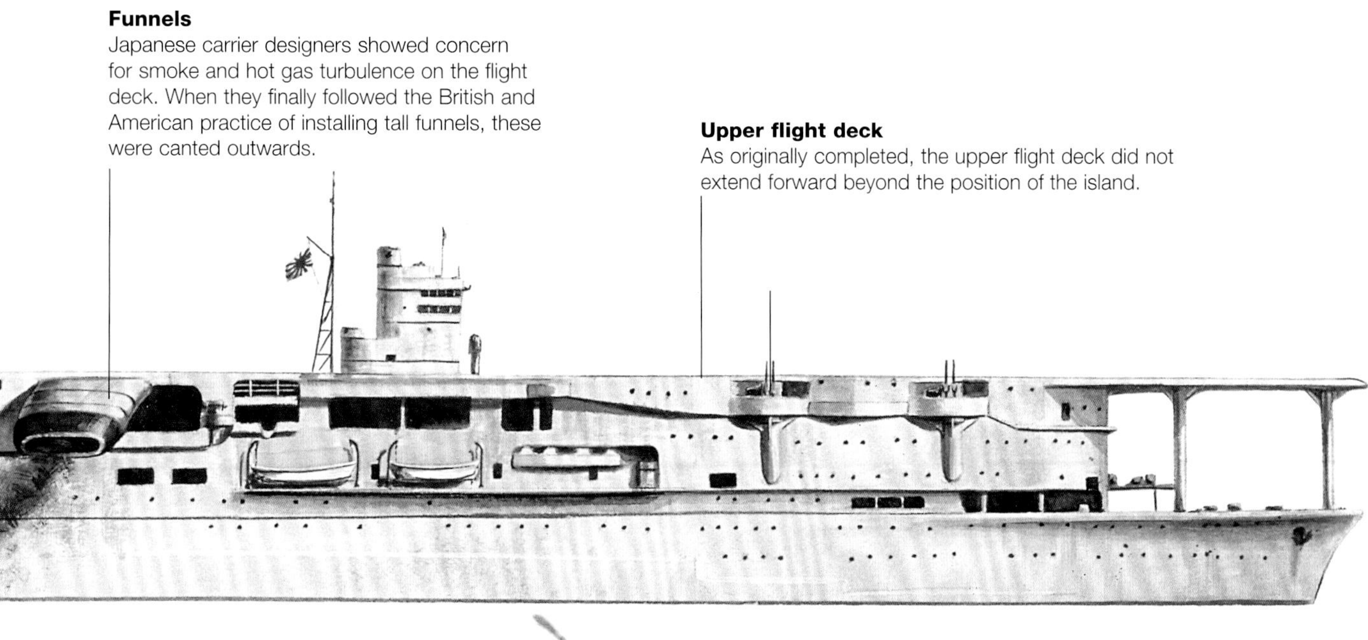

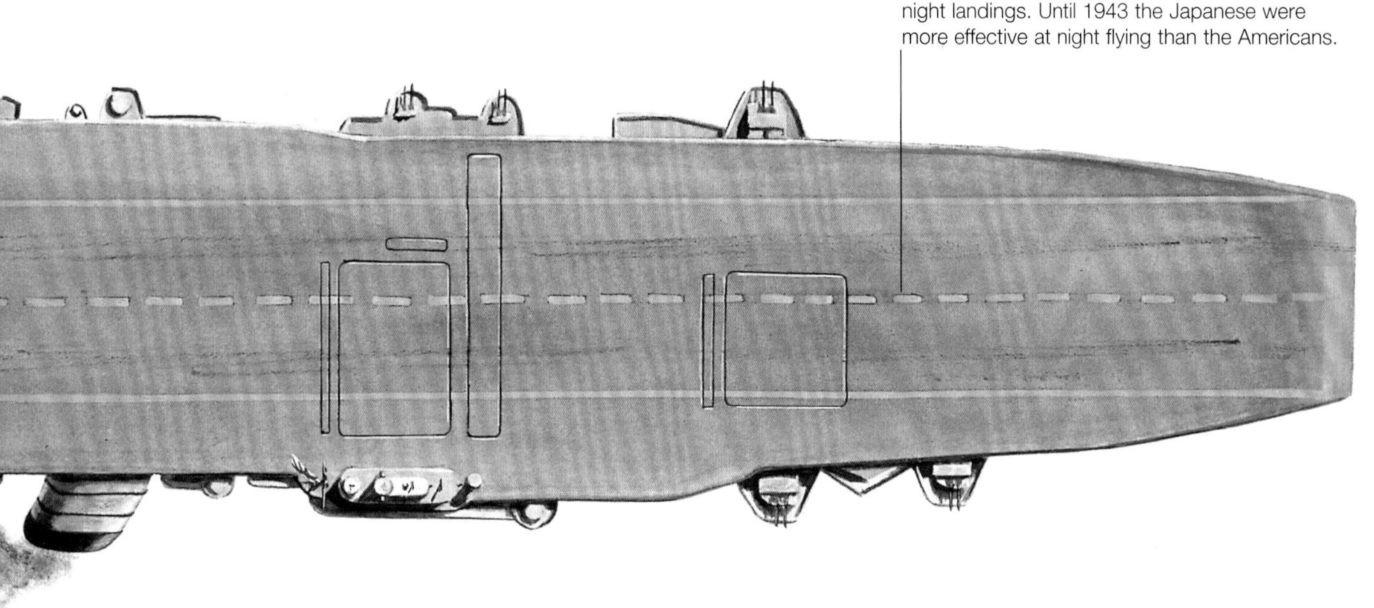

Aerial view of *Kaga* in the early 1930s, before the full-length flight deck was fitted.

It had three flight decks in the original configuration, all mounted above the original hull and giving the ship a towering look even for a carrier. A small island unit was positioned to starboard but this was removed at a very early stage to make the ship a complete flat-top with no structure to impede the uppermost flight deck, 171.2m (561ft 8in) long and intended primarily for landings. The flight deck and hangar sides were not armoured. The ship was heavily armed with ten 203mm (8in) guns and 16 120mm (4.7in) guns, a cruiser-type armament again similar to that of the two American fleet carriers.

Specification

Dimensions:	Length: 247.5m (812ft); Beam: 32.6m (107ft); Draught: 9.45m (31ft)
Displacement:	38,811 tonnes (38,200 tons), 43,222 tonnes (42,541 tons) full load
Propulsion:	8 Kampon boilers, 4 Kampon geared turbines, four shafts; 95,002kW (127,400shp)
Speed:	28 knots (52km/h; 32mph)
Range:	10,000nm (18,500km; 11,500 miles) at 16 knots (29.6km/h; 18.4mph)
Armament:	10 203mm (8in), 16 127mm (5in), 22 25mm AA guns
Aircraft:	90
Complement:	1708

A thorough reconstruction of the upperworks was made in 1934–35. *Kaga* emerged with a lengthened hull, a single flight deck of 250 x 32.6m (812 x 106ft) laid with longitudinal wood planking above a thin steel base, and a displacement increased by around 8128 tonnes (8000 tons). A third aircraft lift was installed and the exits from the boiler uptakes were replaced by a single midships funnel to starboard, canted outwards and downwards to keep the flight deck clear. Removal of the lower take-off decks enabled the hangars to be enlarged and gave the ship capacity to hold 90 aircraft. There was no catapult, and in fact no Japanese carriers of the 1920s and 1930s actually carried a catapult. *Kaga* retained all ten of the 203mm (8in) guns, but the four originally located in twin turrets were moved to casemates under the flight deck alongside the other six.

Pearl Harbor and Midway

Kaga was one of the six carriers of the First Air Fleet, which mounted the attack on the US fleet at Pearl Harbor on 7 December 1941. As Japanese forces spread across the Pacific islands, *Kaga* provided air support and supplies in operations against the Dutch East Indies and New Guinea. It was one of four carriers in the fleet commanded by Admiral Nagumo at the Battle of Midway. On 4 June

1942 at 10.22 it was attacked by dive-bombers from USS *Enterprise* and hit by at least four bombs, three 225kg (500lb) and one 450kg (1000lb). Two broke through to the upper hangar, causing explosions and fires.

The uncontrollable conflagration aboard *Kaga* could partly be attributed to Japanese carrier design of the time. According to plan, to fight a fire in the enclosed hangar the damage control team was to pull heavy fire curtains intended to isolate sections of the hangar. However, fires occurring in multiple areas of the hangar made this impossible. Furthermore, a single water main running along the ship that supplied water for firefighting was destroyed in one of the explosions, while avgas fuel lines were ruptured, spilling oil. Finally, the hangar at the time was stocked with ammunition moved up ready for loading on the planes; in this enclosed space, without an opening directly to the exterior, the crew simply had no way to move the heavy bombs and torpedoes away from the fires. By 17.00 the surviving crew was evacuated, and the still-burning hulk was sunk at 19.25 by two torpedoes from the escort destroyer *Hagikaze*. In total 811 men were lost.

The carriers *Akagi* and *Sōryū* were sunk in the same attack. Parts of *Kaga*'s remains were identified in September 1999, lying 5916m (17,000ft) below the surface.

Landing strategies

Air operations on the Japanese carriers were carefully thought out. A system of mirrors and lights, although not as efficient as post-war optronic guidance, was devised as a landing guide. A steam valve could be opened to show the wind direction and a system of flags controlled aircraft movements. Take-offs could be made with only a 20-second interval. To indicate clear for landing, a black ball was hoisted with numbered indicators to give the wind speed, and a look-out signalled with a red flag to order touch-and-go, or a black H to tell the pilot his tail hook was not down. Often the after deck was painted with red and white stripes to help the pilot line up for landing, and some carriers had a white circle mark to show the position of the rearmost arrester wire.

***Kaga* during exercises in 1937. The crowded flight deck holds Nakajima A2N, Aichi D1A and Mitsubishi B2M planes.**

HMS Glorious (1930)

Sister ship to HMS *Furious* and *Courageous*, *Glorious* became one of the few carriers to be sunk by gunfire from a surface ship, rather than by aircraft or submarines, in an encounter with *Scharnhorst* that remains controversial.

Laid down on 1 May 1915 at Harland & Wolff, Belfast, and launched on 20 April 1916, *Glorious* was first commissioned as a light battlecruiser on 14 October 1916. In this form the ship saw action in the engagement at Heligoland Bight on 17 November 1917. The *Courageous*-class design had significant weaknesses and did not find a place in the Royal Navy's post-war dispositions. *Glorious* and *Courageous* both were converted to carriers; *Glorious* underwent conversion between 1924 and 1930 at the RN Dockyards of Rosyth and Devonport, completed at the latter yard on

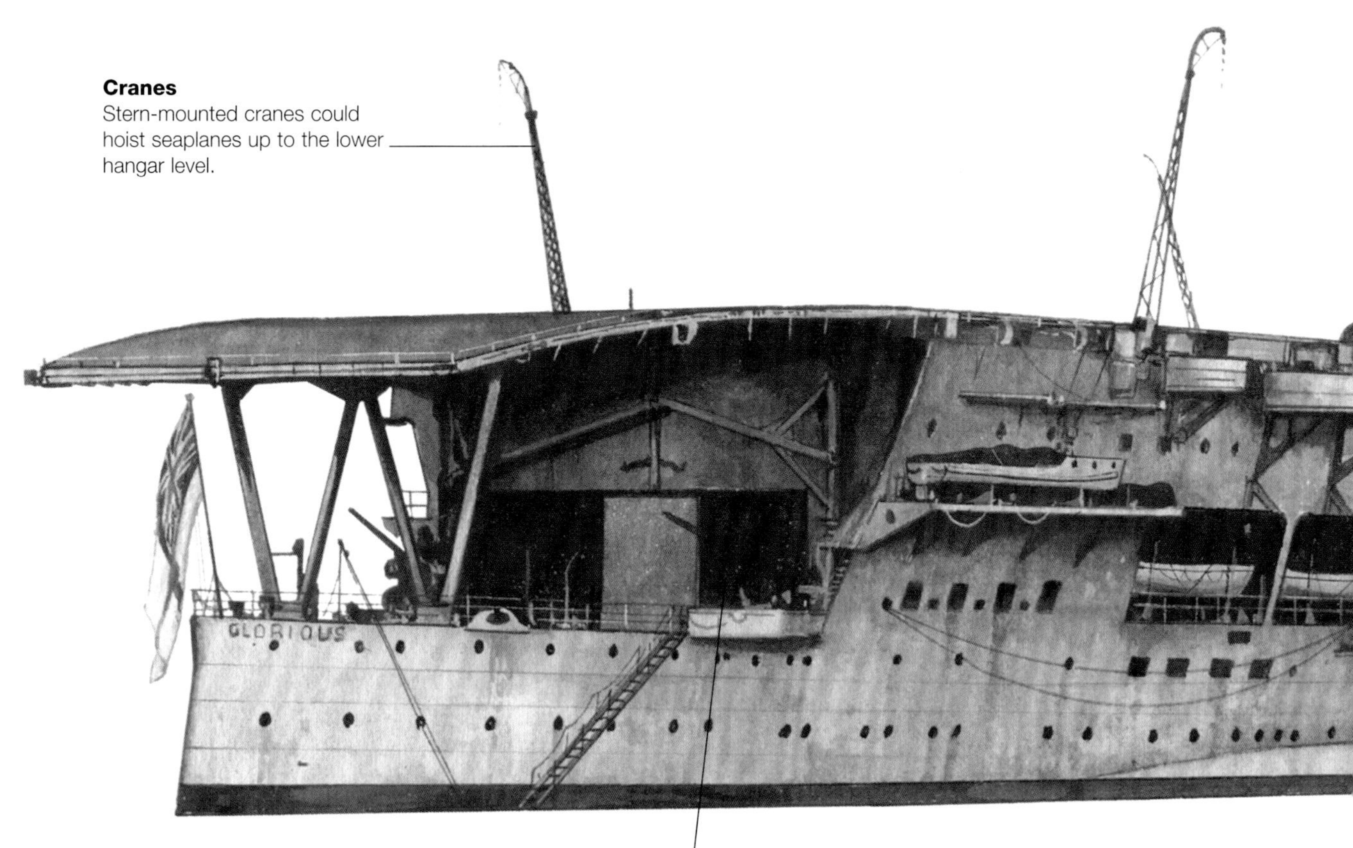

Cranes
Stern-mounted cranes could hoist seaplanes up to the lower hangar level.

Access points
Access hatches were provided forward and aft of the conning tower. The airlock and diving compartments are located just behind the bows.

24 February 1930. Everything above the main deck was removed and the hull sides raised by 9.7m (32ft) to provide two hangar decks 167.6m (550ft) long.

The upper hangar deck initially opened on to a fly-off deck built above the forecastle, enabling planes to take off and land at the same time. The main flight deck incorporated an island with a tall funnel and pole mast. Two aircraft lifts were installed forward and aft. An arrangement of 18 Yarrow water-tube boilers and four geared turbines driving four screws gave it a top speed of 32 knots (59.2km/h; 36.8mph) in its cruiser form; the increased displacement of some 6096 tonnes (6000 tons) as a carrier reduced this to slightly under 30 knots (55.5km/h; 34.5mph). The armour was light for a large warship, with a waterline belt of 51–76mm (2–3in), 19–25mm (0.75–1in) on the main deck and 51–76mm (2–3in) on the bulkheads. *Glorious*, like *Courageous,* could carry and service four squadrons of aircraft, up to 36 planes in total. For defence it carried 16 120mm (4.7in) dual-purpose guns mounted in single turrets.

***Glorious* depicted from the starboard quarter. Comparison with HMS *Eagle* shows the continuing evolution of the island design on British carriers.**

The Gloster Sea Gladiator was a 1938 naval variant of the proven but obsolescent Gladiator fighter. The type gained renown in the defence of Malta, 1940–42.

Relieving *Courageous* in the Mediterranean Fleet in 1930, *Glorious* remained in the Mediterranean until 1939, and was based at Alexandria when war was declared on 3 September. In October it was directed to the Indian Ocean as part of a 'Hunting Force' seeking the German commerce raider *Graf Spee* without success. Back in the Mediterranean in January 1940 it underwent a refit at the Malta naval dockyard, and immediately on completion of this was deployed to the Home Fleet following the German invasion of Norway. Embarking RAF Gloster Gladiator biplane fighters and Blackburn B-24 Skua fighter-bombers, it left Scapa Flow on 23 April with a naval force including the carrier *Ark Royal*, two cruisers and six destroyers to provide sea support and air cover for landings at Narvik. In a series of to-and-fro movements between then and 8 June it passed between Scotland and Norway several times.

On 18 May it was off the north Norwegian coast with HMS *Furious* and *Ark Royal*, the first time three RN carriers had joined in a combat mission. *Glorious* flew off Gladiators and Sea Hurricanes to operate from British-held shore bases. By the beginning of June, the failure of the British attempt to hold northern Norway was obvious and the evacuation of 25,000 troops was accomplished between 3 and 8 June. Landed planes were re-embarked, touching down on the carrier without the use of hooks and arrester wires.

Specification

Dimensions:	Length: 239.8m (786ft 9in); Beam: 27.6m (90ft 6in); Draught: 8.5m (27ft 9in)
Displacement:	25,370 tonnes (24,970 tons); 27,859 tonnes (27,419 tons) full load
Propulsion:	18 Yarrow boilers, 4 geared turbines, 4 shafts; 67,113kW (90,000shp)
Speed:	30 knots (55.5km/h; 34.5mph)
Range:	6000nm (11,000km; 6900 miles) at 20 knots (37km/h; 23mph)
Armament:	16 120mm (4.7in) DP guns
Aircraft:	48
Complement:	1283

Norwegian disaster

On 8 June *Glorious* left the Narvik area at 02.53, carrying around 20 RAF Gladiators and Hurricanes in addition to ten fighters and five torpedo bombers of Fleet Air Arm Squadrons 802 and 823. The carrier had requested and received permission to steam independently to Scapa Flow, escorted only by two destroyers, *Acasta* and *Ardent*. A German battle squadron formed of battlecruisers *Scharnhorst* and *Gneisenau* and the heavy cruiser *Hipper* had been dispatched on 4 June as Operation Juno to bombard British positions at Narvik, and at 16.00 on the 8th, the two battlecruisers sighted *Glorious* and closed in to attack. Despite being in an extremely hazardous sea area, the carrier had no look-out planes in the air or ready for take-off and was slow to identify the enemy ships, and proceeding only at fourth level of readiness. Desperate attempts by the destroyers to lay smokescreens and attack the capital ships with gunfire and torpedoes could not save *Glorious*, already hit by *Scharnhorst*'s third salvo and on fire. Both destroyers were sunk and further shelling by *Scharnhorst*'s 280mm (11in) guns sank *Glorious* at 18.10. In total 1474 naval and 59 RAF personnel were lost.

The reason for *Glorious*'s permission to proceed alone was long officially given as shortage of fuel. It was only in 1999 that researchers into the ship's fate uncovered evidence suggesting that its commanding officer, Captain Guy D'Oyly Hughes, had requested permission because he was in a hurry to get back to Scapa Flow for the court martial of the ship's Commander (Air), who had been left at Scapa under arrest for refusing to allow the ship's Swordfish torpedo bombers to be launched against poorly-defined shore targets. This was a task for which they were completely unsuited. There had been other dissensions between the captain and the air arm officers. The evidence remains confused as to whether the carrier was ordered to Scapa Flow either as the nearest fuelling point, or because the Commander-in-Chief of the Home Fleet wished to have the court martial held under his flag (the accused officer was eventually completely exonerated), or because the ship's captain requested it.

Fuel limitations

On active service, particularly operating in stormy waters and frequently needing to apply full power, the 18 boilers on *Glorious* could consume from 610 to 711 tonnes (600–700 tons) of oil a day, setting strict limits to the carrier's time at sea unless it was accompanied by a fleet oiler which could replenish the bunkers. This would have been problematic in a combat situation, apart from the fact that the tanker's top speed would be less than two-thirds that of the carrier. As a result *Glorious* had to make return trips from the Norwegian Sea to Scapa Flow every five or six days, taking it off station and requiring escort protection. Millions of gallons of oil were stored at all main naval bases, requiring regular topping up from fleet tankers.

A feature of *Glorious* was the angled platform that could be swung out to port over the flight deck and was presumably intended as a flying control station.

Hiryū (1937)

The Imperial Japanese Navy was building up its carrier force in the late 1930s, with *Sōryū* and *Hiryū* as fast carriers added to the fleet in 1937 and 1939. Both were to become victims of the Battle of Midway.

Hiryū and *Sōryū* were sister ships, both often referred to as *Sōryū*-class, although *Hiryū* was sufficiently different in details to the earlier ship as to really form a separate or sub-class. Its name means Blue Dragon, and *Sōryū* was laid down at the Kaigun Kosho Yard at Kure on 20 November 1934, launched on 23 December 1935 and commissioned on 29 January 1937. Although designed from the start as a carrier, the ship had a conventional bow with the forward

Both ships had similar tower-type islands, although differently located, and *Hiryū*'s had an additional deck level. Both had masts rising from flight-deck level, although again of different design.

Fire curtains
Fire curtains and insulation on carriers of all navies in the 1930s and 1940s made extensive use of asbestos, whose toxic properties were not realized at the time.

Hangars
Both *Sōryū* and *Hiryū* retained the two-level enclosed hangar design of earlier carriers like *Kaga*. The height of the lower hangar at 4.3m (14ft) restricted the type of plane that could be carried.

part of the flight deck extended over it on stanchions; the stern was treated in a similar way.

Hiryū, meaning Flying Dragon, was of slightly larger dimensions than *Sōryū*, and was built at Yokosuka Naval Dockyard. It was laid down on 8 July 1936, launched on 16 November 1937 and commissioned on 5 July 1939. Experience with earlier carriers and events like the 'Fourth Fleet Incident' (see page 41) led to many modifications to the design, including a stronger hull framework and a raised forecastle deck. The island, placed well forward on *Sōryū*, was positioned amidships on *Hiryū*. Both were of minimal size, but unlike *Sōryū* and all other carriers except *Akagi*, *Hiryū*'s island was on the port side. On both ships the boiler uptakes emerged to starboard at right angles to the hull. They were very fast, with eight Kampon boilers supplying steam to four geared steam turbines, giving a top speed of 34.3 knots (63.5km/h; 39.4mph).

Hiryū had better armour protection: 89–150mm (3.5–5.9in) belt armour compared to *Sōryū*'s 46mm (1.8in). Both had deck armour of 30mm (1.2in), rising to 50mm (2in) over

Sōryū was slightly smaller in overall dimensions than _Hiryū_, but the main difference between the two sister ships was the location of the island. _Sōryū_'s was positioned to starboard.

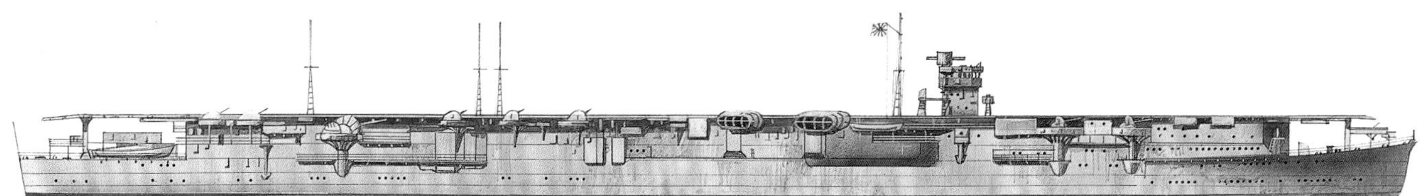

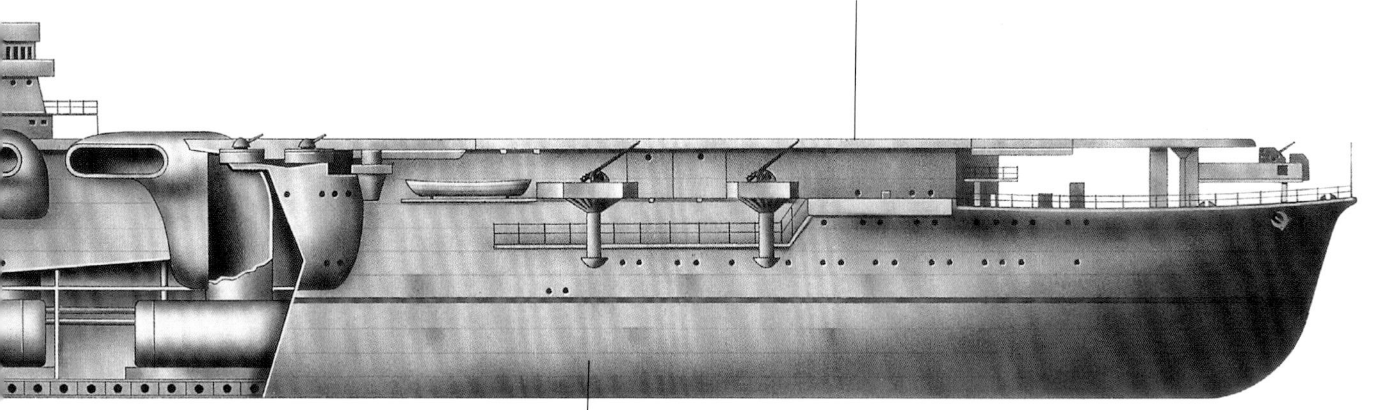

Rising sun
A large *Hinomaru* or rising sun was painted on *Hiryū*'s flight deck, ironically providing a 'bullseye' target for US dive-bombers.

Beam
Hiryū's beam was 1.2m (4ft) greater than *Sōryū*'s, giving the ship a 20 per cent increase in interior space as well as greater stability.

A Mitsubishi A6M2 'Zero' bomber, flown from *Hiryū*, which took part in the Pearl Harbor attack, 7 December 1941. The highly successful A6M long-range 'Zero' gained its nickname from the last digit of 2600: the Japanese imperial year. The Allies' code name for it was Zeke.

the machinery and magazines, and both were fitted with six 127mm (5in) DP guns mounted laterally, three to each side. *Sōryū* also had 28 25mm AA guns in double mounts, while *Hiryū* had seven triple and five twin mounts. *Hiryū* carried 73 aircraft compared to *Sōryū*'s 63 (plus eight in dismantled form), with both ships carrying a combination of D3A 'Val' dive-bombers, B5N 'Kate' torpedo bombers and A6M 'Zero' fighters. *Sōryū* was the first carrier to fly the Yokosuka D4Y1 Suisei dive-bomber and its reconnaissance version, D4Y1-C.

Specification (*Hiryū*)

Dimensions:	Length: 227.4m (746ft 1in); Beam: 22.3m (73ft 2in); Draught: 7.9m (26ft)
Displacement:	17,577 tonnes (17,300 tons); 22,403 tonnes (20,250 tons) full load
Propulsion:	8 Kampon Ro boilers, 4 geared turbines, 4 shafts; 114,000kW (153,000shp)
Speed:	34.3 knots (63.5km/h; 39.5mph)
Range:	10,330nm (19,130km; 11,890 miles) at 18 knots (33.3km/h; 20.7mph)
Armament:	12 127mm (5in), 31 25mm AA guns
Aircraft:	73
Complement:	1100

Hiryū's first military mission was in support of the Japanese invasion of French Indo-China in June 1940. In the Pacific War the two ships took part largely in the same missions as the Second Carrier Division of the First Air Fleet, from the Pearl Harbor attack to Midway. Returning from Pearl Harbor, their planes were in action at Wake Island where US Marines were resisting Japanese attack. Planes from *Hiryū* bombed Darwin, Australia, on 19 February 1942, and helped sink the British carrier *Hermes* and the heavy cruisers *Cornwall* and *Dorsetshire* off Ceylon (Sri Lanka) in the course of the successful 'Indian Ocean Raid' (31 March–10 April 1942).

Battle of Midway

Both ships formed part of Vice Admiral Chuichi Nagumo's First Carrier Striking Force, the Kido Butai, deployed on 27 May 1942 to Midway Island as spearhead of a major strategic operation. The invasion of Midway, held by a small US garrison, was intended to draw out the American carriers, which would then be overwhelmed in a surprise attack from Yamamoto's main battle fleet. The grand plan was forestalled by US interception and decoding of IJN radio signals, and the trap was sprung by the Americans, with *Yorktown*, *Enterprise* and *Hornet* lying in wait.

On the morning of 4 June the Japanese carriers found themselves under intensive attack from carrier-borne dive-bombers and high-flying B17 bombers. At first the well-coordinated Japanese air defence beat off the attacks from *Yorktown* but at around 10.22, with their combat air patrol at low level, they were surprised by the simultaneous strikes from *Enterprise* and *Yorktown*, which in a matter of minutes put *Sōryū*, *Akagi* and *Kaga* out of action. *Sōryū*, with its surviving crew evacuated, was sunk by the escort destroyer *Isokaze* at 19.13, with its captain refusing to leave. It had lost 718 crew. *Hiryū*, flagship of Rear Admiral Yamaguchi in Carrier Division 2, well to the north of the other carriers, was the only one left operational.

Yamaguchi ordered two attack waves, at 10.50 and 13.30. The first wave of dive-bombers shadowed US planes that were returning to *Yorktown*, which itself was looking for *Hiryū*. Six of the 18 Japanese planes penetrated the defensive barrage and made three direct hits. The second wave comprised of torpedo bombers made two hits. *Hiryū* remained in the thick of fighting under waves of attack from *Yorktown* and *Enterprise*, and was struck by four 450kg (1000lb) bombs just after 17.00. All landed forward and the forward elevator was blown out against the bridge. Although blazing from stem to stern, *Hiryū* continued to give AA fire. The damage was too great for the ship to be salvable and the order to abandon was given at 03.15 on 5 June. Torpedoes from the escort destroyer *Makigumo* failed to sink the carrier immediately. With Yamaguchi and the ship's captain Tomeo Kaku choosing to remain on board, *Hiryū* finally sank at 09.12.

The Fourth Fleet Incident

In September 1935, many Japanese naval units were engaged in war game exercises between Honshu and the Kurile Islands. A 'Blue Fleet' formed from the First and Second Fleets was pitted against the Fourth or 'Red' Fleet. On the 26th, the Red Fleet was warned of a typhoon storm sweeping towards it. With no time to make for shelter, the ships reduced speed to 10 knots (18.5km/h; 11.5mph), secured everything, and prepared to ride out the storm. Encountering winds of 145km/h (90mph) and waves 15–18m (45–60ft) high, many ships suffered serious structural damage, including the carriers *Hōshō* and *Ryūjō*. Both the hull designs and construction techniques (including much electric welding) of recent ships were shown to be incapable of withstanding such conditions. A thorough reappraisal was made and all new designs were revised, including those of *Sōryū* and *Hiryū*. Although this caused considerable delays to the building programme, it meant that by 1941 the IJN's ships were far more seaworthy than they had been six years earlier.

***Hiryū* making speed during its sea trials in April 1939. Both it and *Sōryū* were fast ships, capable of 34 knots (39mph; 63km/h) or more.**

USS Yorktown (1937)

The first of the US Navy's large purpose-built carriers, *Yorktown* saw fierce action in the Pacific War. Fatally crippled in the Battle of Midway, it was abandoned and subsequently torpedoed.

The USN's first ship to be built as a carrier from the keel up was USS *Ranger* (1931), displacing 15,838 tonnes (15,589 tons) fully loaded, which, although smaller than *Lexington* and *Saratoga,* could carry almost as many planes – 86 against 91. Experience with *Ranger* convinced the Navy Board that carriers should be bigger, more powerful, faster and fitted with anti-torpedo protection through internal

Yorktown in port profile and in aerial plan, prior to 1942. As the number of carriers grew, it was necessary to designate the ship's identity as a guide to incoming pilots.

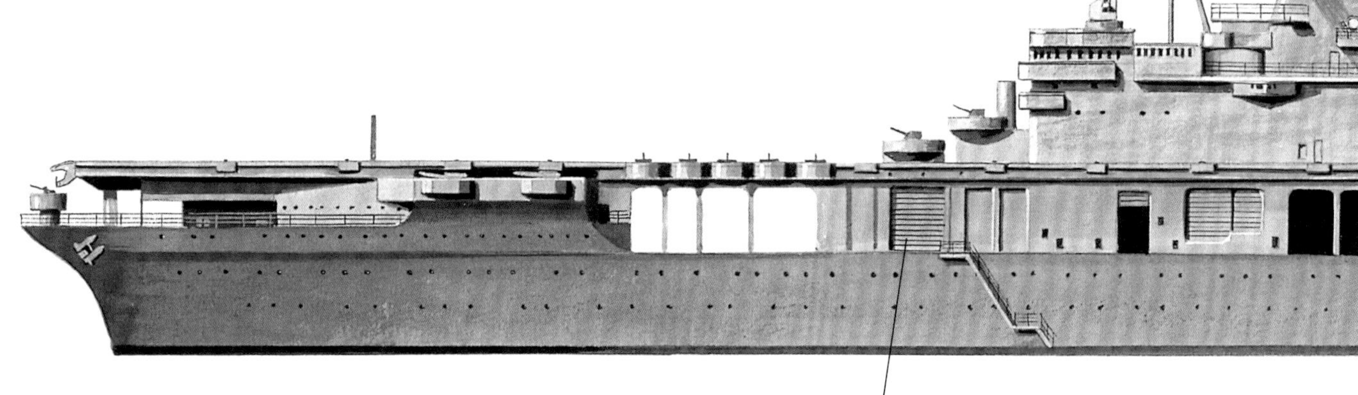

Crash barriers
Crash barriers were mounted forward of the forward elevator and at the forward end of the island.

Catapult
Until 1943 a lateral-firing catapult was installed on the hangar deck for use in emergencies.

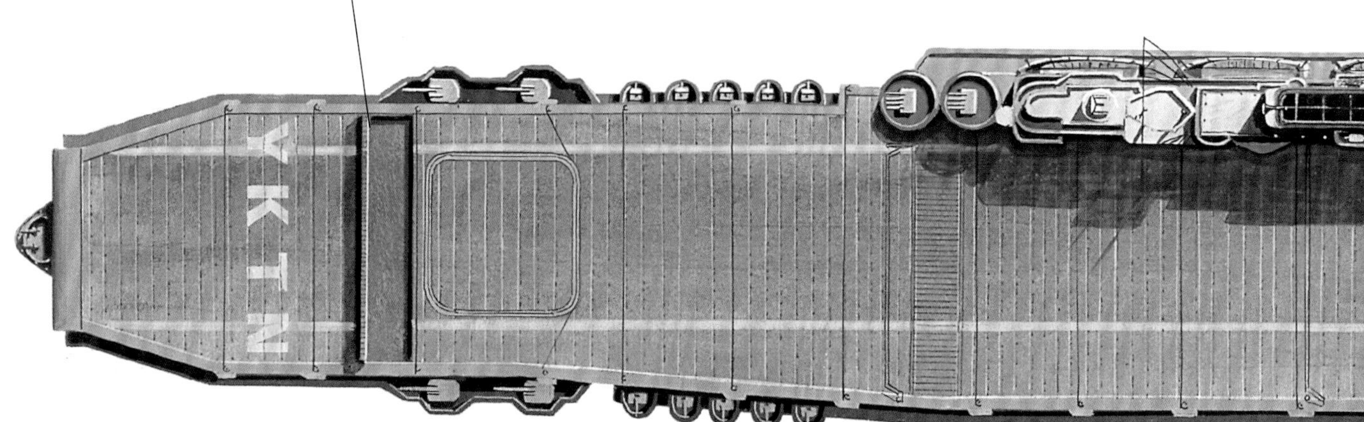

bulkheads and watertight compartments as well as hull armour. Island structures for better command and control were also considered essential. *Yorktown* (CV-5) was the first ship to benefit from these conclusions, although it had to be designed within the limits fixed by the Naval Treaty of 1922, with a displacement of 25,400 tonnes (25,000 tons), permitting a complement of 72 aircraft. Constructed at Newport News Shipbuilding & Dry Dock Co., it was laid down on 31 May 1934, launched on 4 April 1936 and commissioned on 30 September 1937.

On all US carriers from *Ranger* to CVL-49, *Wright* (1947), the hangar deck was the main deck, providing structural strength. On *Yorktown* it was not armoured. The five openings to starboard and six to port could be closed with roller overhead doors. Internal hull arrangements were worked out specifically for carriers, with three transverse bulkheads and partial longitudinal bulkheads protecting the engine rooms, fuel tanks and ammunition magazines. Specially treated non-splinter steel was used in the bulkheads. The fourth deck was the only one to be armoured with 38mm (1.5in) plate. Three express-type aircraft elevators were fitted. Two catapults were mounted on the flight deck, and *Yorktown* had sets of arresting gear at both bow and stern.

Nine boilers were installed in three separate rooms abreast on the principle that even if the outer six were put out of action, the inner three could still supply power. The boilers were three-drum express types, rated to 28kg/cm^2

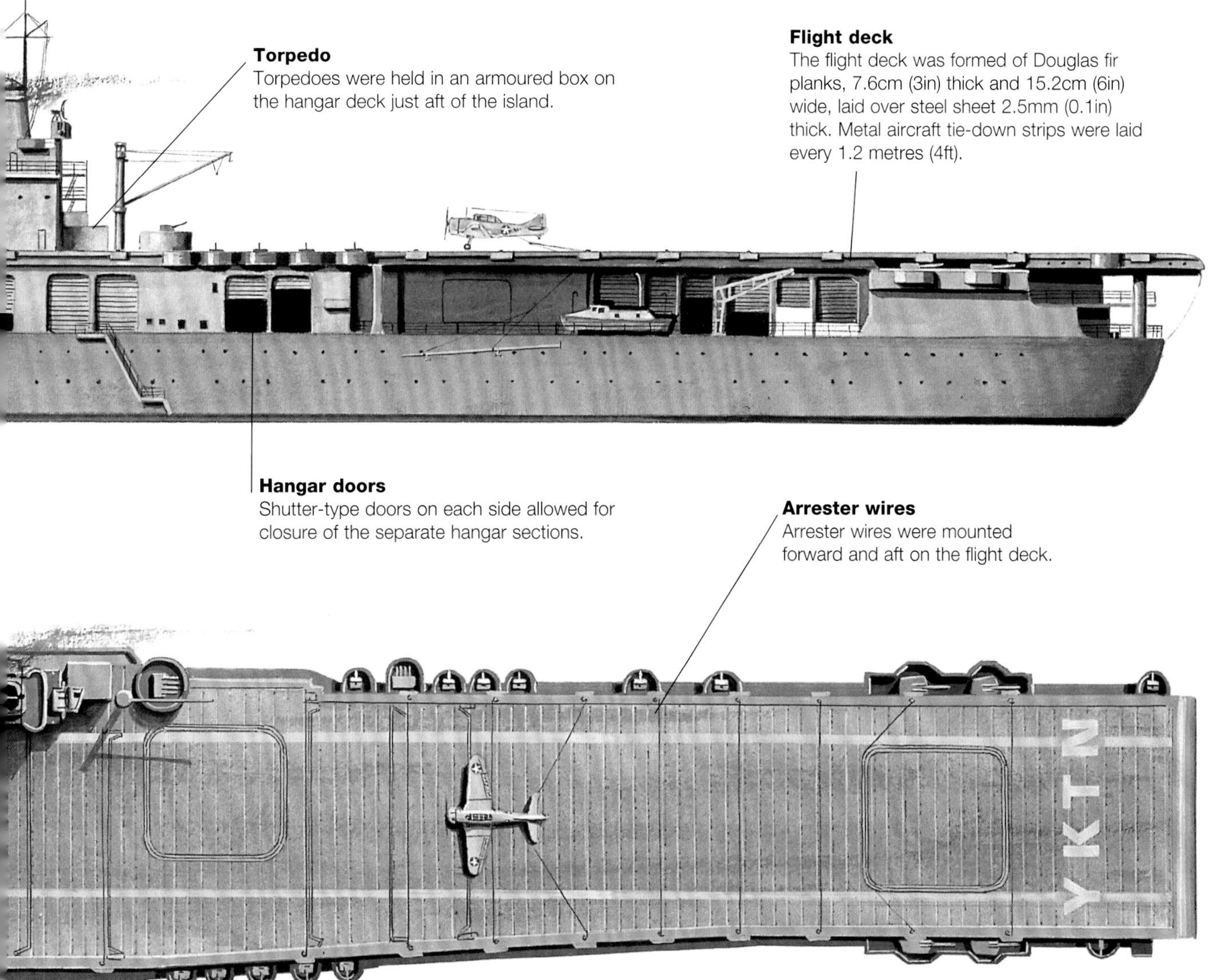

The Curtiss SBC Helldiver dive-bomber was the last biplane type acquired by the US Navy, in 1938. The two-seater was in active service until 1944.

(400psi), and steam was passed from the forward six to the three aft, which were fitted with superheaters to take the temperature up to 315°C (599°F). Four turbines drove the shafts through single reduction gears. The ship's electric plant could generate 4000kW, with an emergency generator giving 400kW. External armour of 82mm (3.25in) was provided below fourth deck level, protecting the fuel tanks and ammunition, and 70mm (2.75in) for the engine space, forming an armoured box, with 102mm (4in) transverse bulkheads at each end.

Specification as commissioned

Dimensions:	Length: 251.4m (824ft 9in); Beam: 33.4m (109ft 6in); Draught: 7.9 m (25ft 11in)
Displacement:	20,100 tonnes (19,800 tons); 25,900 tonnes (25,500 tons) full load
Propulsion:	9 B&W boilers, 4 Parsons turbines; 89,000kW (120,000shp)
Speed:	32.5 knots (60.2km/h; 37.4mph)
Range:	12,500nm (23,200km; 14,400 miles) at 15 knots (27.7km/h; 17.2mph)
Armament:	8 127mm (5in) 38 cal guns, 4 quad 280mm (1.1in) 75 cal guns, 24 .50 cal machine guns
Aircraft:	90
Complement:	2217

After a traditional shake-down cruise to the Caribbean in January–March 1938, the ship joined with USS *Enterprise* and other vessels in intensive drills and 'problem-solving' exercises off the USA's East Coast. These exercises were of great importance and value in developing the integration of carriers – still an unknown and doubtful quantity to many experienced naval officers – with other warships in a powerful sea/air task force. From April 1939 *Yorktown* joined the Pacific Fleet at San Diego. On 20 April 1941, it left Pearl Harbor for the Atlantic, via Panama, and from then until December, with a supporting battleship, cruiser and destroyer group, was deployed in the Atlantic Ocean, ensuring the security of the American coast and the safety of American ships.

Battle of the Coral Sea

Following the Pearl Harbor attack it was immediately ordered to the Pacific, arriving in San Diego on 30 December and installed as flagship of Task Force 17 under Rear Admiral Frank J. Fletcher. Its first mission was carrying Marine troops to Samoa, then joining USS *Enterprise* (Task Force 8) in the real thing: launching air attacks against Japanese positions on the Gilbert and Marshall Islands, as their invasion forces spread across the Pacific islands. Its first major action came in the Battle of the Coral Sea, 4–8 May 1942, intended to stem the Japanese aim to capture Port Moresby in New Guinea and Tulagi in the Southern Solomons. By then ship and air crews had gained a great deal of experience that served them well in this first ever battle between carriers.

USS *Lexington* was sunk and *Yorktown* sustained serious damage when a 250kg (551lb) bomb went through the flight deck and two further decks before exploding. The

radar and refrigeration systems were put out of action and a series of watertight bulkheads was destroyed. Near-miss explosions opened up seams in the outer hull and sprang leaks in the fuel bunkers. The Japanese believed it had been sunk. Back in Pearl Harbor, *Yorktown* was dry-docked on 27 May for an estimated two weeks' repair work, but events were moving fast, and at the order of Admiral Chester Nimitz this was cut to just two days – Nimitz, with only two active carriers, *Hornet* and *Enterprise*, needed *Yorktown*. Only basic patch-up repair was possible before the ship was deployed as Fletcher's flagship in Task Force 17, dispatched with Task Force 16 to intercept the Japanese armada converging on Midway Island.

Admiral Yamamoto and his staff had planned the invasion deliberately to draw out the depleted American carrier force in defence of Midway and annihilate it. American codebreakers picked up the Japanese signals and were prepared for this. Off Midway on 4 June *Yorktown* sent out reconnaissance planes, confirming the Japanese positions, and had to wait to land them before following the other carriers into battle. There was some confusion due to this separation. The initial American attack by torpedo bombers was turned back with massive losses, and the SBD Dauntless dive-bombers from both *Enterprise* and *Yorktown* reached the Japanese carriers at the same time. Their onslaught was devastatingly successful, reducing *Akagi*, *Kaga* and *Sōryū* to flaming hulks. Only *Hiryū* was able to strike back, its dive-bombers making two strikes on *Yorktown*, knocking out its propulsive power for an hour and reducing speed to 20 knots (37km/h; 23mph) when restored.

Hiryū's second wave of torpedo bombers made two hits in the carrier's port side, and again all power was lost. With the ship listing towards capsize point, the order to abandon was given, but *Yorktown* remained afloat and a salvage party was put on board and it was put under tow. The destroyer USS *Hammam* was placed alongside to provide power. At 15.36 on 6 June, Japanese submarine I-168 evaded the destroyer escorts and fired a spread of torpedoes at the carrier. *Hammam* was hit and sank almost immediately, and *Yorktown* was struck by two further torpedoes, and again had to be abandoned. At 07.00 on 7 June the carrier tilted heavily to port, capsized and sank. Its loss was a serious blow to the Allies' naval strength, but Midway was a decisive victory and a turning point in the Pacific War.

In May 1998 the hull of *Yorktown* was discovered, upright on the seabed at a depth of 4.8km (3 miles) below the Pacific.

Smoke billows up after *Yorktown* is struck by a Japanese dive-bomber in the Battle of Midway, June 1942.

Launch catapults

***Yorktown* was the first US carrier to use hydraulic catapults, in which hydraulic fluid under high pressure was released into a cylinder containing a piston. The piston was connected to a releasable shuttle attached to the aircraft. The first US Navy catapult used compressed air to give the plane velocity, and other pioneer systems used gunpowder or cordite. One solution was an electrically driven flywheel device, installed on *Lexington* and *Saratoga* but removed in 1931. Catapults on through-deck carriers were not at first considered essential as the aircraft in use were lightweight and had slow take-off speeds. As planes became heavier and bigger payloads were needed, catapults became an important part of the carrier's equipment, and in 1934 development of the Type H hydraulic catapult began, which with improvements would remain in use until the advent of the steam catapult in the 1950s.**

USS Enterprise (1938)

The seventh US ship to carry the name, the 'Big E' took a prominent part in all the great Pacific campaigns of World War II, surviving bombs and kamikaze attacks to gain both battle scars and stars as the most decorated US ship of the war.

With USS *Yorktown*, *Enterprise* (CV-6) formed a class of two, built side by side at Newport News Shipbuilding & Dry Dock Co. *Enterprise* was laid down on 16 July 1934, launched on 3 October 1936 and commissioned on 12 May 1938. The *Yorktown* class followed USS *Ranger* (CV-4, 1934) in being designed as carriers from the start, and so able to carry more aircraft and function more effectively. *Enterprise* carried as many aircraft as *Lexington* but had only half the older ship's displacement. They followed earlier types in having the flight deck built above the main hull, with open forecastle and stern decks, but were larger than *Ranger* while remaining within treaty limits. By this time the starboard-located island, combining navigation and air control stations with masts, communications aerials and a single massive funnel, were fully established features of American carriers. Three elevators were fitted, and two flight deck catapults plus a single hangar deck catapult. Protective armour was fitted in a waterline belt of 5–10mm (2–4in), 10mm (4in) on bulkheads and around the steering gear. The engine rooms held nine Babcock & Wilcox boilers, powering four Parsons geared turbines and driving four shafts, giving a maximum speed of 32.5

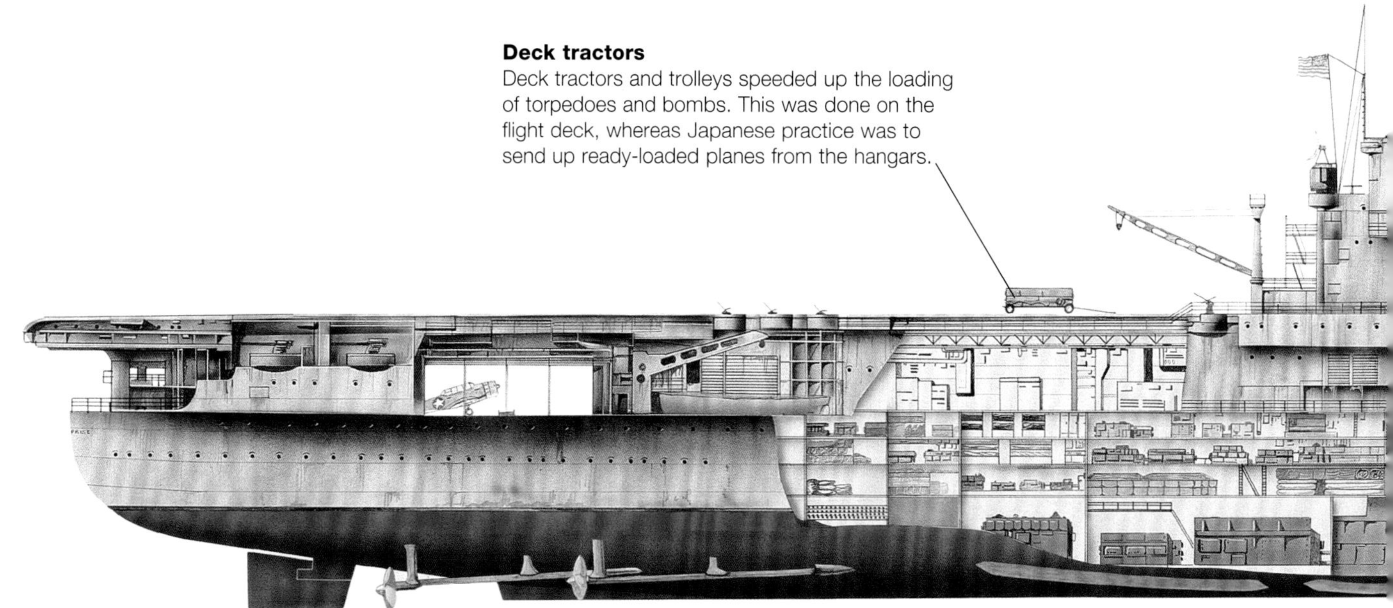

knots (60.2km/h; 37.4mph). Speeds of this order were now part of the basic requirement for USN carriers, both for maximizing launch and landing efficiency and for rapid movement that a submarine of the time could not match.

Enterprise originally was armed with eight 127mm (5in) guns in single mounts, four quad 28mm (1.1in) guns and 24 .50 calibre machine guns. Radar equipment (RCA CXAM-1 type) was fitted early on in 1941. The nominal complement of aircraft was 96, with 18 fighters, 36 torpedo bombers, 37 dive-bombers and five planes classified as general purpose, which might include reconnaissance or minelaying.

Enterprise's first cruise was a shakedown trip to Rio de Janeiro. From April 1939 it was assigned to the Pacific Fleet at San Diego, patrolling the ocean between there and the new US naval base at Pearl Harbor. In December 1941 it was ferrying planes to Guam and Wake Island and was 241km (150 miles) from Pearl Harbor when the Japanese attack was made. Planes flown off for return to the Luke Field land base were misidentified as a renewed Japanese assault and four were mistakenly shot down. Fruitless pursuit of the Japanese Task Force was mounted, but *Enterprise* planes sank the Japanese submarine I-70 on 10 December, the first in a long series of successes.

In the battles of 1942 the USN carriers emerged from their role as plane ferries, scouting and escort craft to prove themselves prime fighting ships in the successive battles of the Coral Sea, Midway, the Eastern Solomons, Santa Cruz and Guadalcanal. At Midway, *Enterprise* was the flagship of Rear Admiral Raymond A. Spruance in Task Force 16. In the Battle of the Eastern Solomons on 24–25 August, the ship suffered serious damage from three bomb hits and several near misses, and 74 crew were killed. At Santa

The profile shows the ship in post-1941 form, with CXAM-1 radar mounted on the tripod mast above the signals shelter.

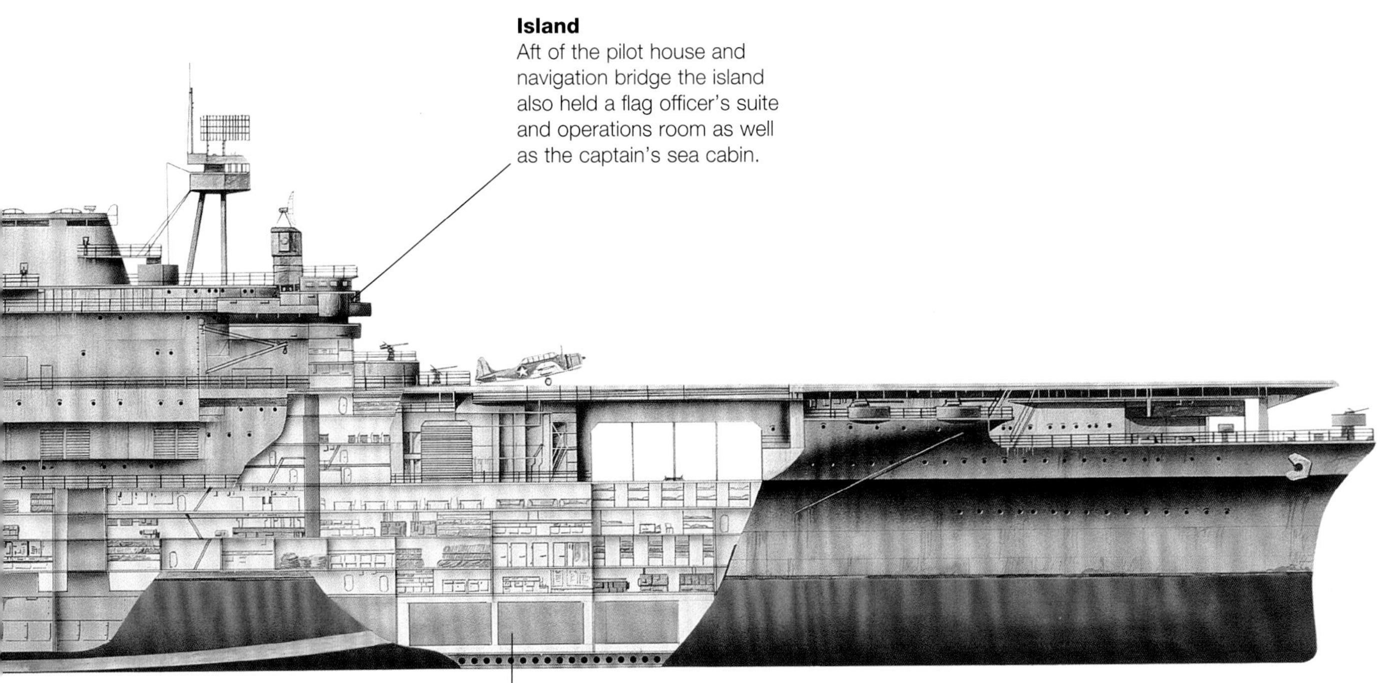

Enterprise after RCA-CXAM radar had been fitted. The absence of aircraft suggests it has accomplished a delivery trip, perhaps in late 1941.

Cruz, 26 October, it was hit twice by bombs that killed 44 crew, but remained in action, taking on board many planes from USS *Hornet*, which was sunk in the battle. Altogether it had taken six hits from Japanese bombs and lost over 300 crew by 26 October. At that time *Enterprise* was the only operational carrier in the Pacific until *Saratoga* returned to active service on 5 December. In May–July 1943 essential repairs were made at Pearl Harbor before the ship returned to Bremerton naval base for a refit. This included the fitting of an anti-torpedo blister belt and installation of AA batteries as well as radar control for the 127mm (5in) and 40mm (1.5in) guns. The flight deck was extended by 5.5m (18ft) and widened by 1.5m (4ft 11in).

Specification (as of October 1943)

Dimensions:	Length: 251.4m (824ft 9in); Beam: 34.9m (114ft 5in); Draught: 7.9m (25ft 11in)
Displacement:	21,336 tonnes (21,000 tons); 32,573 tonnes (32,060 tons) full load
Propulsion:	9 B&W boilers, 4 Parsons geared turbines, 4 shafts; 89,484kW (120,000shp)
Speed:	32.5 knots (60.2km/h; 37.4mph)
Range:	12,000nm (23,200km; 14,400 miles) at 15 knots (27.7km/h; 17.2mph)
Armament:	8 127mm (5in) 38 cal guns, 8 twin and 6 quad 40mm Bofors guns, 50 20mm Oerlikon guns
Aircraft:	90
Complement:	2217

Fleet actions

On return to Pearl Harbor on 6 November 1943, *Enterprise* was now part of a formidable carrier fleet some 14 strong, including six new fleet carriers, and a year of intense action followed as the Allied forces gradually reversed the Japanese invasion successes of 1942. Support of troop landings took *Enterprise* to the Marshall Islands, Kwajalein Atoll, the fortified island of Truk, Majuro Atoll and the coast of New Guinea in hard-fought battles on land and sea. At Truk in February 1944 it launched the first night attack by carrier-based bombers, radar-directed, and was the first US carrier equipped for continuous 24-hour action, having its hull number altered to CV(N) for Night, in recognition. In mid-year, with a massive offensive about to close in on

Japan's inner defences, *Enterprise* took part in the last carrier battle in the Philippine Sea on 19–20 June 1944. In intense combat, three Japanese carriers, *Shō kaku*, *Hiyō* and *Taihō* , were sunk by American aircraft and submarines and 426 Japanese naval aircraft were destroyed. This assured the USA's air supremacy over the Pacific, but from October that year kamikaze attacks began, and although only around seven in 100 made a successful strike, they were a dangerous new factor, and AA defences were heightened. Ranging the western Pacific from the Chinese coast to Iwo Jima, Ulithi Atoll and ever closer to the Japanese mainland, from 10 February *Enterprise* was launching regular raids on Japan's home islands. This proximity to Japan made the American ships vulnerable to land-based air strikes, including intensive suicide attacks.

Between Ulithi Atoll and Okinawa, on 20 March *Enterprise* was forced back to Ulithi for repairs after a bomb hit, and accidental damage from shells fired by escort craft; and then it was the victim of two successful kamikaze strikes on 11 April and 13 May. With the forward elevator wrecked, a hectic and distinguished war career was brought to an end and the ship was directed to Puget Sound for repairs.

Enterprise was one of the ships used in late 1945–46 for Operation Magic Carpet, the hangars fitted with thousands of temporary berths, making four voyages to bring US troops back from Pearl Harbor and Europe, then placed on reserve that year and decommissioned on 17 February 1947. In October 1952 it was redesignated as an attack carrier, CVA-6, and again on 8 August 1953 as CVS-6, an anti-submarine carrier. Efforts in 1956 to preserve the ship, now condemned as obsolete, did not succeed and it was finally broken up in 1958.

Enterprise's war record encompassed the destruction of 911 enemy aircraft, the sinking of 71 ships and severe damage to a further 192. It gained the greatest number of battle honours of any US warship, including 20 battle stars.

Naming conventions

Prior to 1942, USN carrier air groups were named for the ship, so there was an *Enterprise* air group, with its component squadrons identified by the ship's hull number: VF-6 for the fighters, VB-6 for the dive-bombers, VT-6 for the torpedo bombers and VS-6 for scout planes. In wartime, however, planes were frequently exchanged and relocated, sometimes to land bases; and with carrier sinkings, surviving aircraft had to be found new homes. A new nomenclature gradually emerged, centred on the concept of numbered Air Groups. At first these still carried a particular ship's number, but this was changed on the realization that this could give the Japanese a clue as to a carrier's whereabouts. Random numbers were then applied. In the later stages of the war *Enterprise* flew planes of Air Groups 10 and 20, and Night Air Group 90.

The Douglas TBD Devastator torpedo bomber entered service in 1937. Its wings had hydraulic folding mechanisms. Involved in the battles of 1942, it was supplanted by more modern aircraft in the later years of World War II.

HMS Ark Royal (1938)

The third *Ark Royal*, the first carrier to bear the name, saw intensive action in the early part of World War II in the Atlantic, the Norwegian Sea and finally the Mediterranean.

Design work on a new carrier had begun in 1931, and by the time of commissioning, *Ark Royal* embodied all that the Royal Navy had learned about carrier design and operation in the previous 20 years. This was the first carrier to be designed in an integrated way with hangar and flight decks as part of the hull structure, not built up on top of it. Laid

Though massive in appearance from the starboard side, the minimal space occupied by *Ark Royal*'s island is clearly seen from the plan view: it is hardly wider than the ship's funnel.

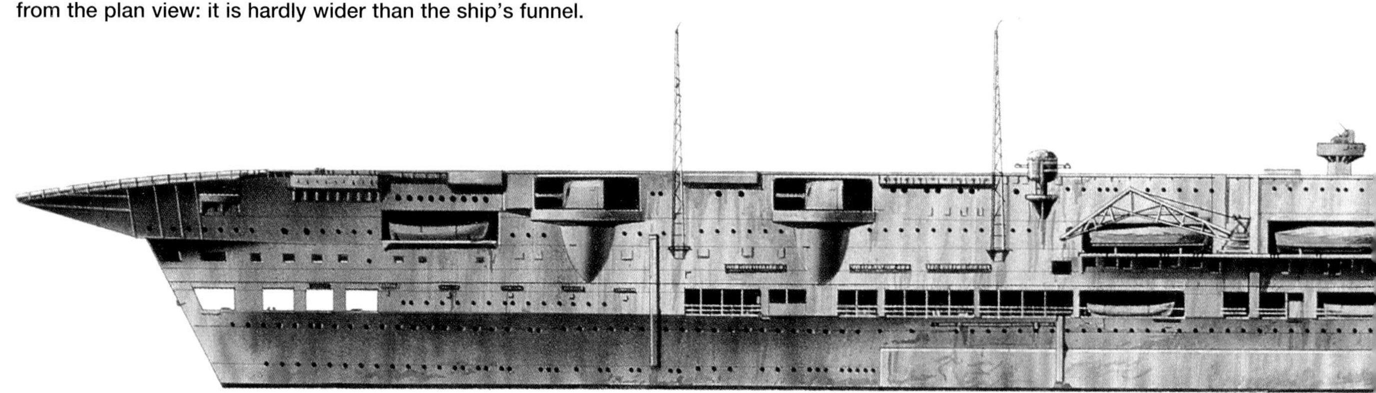

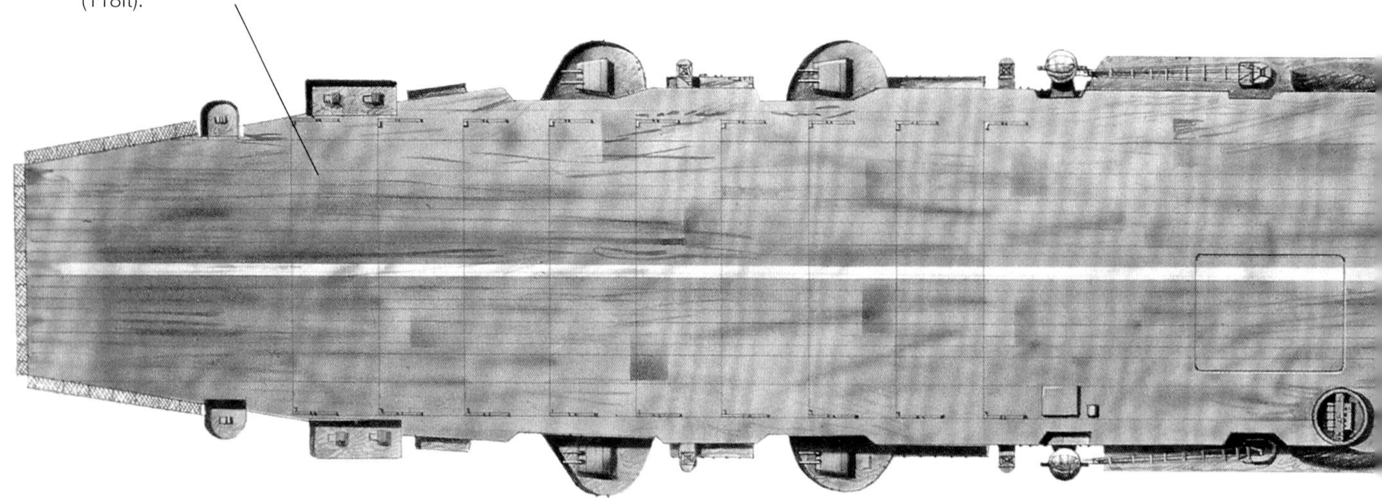

Flight deck
Ark Royal's flight deck was 20m (66ft) above the waterline. Its length exceeded that of the keel by 36m (118ft).

down at Cammell Laird's yard, Birkenhead, England, on 16 September 1935 and launched on 13 April 1937, it cost £3,215,000 to build and was commissioned into the fleet on 16 December 1938. A full-length flight deck was fitted with an island bridge deck, conning tower and a single funnel. To save weight the hull was part-welded, and not heavily armoured. This *Ark Royal* was the last RN carrier not to have an armoured flight deck. Its hull protection was a 8.9cm (3.5in) side belt and 114mm (4.5in) above the machinery and magazines. Six Admiralty three-drum boilers in three separate engine rooms provided steam for three Parsons geared turbines, driving three shafts.

For defence the ship carried 16 110mm (4.5in) DP guns in twin turrets, 32 40mm (2-pdr) in four mountings and eight .50 calibre heavy machine guns. Three lifts served the two hangar decks. Two cranes were fitted for recovery of seaplanes from the surface. A new arrester gear arrangement was also fitted, and a crash barrier was installed for the first time on a British carrier. Although the original design was to provide for 72 planes, the completed

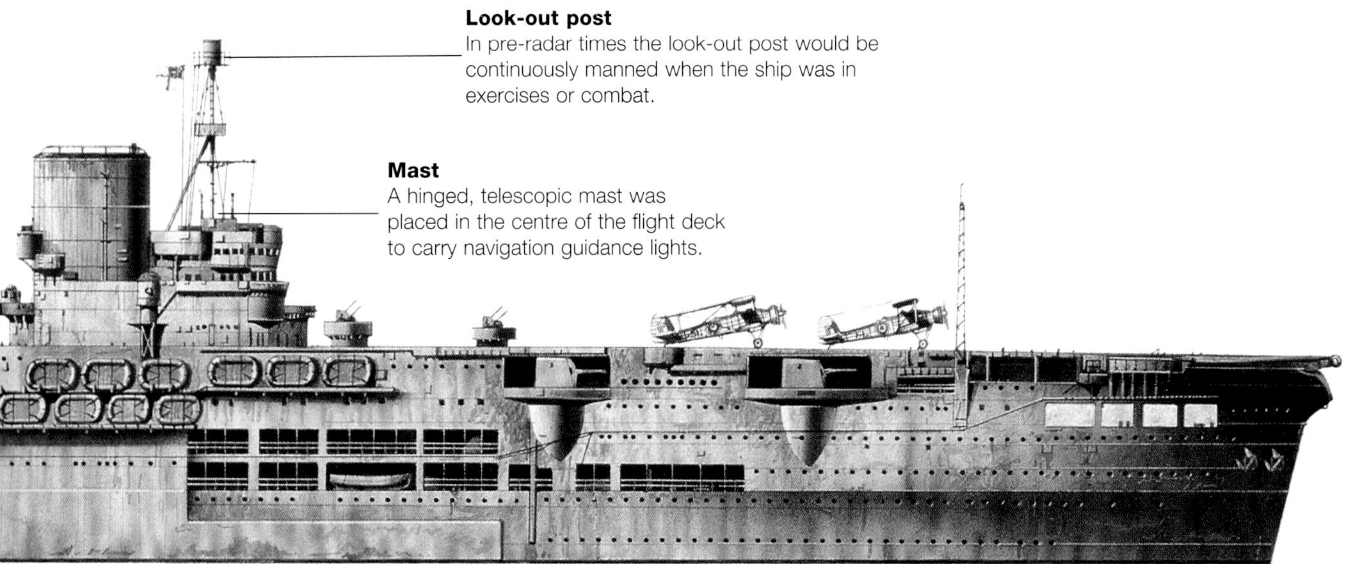

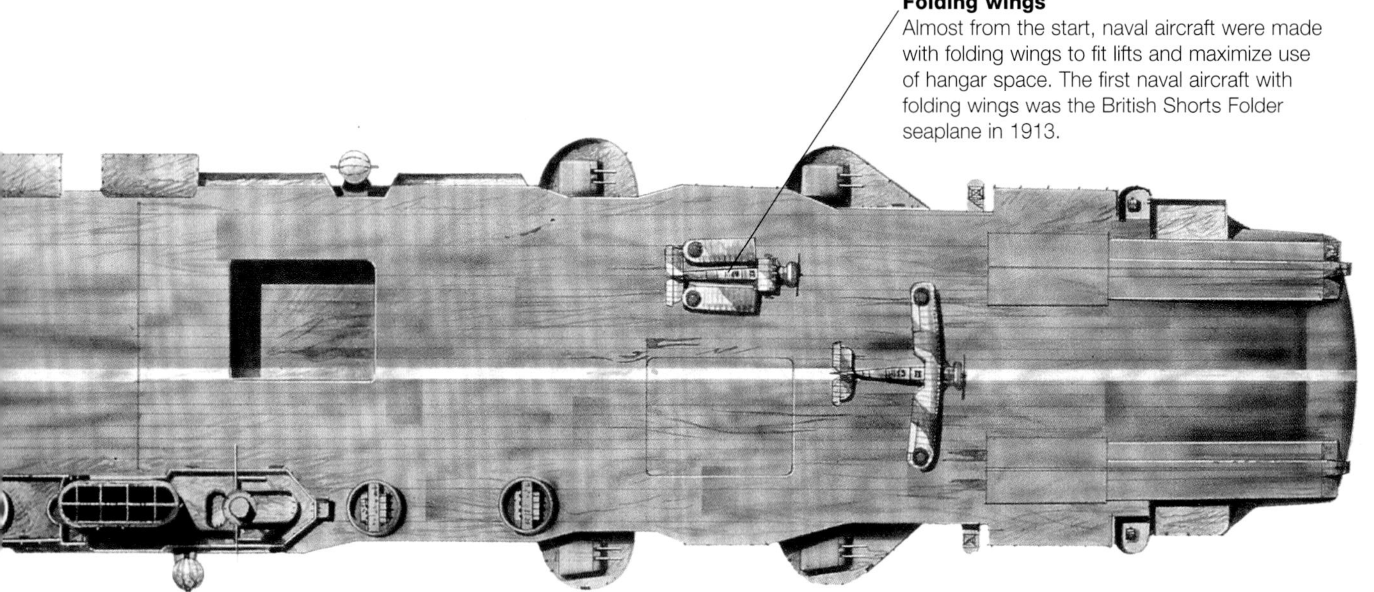

Forward profile, with a Fairey Swordfish torpedo bomber poised on the bow.

Specification

Dimensions:	Length: 208m (682ft); Beam: 28.9m (94ft 10in); Draught: 8.73m (27ft 10in)
Displacement:	22,352 tonnes (22,000 tons); 28,163 tonnes (27,720 tons) full load
Propulsion:	6 Admiralty boilers, 3 Parsons geared turbines; 76,807kW (103,000shp)
Speed:	31 knots (57km/h; 36mph)
Range:	7600nm (14,100km; 8700 miles) at 20 knots (37km/h; 23mph)
Armament:	16 110mm (4.5in) DP guns, 32 2-pdr 40mm (1.57in) pom-pom guns, 12.7mm (32.5in) AA machine guns
Aircraft:	60
Complement:	1580

ship only held 60, and as aircraft became larger and heavier by 1941 this was reduced to 54 (the *Illustrious* held only 36). *Ark Royal* flew Blackburn Skuas, usable as fighters and dive-bombers with a 225kg (500lb) payload, Blackburn Rocs, also dual purpose but more effective in fighter mode, and Fairey Swordfish torpedo bomber/reconnaissance planes, which could launch a 731kg (1610lb), 457mm (18in) diameter torpedo or drop a 681kg (1500lb) bomb.

Home Fleet service

Ark Royal was attached to the Home Fleet and was in immediate action from the outbreak of World War II. It narrowly avoided torpedoes from U-boat Type IXA U39 off Rockall on 14 September 1939: the submarine was sunk by the destroyer escorts. Its planes downed a German flying boat in the North Sea 12 days later. With HMS *Renown* it went to the South Atlantic in pursuit of the pocket battleship *Graf Spee*, and was based at Freetown, Sierra Leone, until February 1940. A brief spell in the Mediterranean was followed by participation in support of the unsuccessful landing in northern Norway in April, and a return to the Mediterranean where it was part of Force H in Operation Catapult, the attack on the Vichy French fleet at Mers el-Kebir on 3 July.

The battlecruiser *Dunkerque*, already damaged, was destroyed by *Ark Royal's* planes on 4 July. When Italy declared war on 10 June 1940, *Ark Royal* launched attacks on Italian airfields as part of the struggle to preserve British supply lines. Always on the move, the *Ark* supported the Free French in the effort to take Dakar in September 1940, returned to Liverpool for maintenance work in October and was back in the Mediterranean in November. Early in 1941 it delivered desperately needed fighters to Malta, then was deployed to the Atlantic to search for the battleships *Scharnhorst* and *Gneisenau*. In May the hunt changed to *Bismarck*. Swordfish planes launched and landed in stormy conditions with the flight deck pitching 15m (50ft) and more. It kept the German battleship under surveillance on 26 and 27 May and fired the torpedoes that disabled its steering gear.

After the sinking of *Bismarck*, *Ark Royal* returned to the Mediterranean and the campaign to hold Malta. At 15.41 on 13 November 1941 it was sailing in line with the battleship *Malaya*, the carrier *Furious* and six destroyers.

Ark Royal seen from the port side, in original condition, June 1938.

U-boats were shadowing the force, and *Ark Royal* was launching and landing Swordfish for reconnaissance when it was struck amidships on the starboard side, just below the island and 5m (16ft 5in) beneath the waterline by a torpedo from Type VIIC submarine U-81, about 48km (30 miles) east of Gibraltar.

Most of the crew were evacuated onto the escort ships, and the *Ark Royal* was taken under tow by two Gibraltar tugs. A damage control team struggled all night to keep the ship afloat, but by 04.30 on 14 June they were forced to abandon it, listing heavily and eventually sinking vertically, stern first, at 06.24. German propaganda had several times claimed the sinking of the elusive *Ark*, but this time it was true. A single member of the crew was killed by the torpedo strike. In autumn 2002 the remains were located by a Hugin 3000 AUV (autonomous underwater vehicle).

Ark Royal had been a model for the *Illustrious* class, and the failure of its torpedo protection caused rapid design changes in new carriers along with improved damage control systems and practice, and the provision of diesel generators to provide electric power in the event of a mechanical failure.

The Fleet Air Arm

When the Royal Air Force was formed on 1 April 1918 (formerly the Royal Flying Corps), naval aviation was transferred to it, giving it the 55,000 personnel of the Naval Air Service and around 2500 aircraft, mostly small seaplanes. It was intended that the Navy would provide the carriers and that the RAF would supply the aircraft, flying crews and maintenance teams. This was a most unfortunate decision. The Royal Navy had taken a pioneering role in naval aviation and now found itself reduced to a transport service, with little say in the planning and design of aircraft that were essentially weapons of naval strategy. Despite the increasingly obvious problems of managing naval aviation through two separate services, it was 1937 before the Fleet Air Arm once again became an integral part of the Royal Navy.

USS Wasp (1940)

The last of the 'treaty carriers' whose size was restricted by the 1922 Naval Treaty, and the last US carrier to be commissioned before America entered World War II, *Wasp* was the only ship of its class.

Intended as a replacement for the USN's first carrier, *Langley*, and designated CV-7, *Wasp*, the seventh US warship to bear the name, was laid down at the Bethlehem Steel Co.'s Fore River Shipyard, Quincy, Massachusetts, on 1 April 1936, launched on 4 April 1939 and commissioned on 25 April 1940. In October 1940, after further trials and training, it joined the fleet. Its dimensions and capacity were governed by the 1922 Naval Treaty, whose rules the USA, as sponsor nation of the treaty, upheld more strictly than Germany or Japan. The new carrier was to be only about three-quarters the displacement of *Enterprise*, and its cost was $20 million.

Efforts to save weight had to balance military capacity against survivability, with some compromise on the latter. Belt armour of 102mm (4in) thickness was fitted amidships, and the main deck, below the flight deck, had

Wasp's profile shows that its design continued the practice of building the flight deck as a superstructure above the hull.

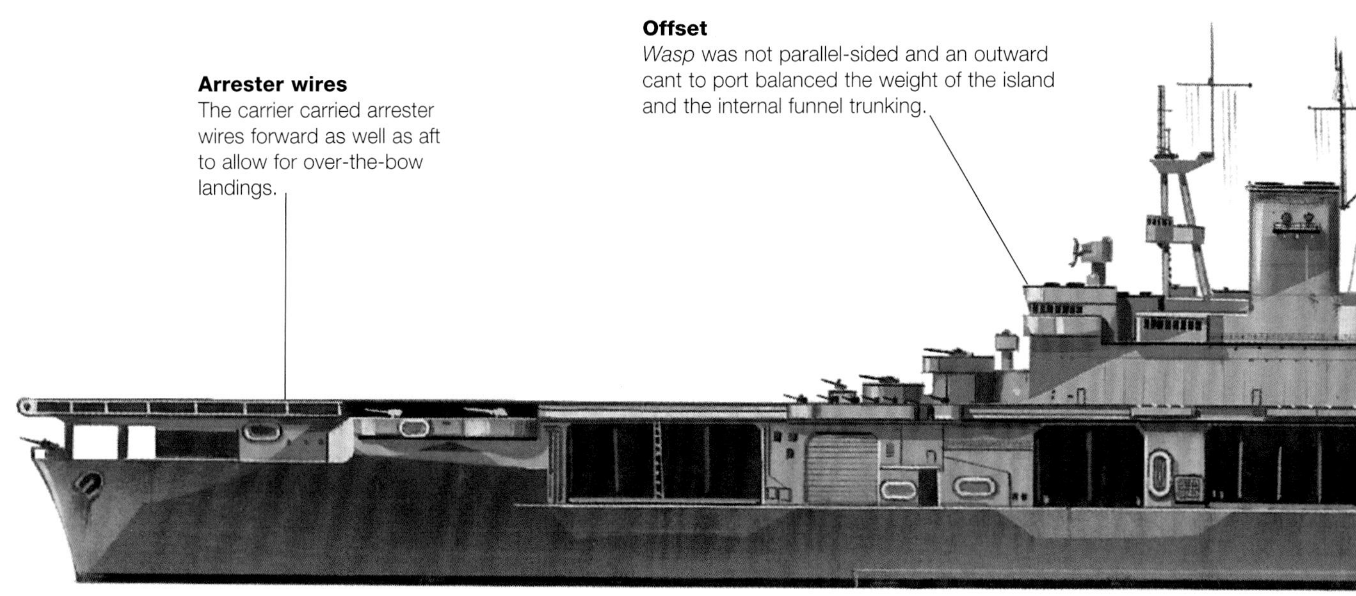

38mm (1.5in) plating. This modest protection turned out to be inadequate. *Wasp* was also given less powerful machinery than *Enterprise*. Six boilers working at 39.7kg/cm^2 (565psi) powered two Parsons steam turbines, driving two shafts. This helped keep down the carrier's displacement, at a cost of around three knots of speed, although the maximum was a respectable 29.5 knots (54.6km/h; 33.9mph). The ship's design was very much on the conventional pattern, with the forward flight deck built above an open forecastle deck and a similar arrangement aft above the quarterdeck. Overall length of the flight deck was 225.9m (741ft 3in). A substantial funnel rose above the island between two masts.

Wasp was the first carrier fitted with a deck edge elevator, on the port side level with the island, in addition to two inboard, and this turned out to be a useful innovation. Two catapults were fitted on the flight deck and two on the hangar deck, all hydraulically operated. For its own defence the ship had eight 130mm (5in) 38 calibre guns, with 16 28mm (1.1in) 75 calibre AA cannon and 24 12.7mm (.5in) heavy machine guns. Most of the latter were replaced by 20mm (.787in) AA guns in January 1942. This was also the first US Navy ship to be fitted with CXAM-1 air search radar, in March 1941. Though regarded as a 'light' carrier, *Wasp*'s design allowed it to embark over 70 aircraft. By comparison, British fleet carriers under design at the same time held many fewer aircraft but were much more substantial ships.

Atlantic patrols

In October 1940 *Wasp* was assigned to Carrier Division 3 and engaged in flight-testing of Army Air Corps fighters, establishing that a carrier could cope with planes built for land bases. On 28 July 1941, *Wasp* sailed for Iceland with 33 Army aircraft, then returned to Norfolk for more carrier qualifications and other flight training. From 6 September

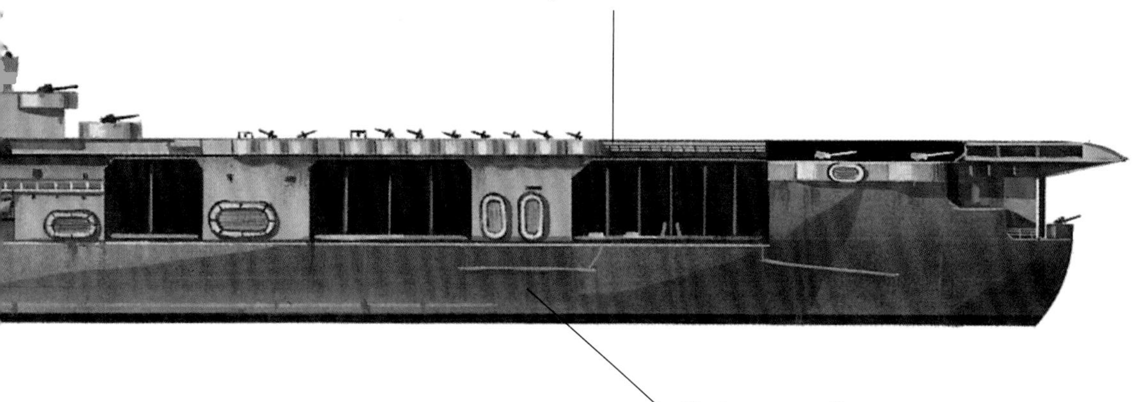

Deck elevator
The deck edge elevator was fitted as an experiment but was quickly recognized as a great help in flight deck and hangar operations.

Marine camouflage
Wasp in dark grey Measure 1 camouflage paint, before the 1941 refit that saw a CXAM-1 radar fitted to the mast.

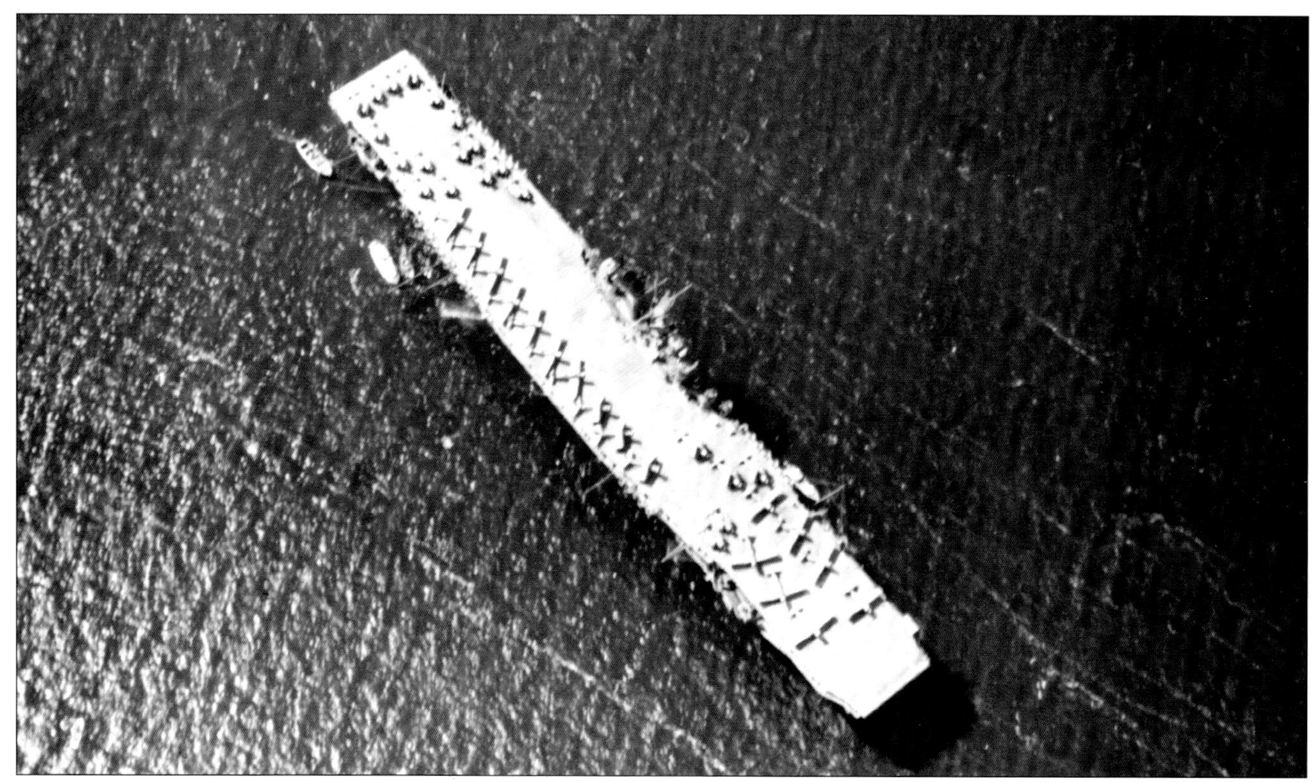

Aerial view of *Wasp*, at a Pacific location, June 1942. A month earlier the deck was filled with Royal Air Force Spitfires.

Specification

Dimensions:	Length: 210m (688ft); Beam: 24.6m (80ft 9in); Draught: 6.1m (20ft)
Displacement:	14,900 tonnes (14,700 tons); 19,423 tonnes (19,116 tons) full load
Propulsion:	6 boilers, 2 steam turbines, 2 shafts; 52,000kW (70,000shp)
Speed:	29.5 knots (54.6km/h; 33.9mph)
Range:	12,000nm (22,000km; 14,000 miles) at 15 knots (27.7km/h; 17.2mph)
Armament:	8 127mm (5in) 38 cal guns; 16 28mm (1.1in) 75 cal guns, 24 .50in machine guns
Aircraft:	70+
Complement:	2167

it was on patrol "to enforce the neutrality of the United States in the Atlantic." With other American warships, it escorted British merchant ships in convoys as far as mid-ocean. When the Japanese attacked Pearl Harbor on 7 December 1941, *Wasp* was at Grassy Bay, Bermuda, and was not immediately sent to the Pacific, since a strong naval presence was required in the Caribbean where certain islands were French colonial possessions whose allegiance was being demanded by the Vichy government, and that harboured French warships.

Once the tension with French forces had lessened, it went to Norfolk Navy Yard in Portsmouth, Virginia, for an overhaul that lasted until 14 January 1942. After further coastal patrols, on 26 March the ship was deployed to Britain with Task Force 39 as a reinforcement for the hard-pressed Royal Navy. Stopping at Scapa Flow and Glasgow, it took on the mission to ferry 47 Spitfire fighters to the British island colony of Malta in the Mediterranean, with an escort of Force W of the Royal Navy and two American destroyers. The mission was successful, although many of the Spitfires were later destroyed on the ground by German bombs. *Wasp* was also carrying 12 Grumman F4F Wildcats of Fighter Squadron VF-71 as

Wasp in 1942, carrying Spitfires to Malta. The carrier made two trips on this hazardous mission.

Torpedo attack

Torpedoes were important weapons to carriers. Their planes could launch them against hostile ships, but they themselves were vulnerable to both aerial and submarine-fired torpedoes. The most deadly and feared torpedo of World War II was the Japanese Type 93 'Long Lance' and its smaller version, the 533mm (21in) Type 95, fired from destroyers and submarines respectively. The Type 93 had a range of 10km (6.2 miles) at a speed of 45 knots (83km/h; 52mph) with a 490kg (1080lb) warhead. Type 95, which disabled *Wasp*, had the same range and speed, with a 404kg (893lb) warhead. American torpedo bombers were armed with the Mk 13 aerial torpedo, of 569mm (22.4in) diameter and with a 272kg (600lb) warhead, which in the early years of the war had poor reliability, with only around 30 per cent giving satisfactory performance. By 1944, after numerous modifications, their performance had vastly improved.

its own combat air patrol flight. On 3 May 1942, *Wasp* delivered a second group of Spitfires to Malta in company with the British carrier *Eagle*.

With the loss of *Lexington* and *Yorktown* seriously weakening the US Navy's carrier force in the Pacific, *Wasp* was directed to that ocean in June 1942, embarking F4F Wildcat fighters, SBD-3 Dauntless dive-bombers and TBF Avenger torpedo bombers at San Diego. It supported the Marine landings on Guadalcanal on 7–8 August with combat air patrols and strikes on enemy bases. On 15 September, with USS *Hornet*, *Wasp* was again giving air protection to Marine transports when at 14.44 it took massive hits from three 'Long Lance' Type 95 torpedoes fired from Japanese submarine I-19, striking through the armour close to the forwards magazine and fuel storage areas. Fires spread too rapidly to be controllable, and successive explosions prevented escort ships from coming in close. At 15.20 the order to abandon ship was given, and finally the fire-racked hulk was sunk by torpedoes from USS *Landsdowne*. With it went 45 planes, although 25 out of 26 airborne planes were recovered by *Hornet*. Of the ship's crew, 193 lost their lives. The *Essex*-class carrier CV-18, on the stocks at Fore River as USS *Oriskany*, had its name changed to *Wasp* in honour of its predecessor from the same yard.

CAM and MAC Ships (1941)

Pressed into action as convoy protection vessels, the CAM and MAC ships had an important role in the Battle of the Atlantic, where warfare was conducted on three levels – sea surface, undersea and in the air.

Apart from occasional German forays like that of *Scharnhorst* and *Gneisenau*, as well as lone surface raiders, the Allied navies maintained control of the Atlantic Ocean's surface routes. However, the same was not true below the surface, where U-boats from their bases in Western France could patrol far into the ocean, assembling as 'wolf packs' to attack convoys. In a highly co-ordinated campaign, information on convoy locations, movements and escorts was passed to U-boat HQ and on via the Enigma code system to the submarines. The key to this system was the Focke Wulf FW200 Kondor reconnaissance plane, a four-engined craft with a 2000-nautical mile (3700-km;

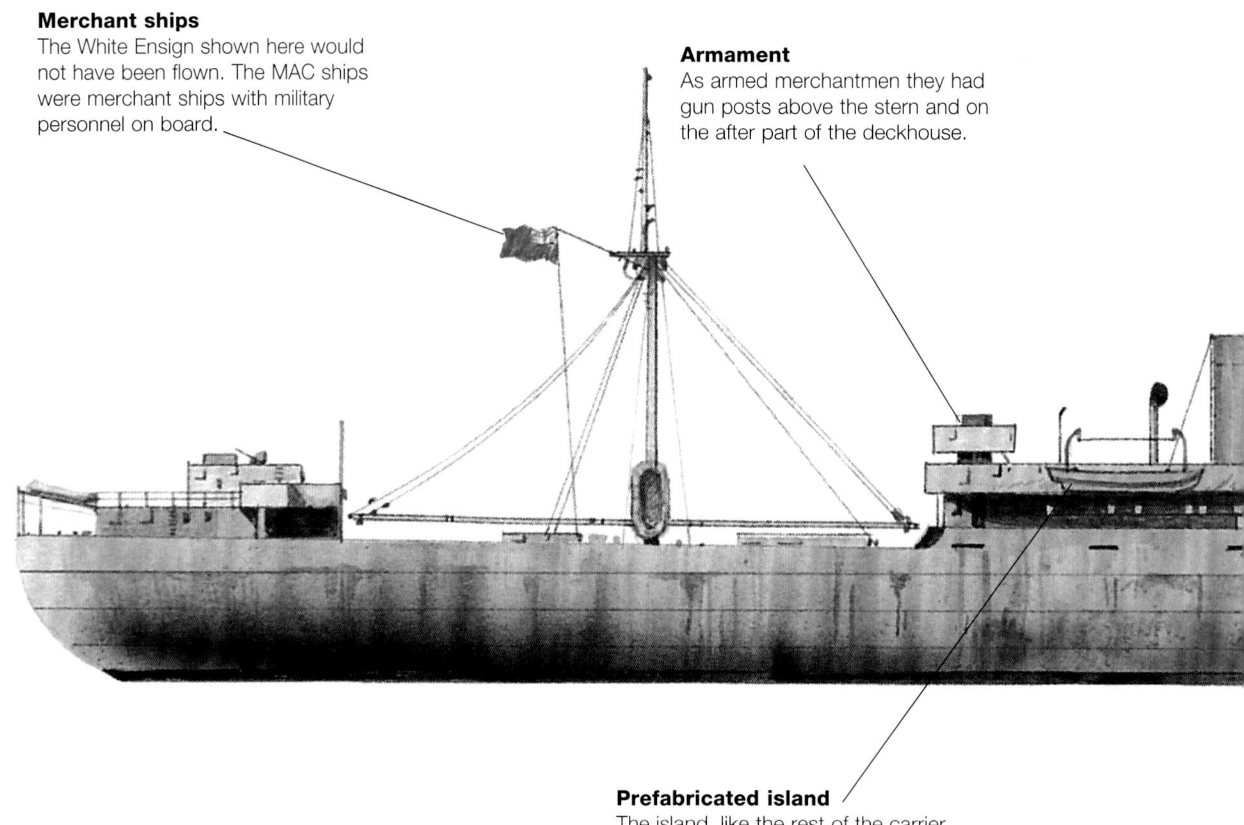

2300-mile) range. Based in Western France and Norway, they could sweep a wide extent of ocean and bring back intelligence of a convoy's position and direction.

The Kondor, although armed, was vulnerable to air attack, but in 1941 the Royal Navy had no carriers to spare to mount Atlantic patrols. Instead, in a spirit of make-do, the idea of the CAM or Catapult Aircraft Merchant ship was developed. Ships were already available: what was needed was a system mounted on the forecastle to launch a fighter plane with the speed, armament and manoeuvrability to down a FW 200, or the Junkers 88 and Heinkel 111 bombers that attacked Russia-bound convoys from bases in Norway.

There was undoubtedly an underlying element of desperation to the scheme, which was rolled out as a quick stopgap while escort carriers were still under conversion or construction. While in no way seen as a kamikaze-type campaign as used by the Japanese in the late stages of the war, it required an airman of exceptional skill, nerve and courage to be catapulted off a ship with no prospect of

A typical CAM ship. Some were given names beginning with Empire, though not all 'Empire' ships were fitted with catapults.

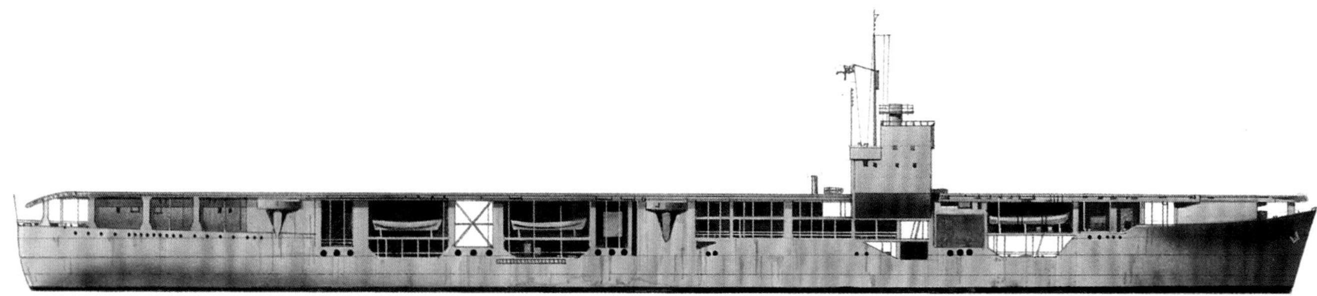

Profile of a *Rapana*-type tanker converted to MAC ship. The white naval ensign is incorrect: these were designated as merchant vessels. The island, like the rest of the carrier structure, was made as much as possible of prefabricated parts.

landing back on it – he could possibly find a landing ground if not too far from a friendly coast, but more likely he would have to ditch his plane and hope to be picked up out of the water by one of the convoy escorts. The chosen aircraft was the Hurricane Mk 1A, of which 50 were adapted with reinforced frames for firing from catapults as Sea Hurricanes. A further 50 Hurricanes were built in Canada for the purpose.

Merchant carriers

Altogether 35 merchant ships were fitted with bow catapults that used a cordite-powered rocket to drive a launch trolley. Not officially designated as Royal Navy warships, they flew the Red Ensign and were not commanded by naval officers.

Specification (MAC tanker MV Ancylus)

Dimensions:	Length: 142m (465ft); Beam: 18m (59ft); Draught: 8.4m (27ft 6in)
Displacement:	8145 tonnes (8017 tons); 16,256 tonnes (16,000 tons) full load
Propulsion:	Diesel engine, single shaft; 2610kW (3500bhp)
Speed:	13 knots (24km/h; 15mph)
Range:	10,000nm (18,520km; 11,510 miles)
Armament:	1 100mm (4in) gun; 8 20mm (.787in) AA guns
Aircraft:	3
Complement:	100

The pilots were RAF men and a special RAF unit was formed on 5 May 1941, known as the Merchant Service Fighter Unit (MSFU). Five naval vessels were similarly equipped, known as Fighter Catapult Ships (FCS) and flying Fleet Air Arm Fairey Fulmars. The CAM ships carried two Hurricanes and two pilots.

Operations began on 27 May 1941 with CAM ship *Michael E.* escorting a westbound convoy: an unlucky start as it was sunk by a torpedo from Type IXB U-108 on 2 June. By July that year there were 16 vessels in action, and the first effective result was on 2 August 1941 when Lieut. R.W.H. Everett, a Royal Naval Reservist, launched from FCS *Maplin*, shot down a FW200, ditched his plane and was rescued by a destroyer. On 1 November 1941 a Hurricane from CAM *Empire Foam* chased off but failed to destroy a Kondor. The Kondor could lose two engines and still fly home, and successes were comparatively rare.

In winter conditions CAM operations had to be suspended but they resumed in March 1942. By early 1943 escort carriers were being deployed and the CAM operation came to an end. The MSFU was disbanded on 8 June but some CAMs were still at sea and Hurricanes flying from *Empire Darwin* and *Empire Tide* destroyed two Kondors on 28 July 1943. In total 12 CAM ships were sunk, eight planes were lost and eight German planes destroyed. The greatest importance of the CAM ships was in boosting the confidence of convoy seamen, and in convincing public opinion in Britain that something was being done to counter the U-boat menace.

MAC (Merchant Aircraft Carrier) ships were a more highly developed form of the CAM ship. Converted bulk carriers, mostly originally built as grain ships and oil tankers, they were both cargo carriers and capable of launching and landing assault planes. The 19 'Empire' named ships flew

Swordfish Mk I and Mk II torpedo bombers whose biplane construction allowed take-off at lower speeds than Sea Hurricanes: catapults were not fitted to the MACs. With a continuous flight deck of minimum dimensions 120m (390ft) by 19m (62ft), two arrester wires and an emergency barrier, they had a minimal conning post set well forward to starboard and a single pole mast. Up to four aircraft were carried, and some had a lift from hangar to flight deck.

Like the CAM ships they flew the Red Ensign and the servicemen on board wore merchant navy badges. They were motor ships, which could more easily dispense with a funnel to allow for an unimpeded flush deck. In all 19 were converted and gave more substantial protection to convoys than the CAM ships could. They were lightly armed, but sailed with naval destroyers and corvettes with AA batteries and anti-submarine defences. Apart from convoy escort duties they were also used to ferry aircraft across the Atlantic in the preparations for D-Day in 1944, and the tanker MACs were also used to refuel other ships at sea.

Some 4000 sorties were flown from the MAC ships but the only submarine casualty was the Free French submarine minelayer *La Perle*, sunk in error by Swordfish from *Empire MacCallum* on 8 July 1944. Claims have been made that no convoy escorted by a MAC ship lost a vessel, but this is not the case. However, there is no doubt that the presence of a MAC ship was an effective deterrent both to U-boats and to aircraft. All 19 survived the war and were reconverted to normal merchant craft in 1945 and 1946.

Ten Mac ships were given 'Mac' names prefixed by *Empire*, and the other nine were not new vessels but converted tankers of the Royal Dutch Shell Company, known after the class leader as the *Rapana*-class. Two were Dutch-registered and can claim to have been the Netherlands' first aircraft carriers.

Tanker conversion

The Admiralty was at first reluctant to use tankers as MAC ships, but the suitability of the tanker design finally overrode concern about the fire hazard. Tanker MACs, unlike the grain ships, did not have hangars built beneath the flight deck, and carried three aircraft on the flat top. One of the hull oil tanks was used to store avgas for the planes. Some were provided with refuelling-at-sea apparatus that could be streamed over the stern. Although the MACs had no catapult, they did use rocket-assisted take-off gear (RATOG) to enable the Swordfish to get into the air with two 113.5kg (250lb) depth charges and four marine markers. This was fitted aft of the main undercarriage strut.

***Empire MacAndrew*, a grain ship converted to merchant aircraft carrier, seen at Greenock, Scotland, 13 July 1943, soon after completion.**

HMS Audacity (1941)

There was a touch of audacity in the action of converting the German merchant ship *Hannover*, seized in the Atlantic in March 1940, into the first British escort carrier. Its brief career as a warship clearly showed the value of such ships.

Cargo
Fairey Swordfish shown on deck. *Audacity* was the first British carrier to operate Grumman Martlet Mk II fighters. The F4F Wildcat was renamed Martlet by its British users, but from March 1944 the Royal Navy also used the Wildcat name.

MS *Hannover* was a new vessel in 1939, launched in March at the Vulkan Yard in Bremen for the Norddeutscher Lloyd shipping company as a refrigerated cargo liner running between South America and Germany. The start of war between Germany and Britain found it

Deck construction
The flight deck was wood-surfaced, unlike standard RN carriers, in the interest of rapid construction, saving of steel and reducing top weight. In action it was painted in camouflage colours.

Ballast
Unlike the CAM and MAC ships *Audacity* carried no cargo and required 3048 tonnes (3000 tons) of ballast to maintain stability.

on the west side of the Atlantic, and it first headed for Curaçao in the Dutch Antilles. While making a return across the Atlantic with two other cargo steamers, it was intercepted on 8 March 1940 by the light cruiser HMS *Dunedin* and the Canadian destroyer HMCS *Assiniboine*, mounting the outermost edge blockade of the British blockade of German ports.

The crew abandoned ship, attempted to scuttle it and also set fire to the deckhouse, but a boarding party from *Dunedin* succeeded in salving the ship – a saga in itself, requiring immense effort, initiative and courage – and *Dunedin* towed it to Kingston, Jamaica, where it was renamed *Sinbad*. The damage was light enough for the ship to be sailed to Britain, where it was renamed *Empire*

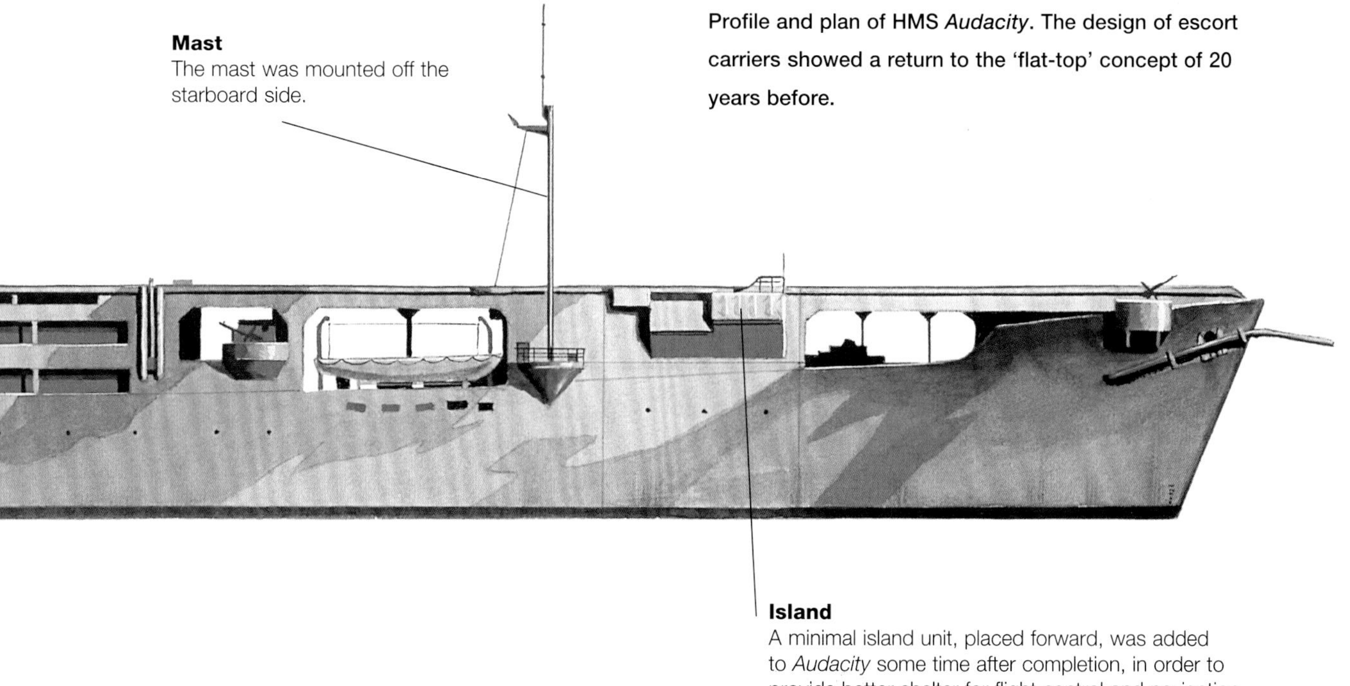

Profile and plan of HMS *Audacity*. The design of escort carriers showed a return to the 'flat-top' concept of 20 years before.

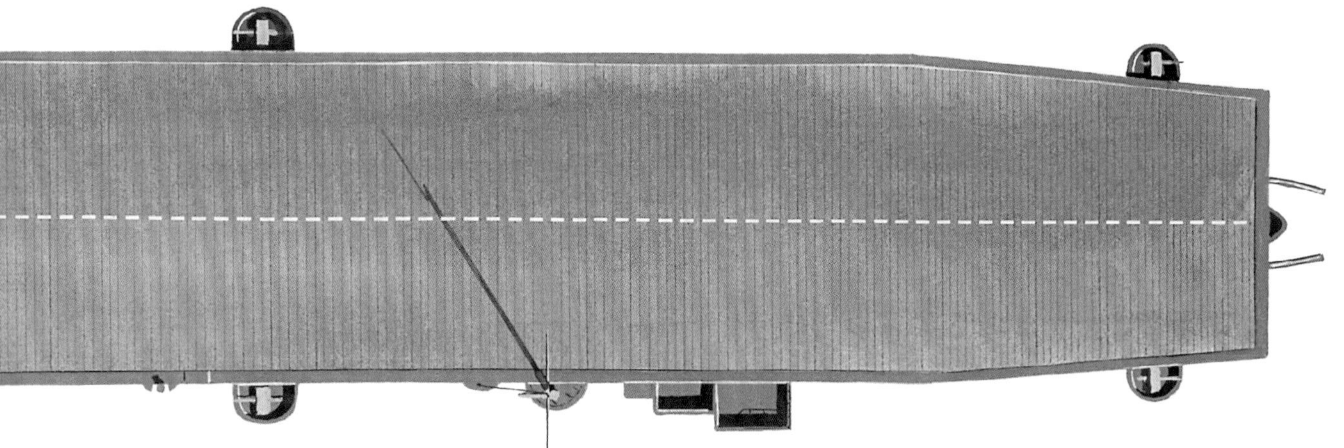

HMS Audacity

HMS *Archer* was one of two US-built carrier conversions on a CM-3 type cargo ship hull, the *Long Island*-class, designated as an auxiliary carrier (AVG). Commissioned into the RN on 17 November 1941, it shows a different conversion style to *Audacity* and to the *Attacker*-class (see opposite below). Unlike *Audacity* it had a lift and could carry 15 aircraft.

HMS *Nairana* was first of a class of three escort carriers built in the UK on merchant ship hulls. Entering service on 26 November 1943, it carried up to 20 aircraft and escorted Arctic and Atlantic convoys. From 1946 to 1948 it was loaned to the Royal Netherlands Navy as *Karel Doorman*. After 1948 it was reconverted to a merchant ship as MV *Port Victor*.

Audacity, intended first for conversion to an armed ocean boarding ship. With growing realization of the value of, and need for, convoy escort carriers, the plan was changed and on 13 January 1941 conversion into escort carrier form began at the Blyth Shipbuilding & Dry Dock Co. in Northumberland.

The fact that *Empire Audacity* was a motor ship was a key factor in its choice. It had a MAN 7-cylinder diesel engine driving a single shaft, and the exhaust gases could readily be trunked outwards at a 90° angle without the need for a funnel. Its speed of 14.5 knots (26.8km/h; 16.6mph) was more than adequate for convoy protection: most convoys proceeded at 10 knots (18.5km/h; 11.5mph) or less. With the fire-damaged superstructure removed along with masts, derricks and everything above deck level, a wooden flight deck 138m (453ft) long was laid, with three arrester wires mounted.

Specifications as carrier

Dimensions:	Length: 142.4m (467ft 3in); Beam: 17.15m (56ft 3in); Draught: 8.4m (27ft 6in)
Displacement:	10,230 tonnes (10,068 tons); 12,192 tonnes (12,000 tons) full load
Propulsion:	7-cylinder MAN diesel, single shaft; 3900kW (5200bhp)
Speed:	15 knots (28km/h; 17mph)
Range:	Not known
Armament:	1 102mm (4in) gun, 4 2-pdr AA guns, 4 20mm (.787in) AA guns
Aircraft:	6
Complement:	480

'Flat-top'

Audacity was a complete 'flat-top' with no island, only an open conning post at flight deck level. There was no hangar deck and the aircraft were parked and refuelled on the open flight deck. To keep the ship stable, 3048 tonnes (3000 tons) of ballast were loaded. No armour was installed, and defence consisted of one 102mm (4in) gun, one 6-pdr, four 2-pdr AA guns and four 20mm (.787in) AA guns. Air warning Type 79B radar was installed, enabling the ship to detect incoming planes and to track its own aircraft for up to 120km (75 miles). Conversion was completed on 20 June 1941 and the vessel was commissioned as *Empire Audacity*, but the 'Empire' was dropped on 31 July as the ship was not a member of the new *Empire*-class of merchant aircraft carrier being developed at that time. Unlike these, *Audacity* was officially a warship, with a navy crew and naval command.

The first deck landing was made on 10 July 1941. With six (some accounts make it eight, which was the maximum number it could carry) Grumman Martlet fighters of 802 Squadron, Fleet Air Arm, *Audacity* was assigned to Western Approaches Command and entered convoy escort duty between Gibraltar and Britain on 13 September 1941. Its planes shot down five Focke-Wulf FW-200 Kondor long-range reconnaissance planes and participated in the sinking of Type IXC U-131 on 17 December.

In December 1941, Convoy HG 76 was formed to sail from Gibraltar to Britain. With 32 merchant ships it had 12 escort vessels plus *Audacity*. German agents based at Algeciras, Spain, kept permanent watch on movements from Gibraltar, alerting U-Boat Command, and after departure on 14 December the convoy was soon under attack from German air and submarine units in a running battle that lasted six days. Off the Portuguese coast six U-boats closed in and the convoy escorts destroyed three. On 21 December *Audacity*'s Martlets drove off two Kondors. That night it was at some distance from the convoy – a necessity when launching and landing aircraft – when at 21.37 it was hit by one of four torpedoes fired by the Type VIIC U-751, disabling the steering and slowing the ship, enabling the U-boat to strike the forward part of the hull with two further torpedoes at 21.45.

Audacity sank by the bow, the stern rising to the vertical and its planes falling from the deck. It foundered at 22.10, with the loss of 73 crew members, most of them drowned. Despite being in many ways a makeshift design, in its brief time in action *Audacity* conclusively proved the value of the escort carrier in reconnaissance, defence and attack roles. Evidence at the inquiries into the ship's loss showed how liaison between the escort corvettes and destroyers and the escort carrier could extend the convoy's early warning area by many miles, and exert a substantial deterrent effect on enemy submarines and aircraft.

Transport, escort and attack carriers

Between August 1942 and June 1943 18 purpose-built escort carriers were built in the USA and supplied both to the US Navy as the *Bogue*-class (CVE) and the Royal Navy as the *Attacker*-class. The RN had eight, supplied on lend-lease terms to Britain. Based on a cargo ship hull design (Maritime Commission Type C-3) adapted to form a light carrier with hangar deck and lifts, they could hold 24 aircraft. A further 24 were built in 1943–44, of which all but one were transferred to the Royal Navy, known as the *Ameer* or *Ruler*-class. In the course of the war they functioned variously as transport, escort and attack carriers. While all went through modification before commissioning in the British fleet, RN sailors were pleasantly surprised by the standard of crew accommodation on a US warship, with bunks and cabins instead of mess-decks and hammocks.

USS *Bogue* (CVE-9), commissioned on 26 September 1942, was lead ship of the *Bogue* class of escort carrier, known in the British Navy as the *Attacker* class.

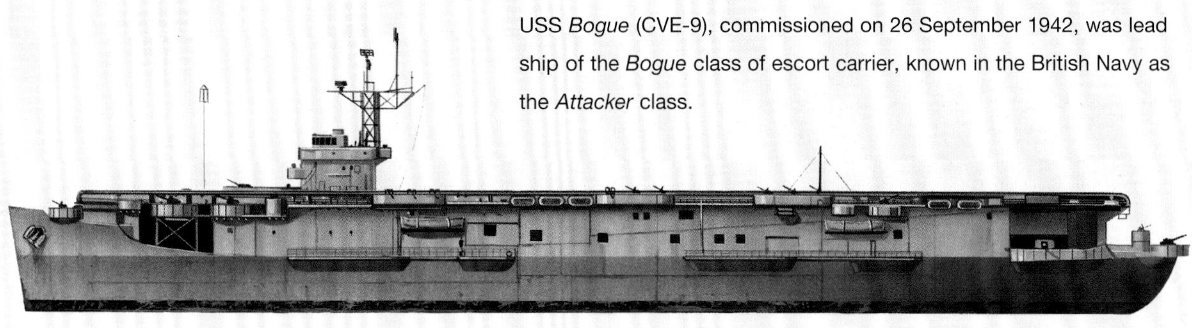

Shōkaku (1941)

The large carriers *Shōkaku* and *Zuikaku* were key elements in Japan's Pacific war plan. With long-range and high endurance capacity, and able to hold 84 aircraft, they were considered to be battle-winners for the Imperial Navy.

Shōkaku, 'Soaring Crane', and *Zuikaku*, 'Fortunate Crane', were very new when the long-brewing Pacific War started in December 1941. *Shōkaku* was laid down on 12 December 1937 at the Yokosuka naval dockyard, launched on 1 June 1939 and commissioned on 8 August 1941. *Zuikaku* was built at the same time at the Kawasaki yard, Kobe, and commissioned on 25 September 1941. Both were intended to serve in conjunction with heavy battleships of the *Yamato*-class.

At a late design stage the island position was switched from port to starboard. There was no funnel: two exhaust uptakes were mounted on the starboard side and angled downwards. The ships had enclosed two-level hangar decks, with three centreline aircraft lifts. These were intended to the first Japanese carriers to be fitted with catapults, but although mountings were laid, catapults were never fitted. Nine Type 4 arrester wires were fitted, three forward and six aft, worked by an electrical drum-and-rotor 6-pole stator, and three crash barriers worked by pneumatic-hydraulic cylinders.

The ships were well armoured to ensure battle survivability, with a 165mm (6.5in) belt by the magazines and 46mm (1.8in) by the machine rooms. The lower hangar deck was the armoured one, with 66mm (2.6in) armour over Ducol steel plate. Four sets of longitudinal bulkheads protected the lower hull against torpedo attack up to a force of 200kg (440lb) of TNT. Protection for the magazines was made to resist the impact of a 800kg (1760lb) bomb

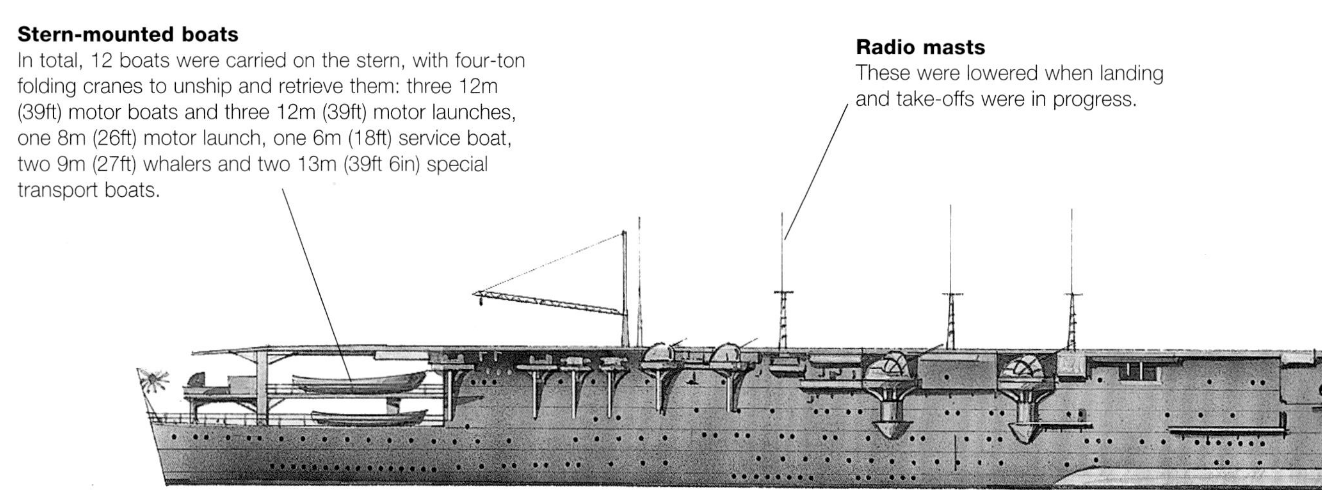

The very long, low profiles of *Shōkaku* and *Zuikaku* were not deliberately planned to minimize radar detection, but it certainly helped. In daylight combat, they presented a substantial target area.

The Aichi D3A1 Model 11 'Val' dive bomber carried a 113kg (250lb) bomb under the fuselage and two 60kg (132lb) bombs under the wings.

released from 3050m (10,000ft). The machinery consisted of eight Kampon Model B boilers powering four geared turbines, giving a high maximum speed of 34.5 knots (63.8km/h; 39.7mph). The main and auxiliary steering gear was hydraulically powered, with electric drive; the fore and aft anchor windlasses were also electrically powered.

The main defence armament was 16 127mm (5in) Type 98 AA guns, mounted laterally in twin mounts on sponsons, and backed up by 36 25mm Type 90 AA guns. Both ships were fitted with sonar listening devices during construction, consisting both of Type 91 Mod 4 passive and Type 97 hydrophones, which to some extent made up for the lack of radar. There was capacity for 72 aircraft plus a further 12 partially dismantled in reserve.

Carrier Division 5

From 7 October 1941 both ships formed Carrier Division 5, part of Admiral Chuichi Nagumo's First Air Fleet sent to make the surprise attack on Pearl Harbor, and joined in both strike waves. In January 1942 they were involved in the capture of Rabaul and in the early Spring were deployed across a wide expanse of the Pacific and Indian Oceans, including the raid on Trincomalee that sank two British cruisers and the carrier HMS *Hermes* (9 April). They also gave support to the Japanese landing on New Guinea. Both took part in the hard-fought Battle of the Coral Sea on 7–8 May, including a risky and unsuccessful nightfall attack on the 7th that lost seven planes for no results (this was the occasion when six Japanese planes mistook USS *Yorktown*

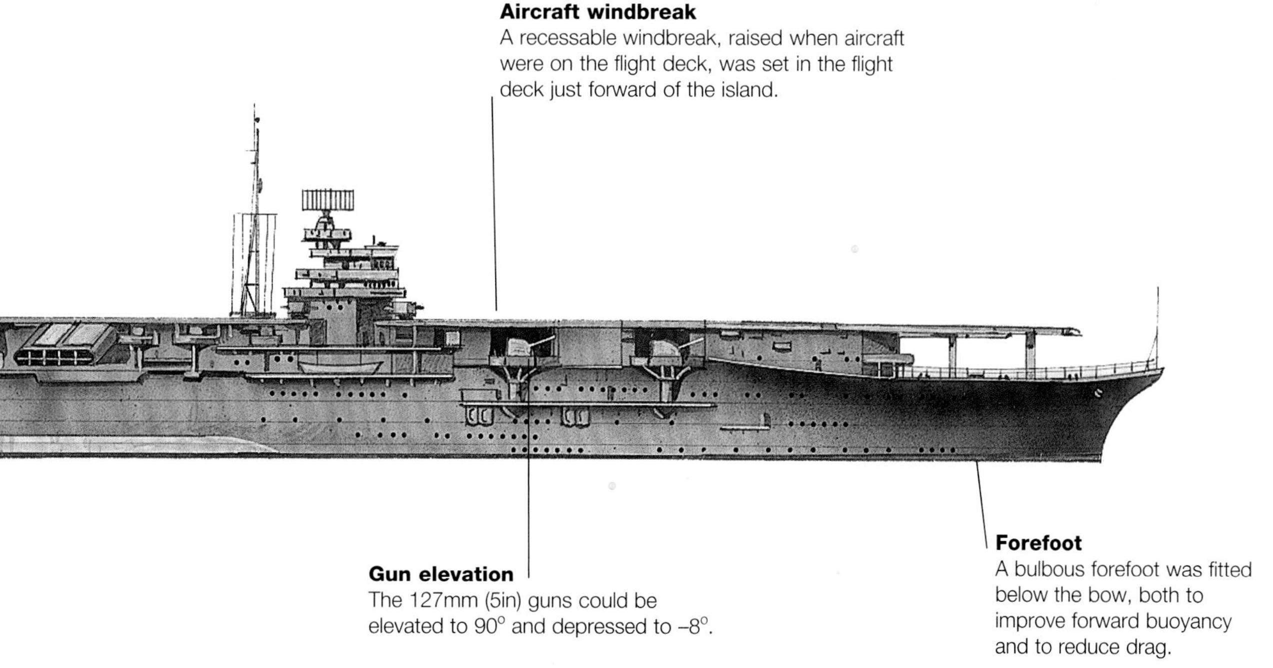

for *Shōkaku* or *Zuikaku* in the semi-dark and almost landed). *Shōkaku*, hit by two 454kg (1000lb) bombs on the morning of the 8th, was forced to leave the battle and head for the Truk base, dodging eight US submarines while en route, and *Zuikaku* landed many of its sister ship's strike planes following their attacks on USS *Lexington* and *Yorktown*. *Shōkaku* returned to Kure for repair, and *Zuikaku* went on patrol and support missions off the Aleutian Islands, so neither was present in the Battle of Midway in early June.

Specification

Dimensions:	Length: 257.5m (844ft 10in); Beam: 29m (95ft 2in); Draught: 9.3m (30ft 7in)
Displacement:	26,086 tonnes (25,675 tons); 32,619 tonnes (32,105 tons) full load
Propulsion:	8 boilers, 4 Kampon geared turbines, 4 shafts; 120,000kW (160,000shp)
Speed:	34.5 knots (64km/h; 39.7mph)
Range:	9700nm (18,000km; 11,200 miles) at 18 knots (33.3km/h; 20.7mph)
Armament (original):	8 Type 89 127mm (5in) 40-cal twin HA guns; 12 Type 96 triple 25mm machine guns
Aircraft:	84
Complement:	1660

***Shōkaku*'s wake shows a tight turn in the effort to evade dive-bomb attacks from USS *Yorktown* on 8 May 1942. The forward area is already on fire.**

On 15 August 1942 the two ships again operated together, with *Shōkaku* as flagship of Admiral Chūichi Nagumo in Carrier Division 1 for the invasion of Guadalcanal. On 24 August in the Battle of the Eastern Solomons, the two big Japanese carriers were in conflict with USS *Enterprise* and *Saratoga*. In the Battle of Santa Cruz, 26–27 October, *Shōkaku* and *Zuikaku* engaged USS *Hornet* and *Enterprise* in a fierce battle that left *Shōkaku* on fire and unable to continue action, although its machinery was unaffected. Again *Zuikaku*, justifying its name, remained on the scene, taking on board numerous aircraft launched from *Shōkaku*.

In mid-1942 *Shōkaku* had a type 21 air warning radar fitted above the Type 24 fire control director on the island, protected by a spherical splinter shield. On *Zuikaku* the director was removed to enable a larger Type 21 antenna. In 1944 a second Type 21 was placed on the port aft section of the flight deck, and both ships had Type 13 air search radar fitted on the mainmast. The AA batteries were augmented and 120mm (4.7in) rocket launchers fitted. With the carriers *Jun'yō* and *Zuihō*, *Zuikaku* supported the evacuation of Guadalcanal in early February 1943, and from 25 May it was again partnered by *Shōkaku* in patrols between Japanese home bases and Truk Lagoon, the central Pacific base of the Combined Fleet. On 13 February 1944 the two carriers arrived in Singapore, which was intended to become a major forward base for Japanese strikes. *Shōkaku* remained there while *Zuikaku* returned to Kure, then came back on a plane-ferrying voyage.

On 18–20 June 1944, *Shōkaku*, *Zuikaku* and *Taihō* as Carrier Division 1 were in action in the Battle of the Philippine Sea. At 11.22 on the 19th, US submarine *Cavalla* fired six torpedoes at *Shōkaku*, of which at least three and perhaps four struck the ship while aircraft refuelling was under way. Damage control teams made desperate efforts to contain the resulting fires but aerial bombing continued and at 14.08 a bomb delivered what turned out to be the final blow. As the ship tilted many of the crew, mustered for abandoning, fell into the blazing elevator pit: 1263 died and 570 survived. At 14.32 *Taihō* was put totally out of action by a huge explosion of fuel vapour. *Zuikaku* was the only surviving carrier, landing as many planes as it could, but 244 out of 374 launched were lost along with the two carriers: a disastrous blow from which the Imperial Navy's air arm never recovered. The battle continued, with *Zuikaku* subject to intense attack from USS *Hornet*, *Yorktown* and *Belleau Wood*. A direct hit from a 113kg (250lb) bomb started a fire in No.1 hangar, but it was contained and the ship remained operational. It spent 18 days in dry dock at Kure, receiving augmented AA armament and modifications to the mainmast as well as essential repairs.

By 20 October 1944 *Zuikaku* was still fielding 65 aircraft, and on the 24th as Admiral Ozawa's flagship in the Battle of Leyte Gulf it launched the last attack wave from a Japanese carrier force, along with the three light carriers of the Mobile Fleet, *Zuihō*, *Chitose* and *Chiyoda* – a total of 72 aircraft. Early on the following day *Zuikaku* was attacked off Cape Engano by planes from USN Task Force 38. Struck by three 113kg (250lb) bombs, and a torpedo on the port side, the ship made its way forward at 23 knots (42.5km/h; 26.4mph) on two shafts. Unable to escape continuous attacks, despite maintaining heavy AA fire, it took six more torpedo hits in ten minutes between 13.15 and 13.25. At 13.58, with the ship about to sink, the order to abandon was given. Last survivor of the Pearl Harbor attack carriers, *Zuikaku* sank at 14.14 with the loss of 743 lives, while 862 were rescued by escort ships.

Vapour explosions

Aviation fuel tanks in Japanese carriers were not independently installed and protected by water-filled spaces, but integral with the hull and so far more prone to shocks and leakage. Following the loss of *Kaga* at Midway, concrete protection was applied to the fuel tanks on *Shōkaku* and *Zuikaku*, although this was of limited value against leaking vapour. Historians have pointed out that *Shōkaku*, *Taiyō* and *Hiyō* all suffered similar vapour-induced explosions after torpedo attacks. Japan was pumping oil at Tarakan Island off Borneo, but lack of tankers reduced the amount that could be refined, and the carriers were burning unrefined Tarakan crude that gave off more flammable vapour than refined oil did.

Zuikaku, photographed in 1941.

HMS Indomitable (1941)

A ruggedly built and well-equipped fleet carrier, *Indomitable* was the fourth member of a class with a distinguished service record through World War II and into the 1950s.

Indomitable underwent numerous modifications post-1945, but it never acquired an angled flight deck.

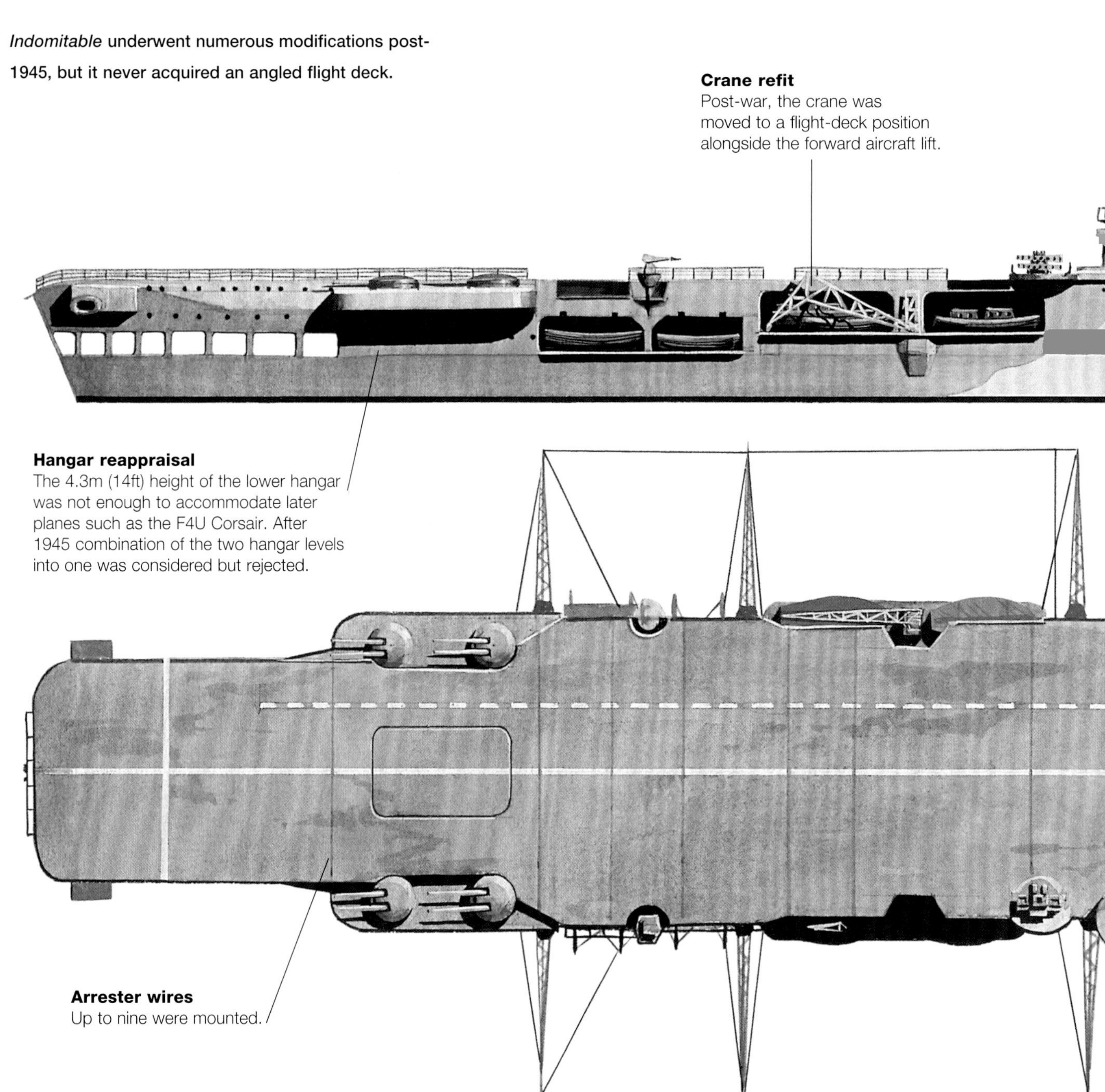

Indomitable was laid down at the Vickers Armstrong yard in Barrow-in-Furness, Cumbria, on 10 November 1937, launched on 29 March 1940 and commissioned on 10 October 1941. Its design history began in 1936 with the plan for HMS *Illustrious*, intended to be the leader of a class of fleet carriers. *Illustrious*, launched on 5 April 1939 and commissioned on 25 May 1940, embodied a new principle adopted by the Royal Navy that a carrier should be a strongly armoured vessel capable of sustaining damage without being put out of action, and that its aircraft, as prime weapons, should also be protected from hostile fire. This resulted in the hangar being constructed as a great armoured box. Effective fire protection systems were installed, including two sets of asbestos curtains, ventilation fans and drains for the sea-water sprinkler system.

While the fighting and survival qualities of the ship were improved compared to its immediate predecessor *Ark Royal*, its aircraft capacity was considerably reduced to a maximum of 36 planes. By 1938 the service requirements and design characteristics were being overhauled for the

Carley floats
Multiple Carley floats were carried in addition to the boats because in combat conditions it might be carrying survivors from other ships.

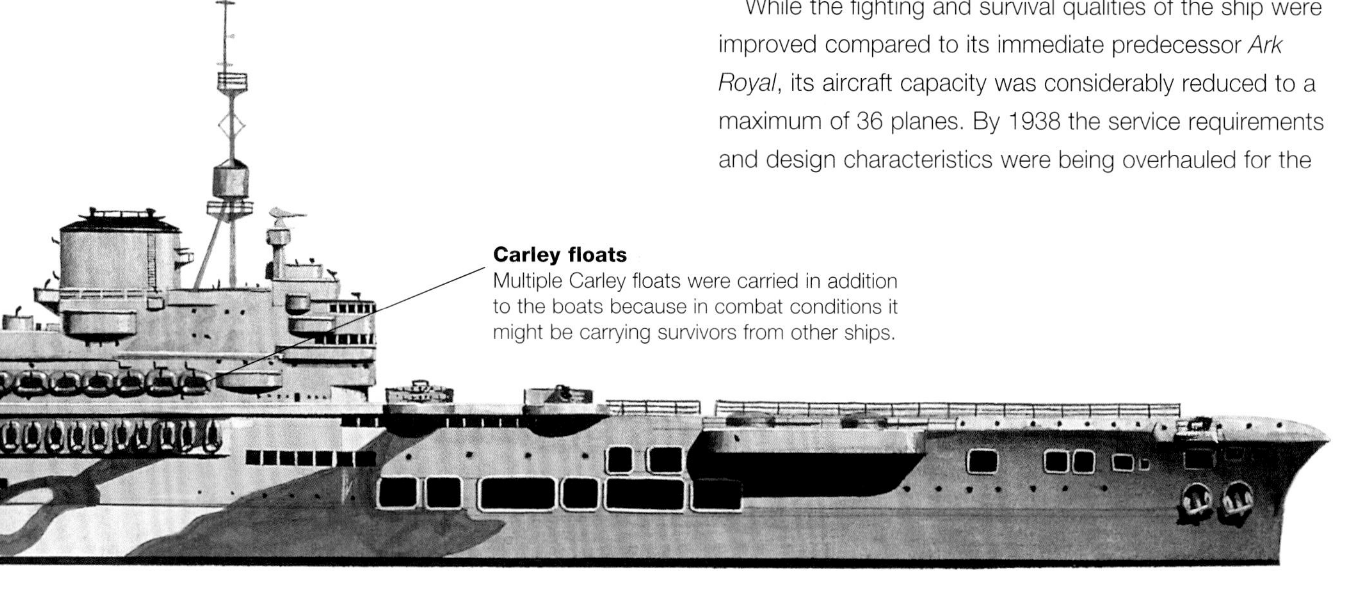

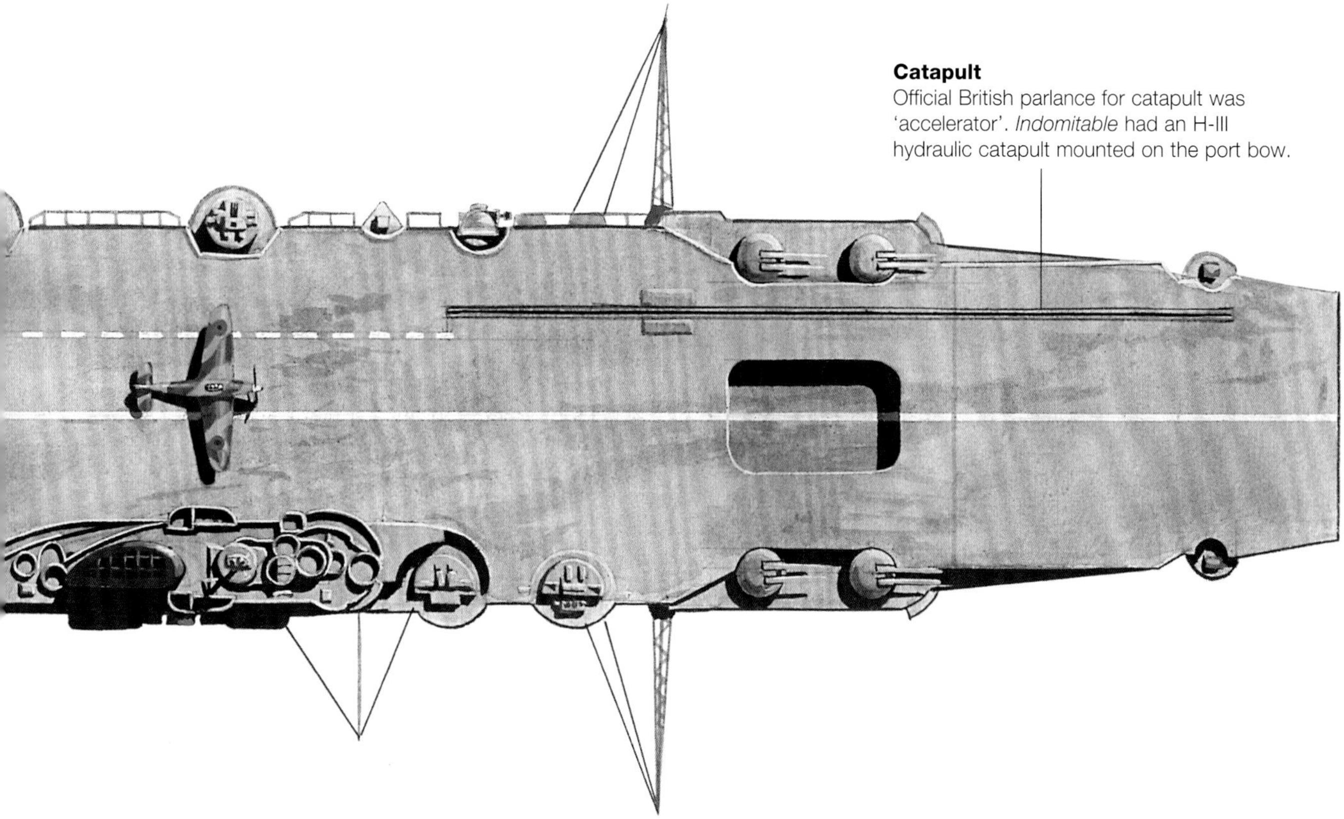

Catapult
Official British parlance for catapult was 'accelerator'. *Indomitable* had an H-III hydraulic catapult mounted on the port bow.

subsequent *Implacable*-class, and this was done in time for *Indomitable*, the fourth and last ship in the *Illustrious*-class, to have its design modified to provide for 48 planes. It also received the improved aircraft lifts and catapult designed for the next generation of carriers. This enhanced offensive capacity was achieved by installing a second hangar deck, 63.4m (208ft) long in the aft section, about half the length of the main hangar. The armoured flight deck was raised by 4m (14ft) to accommodate this, and the armour of the hangar sides reduced from 111mm (4.1in) to 38mm (1.5in), in order to maintain stability and prevent the vessel from being top-heavy. Even so, at full load *Indomitable* displaced 30,206 tonnes (29,730 tons) compared to *Illustrious's* 29,058 tonnes (28,600 tons). It was 3m (15ft) longer than *Illustrious*, and shared the class's full-height hurricane bow with the flight deck extending over it in a distinctive turned down lip, also a tall, narrow island and a single oblong funnel.

The stayed pole mast underwent several modifications in the course of World War II and later, as new communications and sensor equipment was installed. Six boilers supplied steam to three Parsons geared turbines driving three shafts, with a single rudder set aft of the screws. Its AA defences were 16 114mm (4.5in) guns, 48 2-pdr and ten 20mm guns. The original air wing was formed of 22 Sea Hurricanes, 12 Martlets and 16 Albacores. In 1943 it was 40 Supermarine Seafires and 15 Albacores.

Specification (Original)

Dimensions:	Length: 230m (754ft 7in); Beam: 29.2m (95ft 10in); Draught: 8.8m (29ft)
Displacement:	23,368 tonnes (23,000 tons); 30,206 tonnes (29,730 tons) full load
Propulsion:	6 boilers, Parsons geared turbines, 3 shafts; 83,000kW (111,000shp)
Speed:	30.5 knots (56km/h; 35mph)
Range:	11,000nm (20,000km; 13,000 miles) at 14 knots (25.9km/h; 16.1mph)
Armament:	16 110mm (4.5in) guns, 48 2-pdr and 10 20mm AA guns
Aircraft:	48
Complement:	1600

East Asia duty

Indomitable's first voyage after commissioning was to Jamaica. It was then intended to steam to Singapore to join HMS *Prince of Wales* and *Repulse* in Force Z to defend the island city, but on leaving on 3 November the ship grounded, coming off again under its own power, but it had to turn northwards to Norfolk, Virginia, for repairs. This delay prevented it from being present off Malaya when the other two ships were sunk by air attack on 10 December. Whether *Indomitable*'s planes would have been enough to change the outcome is generally considered unlikely. Arriving in eastern waters in January, it diverted to Port Sudan without its own air wing to take on 50 RAF Hurricanes of 258 (F) and 252 (F) Squadrons for the defence of Singapore, but the city fell to Japan on 15 February. Based with the British fleet at Trincomalee in January 1942, *Indomitable* continued to transport Hurricane fighters between Ceylon, Singapore and Java.

With HMS *Illustrious* it attacked the Vichy French port of Diego Suarez on Madagascar, a potential Japanese submarine base, on 5–8 May. In summer 1942 it returned to European waters to join in convoy support for Operation Pedestal, the convoy system that kept Malta supplied, and was hit by three 500kg (1100lb) bombs, severely damaging the flight deck, and was again sent to the USA for repair. On return to Britain in February 1943 it acquired aircraft warning radar Type 218B and Type 79, and was then deployed with the Home Fleet until sent again to the Mediterranean with Force H on convoy protection in July, and support Allied landings on Sicily. Struck by an aerial torpedo from a misidentified Italian bomber on 16 July, it again was directed to the USA for repair at Norfolk Navy Yard, where it also acquired American SM1 and SG radar.

On return to the Royal Navy in May 1944 it re-embarked a new air wing of F6F fighters (1839 and 1844 Squadrons): the first Hellcats to serve with the Fleet Air Arm. In July 1944 it again joined the Eastern Fleet at Trincomalee and was in action in the Pacific, off Sumatra and Taiwan into 1945. From February to August it was assigned to US naval command, with Task Force

HMS *Indomitable* manoeuvred by tugs to enter Rosyth Naval Dockyard on 6 May 1944. It has brought Grumman TBF Avenger torpedo bombers from the United States.

113, then TF 57, supporting troop landings on Okinawa. On 1 April a kamikaze strike caused serious damage to the island, killing 14 of the crew, but effective damage control had the flight deck cleared for continuing action within an hour. May 1945 was a troubled month for *Indomitable*, hit by further kamikaze strikes on the 4th and 9th, and colliding on the 20th with the destroyer HMS *Quilliam*, but the ship remained operational until June when it was sent to Sydney for repairs and refit, returning to the fleet to join in the liberation of Hong Kong on 30 August.

On 12 December 1945 *Indomitable* returned to Britain. In 1946 it was placed in reserve but recommissioned and extensively modernized, with new bow and stern sections, during the Korean War period, 1950–53. An explosion on board on 3 February 1953 was caused by a leak of aviation fuel, and the spread of inflammable vapour resulted in nine deaths. By unfortunate chance the explosion was caused by a safety precaution, when the ventilation fans were shut down and arcing brought sparks in one or more of their electric motors. *Indomitable* was struck from the Navy list in 1955, and scrapped in October that year.

Strike power

***Indomitable* in effect formed an interim design between the *Illustrious*- and *Implacable*-classes. *Implacable* (in service from 1944 to 1955) was slightly larger and faster, also with two hangar decks, but with hangar-side armour of 51mm (2in). It had more powerful engines, with eight boilers and four shafts, and made a faster speed of 32.5 knots (60.2km/h; 37.4mph). Most importantly, it could carry up to 81 aircraft, giving it considerably greater strike power.**

USS Sangamon (1942)

Sangamon was first of a class of escort carriers that would play essential supporting roles in achieving the US Navy's dominance in the Pacific.

Sangamon had a dual career with the US Navy, first as a fleet oiler, then as the Navy's first escort carrier. Laid down on 13 March 1939 at the Federal Shipbuilding & Drydock Co., Kearny, New Jersey, for Standard Oil's fleet as *Esso*

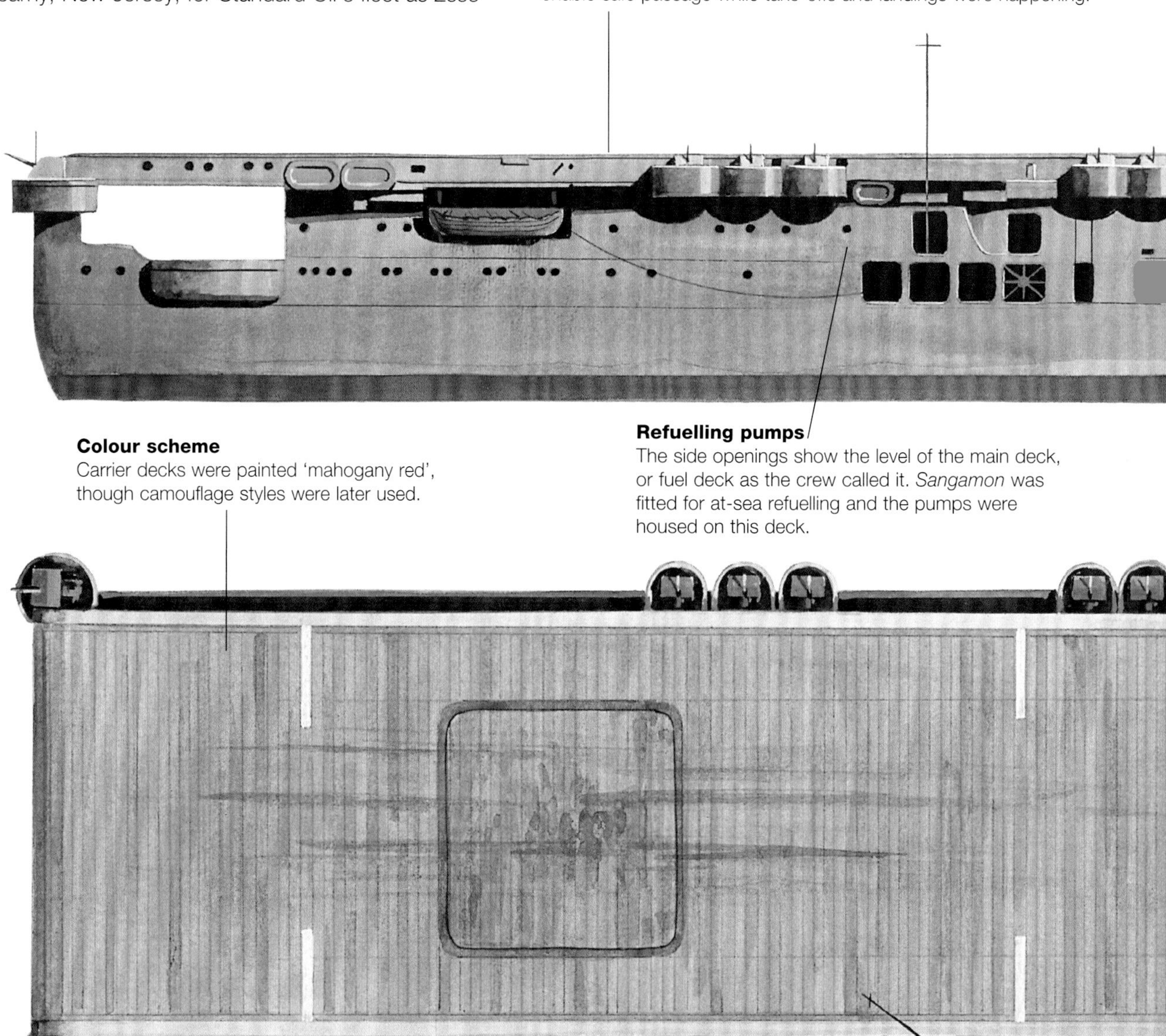

Trenton, one of a group known as the *Cimarron*-class, it was launched on 4 November the same year. The Navy purchased it on 22 October 1940, giving it the designation AO28 and changing the name to *Sangamon* on 12 April 1941. From December 1941 there was a search under way for ships or hulls suitable for rapid conversion to carriers, with tankers and bulk carriers considered the best possibilities. *Sangamon* was picked, given the designation AVG-26 on 14 February 1942, underwent reconfiguration as a carrier at Newport News and was commissioned as an auxiliary carrier on 25 August, with its designation letters altered to ACV. Within five months its appearance,

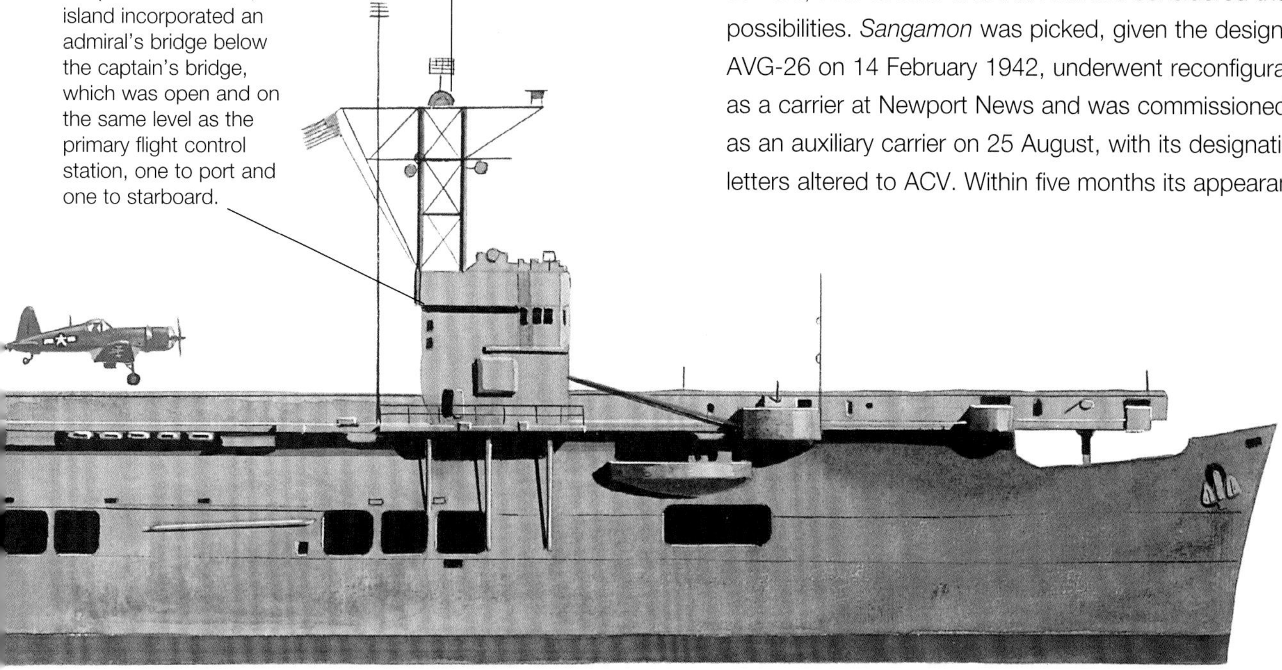

Mast
The lattice mast was modified several times as further radar equipment was installed.

Island
Despite its small size, the island incorporated an admiral's bridge below the captain's bridge, which was open and on the same level as the primary flight control station, one to port and one to starboard.

***Sangamon* was lead ship of a class of four 'Cimarron' type tankers converted to carriers.**

Flight deck
This extended well beyond the hull to port and starboard, with a maximum width of 12m (39ft) more than the ship's beam.

USS Sangamon

Port-side profile of a *Sangamon*-class carrier. The others were *Suwannee*, *Santee* and *Chenango*.

of standard tanker type with forward and aft well decks separated by a central bridge, was altered dramatically, with a virtually full-length flight deck built up above a hangar floor on the main deck, two plane elevators and a small island set well forward on the starboard side. A single catapult was fitted originally, with a second added in 1944. Three sister ships with similar hulls of T-3 type were also converted, forming a class of four.

The rugged internal hull construction, braced to support oil tanks without rupturing, and the length and stability of the ships, were important factors in their choice and they proved to be very successful. The 153m (502ft) flight deck enabled them to fly Grumman F6F Hellcat fighters, unlike other escort carriers. Unlike British merchant conversions, they were not motor ships but driven by steam turbines, and low-level funnels were fitted to port and starboard at the stern above the engine room. No armour was fitted, except for some protection around the magazine, where 687 tonnes (676 tons) of ammunition were stored, and they had limited AA armament at first, as the intention was that they would always be accompanied by destroyers or other armed escort ships.

Ultimately *Sangamon* had two 127mm (5in) guns in single turrets, four twin 40mm AA guns and 12 20mm AA cannon. A large oil tank capacity was retained, giving the type an unusually wide operational range and the capacity to refuel other ships in their Task Groups when required. SG search radar was fitted. They could carry up to 36 aircraft, with a typical air wing consisting of up to 18 Grumman Wildcats and from 12 to 18 TBF Avengers. *Sangamon* also carried SBD-3 Dauntless dive-bombers on some operations: ships of this class were the only escort carriers to fly dive-bombers. In the course of overhauls, the ship's appearance underwent slight modifications. Its final refit, at Bremerton, Washington, included provision of a fighter director radar, making the ship the first escort carrier to stage night-flying operations.

Specification

Dimensions:	Length: 169m (553ft); Beam: 23m (75ft); Draught: 9.8m (32ft)
Displacement:	11,582 tonnes (11,400 tons); 24,663 tonnes (24,275 tons) full load
Propulsion:	4 boilers, 2 steam turbines, 2 shafts; 10,067kW (13,500shp)
Speed:	18 knots (33km/h; 21mph)
Range:	23,920nm (43,000km; 26,783 miles) at 15 knots (27.7km/h; 17.2mph)
Armament (original):	2 127mm (5in) 38 cal guns, 2 quad, 7 twin 40mm 56 cal and 21 single 20mm 70 cal AA guns
Aircraft:	32
Complement:	1080

Task Force 34

The first deployment of *Sangamon* was with Task Force 34 in October 1942 in the Mediterranean, supporting the Operation Torch landings in North Africa with Composite Squadron VC26 flying CAP (combat air protection), ground support and anti-submarine missions. From mid-January 1943 it was with the Pacific Fleet in Carrier Division 22, on convoy escort and landing support duties. On 15 July 1943 it was redesignated CVE-26; and in September it went to Mare Island yard for an overhaul that included new flight deck gear and a combat information centre, returning to the

A profile view of *Sangamon* at a late stage of World War II.

war zone with VC27 as its air wing. A serious fire broke out on board on 25 January 1944 when a landing plane failed to catch an arrester wire and broke through the emergency barrier. Seven men died. *Sangamon* made emergency repairs and continued in action at Kwajalein and Eniwetok until 24 February, when it returned to Pearl Harbor for two weeks' repair.

Despite its speed deficiency, it worked from March to October with Task Forces TF 53 and TF 52 in the assaults on Saipan and Guam, as well as the Battle of the Philippine Sea. In October it was assigned to Task Group 77.4, formed of no less than 18 escort carriers in three sub-groups, as flagship of Rear Admiral Thomas L. Sprague. In the Battle of Leyte Gulf its aircraft were engaged in the conflict, and it continued in attack rather than escort mode into 1945. On the evening of 4 May 1945 one of a flight of Japanese kamikaze planes crashed on to *Sangamon*, causing heavy damage and starting fires. There were 86 fatalities. Also badly damaged was the destroyer USS *Hudson* as it came alongside to give aid. The edge of the carrier's flight deck ripped away part of its bridge and a burning plane pushed off *Sangamon* fell onto its stern, causing the depth charges mounted there to explode. The carrier was ordered back to its home port of Norfolk, Virginia, to undergo repairs. The war ended before these were completed, leaving the ship superfluous to the Navy's requirements. On 1 November 1945 it was removed from the navy list. Reinstated as a merchant ship, it operated for various owners until 1960 when it was scrapped at Osaka, Japan.

Nautical historians consider the *Sangamon*-class as equal to the purpose-built CVL light carriers that succeeded them, and perhaps in some ways superior in all respects save speed. With a maximum of 18 knots (33.3km/h; 20.7mph) they could not keep up with fast Task Groups, but that still left a wide range of potential duties. The 41 battle stars earned by the quartet are a testimony to that.

Leyte landings

In all, the United States built 122 escort carriers in the course of World War II. Over 40 were passed on to the British Navy. Often known as 'jeep carriers' and built on merchant-navy style hulls, they played a largely unglamorous but not undangerous role in ASW warfare in the Atlantic and Pacific Oceans. They were also heavily used for ferrying planes across the oceans. But on several occasions they found themselves in the heat of battle, as when Task Force 3, with six escort carriers, defended the US Army landings on Leyte against sustained attack from Japanese battleships and cruisers in October 1944.

Jun'yō (1942)

***Jun'yō* was laid down as a passenger liner and underwent conversion to a carrier in order to boost Japan's already considerable naval air power. It was one of two Japanese carriers to survive action in World War II.**

The ship was planned as *Kashiwara Maru* for NYK Lines, and laid down at Mitsubishi Heavy Industries Shipyard in Nagasaki on 20 March 1939. It was one of a number of ships, including its sister carrier *Hiyo*, built as a 'shadow fleet' that could rapidly be converted into warships. From the start the hull design was specifically built for conversion to a carrier.

Features not normally found on a civilian ship included a double hull, seatings for transverse and longitudinal bulkheads, a main deck of 25mm (1in) steel, extra-large fuel bunkers and turbine machinery. The already assembled hull was purchased for carrier conversion in February 1941 and launched on 26 June. *Jun'yō*, meaning 'Peregrine Falcon', was commissioned on 3 May 1942 and assigned to the Second Carrier Striking Force.

Hiyō and *Jun'yō* had the largest islands yet seen on Japanese carriers, sponsoned out to leave a clear flight deck, and with funnels integrated with the superstructure for the first time. The power-plant was four Mitsubishi steam boilers supplying Mitsubishi turbines with two screws. This was not a standard naval rig: effectively it was a hybrid system, with the boilers designed for warships and the turbines part of the original merchant design. Though *Jun'yō* made 26 knots (48.1km/h; 29.9mph) on trials, that was considerably slower than the fleet carriers. The flight deck was wood-paved as with other Japanese carriers, and two elevators were installed, one for each of the two hangars. Relatively light armour was applied, 20mm (0.8in) to the main deck with two layers of 25mm (1in) steel above the machinery room and the same around the magazines.

Although a 'conversion' from a passenger liner, the ship was deliberately planned as a potential warship.

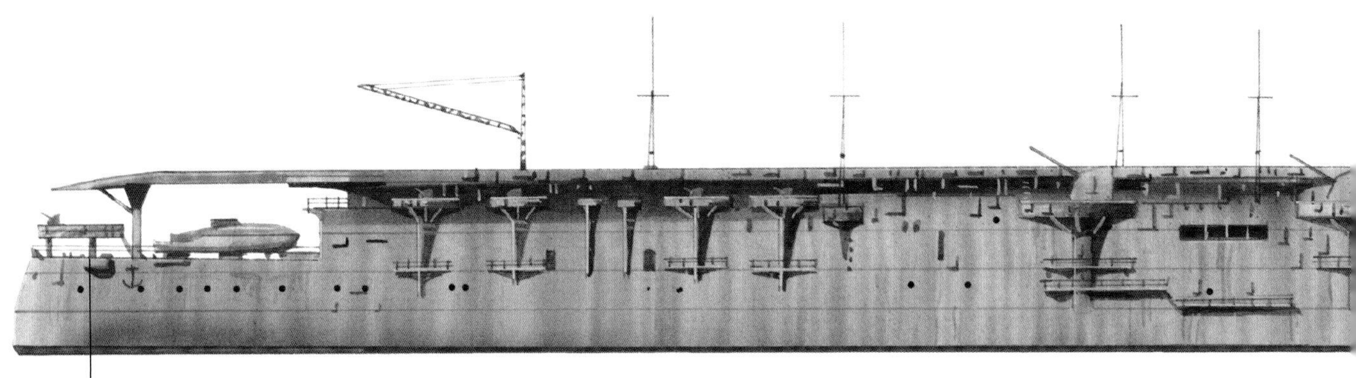

Rocket placement
In September 1944 six racks of 30-tube launchers for 127mm (5in) phosphorus rockets were fitted, three on each side, on stern sponsons. These rockets were armed with multiple incendiary shrapnel charges on a time fuse.

In March 1944 additional concrete protection was applied around the aviation fuel tanks in an attempt to contain the leakage and build-up of oil vapour that had been the bane of other Japanese carriers. Three twin 127mm (5in) Type 89 gun mounts were supplied on each side and the original armament also comprised eight triple 25mm (1in) guns. A further four were added in the summer of 1943. As the frequency and intensity of US air attack grew, additional armament was fitted. After the Philippine Sea battle *Jun'yō* carried a total of 79 25mm guns. Six 28-barrel 115mm (4.7in) incendiary rocket launchers were fitted on sponsons late in the war, three on each side of the aft flight deck. *Jun'yō* carried 48 planes ready to fly, plus five in kit form: 12 Mitsubishi Type Zero A6M fighters, 18 Aichi Type 99 D3A bombers and 18 Nakajima Type 97 B5N attack planes, known to Allied Intelligence as 'Zeke', 'Val' and 'Kate' types respectively.

***Jun'yō* anchored at Sasebo naval base, southern Japan, in 1945.**

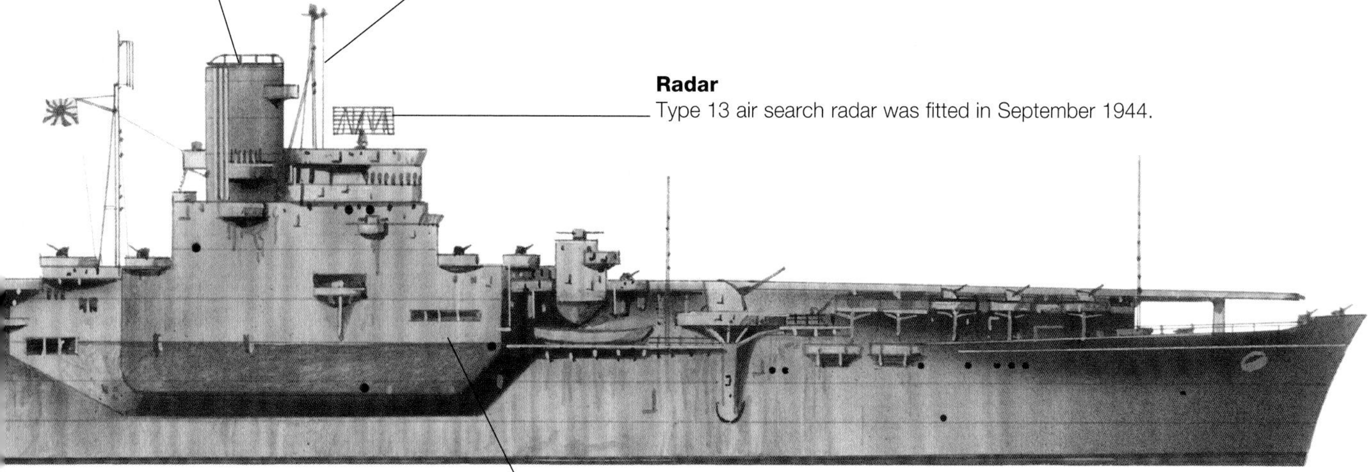

Gas dispersion
Jun'yō's funnel was angled out to starboard at 25° to help in dispersing hot gases away from the flight deck.

Mast positioning
Unusually, the mainmast was positioned aft of the funnel, though a small mast was mounted at a later stage just forward of it.

Radar
Type 13 air search radar was fitted in September 1944.

Island
This was almost entirely sponson-supported.

Jun'yō

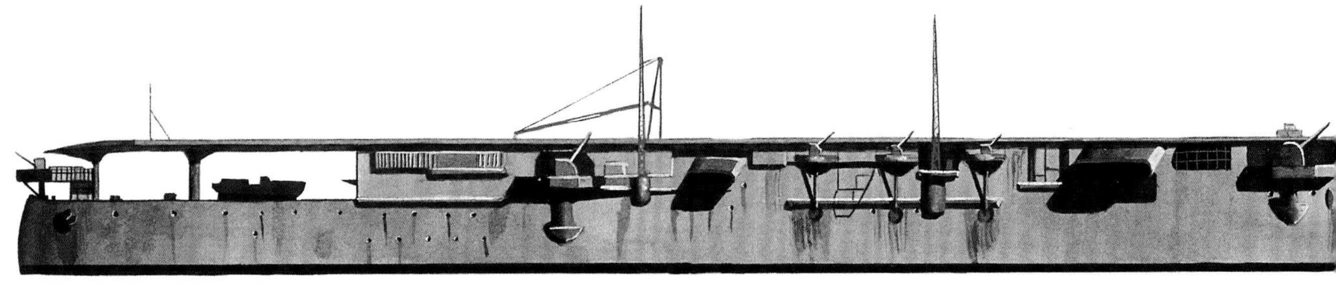

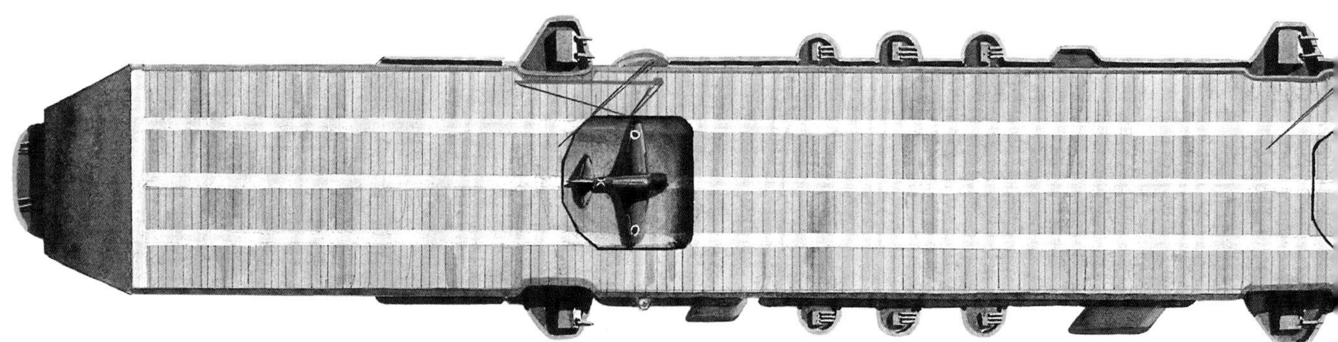

Aleutian attack

Jun'yō was regarded as an auxiliary rather than a fleet carrier, although from the first it was involved in attack operations, and on several occasions operated in concert with *Hiyō*. Its first action was in the invasion and takeover of successive Pacific island groups, notably the assault on the Aleutian Islands, between Siberia and Alaska, in June 1942. Aircraft from *Jun'yō* and the light carrier *Ryujō* (commissioned in 1933) attacked the American base at Dutch Harbor in one of the few Japanese assaults on actual US territory, a diversionary strike that was part of the overall strategy centred on Midway. In the Alaskan raid two islands were captured, but otherwise it achieved little except to extend the Pacific battleground and stretch the resources of the Imperial Navy even further. It possibly also spared *Jun'yō* and *Ryujō* from damage or destruction at the simultaneous Battle of Midway.

After Midway, as one of only four large carriers remaining in service, despite its modest speed *Jun'yō* was redesignated as a fleet carrier. In the light of combat experience its aircraft wing was altered to 21 A6M Zero fighters, 12 D3A dive bombers and nine B5N torpedo bombers. During a quick refit at Kure in the second half of July 1942, Type 21 air search radar was fitted on the top of the island, along with two Type 94 high-angle fire control directors.

Jun'yō saw battle action with Carrier Division 2 in the Guadalcanal Campaign in mid- to late October 1942, as flagship of Rear Admiral Kakuji Kakuta after *Hiyō* was disabled on 22 October, launching strikes against USS *Enterprise* and the battleship *South Dakota* in the Battle of Santa Cruz, and helping to sink the carrier *Hornet*. It played a support role in the Second Battle of Guadalcanal on 12–15 November and continued in active service through 1943, with much aircraft ferrying and troop carrying,

Specification

Dimensions:	Length: 219.3m (719ft 7in); Beam: 26.7m (87ft 7in); Draught: 8.15m (26ft 9in)
Displacement:	24,526 tonnes (24,140 tons); 28,753 tonnes (28,300 tons) full load
Propulsion:	6 Mitsubishi boilers, Mitsubishi geared turbines; 41,906kW (56,250shp)
Speed:	26 knots (48km/h; 30mph)
Range:	10,000nm (18,500km; 11,500 miles)
Armament (original):	6 twin 127mm (5in) Type 89 DP guns, 8 triple 25mm (1in) Type 96 AA guns
Aircraft:	53
Complement:	1224

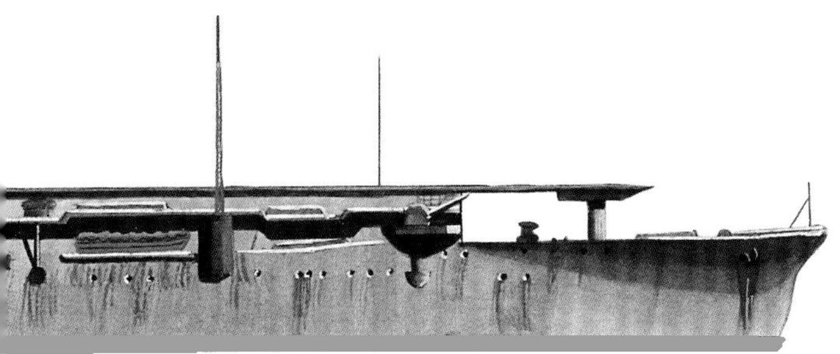

Zuihō, commissioned in 1940, was another pre-planned conversion. It was launched as a submarine tender. Classed as a 'light carrier', it had less than half the displacement of *Jun'yō*. It was sunk in the Battle of Cape Engaño, 25 October 1944.

including the evacuation of troops from Guadalcanal (January–February) and the reinforcement of Rabaul (April). In February–March 1943 two Type 95 directors for the 25mm (1in) AA guns were added, with a second Type 21 air search radar on the port side, outboard of the rear elevator. The ship had a refit at Kure in July–August, receiving a further four Type 96 triple AA mounts. At Singapore on 1 November 1943 its air group was reformed with 24 Zeros, 18 D3A bombers and B5Ns. On 5 November at 05.40 *Jun'yō* was hit by one of six torpedoes from the US submarine *Halibut*, disabling the steering gear, and was towed by the cruiser *Tone* into Kure naval base for repairs.

In February 1944, with the losses of aircraft reaching critical level, *Jun'yō*'s air wing was disbanded, but in May it embarked planes from 652 air group and headed for Okinawa as part of a large battle group comprising Carrier Divisions 2 and 3 and including the super-battleship *Musashi*. In that month four Type 96 triple 25mm AA guns were added, two at the stern and one each forward and aft on the island. At the same time 12 single mounts were added, some of them portable, able to be fixed to tie-down points on the flight deck. In the June 1944 Battle of the Philippine Sea the Japanese lost 244 planes against American losses of 22. *Jun'yō* took several bomb hits on 20 June, damaging the flight deck and island and destroying the funnel.

On 20 June *Hiyō*'s aviation fuel blew up after the ship was torpedoed by aircraft from the USS *Belleau Wood* air group, and it sank. As before, repairs to *Jun'yō* were made rapidly at Kure and it returned to service, with the AA battery reinforced by a further three triple, two twin and 18 single Type 96 25mm guns. All missions were by now transport or troop-carrying missions, as there were no aircraft available. While carrying 200 survivors from the sunken *Musashi*, it was hit again by torpedoes on 9 December 1944 in the East China Sea, from US submarines *Sea Devil* and *Redfish*, but was able to make it to the Sasebo naval base under its own power. Repair was anticipated as Japan was now desperately short of carriers, but also there was now no carrier strategy, and in March 1945 the cost of repairs was deemed too high to be worthwhile. *Jun'yō* remained in harbour, heavily camouflaged and inactive apart from engaging in anti-aircraft fire against American raids. On 5 August it was stripped of all guns for land defences. It was surrendered to the American Navy on 2 September.

On 30 November 1945 *Jun'yō* was removed from the Navy list, and was broken up at Sasebo in 1946–47.

Post-war fate

The only large Japanese carriers to survive World War II were *Jun'yō* and the *Unryū*-class carrier *Katsuragi* (commissioned on 15 October 1944) although both were out of action through damage at the time of Japan's surrender. *Katsuragi* was repaired and used as a troop transport in 1945–46 before being broken up in late 1946. Two other *Unryū*-class carriers, *Kasagi* and *Aso*, had been launched in October and November 1944 respectively, but were still incomplete at the end of the war. The light carrier *Hōshō*, first purpose-built carrier in any navy (commissioned in 1922) also survived the war, in which, apart from a supporting role in the Midway battle, it was used for crew training. It was scrapped in 1946.

USS Independence (1943)

Leader of a class of light carriers, USS *Independence* fought with fast carrier battle groups and was the first night carrier, and ultimately became a target for atom bomb testing.

The attack on Pearl Harbor on 7 December 1941, and the Imperial Japanese Navy's evident air supremacy in the Pacific, resulted in the US Navy Board giving priority to carrier construction. President Franklin D. Roosevelt had previously proposed the conversion of planned light

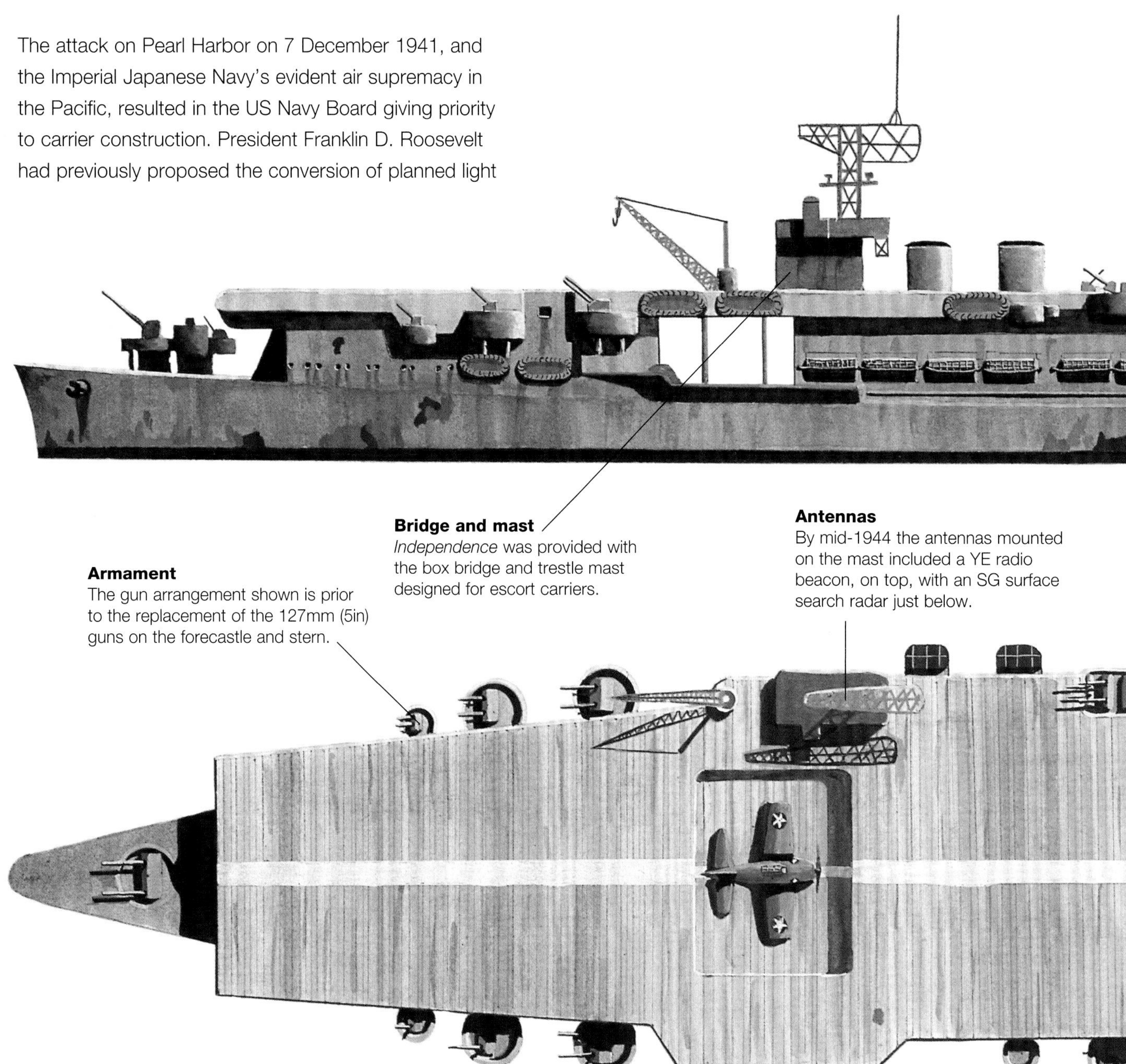

Bridge and mast
Independence was provided with the box bridge and trestle mast designed for escort carriers.

Antennas
By mid-1944 the antennas mounted on the mast included a YE radio beacon, on top, with an SG surface search radar just below.

Armament
The gun arrangement shown is prior to the replacement of the 127mm (5in) guns on the forecastle and stern.

cruisers (the *Cleveland*-class, ordered on 1 July 1940) into carriers but the Navy Board had not agreed, considering that smaller carriers based on cruiser hulls would have serious weaknesses, especially in combat situations. Now the situation had changed and it was appreciated that conversions could be made and brought into action much more rapidly than new fleet carriers, and light carriers were better than no carriers. Nine *Cleveland*-class cruisers were on the stocks, all at the same shipyard, and all were earmarked as carrier conversions. Known as the *Independence*-class after the first to be commissioned, all were in the water and ready for action by the end of 1943. Despite the Navy Board's justifiable concerns, all save *Princeton* survived World War II despite being in intense action much of the time.

The class leader was laid down at the New York Shipbuilding Co., at Camden, New Jersey, on 1 May 1941 as *Amsterdam*, launched as USS *Independence* (CV-22) on 22 August 1942 and commissioned at Philadelphia Naval Base on 14 January 1943. Construction and appearance were quite different from the large fleet carriers. The flight deck, narrowed towards the bow, was 186m (610ft) long. It did not extend over the finely tapered bow, and a 127mm (5in) 38-cal gun was mounted right

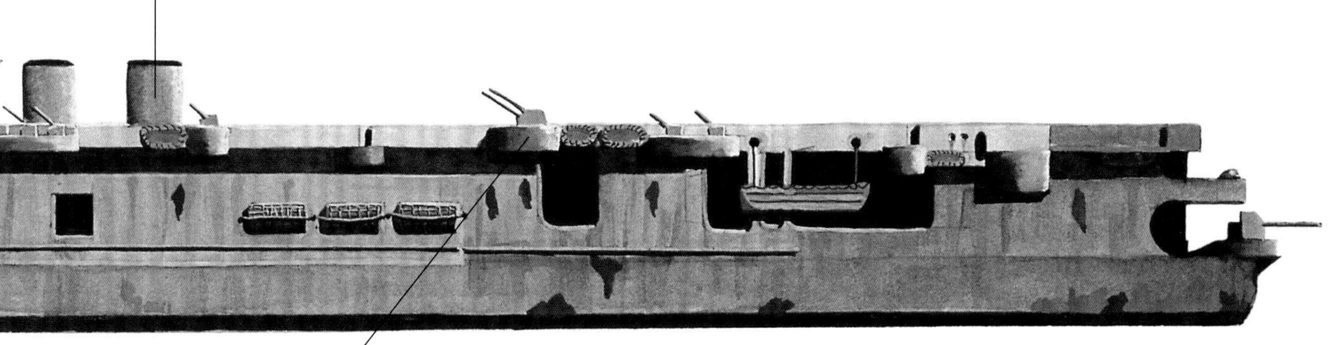

The *Independence*-class's origins as a cruiser design gave it a distinctly different appearance to other American carriers.

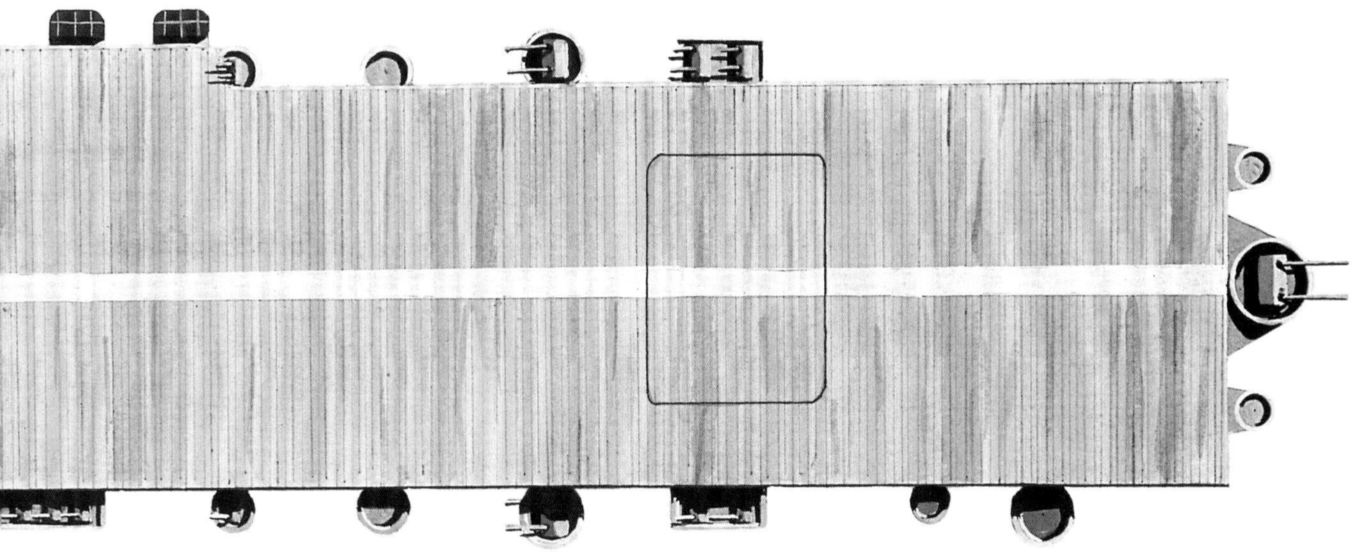

This stern view of *Independence* taken on 30 April 1943 shows the unusual tumble-home hull form of the class.

Specification

Dimensions:	Length: 190m (623ft); Beam: 21.8m (71ft 6in); Draught: 7.4m (24ft 4in)
Displacement:	10,833 tonnes (10,662 tons); 14,987 tonnes (14,751 tons) full load
Propulsion:	4 boilers, GE turbines, 4 shafts; 75,470kW (100,000shp)
Speed:	31 knots (57km/h; 35.6mph)
Range:	13,000nm (24,000km; 14,963 miles) at 15 knots (27.7km/h; 17.2mph)
Armament:	24 40mm, 16 20mm AA guns
Aircraft:	34
Complement:	1569

on the bows (this was removed early on). The freeboard was enclosed from bow to stern. A small starboard island had a trestle mast mounted on its after edge. There was no integral funnel and engine room exhausts were expelled through four starboard vents, projected outwards then hinged upwards at 90°. A shorter secondary mast was mounted forward of the third vent. Two centreline elevators and a single H2-1 hydraulic catapult were fitted. Long bulges were fitted to the hull sides, more in the interest of stability than as anti-torpedo defences.

Independence had no side armour, apart from a 51mm (2in) section protecting the forward magazine. The armoured deck had 51mm (2in) of plate and the bulkheads ranged between 63–127mm (2.5–5in). The *Cleveland* class were designed for speed, which suited their conversion to carriers intended to work with attack and battle groups rather than as escorts or transports. Four Babcock & Wilcox boilers at 44.6kg/cm^2 (634psi) powered four GE geared steam turbines, driving four shafts. The carrier version, with greater displacement, was marginally slower than the cruisers, with a maximum speed of 31 knots (57.4km/h; 35.6mph).

The cruisers were intended to have 127mm (5in) 38-calibre guns, but *Independence* was the only carrier to mount these, and they were removed at San Francisco before the ship entered the war zone, to be replaced by quadruple 40mm (1.5in) mounts. As carriers they had two quadruple and eight dual 40mm AA guns situated in bays alongside the flight deck, and 16 single-barrel 20mm guns. An air wing of 30 planes was planned for the class. *Independence* carried Composite Squadron VC-22, at first with Grumman F6F-3 Hellcat fighters and TBF-1 Avenger torpedo bombers, and also Douglas SBD Dauntless dive-bombers, but the SBDs were not taken into combat as fighter cover and reconnaissance were seen as the ship's primary roles. A typical mix by 1944 would be 24 fighters and eight torpedo bombers. On its final active service it was carrying VF-27 F6F-3 and VT-27 TBM aircraft.

Heavy damage

On 3 July 1943 *Independence* reached San Francisco on its way to join the Pacific fleet. Leaving on 14 July, it was redesignated as a light carrier, CVL-22, on the 15th. From 1 September it engaged with *Essex* and *Yorktown* in heavy raids on Marcus Island, followed by similar attacks on Wake Island. From then on it was in action at Rabaul, the Gilbert Islands and Tarawa. In the course of intense attack by Mitsubishi G4M 'Betty' bombers off Tarawa Atoll, *Independence* was hit on 20 November by a plane-launched torpedo that struck the starboard quarter. The aft engine room and adjacent compartments were flooded, and steering control from the bridge was lost. Damage control response was effective and the ship proceeded under its own power for emergency repairs made by the specialist repair ship USS *Vestal* at Funafuti Atoll. A return to San Francisco had to be made on 2 January 1944 for full repair. A second catapult was installed at this time, and by 3 July the ship was back at Pearl Harbor, beginning training for night-time flying off and landings.

On 29 August it joined Task Force 38, providing night reconnaissance and air cover for the Palaus landings that preceded the taking of Okinawa. As raids were launched on Formosa (Taiwan), the Philippines and Okinawa, *Independence*'s fighters provided day combat air cover as well as the night-time role. As the series of Leyte Gulf battles developed, the ship's planes joined in the attacks that sank the super-battleship *Musashi* and four Japanese carriers, before resuming the operations against bases on the Philippines. On the night of 17–18 December 1944 during a storm, a rack of bombs broke loose in the magazine and began to roll around with the ship. The crew went to emergency stations but the bombs were secured without further mishap. In January 1945 *Independence* supported the Lingayen landings on Luzon and flew sorties from the South China Sea before returning to Pearl Harbor for essential repairs. Its next combat role was the Okinawa landings from 1 April, followed by strikes against Japanese homeland targets, up to the surrender on 15 August.

Independence left Tokyo on 22 September 1945 to return to its home port of San Francisco via Saipan and Guam. From November 1945 to January 1946 it took part in the return of servicemen and prisoners of war to the USA. It was then selected as one of the test vessels to be used in the Operation Crossroads atomic bomb tests of Bikini Atoll. The hull survived two explosions without sinking. Despite being highly radioactive, it was towed first to Kwajalein, then to Pearl Harbor and finally to San Francisco for examination. It was ultimately scuttled with a load of nuclear waste material in the Pacific on 29 January 1951, near the Farallon islands, about 48km (30 miles) off San Francisco.

Post-war recommissions

Alhough built as wartime conversions of light cruisers, several of the *Independence*-class carriers had post-war careers. *Belleau Wood* (CVL-24), placed in reserve in January 1947, was transferred to the French Navy in 1951–60, then returned to the USA for scrapping. *Monterey* (CVL-26) was a training carrier from 1950 to 1956, and an aircraft transport craft (AVT-2) from 1959 to 1970. *Langley* (CVL-27) served with the French Navy as *Lafayette* between 1951 and 1963. *Cabot* (CVL-28) was modernized in 1965–67 and served with the Spanish Navy from 1967 to 1989 as *Dédalo*. *Bataan* (CVL-29), placed on reserve in February 1947, was recommissioned as an ASW carrier between 1950 and 1954.

USS Princeton (1943)

Fourth US Navy ship to bear the name, *Princeton* was originally intended to be a light cruiser but the need for more carriers saw it converted to an *Independence*-class carrier.

The future *Princeton* had been ordered as a light cruiser in July 1940. To be named *Tallahassee*, it was laid down at the New York Shipbuilding Corporation yard, Camden, New Jersey, on 2 June 1941. On 6 February 1942 the change of plan was made, by which time the hull was complete up to the main deck level. As a carrier it was launched on 18 October 1942 and commissioned at the Philadelphia Navy Yard on 25 February 1943 as USS *Princeton* (CV-23). In July 1943 the designation was modified to CVL to indicate its 'light' status.

Princeton's main features were virtually identical to those of *Independence*. Although other class members

***Princeton*'s design gave it the same long, low profile as USS *Independence*.**

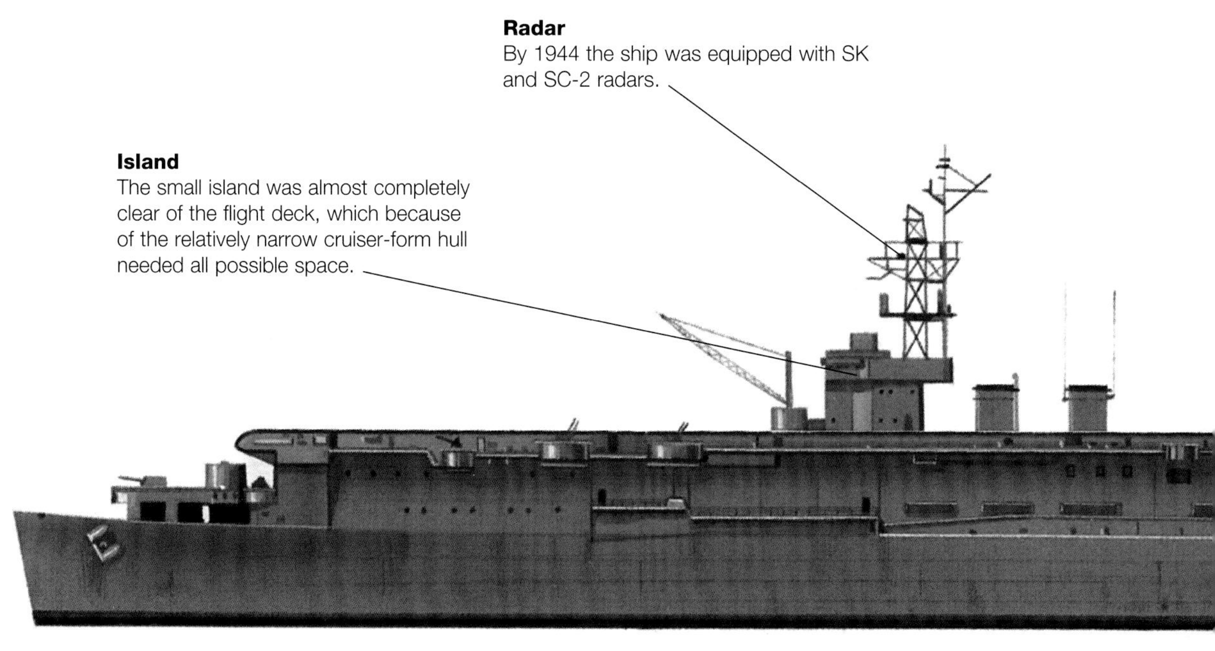

from CVL-24 to CVL-30 carried belt armour of 83–127mm (3.25–5in) with 51mm (2in) main deck armour, *Princeton,* like *Independence,* did not have the belt armour apart from a belt protecting the forward magazine. The main hangar deck had 51mm (2in) armour and the bulkheads 95–127mm (3.75–5in) protection. Two centreline elevators were fitted with one hydraulic catapult. The planned aircraft wing was formed of 30 planes, although the *Independence*-class normally carried around 28: 12 fighters, nine dive-bombers and nine torpedo bombers.

Four American fleet carriers had been sunk in 1942, and the only ones remaining in the Pacific were *Enterprise* and *Saratoga*. *Princeton* was deployed to the Pacific following a shakedown exercise in the Eastern Atlantic, arriving at Pearl Harbor on 9 August 1943, four weeks after *Independence*, and going into combat from the 25th. In August and September it supported the occupation of Baker Island with Task Force 11, acting as flagship of Task Group 11.2. In company with Task Force 15 it made raids on Japanese positions on Makin and Tarawa in September, and with USS *Saratoga* it gave air cover and attack during the US Bougainville landings on 1–2 November. After a return for overhaul at the Puget Sound base at the end of the year, *Princeton* returned to the Central Pacific and joined the TF 58 fast carrier group.

Its movement and actions during 1944 reflect the hard and relentless campaign to push the Japanese back, island group by island group, towards the innermost defensive line around their home islands. In January its planes supported amphibious operations at Kwajalein Atoll and Majuro; in February it was at Eniwetok and again at Kwajalein. March and April saw the ship at the Caroline

Gun tubs
The gun emplacements were known as gun tubs. They were not sponsoned but bracketed out in balcony style.

Measure 21 camouflage
Princeton's paint scheme, here its original dark grey, went through different camouflage types. Measure 21, all-over sea-blue, was frequently used on the large surface areas of carriers. When sunk it was painted in Measure 33/Design 7A.

The Grumman F6F Hellcat was an advance on the F4F Wildcat. As the F6F-3, it began combat duties in August 1943. Hellcats destroyed over 5000 enemy aircraft, more than any other Allied type.

Islands, the Palaus, Woleai and Yap, giving air cover to the Hollandia operation on New Guinea, and attacking the major Japanese central Pacific base at Truk. In May–June it was engaged in the assault on Saipan in the Marianas and raided Guam and other islands still under Japanese occupation, and took part in the Battle of the Philippine Sea, where its planes shot down 30 Japanese bombers and its AA defences downed another three. With only brief returns to bases for replenishment of supplies, in July and August it was back at the Marianas, then deployed to the Philippines, returning eastwards to support the Palau offensive, then back to the Philippines to raid Japanese airfields on Luzon.

Specification

Dimensions:	Length: 189.7m (622ft 6in); Beam: 21.8m (71ft 6in); Draught: 7.9m (26ft)
Displacement:	11,176 tonnes (11,000 tons), 13,208 tonnes (13,000 tons) full load
Propulsion:	GE geared turbines; 2 shafts; 74,570kW (100,000shp)
Speed:	31.6 knots (58.5km/h; 36.4mph)
Range:	12,500nm (23,125km; 14,375 miles) at 15 knots (27.7km/h; 17.2mph)
Armament:	24 40mm (1.5in), 22 20mm AA guns
Aircraft:	34
Complement:	1569

Fast Carrier Task Force

Preparations were under way for landing on the Philippines in October and *Princeton*'s aircraft continued to attack airfields and ground installations as part of Task Group 38.3. Japanese resistance was fierce and counterattacks were made against the fleet assembling in Leyte Gulf. On 24 October, at 09.38 a Yokosuka D4Y 'Judy' dive-bomber succeeded in breaking through AA fire to drop a 226kg (500lb) bomb that pierced the flight deck and exploded on the main deck, causing relatively little damage but starting fires and further explosions. For several hours, with the aid of nearby ships, the crew struggled to contain and put out the fires. Loss of pressure in the fire prevention watermain and failure of the water curtains and sprinklers to work impeded their efforts. There were well-rehearsed drills to counter such scenes, however chaotic they seemed, and Salvage Control Phases I and II were put in hand, which provided for the evacuation of personnel not involved with damage control and engineering.

In a heavy swell, with steering power lost, the drifting carrier collided with the destroyer *Irwin* and cruiser

Birmingham as they sought to place themselves close, damaging both. Then at 15.24 a massive explosion of 400 50kg (110lb) GP bombs held in the C-101B torpedo storage room blew the ship's stern away, aft of Frame 120, along with everything above the main deck from Frame 120 to Frame 105. The task of damage control was now impossible and by 16.00 the ship was burning uncontrollably and without power. All remaining crew on board were evacuated: 1361 were saved and 108 were killed. In the collision and blasts, *Birmingham* was heavily damaged and sustained losses of 233 men. *Princeton*'s hulk was sunk at around 17.50 by two torpedoes from the cruiser USS *Reno,* which detonated the ammunition in the forward magazine.

Sprinkler failure

The inquiry into *Princeton's* loss centred on how a single 226kg (500lb) bomb could have totally disabled the carrier. It noted that the ship's firemain system was well developed, with ample pumping capacity. Had the initial fire that started at 09.50 been quickly contained, the subsequent explosions could have been avoided. But the hangar sprinkler system did not come on, and this was considered the prime cause of the loss of the ship. The reason for the failure could not be established, as the ship's power was functioning at the time. The torpedo stowage area was not intended for the storing of high-explosive bombs and this was described as a 'high risk' practice, but it was noted that even after that explosion the ship remained on an even keel.

USS *Birmingham* comes close to the burning *Princeton* in the effort to control the fires on the carrier, on 24 October 1944.

USS Lexington (1943)

Commissioned in 1943, and claimed as sunk four times, this *Essex*-class carrier had an almost 50-year career, and remains intact and preserved as a naval monument.

Essex (CV-9) was the lead ship of a new generation of fleet carriers and *Lexington* (CV-16) was second in the class to be commissioned. Their construction details were not restricted by treaty, but the design process was curtailed by the need to speed up the building programme after Pearl Harbor. Originally *Essex* was planned for commissioning in 1944, but by the end of 1944 13 of the class were in commission. While the hull of CV-16, intended to carry the name *Cabot*, was on the stocks at the Bethlehem Steel Corp., Quincy,

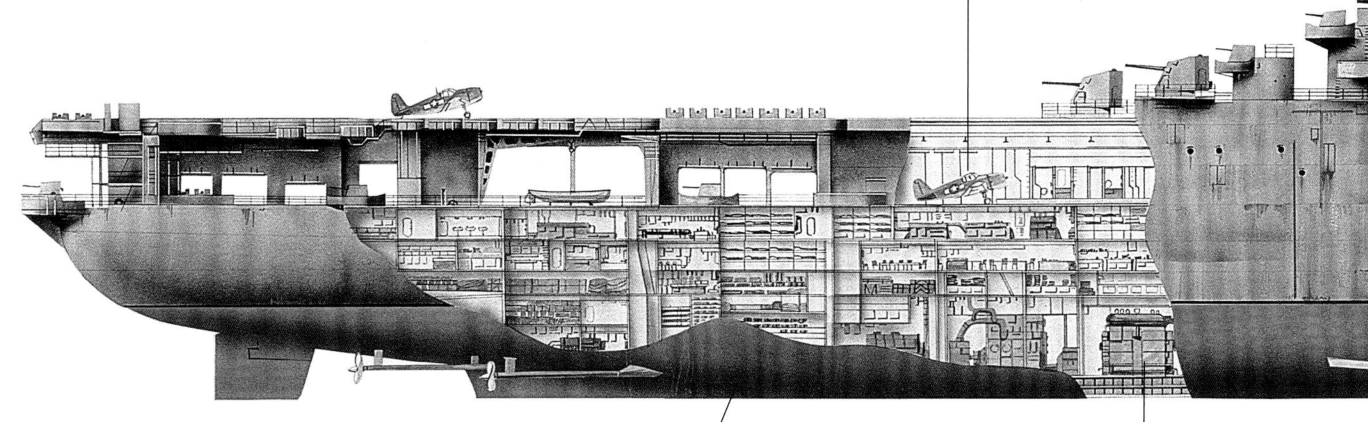

Hangar bays
The three hangar bays had 3600m^2 (40,000 sq ft) of space.

Paint scheme
Lexington usually sported a blue camouflage paint scheme (Measure 33) and this, together with four successive Japanese claims that it had been sunk, gained it the nickname of 'The Blue Ghost'.

Machine rooms
The machinery rooms were arranged *en echelon* (alternately located) for maximum survivability.

Massachusetts, news came of the sinking of USS *Lexington* (CV-2) in the Battle of the Coral Sea, and on 16 June 1942 the ship's name was changed in honour of its predecessor. Laid down on 15 July 1941, it was launched on 26 September 1942 and commissioned at Boston Harbor on 17 February 1943.

The plan of USS *Yorktown* (CV-5) was taken as a basis for the Essexes, but despite the urgency of construction, much experience, thought and new technology went into the design, finally signed off on 20 February 1940 (although the possibility of adaptation to new aircraft types and technology was incorporated, and modification and improvement would go on throughout the war). *Lexington* was built to the specifications and standards of the *Essex*-class as a fleet carrier capable of fielding 90 aircraft. Its machinery was, as with the others, eight M-type Babcock & Wilcox boilers working at 43.5 kg/cm^2 (619psi) and powering four geared steam turbines for the four screws. Four generators were carried, two of 1250kW capacity and two standby generators of 1000kW capacity.

A cutaway profile of *Lexington* gives an indication of the internal complexity and facilities required to operate an *Essex*-class carrier.

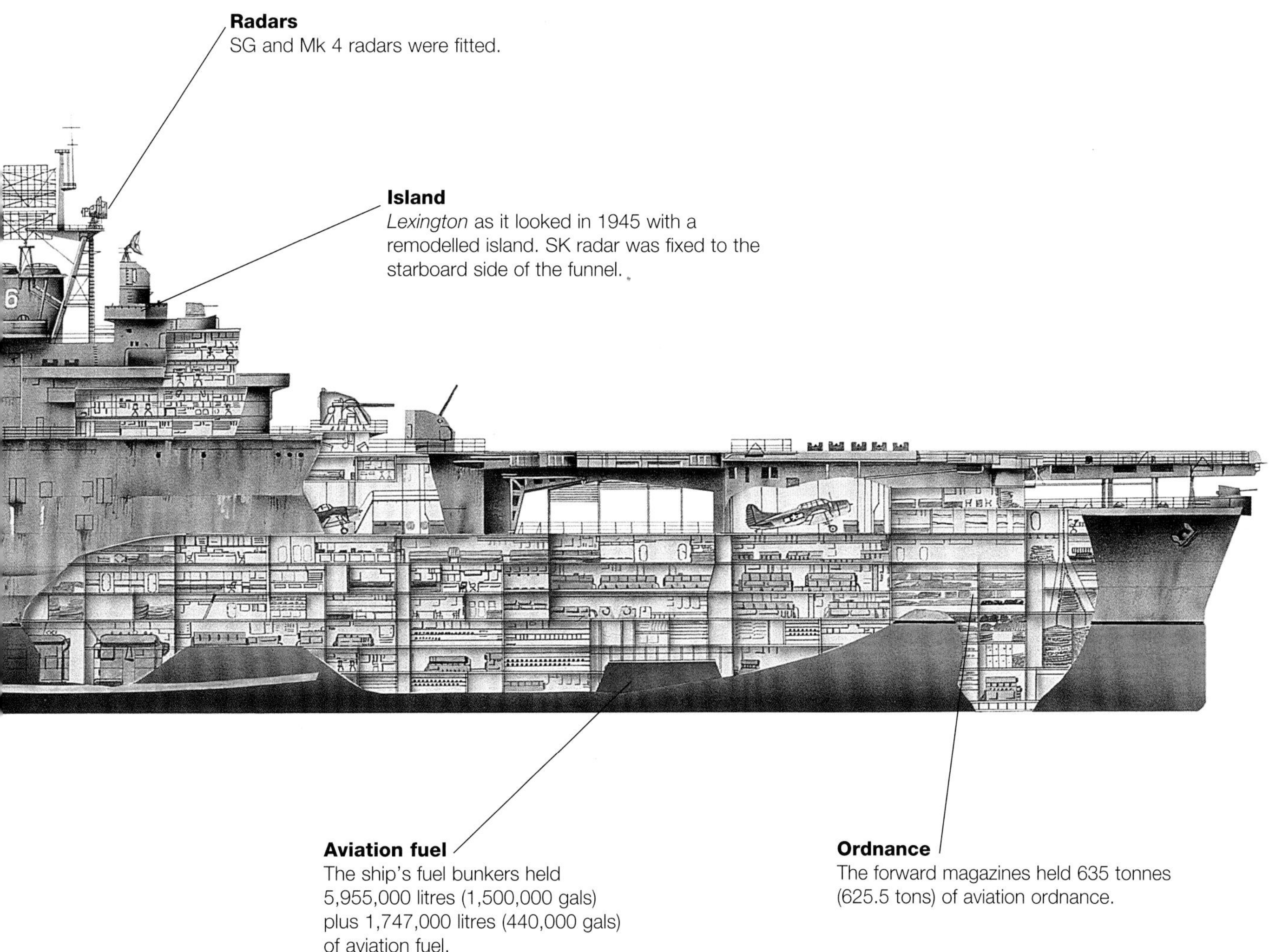

Lexington's appearance after the major modifications carried out between 1953 and 1955.

In accordance with usual practice, it made a training and shakedown cruise on the US East Coast and down to the Caribbean Sea. After a brief return to Boston for maintenance it headed for the Pacific, where the presence of more fast carriers was badly needed if the American drive to turn the tide of events against the Imperial Japanese Navy was going to succeed. Joining the Central Pacific Force (later Fifth Fleet) at Pearl Harbor, from September to November the ship joined in operations in the Gilbert Islands war zone against Tarawa and Wake Island, and against Japanese bases on the Marshall Islands.

At 11.22 on 4 December *Lexington* was hit by a torpedo from a Japanese bomber, knocking out the steering system. Swift damage control work put out the resultant fires and set up a jury system to work the rudder, and it made for Bremerton to undergo repair. From February 1944 it joined TF58, the fast carrier Task Force, as Vice Admiral Marc Mitscher's flagship, making rapid movements between Majuro, New Guinea and Truk in raids on enemy positions and support for Allied landings, dropping sea mines as well as bombs.

Specification (Original Form)

Dimensions:	Length: 250m (820ft); Beam: 28m (93ft); Draught: 10.41m (34ft 2in)
Displacement:	27,534 tonnes (27,100 tons); 36,962 tonnes (36,380 tons) full load
Propulsion:	8 boilers, 4 Westinghouse geared turbines, 4 shafts; 110,00kW (150,000shp)
Speed:	33 knots (61km/h; 38mph)
Range:	15,440nm (28,564km; 17,756 miles) at 15 knots (27.7km/h; 17.2mph)
Armament:	12 127mm (5in) 38-cal guns, 4 twin, 4 single; 8 quad 40mm (1.5in) 56-cal and 46 20mm 78-cal AA guns
Aircraft:	110
Complement:	2600

Battle of the Philippine Sea

Planes from *Lexington* were in action in the Battle of the Philippine Sea, 19–20 June, contributing to what became known as 'the great Marianas Turkey Shoot' in which Japanese aircraft, other than suicide planes, were virtually cleared from the skies, and continued on campaign through that summer, joining in another major battle in Leyte Gulf, where they helped sink the battleship *Musashi* and light carriers *Chitose* and *Zuihō*, and on their own sank the fleet carrier *Zuikaku* on 24–25 October. On

25 October a kamikaze plane struck the flight deck close to the island while operations were going on, but failed to stop the launching and landing of *Lexington*'s aircraft. Repairs were made at the Ulithi Atoll base and the ship was back in action by December. By February 1945 it was part of the force closing in on the Japanese home islands. It supported the Marine landings on Iwo Jima before being sent for a much-needed overhaul at Puget Sound naval base.

Returning to join Rear Admiral Thomas F. Sprague's TF38.1, it launched fresh attacks on Japan's homeland, targeting airfields, industry and the naval bases at Kure and Yokosuka during the Pacific War's final phase. A wave of bombers from *Lexington* was in the air on 15 August when news of the Japanese surrender was radioed to them, and they released their bombs into the sea. *Lexington*'s war record was second to none even in the annals of US carriers. It spent a total of 21 months on combat duty, shot down 372 enemy aircraft and destroyed a further 475 on the ground. Its planes sank 304,810 tonnes (300,000 tons) of enemy cargo vessels and damaged a further 609,628 tonnes (600,000 tons). In addition, 15 attacking aircraft were shot down by its guns.

The ship left Tokyo Bay on 3 December 1945 to return to San Francisco with US servicemen on board. With the reduction of the Navy to peacetime strength, *Lexington* was decommissioned on 23 April 1947 and became part of the reserve fleet at Puget Sound. As global tensions increased again, carriers were among the first reserve craft to be recommissioned. *Lexington* was reclassified as an attack carrier, CVA-16, and from September 1953 it underwent two modernization programmes, SCB-27C and SCB-125. The bow was remodelled in full-height 'hurricane bow' format, the island was reshaped in a more streamlined form, an angled flight deck was fitted along with a steam catapult and the existing flight deck was reinforced to take the stresses of heavier jet aircraft landings. This work was completed in August 1955 and on the 15th of that month *Lexington* was recommissioned and moved to the San Diego naval base. It would remain with the Seventh Fleet in the Pacific for six years, contributing to SEATO operations and shows of force during crisis periods with China over Taiwan.

In January 1962 it was deployed to the Mexican Gulf just as the Cuban Missile Crisis was coming to a head; and from December 1962 it was used for pilot training in the Gulf of Mexico, although it was not formally designated as a training carrier (CVT-16) until 1 January 1969, and it continued to function as such until 1991, by which time it was the last *Essex*-class carrier in service and the longest-serving carrier in any navy. Another of its many firsts was to have the first female crew members on a US carrier in August 1980. *Lexington* was decommissioned on 8 November 1991, and has been preserved as a museum ship at Corpus Christi, Texas.

Lexington **under way on 12 November 1943.**

Equipment limitations

As well as *Lexington*, four other former US Navy carriers, along with specimen aircraft of their period, are preserved as museum ships, three of them also *Essex*-class ships. USS *Yorktown* (CV-10) is at Charleston, South Carolina. USS *Intrepid* (CV-11) is at New York City. USS *Hornet* (CV-12) is at Alameda, California. USS *Midway* (CV-41) is at San Diego, California. USS *John F. Kennedy* (CV-67), the last conventionally powered carrier in the US Navy, which was decommissioned in 2007, is held as a potential museum ship. No qualified organization has yet acquired it, but the Rhode Island Aviation Hall of Fame has launched the John F. Kennedy Project in the hope of giving the carrier a permanent home.

USS Intrepid (1943)

Despite being the most frequently hit US carrier in World War II, *Intrepid* served in the US Navy for more than 30 years on missions from Pacific battles to spacecraft recovery, and remains today as one of the four surviving *Essex*-class carriers.

On 10 July 1940, President Franklin D. Roosevelt signed the 'Two-Ocean Navy' Act, affirming the US's aim to have a powerful naval presence both in the Atlantic and Pacific zones, and authorizing funding for three more fleet carriers of the Essex class: *Yorktown*, *Intrepid* and *Hornet*. As American involvement in the war grew more likely, a further seven fleet carriers were approved in the same month. Hull CV-11 was laid down at Newport News, Virginia, on 1 December 1941, a few days before the Pearl Harbor attack, launched as USS *Intrepid* on 26 April 1943 and

Aircraft
The *Intrepid* carried 110 aircraft of various types, including Hellcats and Helldivers.

Flight deck
The flight deck area was 262.8m x 32.9m (862ft 2in x 107ft 11in).

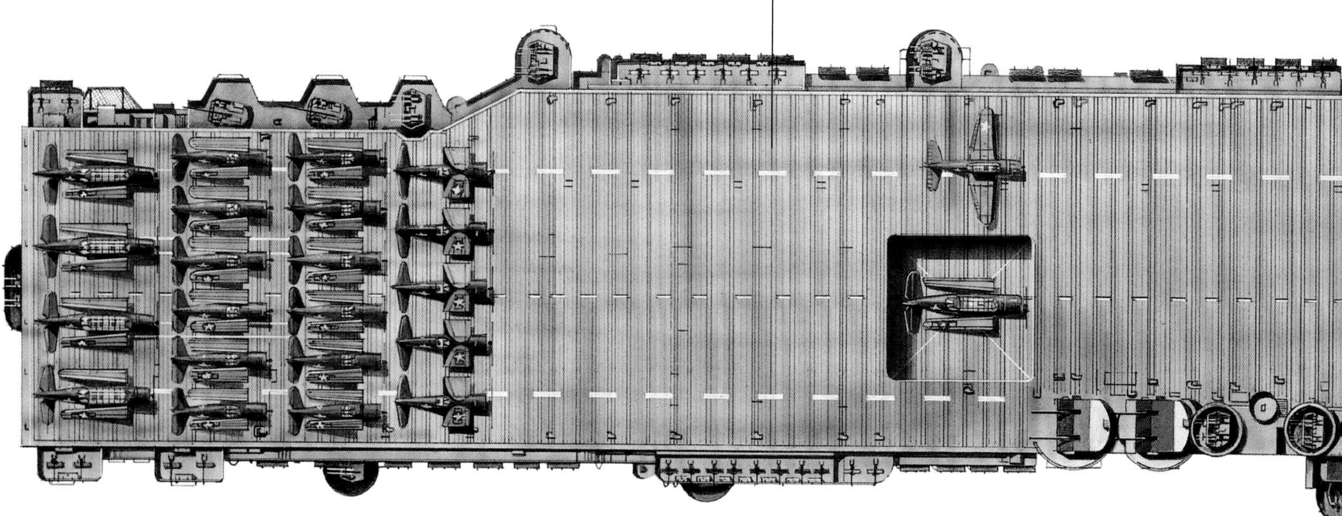

commissioned on 16 August that year. Its first captain was Thomas Lamison Sprague, later to become an admiral of carrier forces.

In design and appearance *Intrepid* followed the basic *Essex* pattern. The strength deck, providing the ship with rigidity, was the hangar deck. This brought the weight of the armour lower in the hull, improving stability, increasing hangar space and requiring less internal bracing. The hangar deck had 63mm (2.5in) armour and below it the fourth deck had 38mm (1.5in). The hangar deck had roll-up doors on all sides, ensuring adequate ventilation and the dispersal of flammable vapour, and also allowing planes to warm up their engines before being lifted for take-off. The hull was divided by bulkheads in an arrangement of watertight compartments, with sets of voids along the sides to absorb

***Intrepid*, fourth USN ship to bear the name, was often known as 'The Fighting I' in tribute to its many battles.**

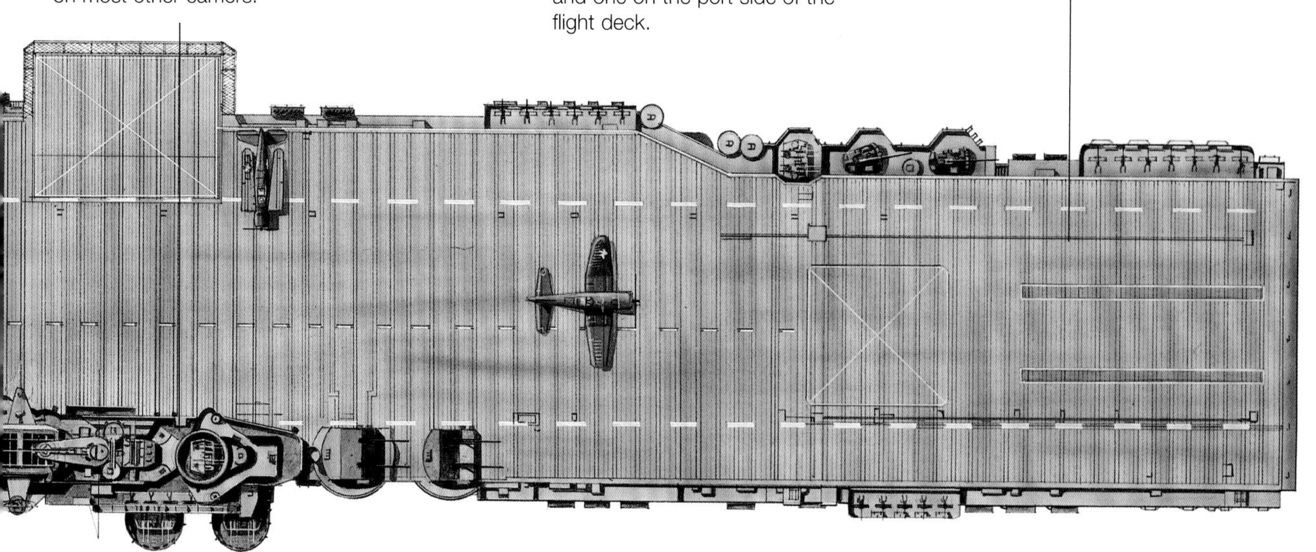

Left and below: forward and aft profiles of USS *Intrepid*.

torpedo or shell strikes. A centreline, mid-hull elevator was dropped from the design, improving structural strength. Side armour varied from 63mm (2.5in) to 102mm (4in).

Intrepid left Norfolk for Pearl Harbor, via San Francisco, on 3 December 1943, and was in action at Kwajalein Atoll from 29 January 1944. On the night of 17 February it was struck by a torpedo, 4.5m (5ft) below the waterline on the starboard quarter, jamming the rudder. Using the port engine and hoisting a makeshift sail to benefit from the wind direction, the ship made Pearl Harbor by the 24th, and went on to Hunter's Point Navy Yard, San Francisco, with a jury rudder to complete repairs. During operations off the Philippines two kamikaze planes struck the ship on 25 November 1944, resulting in 65 members killed, but the ship stayed on station and the resultant fires were put out in less than two hours. Another visit to San Francisco had to be made for repairs. A further kamikaze strike happened on 16 April 1945 off Okinawa; again fires were put out but another trip back to base was necessary.

In the course of the war, in its numerous visits to dry dock for repairs as well as refits, *Intrepid*'s original armament was enhanced by three quadruple 40mm (1.5in) mounts below the island and three more on the port side, plus one each on the starboard quarter and on the stern, as well as 21 additional 21mm (0.8in) mounts. This extension of the AA defences was a response to the increasing frequency of kamikaze attacks.

Reserve role

On 22 March 1947 *Intrepid* was decommissioned and joined the reserve fleet for five years. An SCB 27C reconstruction programme began at Newport News on 9 April 1952 to

Specification

Dimensions:	Length: 250m (820ft); Beam: 28m (93ft); Draught: 10.41m (34ft 2in)
Displacement:	27,534 tonnes (27,100 tons); 36,962 tonnes (36,380 tons) full load
Propulsion:	8 boilers, 4 Westinghouse geared turbines, 4 shafts; 110,00kW (150,000shp)
Speed:	33 knots (61km/h; 38mph)
Range:	15,440nm (28,564km; 17,756 miles) at 15 knots (27.7km/h; 17.2mph)
Armament:	12 127mm (5in) 38-cal guns, 4 twin, 4 single; 8 quad 40mm (1.5in) 56-cal and 46 20mm 78-cal AA guns
Aircraft:	110
Complement:	2600

Intrepid off the Guantanamo Bay, Cuba, naval base in February 1955, between its two modernisations. McDonnell F2H Banshee jet fighters are on the flight deck.

equip *Intrepid* for the era of jet planes and nuclear weapons, and it was reclassed as an attack carrier (CVA-11) in October 1952. Further modernization was done at New York Navy Yard from September 1956 to 2 May 1957, when under programme SCB 125 an angled flight deck was added. Another reclassification made it CVS 11 on 31 March 1962, its purpose now being submarine hunting, reflecting the increasing deployment of Soviet submarines in the Atlantic region. *Intrepid* recovered the space capsule of Project Mercury, with astronaut Scott Carpenter on 24 May 1962, and of *Gemini III*, the US's first manned space flight, on 23 March 1965. Following that the ship underwent a FRAM II life extension refit from March to October, and on completion was deployed to the Vietnam conflict.

Intrepid had three deployments in the Vietnam War as an attack carrier, each with different aircraft groups. From 4 April to 21 November 1966 it shipped Squadrons VA-15 and VAA 95 with A-4 planes and Squadrons VA-165 and VA-176 with A-1 planes. Between 11 May and 30 December 1967 it shipped Squadrons VSF-3 and VA-15 again, and VA-34 with A-4 planes, Squadron VA-145 with A-1s and VF-111 Det 11 with F-8s; finally, from 4 June 1968 to 8 February 1969 with VF-142 and VF-143, both flying F-4s, VA-27 and VA-97 with A-7s, and VA-196 with A6s.

Decommissioned to reserve status on 15 March 1974, the ship was handed over on 27 April 1981 to the Sea, Air, Space Museum in New York City. *Intrepid* spent 24 years moored at Pier 86 on Manhattan's West Side until it was prised out of a 24-year accumulation of silt and moved into dry dock in 2006 to undergo a thorough process of restoration at a cost of some $55 million.

Essex-class variations

The *Essex*-class was separated into two categories, the 14 'long hull' ships, with an overall length of 270m (888ft), and the ten 'short hull' ships that were slightly shorter at 265.8m (872ft). Standard waterline length for both was 250m (820ft). Like *Essex*, *Intrepid* was a short-hull version. Although the long hulls were a design modification introduced in March 1943, one short-hulled ship, *Bon Homme Richard*, was built after that date. It was a variation in bow design, with the longer ships having a 'clipper bow' whose forward projection allowed for the greater length. Two quadruple 40mm (1.5in) gun mounts were placed at the bows of the 'long-hulls'. Even without this distinction, other individual modifications ensured that all *Essex*-class ships ended up with differences of detail.

USS Wasp (1943)

Tenth ship in the *Essex*-class, *Wasp* had an almost 30-year post-war career as an attack carrier, ASW carrier and with the manned space programme.

Wasp (CV-18) was an *Essex*-class carrier, laid down as *Oriskany* at Fore River Shipyard, Quincy, Massachusetts, on 18 March 1942, launched on 17 August 1943 and commissioned on 24 November 1943. Built to the 'short hull' *Essex* design, it followed the standard pattern for the class, including the machinery. Eight Babcock & Wilcox boilers, pressurized to 40kg/cm^2 (565psi) and superheated to 454°C (849°F) powered four Westinghouse geared turbines and four propeller shafts. *En echelon* (alternately located) engine and boiler rooms ensured that if one set of boilers and turbines was flooded or put out of action, the other could still function. The massive strength of the hull

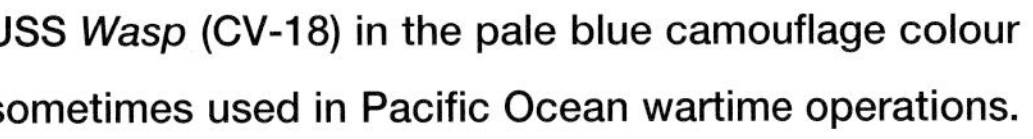

USS *Wasp* (CV-18) in the pale blue camouflage colour sometimes used in Pacific Ocean wartime operations.

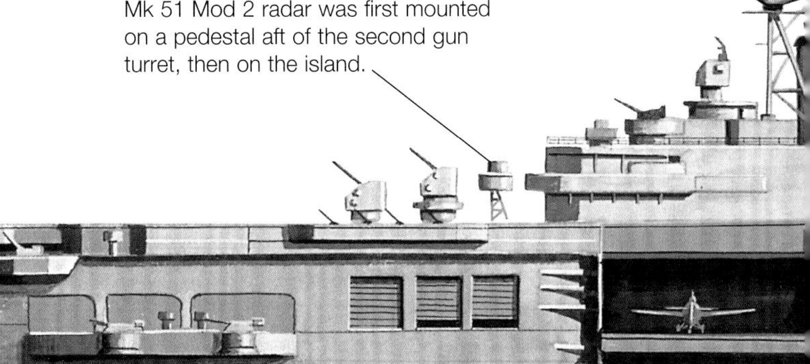

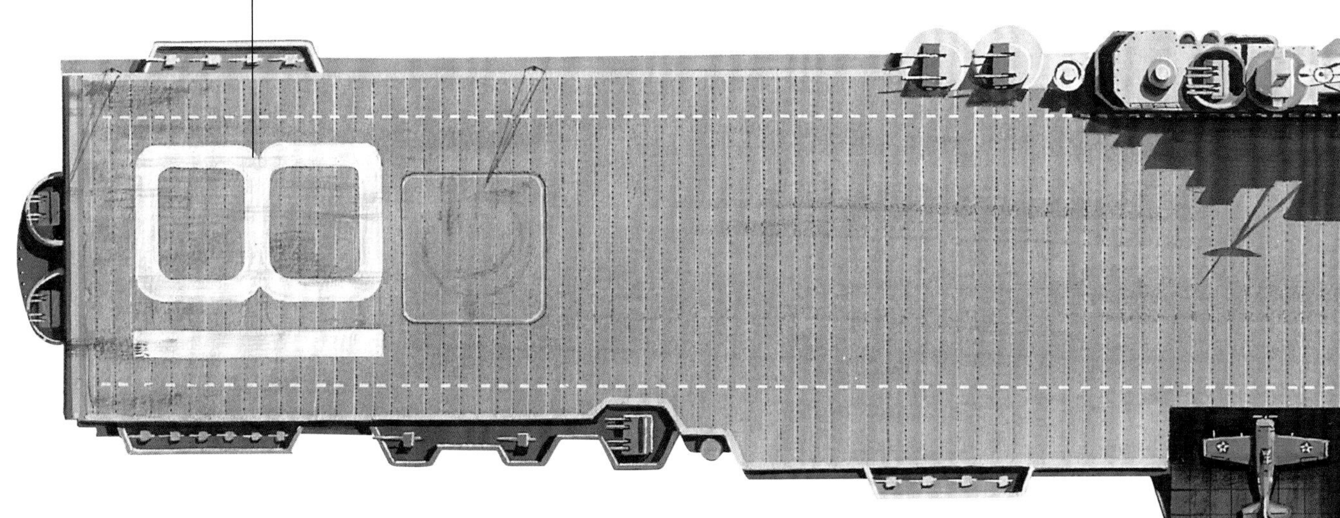

was able to ensure that, despite severe damage from direct hits by bombs, torpedoes and kamikaze planes, none of the *Essex*-class was sunk in combat. Well-planned damage control systems and highly trained damage control crews also played their part in achieving this.

A complement of up to 90 planes was to be carried in four squadrons, plus a fifth in reserve. Careful internal planning enabled the carrying of large stocks of spare parts (25 per cent of total parts), as well as the tools and machinery for rapid repair, all located on hangar deck level. The large stock of planes and the ability to launch them quickly were key features of the design. *Wasp* and the other *Essex*-class ships could put more planes into the air more quickly than any other carriers of World War II, enabling them to mount more intensive bombing strikes and also to provide combat air protection that would outnumber the enemy's defences. The deck edge elevator was a valuable aid here, enabling the transfer of aircraft while the flight deck was still in use.

Pacific deployment

Wasp first went into active service on 10 January 1944 in the Atlantic, serving off the East Coast of the USA until early March 1944, when it was deployed to the Pacific. Its planes made their first combat sorties in May that

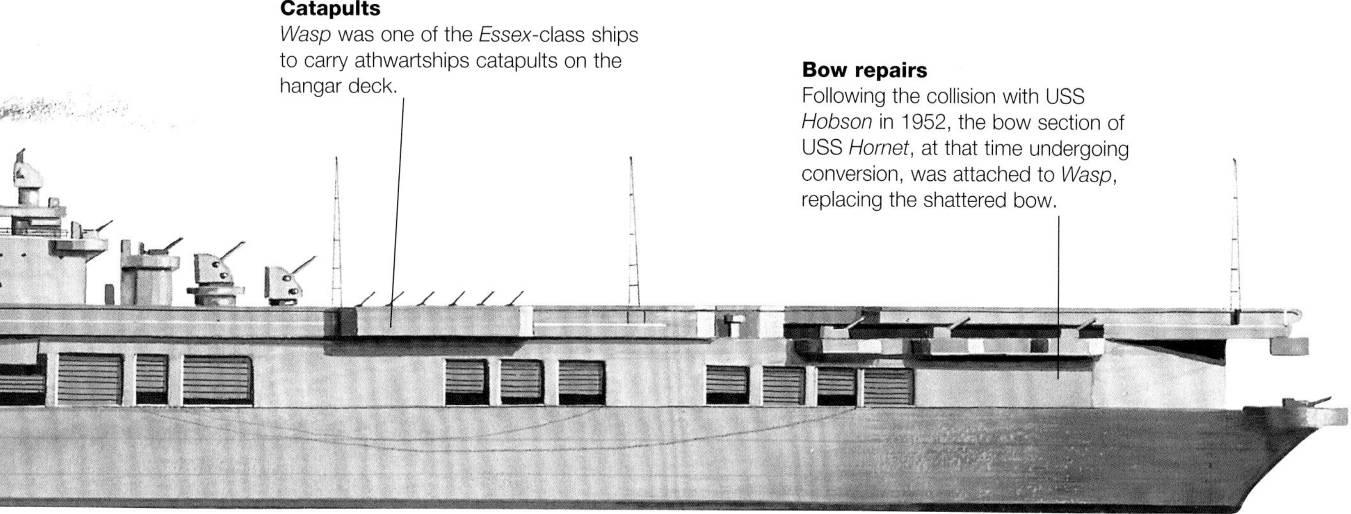

Catapults
Wasp was one of the *Essex*-class ships to carry athwartships catapults on the hangar deck.

Bow repairs
Following the collision with USS *Hobson* in 1952, the bow section of USS *Hornet*, at that time undergoing conversion, was attached to *Wasp*, replacing the shattered bow.

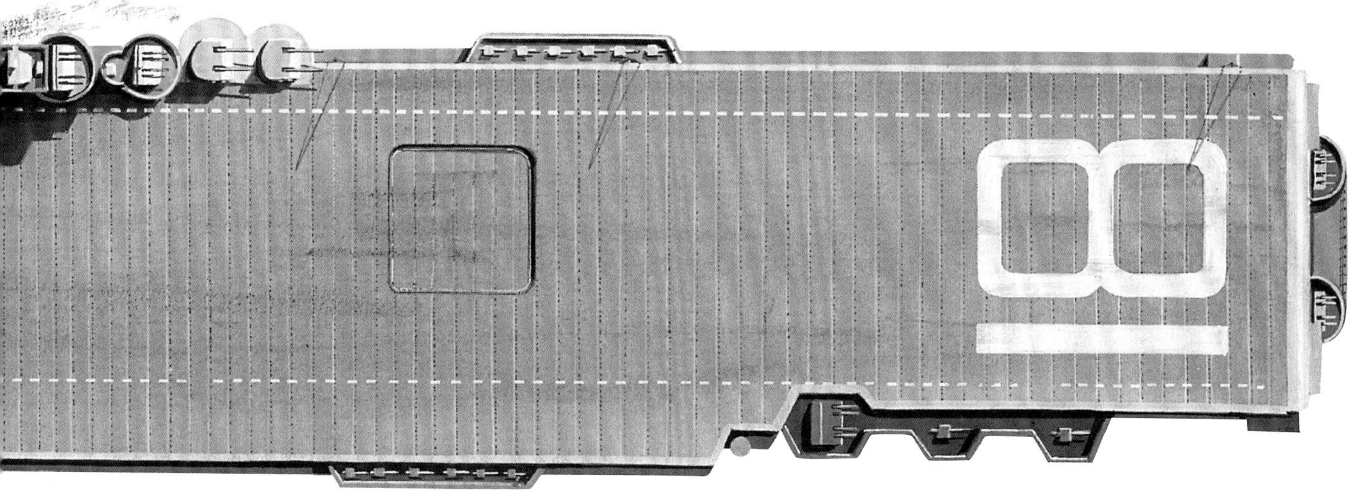

USS *Essex* (CV-9) lead ship of the largest-ever class of aircraft carriers, with 24 launched between 1942 and 1945.

year, attacking Japanese positions on Wake and Marcus Islands and later providing air cover for the occupation of the Marianas Islands. It took part in the Battle of the Philippine Sea, and in July 1944 provided air cover for the invasion of Guam, then in September supported the Allied landings on the Palau Islands. By October *Wasp*'s bombers from Air Group 81 were attacking positions on Taiwan and the northern Philippines, and by February 1945 SB2C Helldivers from *Wasp* were overflying the Japanese home islands. On 19 March 1945 a 226kg (500lb) armour-piercing bomb penetrated the flight deck and the armoured deck, exploding in the crew galley on the third deck and killing 102 of the crew. Flight operations were interrupted for less than half an hour and the ship continued in action.

Between 17 and 23 March its air group shot down 14 Japanese planes, destroyed six on the ground, scored nine bomb hits on Japanese naval ships and shot up a Japanese submarine. It returned to Puget Sound Naval Base for repairs, arriving on 13 April, but was back off Japan just before the surrender, shooting down two attacking Japanese planes on 15 July. *Wasp*'s actions in the Pacific earned the ship eight battle stars. It arrived back in the US on 7 October 1945. *Wasp* then carried 5400 freed Italian prisoners of war back to Italy. By the end of the war with Japan, the ship's original 20mm (.79in) AA guns had been replaced by nine quad 40mm (1.6in) 56-cal Mk I and II, 29 twin 20mm 70-cal and six quad 12.7mm (.5in) AA guns. SK, SC-2 and SM radars were fitted.

Specification

Dimensions:	Length: 250m (820ft); Beam: 28m (93ft); Draught: 10.41m (34ft 2in)
Displacement:	27,534 tonnes (27,100 tons); 36,962 tonnes (36,380 tons) full load
Propulsion:	8 boilers, 4 Westinghouse geared turbines, 4 shafts; 110,00kW (150,000shp)
Speed:	33 knots (61km/h; 38mph)
Range:	15,440nm (28,564km; 17,756 miles) at 15 knots (27.7km/h; 17.2mph)
Armament:	12 127mm (5in) 38-cal guns, 4 twin, 4 single; 8 quad 40mm (1.5in) 56-cal and 46 20mm 78-cal AA guns
Aircraft:	110
Complement:	2600

Reserve role

From 17 February 1947 to 1948 the carrier spent a period in reserve before being brought out for modernization at the New York Navy Yard, to enable it to carry jet planes, and was recommissioned on 28 September 1951. Its displacement was now 41,250 tonnes (40,600 tons) when fully loaded. Eight 127mm (5in) guns were retained, and 14 twin-barrel 76mm (3in) Mk 33 AA guns were mounted. Another 20 years of service followed. Its aircraft complement was now around 80 planes, in a wide range including F4U/FG Corsairs, F6F Hellcats, F7F Tigercats, F8F Bearcats, F9F Panthers and F6U Pirates. *Wasp*'s worst peacetime incident was a collision with the destroyer USS *Hobson* on 26 April 1952 in the Atlantic: the smaller ship sank with the loss of 176 men. With the usual spells for routine refits and dry dockings, including the fitting of an angled flight deck under the SCB-125 Upgrade at San Diego between April and December 1955, the ship was active both in the Pacific and Atlantic areas, and from the later 1950s also in the Mediterranean.

It was redesignated as an anti-submarine carrier (CVS-18) at San Diego on 1 November 1956, carrying AF Guardian ASW planes. In August 1959 reports of an

on-board fire following an accidental explosion revealed that the carrier carried nuclear weapons. In October 1962 *Wasp* was engaged in the blockade of Cuba. In the course of the 1960s it was the main recovery ship in the Atlantic for five US space missions, picking up the *Gemini IV* space capsule and its crew on 7 June 1965. It picked up two space craft within two days in December 1965: *Gemini VI-A* on the 16th and *Gemini VII* on the 18th. It also retrieved *Gemini IX-A* on 6 June 1966 and *Gemini XII* on 15 December 1966. *Wasp* was finally decommissioned on 1 July 1972 and the disarmed hulk was sold for scrapping on 21 May 1973.

***Essex* in action – struck by a kamikaze plane during operations against Luzon, on 25 November 1944.**

Designation explained

American naval aircraft designations began with plane type, as F for fighter, TB for torpedo bomber and SB for scout bomber, followed by an indication of manufacturer (often a code-letter, as with F for Grumman, Y for Consolidated and U for Chance-Vought); sometimes with the initial, as with C for Curtiss and D for Douglas. Subsequent models to the first production run were serial-numbered after the manufacturer's designation, as in F3F, the third Grumman fighter model; evolved versions of a particular model would be distinguished by a hyphen and serial number, as in F3F-2.

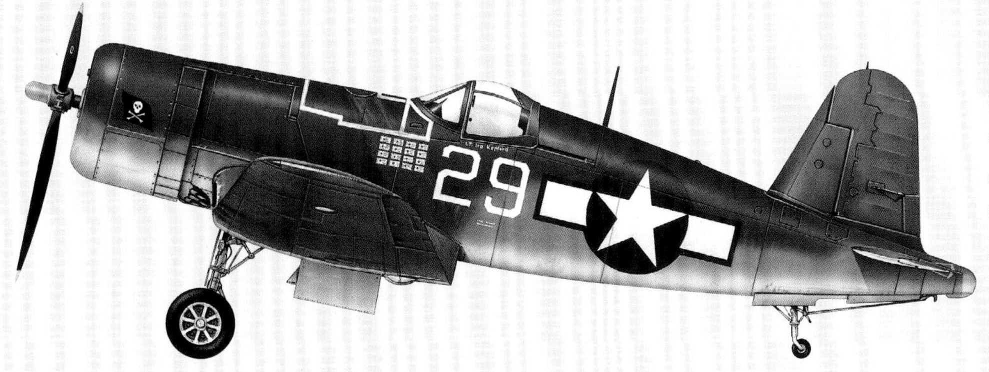

The Vought F4U-1 Corsair, notable for its 'bent-wing' design, was in action from July 1942. The 1D version, shown here, entered service in March 1944.

Taihō (1944)

Marking an advance in Japanese carrier construction and considered unsinkable, *Taihō* was a powerful and formidably armed ship, but its fighting life was destined to last for only three months.

Taihō, meaning 'Great Phoenix', was laid down at the Kawasaki Yard, Kobe, on 10 July 1941 and launched on 7 April 1942. At that time the Imperial Navy was dominant in the Pacific Ocean and may have felt no great urgency about the provision of new carriers. The situation changed with the Battle of Midway, 4–7June, in which four Japanese carriers went down. *Taihō* was still fitting out and two further carriers were quickly ordered, with another five planned. Even so, it was 7 March 1944 before *Taihō* was commissioned, and during 1942–43 the United States added 14 carriers to its Navy. As a result, *Taihō* would go into combat against massive opposition.

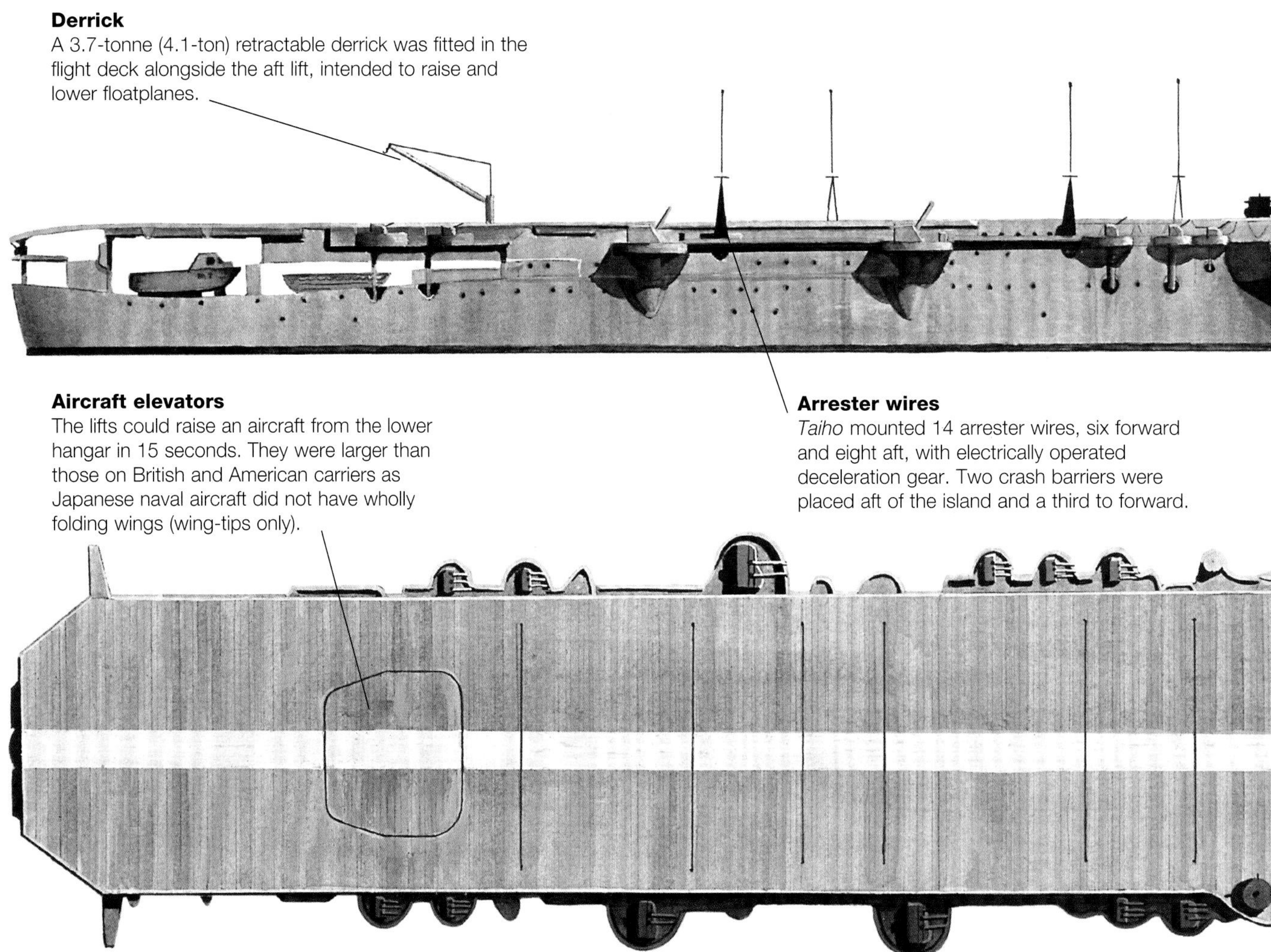

Derrick
A 3.7-tonne (4.1-ton) retractable derrick was fitted in the flight deck alongside the aft lift, intended to raise and lower floatplanes.

Aircraft elevators
The lifts could raise an aircraft from the lower hangar in 15 seconds. They were larger than those on British and American carriers as Japanese naval aircraft did not have wholly folding wings (wing-tips only).

Arrester wires
Taiho mounted 14 arrester wires, six forward and eight aft, with electrically operated deceleration gear. Two crash barriers were placed aft of the island and a third to forward.

Conceived as an improved *Shōkaku*-type in 1939, the design went through important modifications in the course of building. These included the provision of an armoured flight deck, as used by the British Navy. Instead of the hangar and flight decks sitting on top of a hull, the bow and sides were built up to flight deck level and the flight deck itself, longest of any Japanese carrier at 257m (843ft), formed an integral element in providing the hull's strength and integrity. There were upper and lower hangars, the upper one 152m (463ft 4in) long, 22.5m (68ft 6in) wide and 5m (15ft 3in) high, the lower of the same dimensions except for being 45.7cm (18in) longer. As with other Japanese carriers, the hangar decks were enclosed: this was considered an essential precaution both against shipping water in high seas and in showing lights at night, when maintenance work might be going on. Two electrically powered lifts were fitted at opposite ends of the flight deck. The island unit, the first on a Japanese carrier to incorporate fully functional control and command positions, was dominated by a large funnel, canted outwards in the same manner as *Jun'yō*'s, and to maintain balance the flight deck was offset 2m (6.5ft) to port. The tripod mast

***Taihō* took almost two years to fit out after launching, an indication of the difficulties that Japanese industry had in sustaining the huge war effort.**

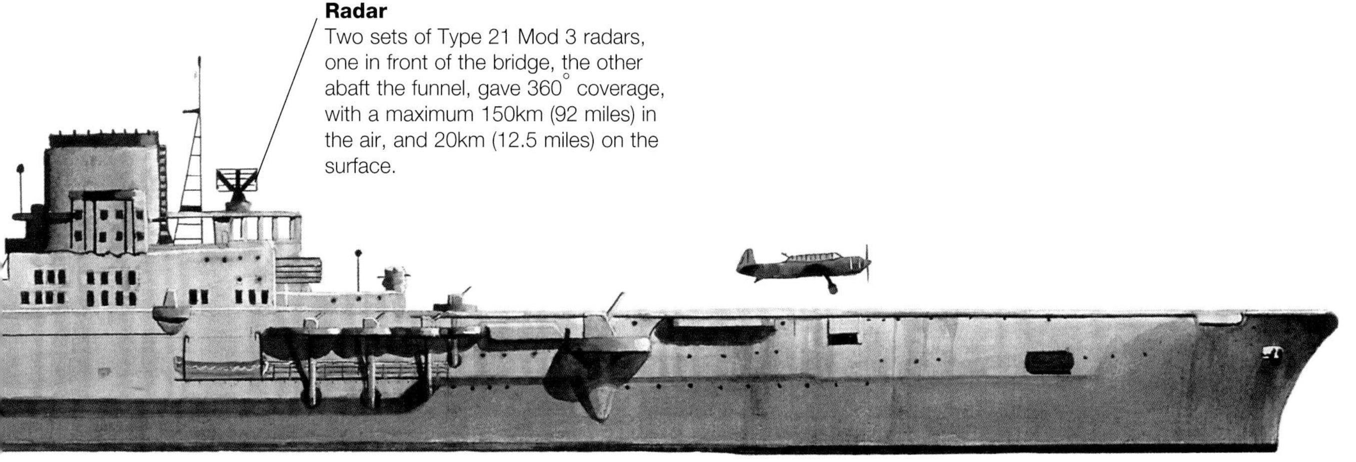

Radar
Two sets of Type 21 Mod 3 radars, one in front of the bridge, the other abaft the funnel, gave 360° coverage, with a maximum 150km (92 miles) in the air, and 20km (12.5 miles) on the surface.

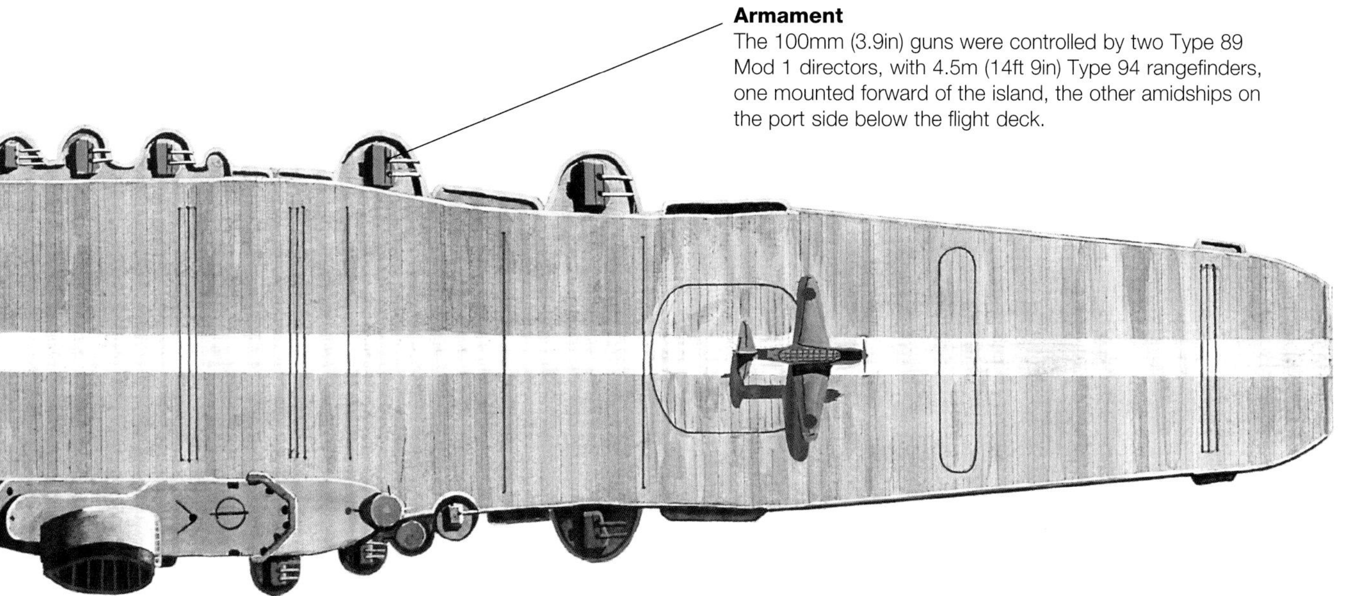

Armament
The 100mm (3.9in) guns were controlled by two Type 89 Mod 1 directors, with 4.5m (14ft 9in) Type 94 rangefinders, one mounted forward of the island, the other amidships on the port side below the flight deck.

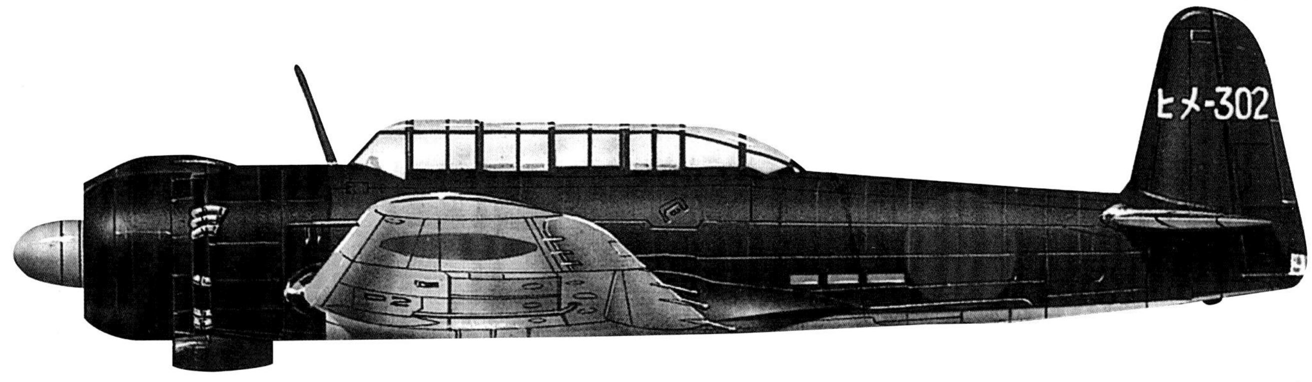

The Nakajima B6N2 Tenzan torpedo bomber (Allied code name Jill) entered service in July 1943. With a three-man crew it carried a 816kg (1800lb) payload.

mounted a Type 13 radar system and two Type 21 Mod 3 radar sets were fitted in front of the bridge and aft of the funnel.

The necessary power to drive the ship at 33-plus knots (61.1+km/h; 37.9+mph) came from eight Kampon boilers and four Kampon geared turbines, with four screws. *Taihō*'s bunkers held 5171 tonnes (5700 tons) of fuel oil and 600,000 litres (132,000 gals) of aviation fuel. The fuel tanks were integrated into the ship's framework. Protection was a major issue as *Taihō* was intended for maximum endurance in the face of attack.

Specification

Dimensions:	Length: 260.6m (855ft); Beam: 27.4m (89ft 11in); Draught: 9.6m (31ft 6in)
Displacement:	29,769 tonnes (29,300 tons); 33,243 tonnes (32,720 tons) full load
Propulsion:	8 Kampon boilers, 4 Kampon geared turbines, 4 shafts; 120,000kW (160,000shp)
Speed:	33.3 knots (61.7km/h; 38.3mph)
Range:	10,000nm (19,000km; 12,000 miles) at 18 knots (33.3km/h; 20.7mph)
Armament:	6 twin 100mm (3.9in) 65-cal Type 98 guns; 17 triple 25mm (1in) AA cannon
Aircraft:	84
Complement:	1751

The main armoured belt, 55mm (2.2in), covered the central section for about half the ship's length, from below the waterline to the level of the lower hangar deck. The air-strip section of the flight deck was protected by 76mm (3in) armour over 19mm (7.5in) steel plate, capable of resisting 500kg (1100lb) bombs, and the lower hangar deck had 32mm (1.2in) armour over 16mm (0.6in) steel plate. As with American, but unlike British carriers, side protection at the level of the hangar decks was not applied. The elevator sides carried 50mm (2in) armour. Heavy protection, from 70mm (2.75in) up to 165mm (6.5in) was applied to the magazines, fuel tanks and steering gear that worked the twin rudders. To help absorb bomb shocks the main deck beams were box-shaped, 70cm (27in) high, with a thin strip of splinter-resistant DCS plate on their bases. The funnel uptakes were lined with 25mm (1in) armour. A 76mm (3in) bulkhead ran the length of the ship, creating a series of watertight compartments on each side. Total armour weight was around 7257 tonnes (8000 tons). For anti-torpedo protection, the lower hull was doubled with the inner spaces filled with water to help absorb and distribute the shock of a hit. Armament consisted of six twin 100mm (3.9in) and 17 triple-barrelled 25mm AA guns.

Taihō carried 75 planes: 27 A6M5a fighters, 27 D4Y1 dive-bombers, 18 B6N2 torpedo bombers and three D4Y1-C reconnaissance planes. Though fewer than the American *Essex*-class, this still gave substantial strike power. It could also have flown the heavier warplanes planned by Japan, such as the B7A 'Grace' attack plane, but these were not available when *Taihō* went into action. It was also expected to function as a refuge ship for planes

from other carriers in the event of their being sunk or badly damaged, and carried fuel supplies in excess of its own air wing's needs. Although the original plan provided for two bow-mounted catapults, *Taihō*, like other Japanese carriers, was not catapult-fitted and planes had to use their own power in unaided take-offs.

Torpedo hit

Crew training on *Taihō* was brief because of the desperate need to bring the ship into combat. As flagship

Aviation advantages

Although Japanese aircraft carriers never employed catapult launchers, and therefore had to rely on their own speed or turning into the wind to launch their aircraft, they were also helped by the fact that the planes themselves were more lightweight than their American and British opponents. This also gave the Japanese planes a somewhat greater range, and thus a tactical advantage, especially in reconnaissance and long-range strikes. On the negative side, it meant a lesser degree of protection to the aircrew and greater liability in the airframe to break up under attack.

Battle of the Philippine Sea, 19 June 1944: a shot-up Japanese plane crashes into the sea close to a Japanese light carrier. *Taihō* was Admiral Ozawa's flagship in the battle.

of the First Fleet it joined in the Battle of the Marianas on 19 June 1944. It had launched its first offensive strike and was bringing up planes for the second wave when at 08.10 a single torpedo of six fired from the US submarine *Albacore* struck the hull, hitting the outer plate of an aviation fuel tank and causing a vapour leak that gradually spread up to the lower hangar. The front lift, directly above the fuel tank, was jammed with the hatch open, preventing further take-offs or landings until a makeshift cover was improvised.

The ship continued to steam at full speed and might have survived, but for the disastrous attempts at fire control. *Taihō*'s destruction was not inevitable if effective damage control procedures had been followed. But with a relatively inexperienced crew, still unfamiliar with the ship, this was hardly possible. Orders given by the chief damage control officer to maximize ventilation and reduce the vapour levels simply allowed the vapour to spread rapidly through the hull. At 14.40 the mixture of heavy fuel vapour and air ignited and virtually blew the huge vessel apart. An hour later the ship capsized, with a death toll of around 1650 of the crew.

Shinano (1944)

Shinano was to have been a _Yamato_-class battleship but changing needs brought conversion to the largest carrier yet built. However, it was sunk even before it went into operational service.

Planned in 1939 as the third battleship of the huge *Yamato*-class, *Shinano* bore the name of an old Japanese prefecture. Its keel was laid at the Yokosuka Naval Arsenal on 4 May 1940, and the hull was largely completed when the decision was taken in mid-1942 to convert the ship

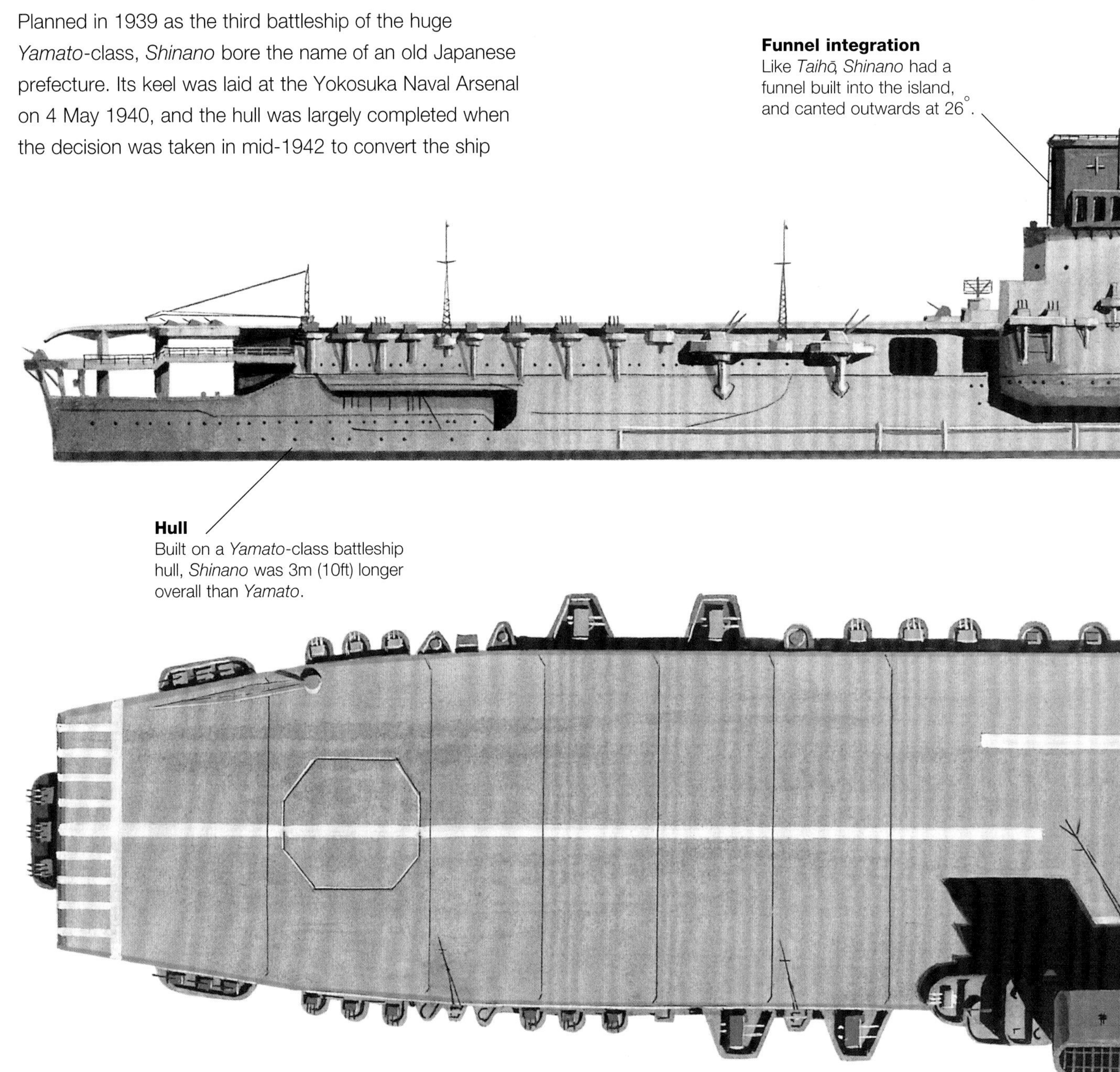

to a carrier following the loss of four carriers at Midway. It was launched on 8 October 1944 and commissioned on 19 November. At that time it was the world's largest aircraft carrier, capable of carrying up to 139 planes. It was conceived as a support and replenishment ship for other carriers, rather than a fleet carrier – at the time of its conversion, plans for *Unryū*-class fleet carriers were also in hand – with repair shops, fuel and equipment stores and other facilities to make it a mobile naval base able to service a fleet at sea. Construction and conversion were accomplished in such secrecy that the US Navy was unaware of the ship's existence.

Shinano retained the battleship bow with the forward flight deck built up on heavy struts above it. The island was placed slightly forward of midships and sponsoned well out to give the maximum flight deck and plane parking area. The funnel was integrated with the island. The flight deck itself was 256m (839ft 11in) long and 40m (131ft 3in) wide and was partly armoured. Like other Japanese carriers, multiple arrester wires were fitted, ten towards the stern and five towards the bow, to allow for forward landings.

The huge *Shinano* was seen as a floating naval base, not unlike the present-day strategic concept of the aircraft carrier.

Armour vulnerability
While the armoured flight deck could resist the impact of 454kg (1000lb) bombs, four Mk 14 torpedoes each with 292kg (643lb) warheads did sufficient damage to the hull, hitting the weak join between the anti-torpedo bulge and the side armour, to ensure the ship's destruction.

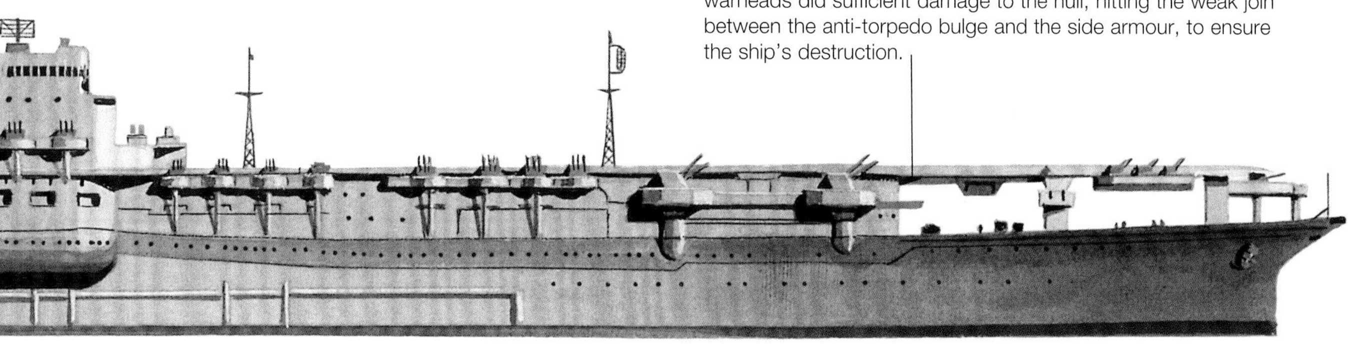

Deck area
The island was almost wholly sponsoned out to provide 10,309m² (115,552sq ft) of flight deck space.

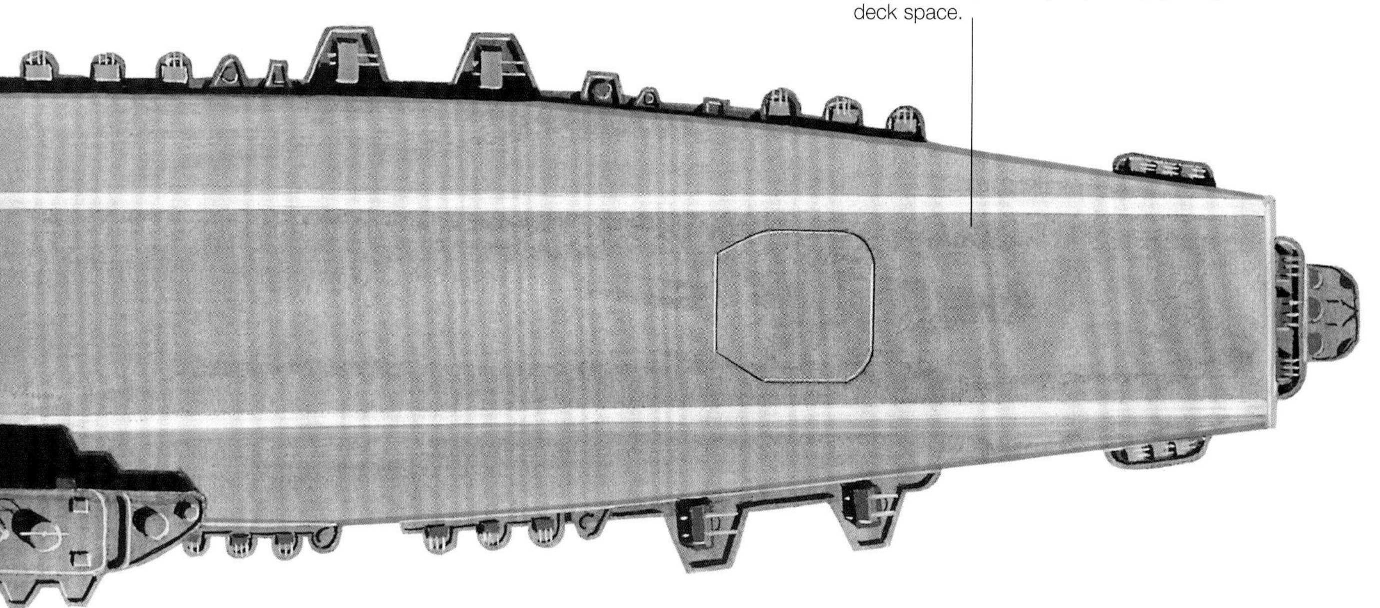

In addition, three dismountable crash barriers were fitted. There were two centreline aircraft lifts. The hangar area, 163.4m by 33.8m (536ft by 111ft) had unarmoured sides and much of it was open-sided – the enclosed hangar sides of earlier carriers had contributed to their destruction – although with a series of fire curtains to close off sections, and ventilation fans to prevent accumulation of explosive fumes. Aircraft repair and maintenance was done at the forward end.

The *Yamato*-class had 400mm (15.7in) belt armour, reduced on *Shinano* to 205mm (8in), and lateral anti-torpedo bulges were fitted, backed up internally by armoured and watertight bulkheads, making a double hull below the waterline and a triple bottom. The main armoured deck was the former battleship main deck, with a maximum of 190mm (7.5in) protection above the engine rooms and magazines. The flight deck, as with *Taihō*, was armoured between the lifts with 75mm (3in) plate, intended to resist penetration by a 500kg (1100lb) bomb. The avgas tanks of plane fuel, capable of holding 720,000 litres (160,000 gals) were isolated within a cofferdam structure, with the void space around filled with 2400 tonnes (2362 tons) of concrete as a precaution against the release of fumes. Power was provided by 12 Kampon boilers, four geared turbines and four shafts. The engines were designed for the *Yamato*-class battleships, and the maximum speed of 27 knots (50km/h; 31mph) was well below the 32 knots (59km/h; 36.8mph) of the *Unryū* (1944) and 33 knots (61.1km/h; 37.9mph) of the American *Essex* carriers.

AA protection came from eight twin 127mm (5in) Type 89 guns, 35 triple 25mm Type 96 guns, and twelve 28-barrel 127mm rocket launchers. Four Type 94 high-angle directors were mounted for the Type 89 guns, two on each side. It would seem that *Shinano* also had Type 22 surface search radar and possibly also Type 13 air search. *Shinano*'s own air wing, never embarked, was to be 47 planes, intended to provide combat air cover in the event of aerial attack, and consisting of 18 Mitsubishi A7M Reppu fighters, 18 Aichi Ryusei bombers and six Nakajima C6N Saiun reconnaissance planes. Five planes were held in storage.

Specification

Dimensions:	Length: 265.8m (872ft 1in); Beam: 36.3m (119ft 1in); Draught: 10.3m (33ft 10in)
Displacement:	65,800 tonnes (64,800 tons); 73,000 tonnes (72,000 tons) full load
Propulsion:	12 Kampon boilers, 4 geared turbines, 4 shafts; 110,000kW (150,000shp)
Speed:	27 knots (50km/h; 31mph)
Range:	10,000nm (19,000km; 12,000 miles)
Armament:	8 twin 127mm (5in) Type 89 guns, 35 triple 25mm Type 96 guns, and 12 28-barrel 127mm rocket launchers
Aircraft:	139
Complement:	2400

Submarine chase

On 1 November an American B-29 Superfortress reconnaissance plane passed above Yokosuka, and fearing that bombing raids on *Shinano* would result, naval command resolved to move the carrier to Kure as early as possible. After hasty sea trials, and with fitting-out uncomplete, it left on 28 November at 18.00 with 300 shipyard workers still on board, and escorted by the destroyers *Isokaze*, *Yukikaze* and *Hamakaze*. At the Kure base, 480km (300 miles) distant, it would complete fitting-out and also embark its air wing. In the hangar were 50 Ohka kamikaze rocket planes and six equally suicidal Shinyo explosive-fitted one-man attack boats, intended for onwards transport to the Philippines battle zone.

By 20.40 the US submarine *Archerfish* picked it up on radar. *Shinano* had already detected the submarine, which was on the surface, but Captain Toshio Abe was confident that the carrier could outrun it. *Archerfish* followed it, a task made easier by *Shinano*'s zigzag course. Although aware of the submarine's proximity, the carrier and escorts forged on, suspecting that others might be closing in. In fact *Archerfish* was alone, and had a further stroke of luck when an overheated bearing in a propeller shaft forced the carrier to drop speed to 18 knots (33.3km/h; 20.7mph). *Archerfish* submerged and prepared to attack as one of *Shinano*'s course changes presented the carrier's whole starboard side. At 03.15 on 29 November six torpedoes were launched, running 10m (30ft) below the surface, and four struck *Shinano*.

Shinano was built on the same hull type as its 'twin', the super-battleship *Yamato*, seen here on sea trials on 20 October 1941. *Yamato* was sunk on 7 April 1945.

Kamikaze cargo

Shinano was transporting 30 Ohka MXY-7 rocket-powered attack aircraft when it was sunk. These were kamikaze craft, essentially human-guided flying bombs, with a 1200kg (2650lb) high-explosive bomb forming the nose of the craft. Normally transported beneath Mitsubishi G4M2e 'Betty' bombers, they would be released and glide towards the target vessel. The pilot would then fire the solid-fuel rocket motors, attaining a diving speed of up to 1000km/h (600mph) on the final approach, and crash-dive his plane on to the target. These planes could not have been launched from any carrier as none had a catapult, and they could not take off or fly any distance under their own power. They would have been offloaded at an island base for launch from bombers.

The carrier immediately began taking in water, but was able to continue at full speed. Captain Abe's aim was to remove it from the risk of further strikes, but the tactic also meant that more water was forced into the hull. The exact extent of failure of the watertight doors and pipework gaskets has been argued over, but it would seem that they were not fully sealed, and the pumping system was certainly not ready for service, meaning that only portable pumps could be used. Counter flooding of the port side was tried, to maintain the ship's trim, but with a steep list already developed to starboard, this failed. Finally at 08.50 on 29 November Abe ordered *Hamakaze* and *Isokaze* to take the carrier under tow, in the hope of beaching it, but the cables snapped under the strain of pulling a 71,120-tonne (70,000-ton) ship already half-awash, and the order to abandon ship was given at 10.18. At 10.57 *Shinano* capsized, taking 1435 men with it, including the captain.

The magnitude of the loss was such that it was not publicly reported, and survivors were held in quarantine. Commander Enright of *Archerfish* did not know of *Shinano*'s existence and believed he had sunk a carrier of the *Shokaku*-class. The US Navy Department was even more incredulous at first, crediting Enright with the sinking of a cruiser, until information on *Shinano* came to light after the war.

USS Midway (1945)

A wartime design but not commissioned until after the conflict had ended, *Midway* was the first of a new generation of USN carriers, and underwent major changes through a working life of almost half a century.

Laid down at Newport News Shipbuilding Co., Virginia, on 27 October 1943, launched on 20 March 1945, *Midway* (CVB-41) was commissioned on 10 September 1945, a month after Japan's surrender, at a construction cost of $86.5 million. Battle conditions of the Pacific War determined the ship's characteristics: more heavily armoured than any of its predecessors, with heavy AA armament, it was the first US carrier class to have an armoured flight deck of 89mm (3.5in). At the same time, it had to have a large air wing, and the ability to make high speed – at least 32 knots (59.2km/h; 36.8mph). A second armoured deck 51mm (2in) thick was installed at the hangar level. Belt armour 4.8m (16ft) high of 193mm (7.6in) thickness was fitted as well as enhanced torpedo protection.

To achieve all these requirements, a much bigger vessel than the *Essex*-class was needed. The hull plan was based on that of the *Montana*-class battleships, planned but never built, providing capacity for 137 aircraft. Two sister ships followed, USS *Coral Sea* (CVB-43) and *Franklin D. Roosevelt*

***Midway*'s bow was built up to flight deck level from the beginning, but it retained the low stern at main-deck level.**

Size
Midway was the largest warship in the world until 1955. An overall width of 31.45m (136ft) prevented it from using the Panama Canal. Atlantic–Pacific transits had to be made via Cape Horn.

Flight deck
Midway class's armoured flight deck was not part of the hull structure, as in British Navy carriers, but part of the ship's superstructure, mounted above the hull. Subsequent US classes followed the British format.

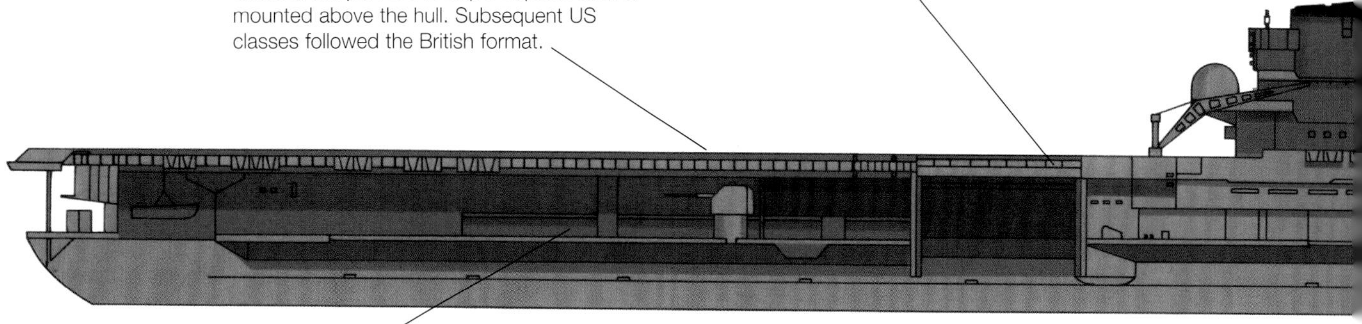

Fuel capacity
Ship and aviation fuel storage capacity was 13.26 million litres (3.5 million gals).

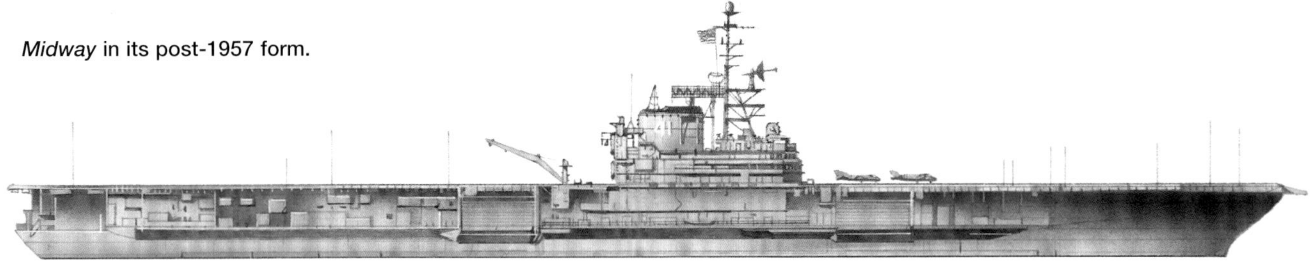
Midway in its post-1957 form.

(CVB-42). These vessels confirmed the status of the fleet carrier as the new capital ship, supplanting the battleship, and would act as flagships and control centres for new task groups in strategic and tactical operations. The engines were among the most powerful yet installed on a ship, with 12 Babcock & Wilcox boilers feeding four Westinghouse geared turbines, consuming fuel at the rate of some 985 litres (260 gals) to the mile. *Midway* was capable of keeping up 33 knots (61.1km/h; 37.9mph) for 140 hours on end, covering over 4600 nautical miles (8520km; 5293 miles) in that time. Eight turbine-powered generators each supplied 1000kW (1341hp) for the electrical systems.

Originally it was planned to fit 203mm (8in) guns, but the need to save weight for the armoured deck and the realization that anti-ship guns on carriers were an outdated concept led to the dropping of this arrangement. All guns were mounted below the flight deck, but as they were mounted on barbettes, and the flight deck was 15m (50ft) above the surface, they commanded a good angle of fire, controlled first from Mk37 directors mounted on cylindrical columns fore and aft of the island.

The primary armament was 18 127mm (5in) guns designed for the *Montana* class and first installed on the Midways, along with 28 Oerlikon 20mm and 84 quad Bofors 40mm. Within two years the Oerlikons were taken out and the Bofors replaced by twin 75mm (3in) AA guns. Three aircraft elevators and two hydraulic catapults were fitted. The air group varied greatly over *Midway*'s five

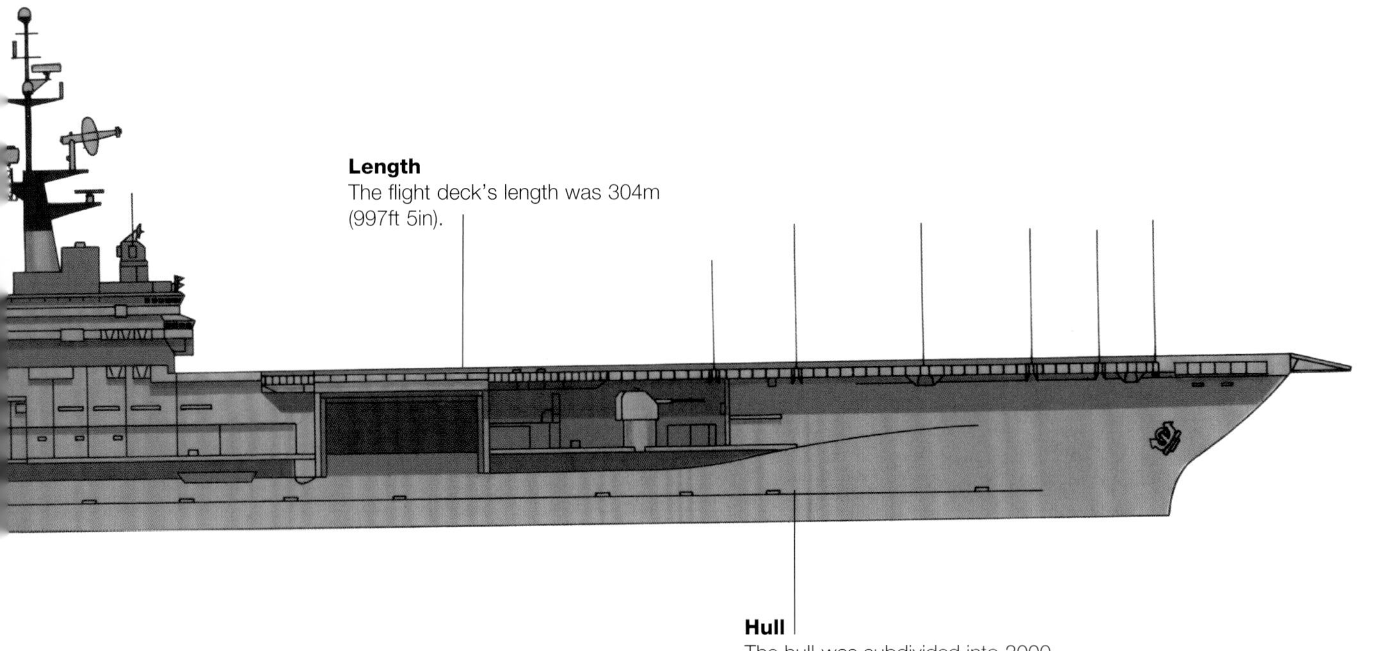

Length
The flight deck's length was 304m (997ft 5in).

Hull
The hull was subdivided into 2000 compartments, with 18 deck levels.

Midway among scattered ice floes in Operation Frostbite, an Arctic cruise in March 1946. On deck are SB2C Helldivers and F4U-4 Corsairs.

decades. As many as 145 single-engined piston-engined planes could be packed in, although as the Navy acquired heavier, larger jets, the number fell to around 85.

Midway was assigned to the Atlantic Fleet and in 1946 was the first US carrier to operate in sub-Arctic winter conditions including sea ice. It participated in early trials of rocket missiles, firing captured German V2s during Operation Sandy in September 1947 and test-firing the Regulus ballistic missile in 1948. In 1949 it was used to show that a carrier could launch the North American AJ Savage bomber, capable of carrying nuclear bombs. From 26 to 29 May 1952, the feasibility of the angled deck concept was demonstrated in tests conducted on a simulated angled deck aboard *Midway* by Naval Air Test Center pilots and Atlantic Fleet pilots in both jet and prop aircraft. Its designation was altered on 1 October 1952 from CVB to CVA, for 'attack' carrier. Up to 1955 the ship made seven cruises in the Atlantic and the Mediterranean as part of NATO exercises.

Specification (1945)

Dimensions:	Length: 295m (968ft); Beam: 34.4m (113ft); Draught: 10.7m (35ft)
Displacement:	45,720 tonnes (45,000 tons); 60,960 tonnes (60,000 tons) full load
Propulsion:	12 boilers, 4 turbines, 4 shafts; 158,000kW (212,000shp)
Speed:	33 knots (61km/h; 38mph)
Range:	12,000nm (22,200km; 13,800 mile)
Armament:	18 127mm (5in) 54-cal Mk 16 guns, 84 Bofors 40mm guns, 68 Oerlikon 20mm AA cannon
Aircraft:	145
Complement:	3443

NATO duty

From December 1954 to January 1955 it undertook a round-the-world cruise, and from the end of June 1955 underwent major alteration at Puget Sound until

October 1957. Under the SBC-110 programme the ship's appearance was greatly altered. An angled flight deck was fitted and the bow was remodelled with plating up to flight-deck height. The aft elevator was taken out and replaced by a deck edge elevator on the starboard side. Steam catapults replaced the hydraulic types. To compensate for the increased weight of these alterations, the belt armour was partially stripped.

From November 1957 onwards *Midway* served in the Pacific and Indian Oceans. In 1965 it was deployed on active combat duties in the Vietnam war zone, flying air strikes into North Vietnam, shooting down three MiG jets but also losing 11 of its own planes. A second, far-reaching upgrade, SCB 101.66, was made at Hunter's Point, California, between April 1966 and 31 January 1970. By this time the *Forrestal*-class carriers were in commission, and *Midway*'s deck space was further increased to maintain capacity with the newcomers.

In 1971 it returned to Vietnam. In October 1973 *Midway* was deployed to station at Yokosuka naval base in Japan, which was a controversial step, not least because of its nuclear armament. During its 17 years at Yokosuka it made several returns to the seas off Vietnam. With the fall of Saigon bringing the Vietnam War to an end, *Midway* acted as a base for USAF helicopters flying off US personnel and South Vietnamese refugees in Operation Frequent Wind, taking around 3000 people on board on 30 April 1975.

Work in progress

Midway has been described as the most-altered of any aircraft carrier to cope with the increasing requirements of heavy jet planes. Deck reinforcement, new steam catapults, new arresting gear, jet blast deflectors and strengthened elevators all were needed. The two major refits transformed the ship's appearance, first with the angled flight deck and then with deck enlargement. Most of its guns were gone by 1963, and by 1990 it was armed with two eight-cell Sea Sparrow missile launchers and two Phalanx CIWS. Final loaded displacement was around 71,120 tonnes (70,000 tons).

Midway in 1963, with angled flight deck and a new generation of naval jets.

Most of the 1980s were spent with the Pacific Fleet. The ship had always had a tendency to roll when seas rose, and in 1986 a refit at Yokosuka removed what remained of the armoured belt round the steering gear, and 92 hollow steel blisters were fitted around the hull to increase freeboard. This reduced the rolling but speeded up the ship's lateral movements, making landings difficult or impossible in heavy seas. On 20 June 1990 while *Midway* was off the Japanese coast, explosions and fire in a store-room for emergency equipment killed three members of the 'Flying Squad' damage control team. This did not prevent the carrier's last operational voyage in November that year, as flagship of naval operations in Operation Desert Storm following the Iraqi invasion of Kuwait, during which it launched over 3000 combat missions from the North Arabian Sea. Having returned to the Pacific, *Midway* also mounted rescue operations for civilians and US military personnel at Clark Air Force Base after the eruption of Mt Pinatubo in the Philippines in June 1991.

Midway was decommissioned on 11 April 1992, and finally stricken from the Naval Register on 17 March 1997. It is now a museum ship at San Diego, California.

YP
5307
07
The

Carriers Since 1945

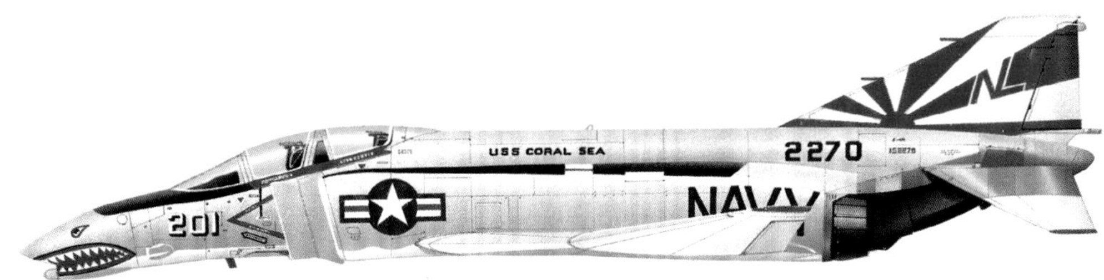

The aircraft carrier continued to have a strategic role after World War II, and with the demise of the battleship and battlecruiser it became the principal capital ship type. The development of the jet aircraft extended its striking range and military capacity. The ships got bigger and bigger and from 1961 some were nuclear-powered. Helicopters became part of the air wing, and in the 1960s the development of vertical take-off and landing (VTOL) jets gave an impetus to the design of smaller carriers, more versatile in function and able to mount amphibious operations. Carriers could now be typified as CATOBAR – catapult-assisted take-off but arrested recovery; STOVL – short take-off and vertical landing; or STOBAR – short take-off but arrested recovery.

Sailors and Marines man the rails as they leave port for a Western Pacific deployment aboard the amphibious assault ship USS *Tarawa* (LHA 1), July 2005.

HMS Eagle (1951)

The Royal Navy's largest carrier yet, *Eagle* played a major role in British and NATO naval operations until the decision to drop fleet carriers was taken.

HMS *Eagle* had a long gestation. Laid down at Harland & Wolff's yard in Belfast on 24 October 1942, it was not launched until 19 March 1946, almost a year after VE Day, and not commissioned until 5 October 1951. Its original name was *Audacious*, intended to be the first of four large carriers, but when two were cancelled after the end of World War II, it was given the name intended for the third in the class. The other one to be completed was *Ark Royal.* Numerous details were updated during the long fitting-out period, but it was completed too soon for an angled flight deck to be installed, and it remained a somewhat old-style ship until its refits in the mid- and late 1950s.

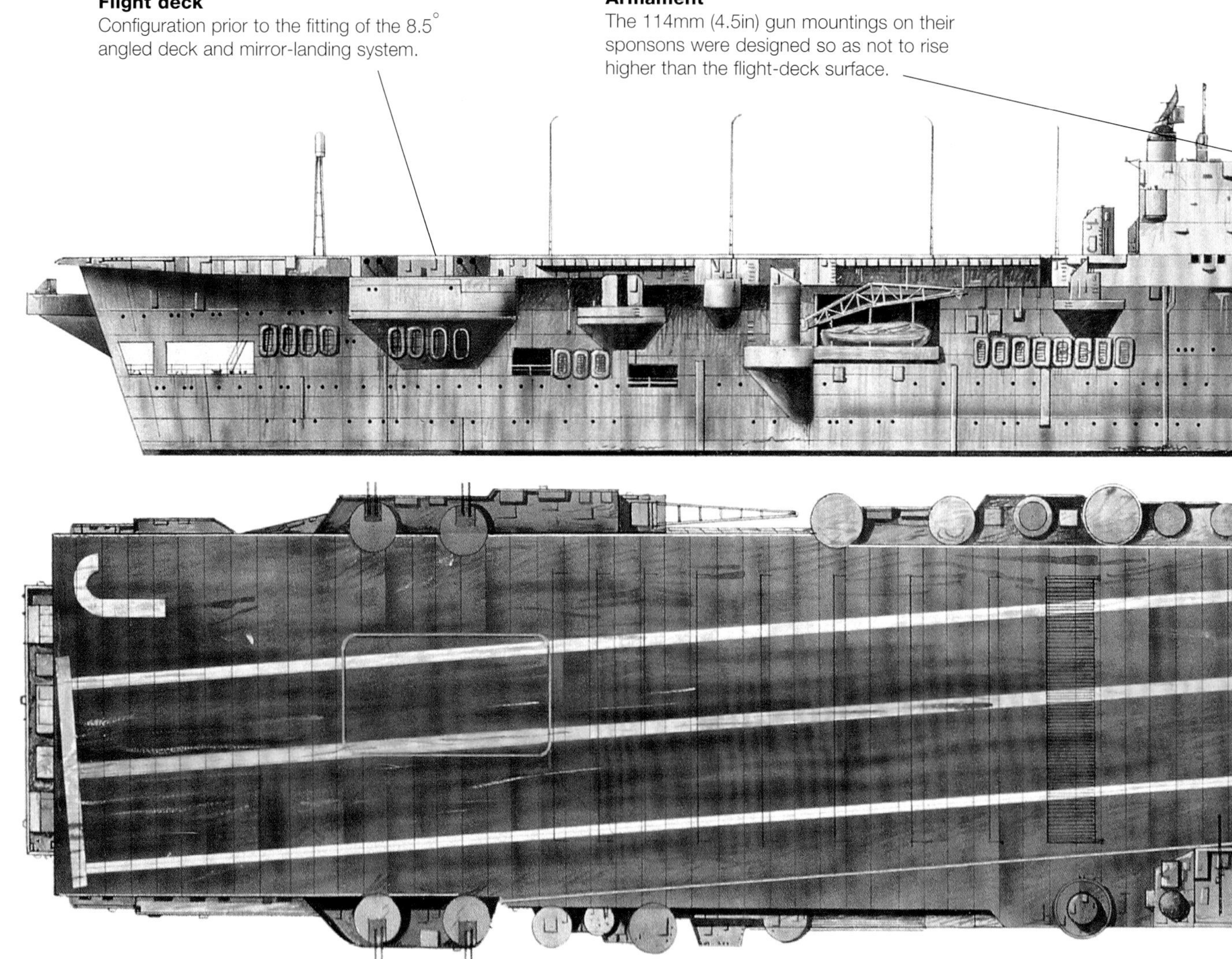

In the established Royal Navy design the hangar was an all-round armoured box structure, beneath a flight deck 25–100mm (1–4in) thick, and with 25mm (1in) sides and deck. Along the waterline 100mm (4in) armour was fitted. As constructed, the ship had 16 114mm (4.5in) guns in twin mountings, and 61 40mm (1.57in) guns, eight in six-barrel mountings, two twin barrels and nine single. *Eagle* was powered by eight Admiralty three-drum boilers and four geared steam turbines with four shafts. Aircraft capacity (pre-1964) was 60, with two hydraulic catapults mounted at the bow.

Eagle joined the Home Fleet in October 1951. In March 1953 it embarked the first operational Sea Hawk squadron, No.806. These planes would form the Fleet Air Arm's main attack force until the 1960s. By this time naval jets were heavier and faster and *Eagle* clearly needed extensive modernization in order to support them. Its sister ship *Ark Royal*, commissioned in 1955, had been fitted with an angled flight deck before its launch, and in 1954–55 *Eagle* was also

***Eagle*'s hurricane bow and long, blank-sided island gave it a massive appearance.**

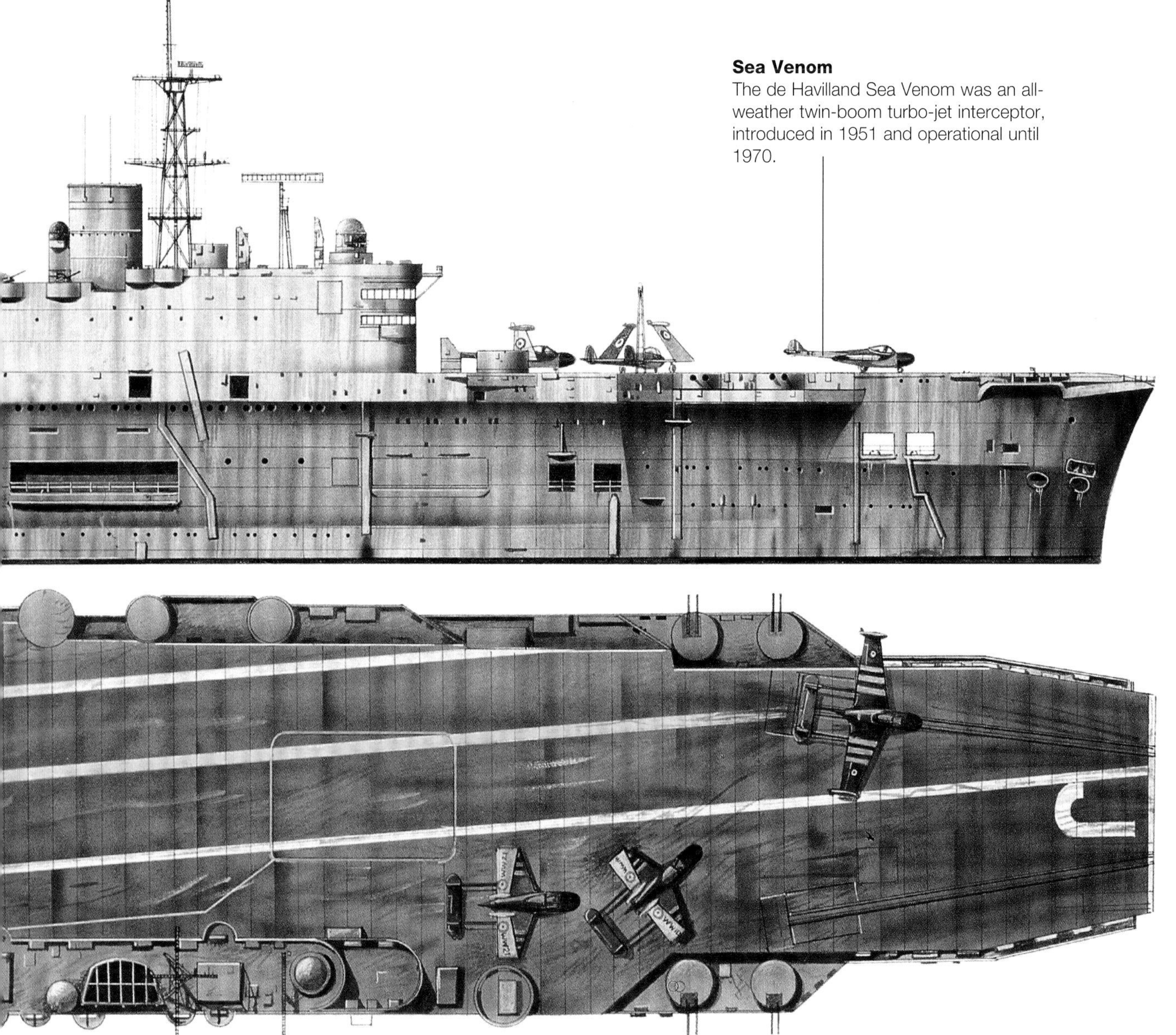

Sea Venom
The de Havilland Sea Venom was an all-weather twin-boom turbo-jet interceptor, introduced in 1951 and operational until 1970.

HMS *Eagle* with crew manning the railings to mark a ceremonial visit to Wellington, New Zealand, in August 1971.

fitted with what was described at the time as a provisional angled deck, at 5.5° from the centreline, with the new mirror landing sight (see box).

In the summer of 1956 the Egyptian government declared nationalization of the Suez Canal and on 5 November the British and French, in collusion with Israel, invaded and occupied the Canal Zone. *Eagle* was the only operational RN carrier in the Mediterranean, carrying 17 Sea Venom FAW-21, 24 Sea Hawk FGA-6, nine Westland Wyvern S-4 and four Douglas Skyraider AEW-1 planes, and two Westland Whirlwind HAR-3 helicopters. The presence of US navy planes (not involved in the military operations) from USS *Coral Sea* and *Randolph* was a complicating issue but the carrier aircraft established air supremacy over Egypt, and in what was otherwise a fruitless campaign confirmed the value of offshore carriers in supporting invasion forces.

From 1959 to 1964 *Eagle* was given an extensive modernization at Devonport Naval Dockyard, although a scheme to extend the hull and install more powerful engines was not pursued. The island was rebuilt, the angle of the flight deck was extended to 8.5° and the deck itself strengthened with 63mm (2.5in) armour. New 3D Type 984 radar was fitted. The hydraulic catapults were replaced by more powerful BS5 steam catapults, and new arrester gear was also fitted. Air conditioning was installed in crew areas, and the electrical system was overhauled with AC generation to supplement the DC circuits: by no means an ideal solution, but the Admiralty was required to hold down the cost of the refit, which ultimately came to £31 million.

Eight of the 114mm (4.5in) guns, mounted forwards, were removed and six Seacat SAM missile launchers installed.

Specification (Original)

Dimensions:	Length: 247.4m (811ft 10in); Beam: 34.4m (112ft 9in); Draught: 10.13m (33ft 3in)
Displacement:	37,400 tonnes (36,800 tons); 47,000 tonnes (46,000 tons) full load
Propulsion:	8 boilers, 4 geared turbines, 4 shafts; 113,000kW (152,000shp)
Speed:	31 knots (57km/h; 36mph)
Range:	7000nm (13,000km; 8050 miles) at 18 knots (33.3km/h; 20.7mph)
Armament:	16 114mm (4.5in) guns, 61 40mm AA guns
Aircraft:	60
Complement:	2500

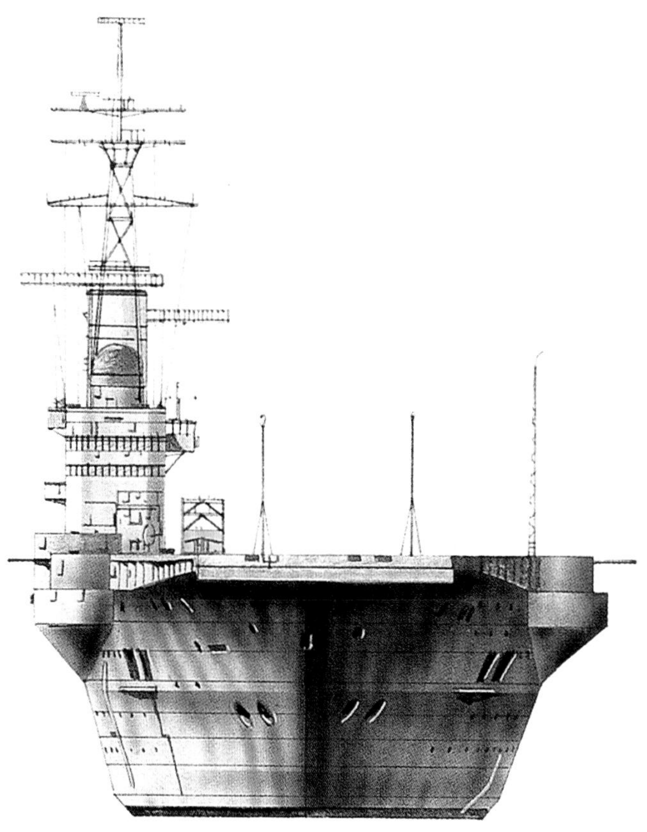

HMS *Eagle* before acquiring an angled flight deck.

These alterations increased the standard displacement by around 7112 tonnes (7000 tons) and presumably impacted on the ship's speed. In 1966–67 further work was done on *Eagle,* including the fitting of an improved DAX II arrester wire as the third and most often used of the catchers.

End of Career

Eagle's history from the mid-1960s mirrors the decline of the Royal Navy's carrier force. The ship was not able to handle US-built Phantom FG1 aircraft, as its jet-blast deflector plates were not sufficiently heat-resistant, and the British government decided that two fleet carriers were more than the country could afford. In late 1970-early 1971 it suffered propeller damage while entering Plymouth Sound. *Eagle* was decommissioned in January 1972. Its last aircraft were 14 S.2 Buccaneers of 800 Squadron, 16 FAW.2 Sea Vixens of 899 Squadron (the RN's last Sea Vixen squadron), four Gannet AEW.3 and one Gannet COD.4 of 849 Squadron, plus five HAS.1 Sea King helicopters of 826 Squadron. Officially placed on reserve, in fact all its reusable equipment had been removed to provide spare and replacement parts for the still-functional *Ark Royal*. Sold for scrapping, it was towed from Devonport to Cairnryan, Scotland, in October 1978. *Ark Royal* followed only two years later.

Tracking Foxtrots

The Royal Navy's Fleet Air Arm was responsible for the three most significant improvements to carrier operation in the age of the jet plane. The concept of the separate angled flight deck was first embodied in *Eagle* and *Ark Royal*, enabling the number of arrester wires to be reduced, parking area barriers to be removed, parking space to be increased and touch-and-go landings safely achieved. The protruding edge of the angled deck made the carrier an irregular-shaped floating platform, requiring very careful manoeuvring especially in canals and dock areas. These ships also introduced the steam catapult, working at a pressure of 24.6kg/cm2 (350psi), and the sighting mirror – a gyro-stabilized mirror in which the approaching pilot sees a battery of lights reflected, showing any deflection from the correct glidepath for landing. The mirror was mounted on a large rigid sponson protruding 3.4m (12ft) from the deck edge.

Eagle at speed, in the late 1960s. On the flight deck are Supermarine Scimitars and Fairey Gannets.

USS Forrestal (1955)

***Forrestal* introduced the concept of the super-carrier and was the lead ship of its class, the last US carriers to be conventionally powered.**

Named for James V. Forrestal, Secretary of the Navy and then Secretary of Defence, who died in 1949, the keel of the ship was laid at Newport News on 14 July 1952, it was launched on 11 December 1954 and commissioned as CVA-59 on 1 October 1955. Its cost was $217 million. *Forrestal* superseded the sunken *Shinano* as the largest carrier yet built in terms of full load displacement. The first carrier specifically planned to fly jet aircraft, including the P2V Neptune patrol bomber that required a bigger carrier than the *Midway*-class to make a landing, it was leader of a class of four that comprised USS *Saratoga* (CVA-60), USS *Ranger* (CVA-61) and USS *Independence* (CVA-62). Tests of a 10m (32ft) scale model had been carried out at the David Taylor Model Basin, Washington DC, to refine the hull design and establish the balancing forces necessary to keep the 68,900-tonne (70,000-ton) ship on an even keel.

In the first plans, the ship was to have a retractable bridge, enabling complete flat-top operations, but the

Forrestal in 1955. The first carrier specifically designed to embark and service jet aircraft, it accomplished 21 successful operational deployments.

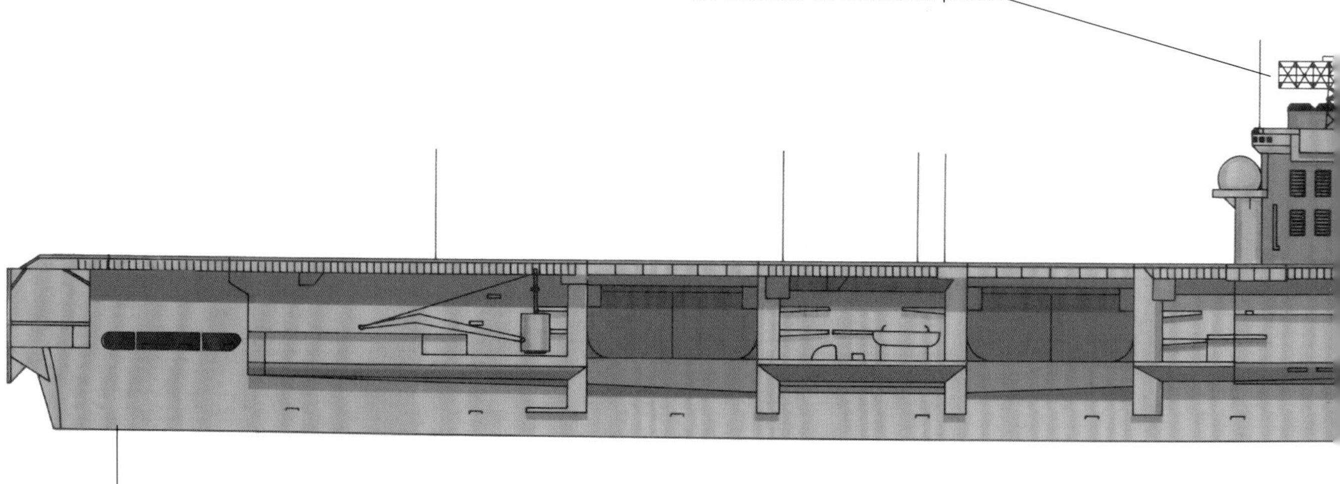

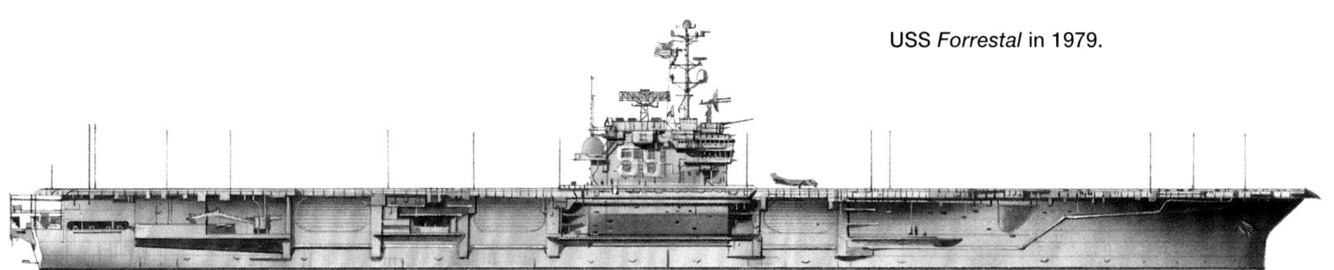

USS *Forrestal* in 1979.

flush deck idea was abandoned and a substantial island was installed with comman and navigation bridges, flight control points and working space for the very extensive range of sensory and communications equipment carried. These rooms particularly required air conditioning, but all accommodation on board was air-conditioned. The flight deck was armoured and, unlike USS *Midway*, it was part of the hull structure, as would be the case on all subsequent USN carriers.

Forrestal was the first American carrier to be launched with an angled flight deck and an optical landing system, the alteration being made while the ship was under construction. The flight deck was reached by four aircraft lifts, three on the starboard deck edge and one on the port edge, making the ship the first carrier with no central elevator. Four catapults, two forward and two amidships on the port side, and four arrester cables were fitted. The hangar deck had no armour. It typically carried 75

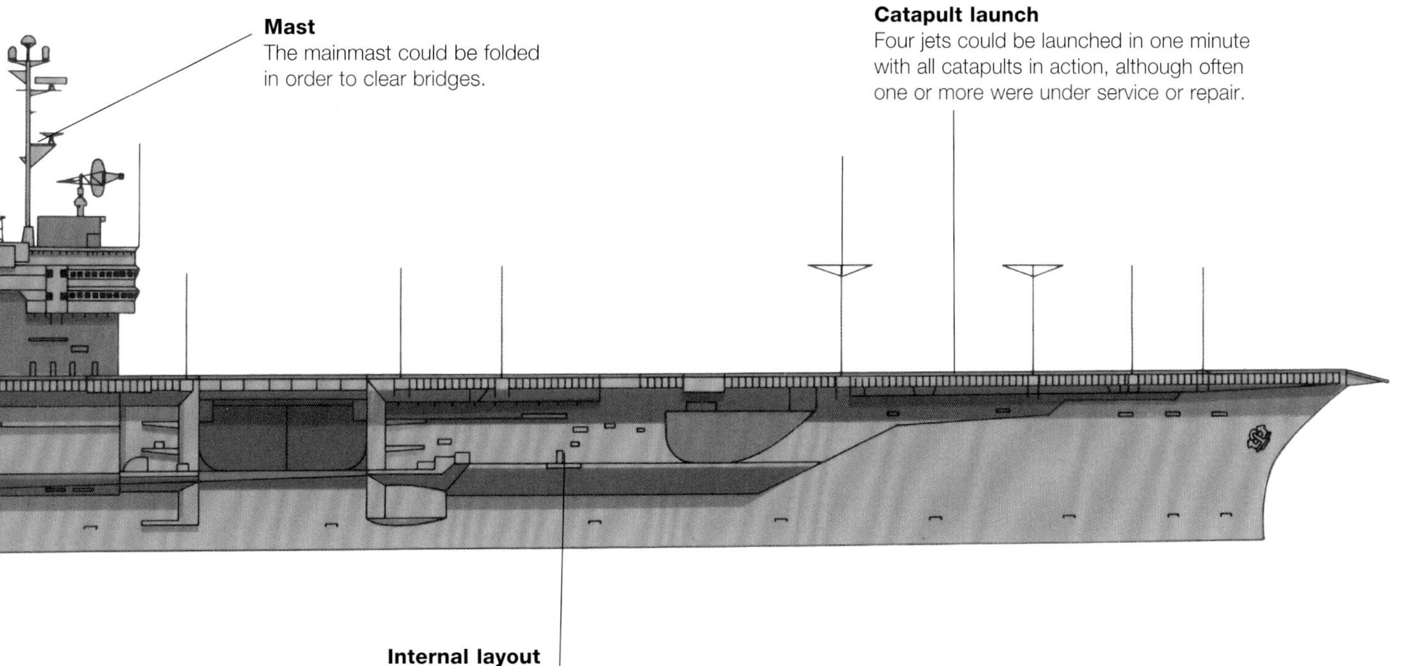

Mast
The mainmast could be folded in order to clear bridges.

Catapult launch
Four jets could be launched in one minute with all catapults in action, although often one or more were under service or repair.

Internal layout
The five-compartment arrangement of the *Permit*-class hull was retained in the design of *Sturgeon*: bow compartment with diesel generator, operations compartment with torpedo room beneath, reactor compartment, auxiliary machinery room no. 2 and engine room.

aircraft although the maximum was 85, and its size and strength enabled it to carry heavy bombers such as the piston-engined P2V-3C Neptune and the AJ-1 Savage turbo-jet. The ship was originally armed with eight 127mm (5in) 54-calibre Mk 2 guns. These were later removed and replaced with three Mk 29 Sea Sparrow missile launchers

Specification

Dimensions:	Length: 326.14m (1070ft); Beam: 39.6m (130ft); Draught: 11.3m (37ft)
Displacement:	60,610 tonnes (59,650 tons); 82,402 tonnes (81,101 tons) full load
Propulsion:	8 B&W boilers, 4 Westinghouse geared turbines, 4 shafts; 190,000kW (280,000shp)
Speed:	33 knots (61km/h; 38mph)
Range:	7995nm (14,806km; 9200 miles)
Armament (original):	8 127mm (5in) 54-cal Mk 42 guns
Aircraft:	85
Complement:	5540

***Forrestal* cruising off the Philippines, August 1967, as American involvement in Vietnam increased.**

and three 20mm Mk 15 Phalanx CIWS. *Forrestal*'s home port was Norfolk, Virginia, and as an intended class leader it was used at first for crew training, essential on a carrier much larger and more fully equipped than any predecessor. In late 1956 *Forrestal* was in the Mediterranean Sea, on alert during the Suez crisis, and until 1966 served either with the Second Fleet in the Atlantic or the Seventh Fleet in the Mediterranean. In the Atlantic it was flagship of Rear Admiral William Ellis's Carrier Division 2, as part of the Project Mercury Recovery Force in February 1962, waiting to pick up astronaut John Glenn, the first American to orbit the Earth.

Combat missions

In June 1967 the ship was deployed to Vietnam, but had only been engaged in combat missions for four and a half days when on 29 July it suffered the worst accident on a US surface ship since World War II. A Zuni rocket, accidentally fired from a F-4 Phantom, struck an armed and loaded A-4 Skyhawk. The resultant series of explosions and fires broke holes in the flight deck and fire and further explosions rapidly spread through the lower decks. At the time the ship was on Yankee Station off the Vietnamese coast and launching combat flights. With the help of sprays from nearby ships the flight deck fire was put out quickly but damage crews fought inside the hull for 24 hours to extinguish the flames. The incident cost the lives of 134 men.

After temporary repairs *Forrestal* proceeded under its own power to Norfolk, Virginia, its home port, for full repair, which was completed on 8 April 1968. In all the ship suffered four serious fires, the others being in July 1972 and two in April 1978. It made 12 further visits to the Mediterranean between 1968 and 1986, but also operated in the North Sea and sub-Arctic (1978). In March 1981 its aircraft flew on interception and combat missions during the missile crisis between Syria and Israel, shooting down two Libyan aircraft after attacks were made on planes from USS *Nimitz*.

The ship was redesignated as simply CV-59 on 30 June 1975, signifying its function as a support carrier rather than a frontline attack ship. On 4 July 1976 it was host ship for the tall ships review in New York Harbor as part of the USA's bi-centennial celebrations. From January 1983 to 20 May 1985 it went through a $550 million service life extension project intended to keep it effective for a further two decades.

Although it was never called on to participate in further armed actions, it was a regular participant in NATO and other US Navy exercises and by 1990 had completed 20 major deployments. Its final mission was from 30 May 1991, providing back-up air power and launching intelligence-gathering flights over Iraq, helping to maintain the 'no fly zone' in the north of that country, returning to the USA on 23 December. On 5 February 1992 its new base was Pensacola, Florida, where it was reclassified as a training carrier, AVT-59. In that capacity it was sent to the Philadelphia Naval Shipyard for a refit, but half-way through the programme, work was terminated by budget cuts. A training carrier was no longer to be maintained.

***Forrestal* executes a sharp turn during tests or manoeuvres, sometime during the 1970s.**

Forrestal was decommissioned on 11 September 1993, and disarmed, but although off the active list it was held at the Newport, Rhode Island, Naval Base until June 2010. Attempts to have it become a museum ship failed to raise enough money, and at first it was scheduled to be sunk as a target, but finally went for scrapping in October 2013. The other three ships of the class, *Saratoga*, *Ranger* and *Independence*, were broken up between 2014 and 2016.

Hercules landing

In a remarkable feat of airmanship, a four-engined KC130F Hercules refuelling plane was landed on the deck of *Forrestal* on 30 October 1963 to become the largest and heaviest plane to land on a carrier. Piloted by Lt James H. Flatley, this was the start of a whole series of test landings and take-offs by the Hercules under different loadings and in varying sea and wind conditions, with a maximum weight, plane plus cargo, of 55 tonnes (54 ton). The tests were to discover whether a 11.3 tonne (11.1 ton) cargo could be carried 4000km (2500 miles) and landed on a carrier at sea, and included 'touch and go' (touching down and immediately taking off again) as well as full-stop landings without the use of arrester wires, and 21 unassisted take-offs. The possibility was firmly established, although in the event smaller planes were used for carrier on-board delivery missions.

HMS Hermes/INS Viraat (1959)

In service with the Royal Navy from 1959 to 1984, *Hermes* achieved fame at home as flagship of the British naval force in the Falklands War of 1982. It then had a second career with the Indian Navy until 2016.

In 1943, among its other plans, the Royal Navy was proposing to build eight carriers to be classed as light fleet carriers. In the event none were completed before the end of hostilities, when four were immediately cancelled. Four others remained on the stocks for several years. First to be launched was HMS *Centaur*, launched in 1954 and giving its name to the class. *Hermes* was the final one, originally destined to be HMS *Elephant* but renamed in honour of its predecessor *Hermes*, sunk in the Pacific in 1942.

As *Elephant*, the ship was laid down at the Vickers Armstrong Yard in Barrow-in-Furness, Cumbria, on 21 June 1944. In mid-1945, with the hull built up to middle-deck level and the main internal bulkheads fitted, work

This profile shows *Hermes* post-1980 with bow ramp and modernized radar systems.

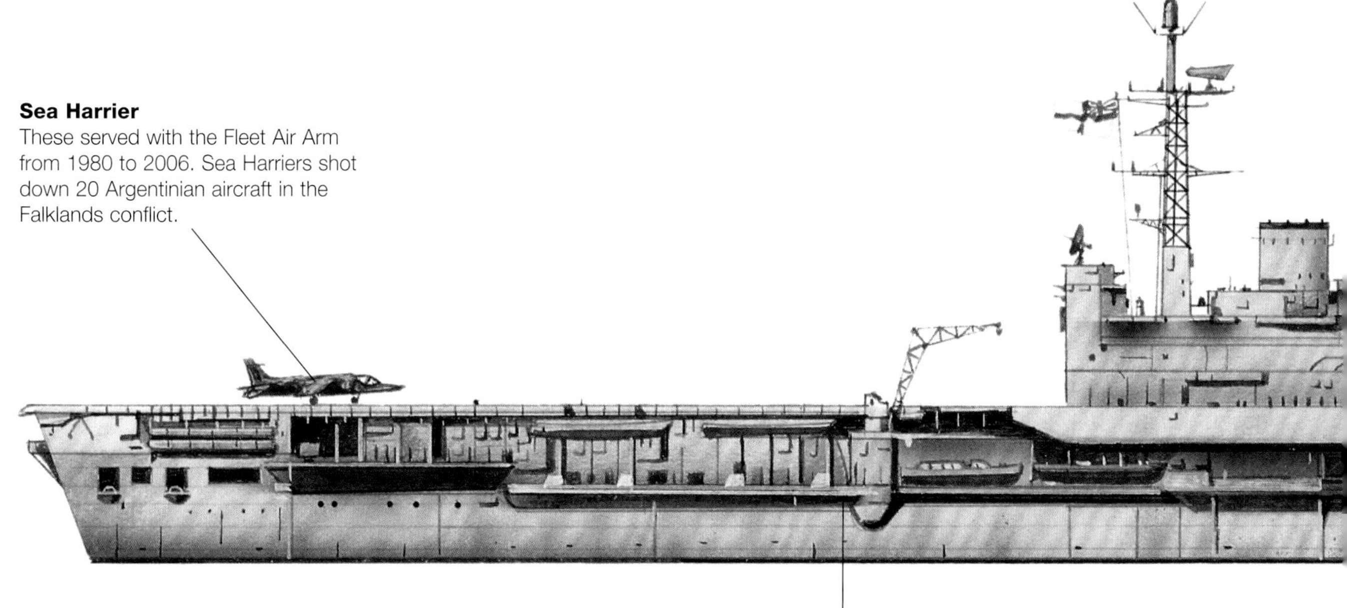

Sea Harrier
These served with the Fleet Air Arm from 1980 to 2006. Sea Harriers shot down 20 Argentinian aircraft in the Falklands conflict.

On-board entertainment
Hermes was probably the only carrier to stage a circus performance in the hangar (October 1961). A horse race was run inside it in March 1976.

was ordered to be stopped, and the steelwork was kept coated in oil to avoid corrosion. In 1949 work resumed to get the vessel into launching mode, and it was launched on 16 February 1953. Fitting-out did not start for another three years, but these were important years in the development of carriers, bringing the angled flight deck, the optical landing system and the guided missile, as well as the jet-powered attack plane.

Extensive strengthening and modification had to be made to the existing hull to instal an angled flight deck, heavy steam catapults and an externally-mounted deck edge lift on the port side. The island was entirely remodelled and the mast was now a pylon structure to carry a 28-ton Type 984 comprehensive display radar antenna. Power came from four Admiralty three-drum boilers supplying steam to two high pressure and two low pressure turbines, turning the two shafts through a gearing mechanism. Each pair of boilers or turbines was unitized to work independently of each other. Accommodation for the crew was far superior to what previous RN ships had to offer, although air conditioning was provided only for the operational rooms.

The originally fitted 114mm (4.5in) guns and most of its 40mm Bofors guns and all 20mm Oerlikon guns were removed and replaced by Firestreak air-to-air missile launchers. Sophisticated new equipment meant that crew numbers jumped from 1500 to 2100. Separate fuel bunkers for jets and piston-engined plans had to be provided as well as heavy oil for the ship itself. The electrical system was changed from DC to AC, powered by two 1000kW (1341hp) turbo-generators and two 360kW (482hp) diesel generators.

From 1959 to 1961 *Hermes* flew de Havilland Sea Vixen fighters of 890 Squadron and Supermarine Scimitars of 803

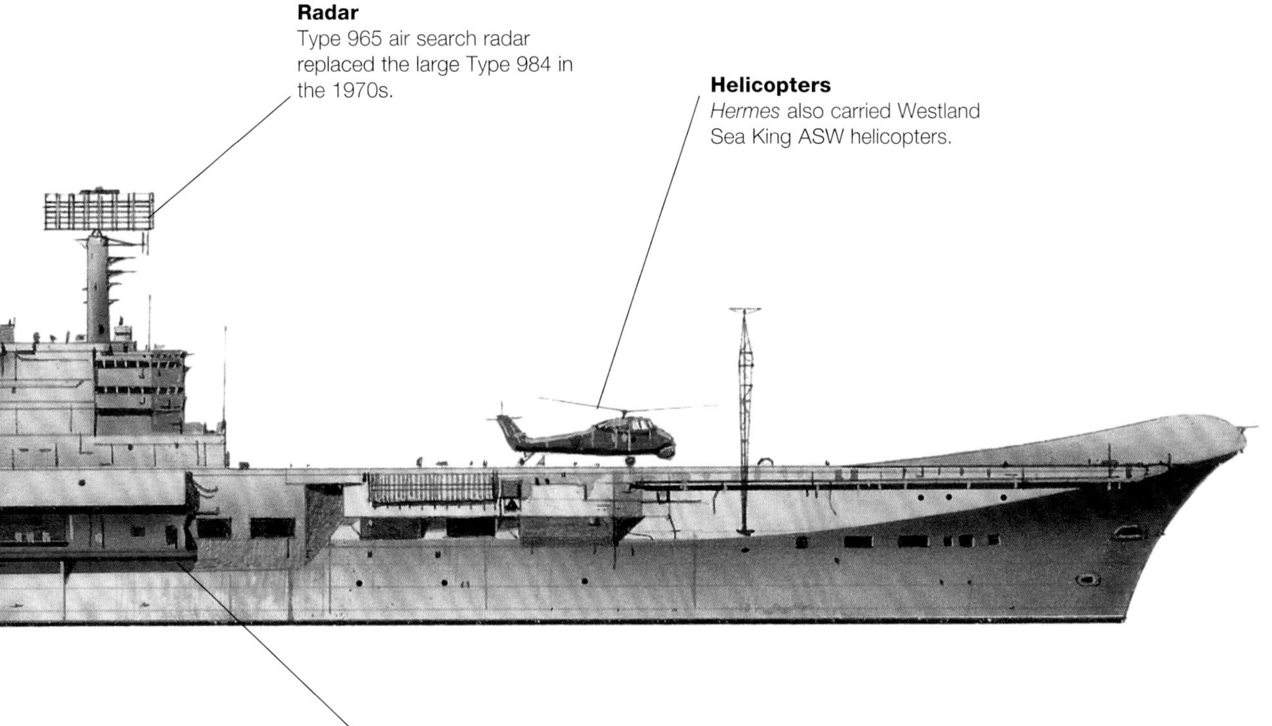

Radar
Type 965 air search radar replaced the large Type 984 in the 1970s.

Helicopters
Hermes also carried Westland Sea King ASW helicopters.

Contamination measures
Hermes was the first British carrier to be designed so that internal accommodation, including the boiler and turbine rooms, could be sealed off and controlled remotely in the event of encountering radioactive contamination.

Hermes after a two-year refit, doing work-up trials in the Moray Firth, Scotland, March 1966.

Specification (original)

Dimensions:	Length: 225.2m (738ft 10in); Beam: 27.4m (90ft); Draught: 8.5m (27ft 11in)
Displacement:	23,000 tonnes (22,638 tons); 28,000 tonnes (27,559 tons) full load
Propulsion:	4 Admiralty 3-drum boilers, 2 Parsons SR geared turbines, 2 shafts; 57,000kW (76,000shp)
Speed:	28 knots (52km/h; 32mph)
Range:	7000nm (13,000km; 8050 miles) at 18 knots (33.3km/h; 20.7mph)
Armament:	10 40mm Bofors AA guns
Aircraft:	30
Complement:	2100

Squadron, seven Blackburn Buccaneer bombers, five turbo-prop Fairey Gannet ASW planes and six Westland Sea King helicopters. In the Falklands/Malvinas war, its air group was 12 Sea Harrier FRS1 and 18 Sea Kings. After 1980 the ship carried up to 28 Sea Harriers and nine Sea Kings.

With fitting out still going on, *Hermes* sailed from Barrow to Southampton in May 1959 and underwent sea trials before returning to Barrow for completion. The final cost was around £19 million, and it was commissioned on 25 November 1959, leaving immediately for a shakedown cruise in the Mediterranean. From 7 November 1960 to 19 April 1961 it made a cruise via the Mediterranean and the Suez Canal to Hong Kong. A refit was made between 11 September 1961 and 24 April 1962, followed by further service in the Mediterranean and another visit to Hong Kong. During the cruise a new propeller was fitted at Singapore Dockyard. *Hermes* went in for a two-year refit at Devonport at the end of 1963, emerging on 28 March 1966, by which time the Royal Navy was scaling down its carrier force and the ship was offered for sale to the Australian Navy, who declined it. The reconditioned

Sea Harrier FRS Mk 1. The Hawker Siddeley (later British Aerospace) single-seater V/STOL multi-role combat plane was in service with the RN Fleet Air Arm between 1981 and 2006.

Hermes carried out extensive tours, taking in Australia and South Africa and places in between until June 1970.

Change of role

From June 1970 to April 1973 it was converted at Devonport into a helicopter carrier at a cost of £15 million, losing its catapults and arresting gear, and air control radar. A further alteration was made in 1976 to make it an anti-submarine support ship at a time when NATO and Soviet submarines were shadowing one another in the Atlantic, followed by yet another change of role after a refit between 20 March 1980 and 12 May 1981, which gave the ship a 12° ski-jump on the port foredeck to enable short take-off Sea Harrier jets to be carried. In April 1982 *Hermes*, now the Royal Navy's largest ship, was scheduled for decommissioning, but instead became flagship of the force sent to the Falkland Islands following Argentina's occupation on 2 April. Hermes launched air strikes against Argentinian ground forces and joined in maintaining a total exclusion zone around the islands, as well as providing hospital facilities and accommodation for crews of ships sunk or damaged.

For two years after the Falkland operations it remained in active commission, then went into reserve in February 1984. In 1985 it was removed from the Navy List. After a second Australian refusal to buy, the Indian Navy acquired the ship on 19 April 1986 after an extensive refit, and renamed it *Viraat*. A further modernization in 1999–2001 was intended to give it another 15 years of service, and included improvements to the propulsion system, new communications equipment, long-range surveillance radar, improvements to the lifts and fire curtains in the hangar. Still flying Sea Harriers, in 2003–04 it was also fitted with Barak SAM missiles.

Although there had been plans to extend its operational life as far as 2020, the need for frequent refits and the commissioning of the ex-Russian *Vikramaditya* carrier in 2013 caused its retiral several years before the commissioning of the home-built carrier *Vikrant*. In autumn 2016 *Viraat* was hulked at Kochi, and towed to Mumbai for ultimate disposal to take place in 2017.

Covert tracking operations

The steam catapult draws its power from the ship's boilers (or reactors), taking steam into accumulator/receiver tubes laid under the deck, with a shuttle to attach the aircraft, a launching valve and a water brake. Steam is admitted to a pressurized receiver tank already partially filled with hot water, and the whole tank rapidly fills with steam under high pressure, 31.6kg/cm2 (450psi) and at a temperature of 480°C (900°F). This steam can be admitted in precise bursts through a launch valve, preset according to the plane's weight and required launch speed, into two cylinders, each containing a piston. The plane is attached to a thrust-exhaust unit with a breakaway link. The plane's engines are turned on to full power and when the catapult controller is satisfied that the pressure is right, the valve is opened and the pistons are forced forward, taking the plane with them. With almost three times the power of the hydro-pneumatic model, the steam catapult can accelerate a plane from standing to 264km/h (165mph) in two seconds.

Clemenceau (1960)

France's first modern aircraft carrier was an important element in President Charles de Gaulle's policy of military independence and boosting national *grandeur*.

The French Navy had five carriers before *Clemenceau*, all of which survived World War II, in which they played hardly any part, and all were obsolete by 1950. *Clemenceau* and its sister ship *Foch* were planned when France still had overseas colonies and had not forsaken an imperial role. Designs were first prepared in 1947 but nothing was done until 1953, when the *Service Technique des Constructions et Armes Navales* dusted them off and began to make enlargements and changes as Project PA54. The keel was laid at Brest Arsenal in May 1954, and the hull was launched on 20 December 1957. Fitting out took almost three years, partly due to problems with the catapult systems. It first landed a plane on 19 September 1960 and was commissioned on 22 November that year, with R98 as its hull designation and Toulon as its home port.

The island had a low integral funnel and was dominated by the pole mast with an array of electronic gear. Advances in carrier design made in the early 1950s were incorporated in *Clemenceau*. It had a flight deck angled at 8.5° to the central axis, with a French version (Type OP3) of the sighting mirror for pilot guidance placed at its outer stern edge. A forward elevator was offset to starboard and an aft elevator at the deck edge, both of 15-tonne

Very much a symbol of French power, *Clemenceau* had many operational deployments, in European and Pacific waters, mostly in support of French actions and policies though also as part of international peacekeeping operations.

(15-ton) capacity. The two Mitchell-Brown BS-5 52m (170ft) steam catapults could put a 12-15 tonne aircraft into the air at 150 knots (277.8km/h; 172.6mph). A crane was mounted on the starboard just abaft of the island. The hangar deck, offset to port, was 152m (499ft) long and 22–24m (72 to 79ft) wide, with a height of 7m (23ft).

Six Indret boilers supplying steam to four turbines, with two shafts and two four-bladed propellers, drove the ship. Electric power was supplied via three turbo-alternators and six MGO V12 SACM diesel alternators. Box-type armour protection 30–50mm (1.2–1.9in) was fitted over the machinery and magazines and 45mm (1.7in) armour was applied to the flight deck. It was well provided with radar and sensors, including air warning DRBV-23B radar, one surface air low-altitude warning DRBV-50 (later DRBV-15), a radome-housed NRBA-50 (later 51) approach radar, a 3-D DRB1-10 air warning radar and DRBN-34 and Decca 1226 navigation radars. Fire control was provided by DRBC-31, then DRBC-32 directors.

On commission, the armament was eight 100mm (4in) turret-mounted guns, and five 127mm machine guns. Four of the turrets were replaced around 1997 by two SACP Crotale EDIR air defence systems with a stock of 52 missiles. *Clemenceau* and *Foch* flew French-

An F-8E(FN) Crusader fighter jet lands on the flight deck of the *Clemenceau*. The *Clemenceau* carried eight Crusaders. The Crusader was the last American fighter with guns as the primary weapon.

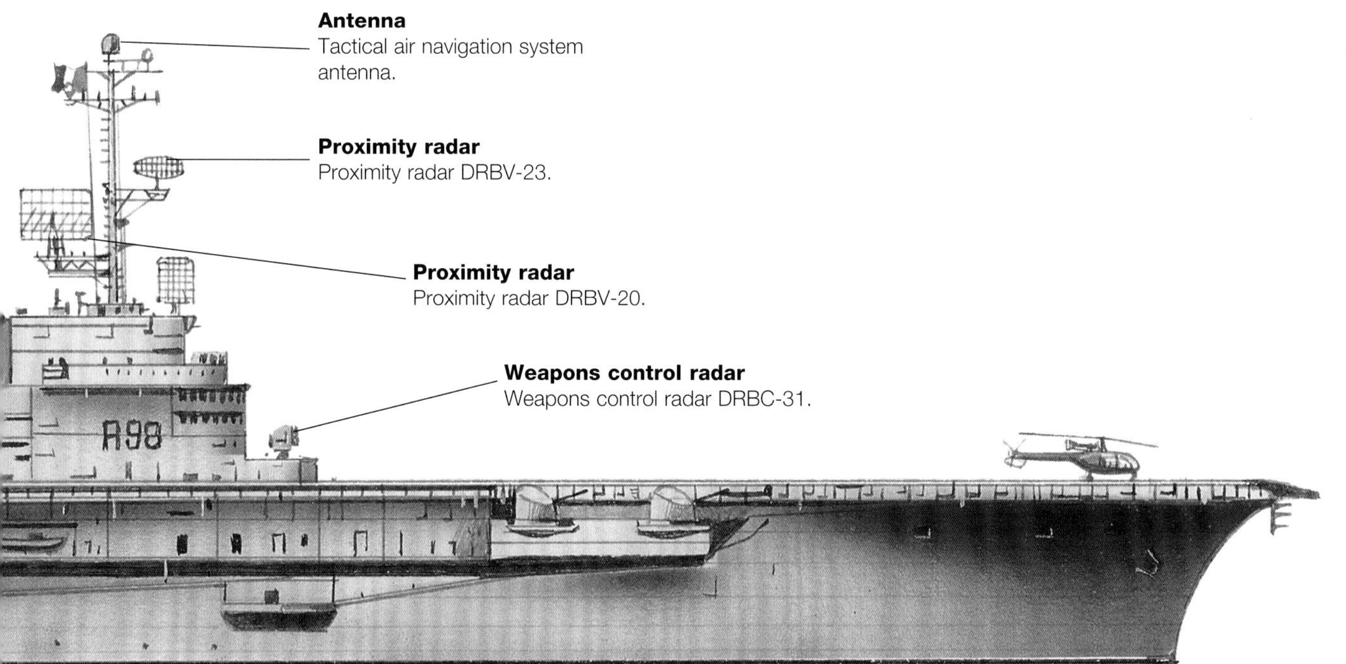

Clemenceau at sea. Its sister ship, *Foch*, is still active in the Brazilian navy today as the *São Paulo*.

Specification

Dimensions:	Length: 265m (869ft); Beam: 51.2m (168ft); Draught: 8.6m (28ft)
Displacement:	22,710 tonnes (22,352 tons); 32,000 tonnes (31,496 tons) full load
Propulsion:	6 Indret boilers, 4 turbines, 2 shafts; 94,000kW (126,000shp)
Speed:	32 knots (59km/h; 37mph)
Range:	7500nm (13,875km; 8625 miles) at 18 knots (33.3km/h; 20.7mph)
Armament:	8 100mm (4in) 55-cal Mod 53 guns
Aircraft:	38
Complement:	1338

built naval aircraft, apart from guests. In the 1960s the air wing was six F-8E (FN) fighters, 18 Etendard IVM fighter-bombers and eight Alizé ASW planes. By 1990 the complement was ten F-8E (FN), 16 Super Etendard, three Etendard IVP, seven Alizé planes and two Alouette III helicopters.

In January–February 1962 it took part in the NATO 'Big Game' exercises with the US 6th Fleet, including carriers *Saratoga* and *Intrepid*, and 'Dawn Breeze VII' in March–April, when it landed British Gannet and Sea Vixen aircraft. Regular exercises and routine patrols continued until January 1966, when it put into Brest for a year-long overhaul.

France left NATO in 1966 and there were no more exercises with the Americans and British until some occasional joint activities in the 1970s and 80s. The carrier engaged in exercises and training operations with some French ex-colonies, such as the Ivory Coast, and took part in most French naval operations across the globe. In 1968 it was with Force Alpha in the Pacific for the conduct of French thermonuclear bomb tests and in 1974–77 it made missions to the Indian Ocean to protect the ex-colony of Djibouti as well as bringing aid to Mauritius after Typhoon Gervaise in February 1975.

Major refit

Between 13 July 1977 and 22 November 1978 a major overhaul saw renewal of the crew accommodation, installation of a new control and command centre, adaptation to carry the Super-Etendard aircraft and provision of capacity to carry nuclear weapons. The Lebanese civil war crisis of 1982–84 brought it to the eastern Mediterranean; and it operated in the Gulf of Oman during the Iran–Iraq war of 1987–88, Operation Prometheus, and was in the Red Sea and Arabian Sea at the end of 1990 in defence of Kuwait against Iraqi invasion.

Between 1993 and 1996, with the collapse of Yugoslavia, it conducted operations in the Adriatic off the Bosnian coast, with USS *America* and HMS *Illustrious*, in support of United Nations peacekeeping troops.

Several refits were made during those years. It went through 'Crusader' modernization in 1966, including the fitting of side bulges, was made capable of operation in a radio-active environment (*capacité nucléaire*) in 1978, and fitted with the French Crotale anti-aircraft defence system in a major refit from 3 September 1985 to 31 October 1986, which also included installation of new engines, enhancement of communication equipment and replacement of the last sets of 100mm (4in) guns by two Crotale EDIR aerial defence systems. A last refit period was from 2 October 1994 to 28 June 1995. The carrier's final cruise was made from 16 July 1997, and it was disarmed in October of the same year.

Against much opposition, *Clemenceau* was sold for scrapping to a Spanish yard on 14 April 2003. An extraordinary saga then ensued, with the hull being towed to India but refused access because of asbestos and other toxic content. Towed back to French waters, it was finally handed over to Able UK at Hartlepool, England, for safe dismantling, a process completed by 31 December 2010. The sister ship, *Foch*, was sold to the Brazilian Navy in 2000 and refitted and recommissioned as *São Paulo*. Flagship of the Brazilian fleet, in 2017 it was due to undergo further modernization to ensure its serviceability to 2030.

Air Wing

The French-designed and built Dassault Etendard fighter entered service in 1962, and both in its IVM strike role and IVP reconnaissance role was carried on *Clemenceau* until 1991. It was replaced in production by the Dassault-Breguet Super-Etendard from June 1978. Armed with French-made Exocet anti-ship missiles, land-based Argentinian Super-Etendards sank the British destroyer *Sheffield* and the supply ship *Atlantic Conveyor* in the Falklands War of April–May 1982. Upgraded versions of the Super-Etendard are still in service. *Clemenceau* also carried the Breguet Alizé propeller-driven ASW aircraft.

A Super Etendard in French Navy livery.

USS Enterprise (1961)

The world's first nuclear-powered carrier, it became the US Navy's third-longest serving surface ship, commissioned from 1961 to 2012, and making a total of 24 active deployments.

The US Congress authorized the building of a nuclear-powered carrier in 1954. Built at the Newport News Shipbuilding Co., the cradle of so many conventionally powered carriers, it was laid down on 4 February 1958, launched on 24 September 1960 and commissioned on 25 November 1961, with the designation CVAN-65 indicating nuclear-driven attack carrier. Five sister ships were planned, but the vast cost of *Enterprise* at $451 million terminated the programme and it remained a one-off. Although the largest carrier yet built, *Enterprise*'s basic design followed the lines brought up to date in the preceding conventionally-powered *Kitty Hawk*-class.

Enterprise's vast surface area allowed for the construction of a square-shaped island rather than the rectangular structure of previous carriers, its upper section built out above a narrower base, with a massive pole mast supporting two broad arms for electronic gear, and carried on a built-out extension of the starboard side that ran around 60 per cent of the hull's length. Design of the island was influenced by the complex SCANFAR phased-array radar system (see below). Belt armour was formed from 203mm (8in) aluminium armour and protection was also applied to the flight deck, hangar, magazines and reactor rooms against torpedo attack (and grounding) was given by a double-hull construction. Four deck-edge elevators were fitted, three to starboard and one to port. Eight Westinghouse A2W nuclear reactors were installed, with two reactors providing power to each of four Westinghouse geared steam turbines to turn the four shafts. Uniquely, the ship had four rudders.

On trial, *Enterprise* reached a speed in excess of 40 knots (74km/h; 46mph). For the ship's defence, RIM-2 Terrier missile launchers had been planned, but on commissioning, *Enterprise* carried no armament apart from

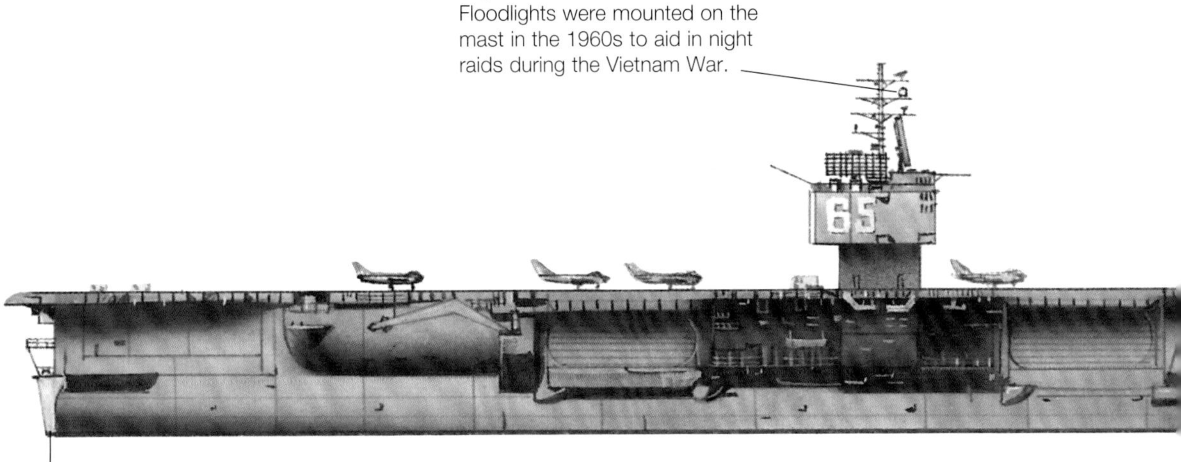

Night raids
Floodlights were mounted on the mast in the 1960s to aid in night raids during the Vietnam War.

Propeller
Four five-blade propellers each weighed 35 tonnes (34 tons).

The North American A-5 Vigilante was a supersonic carrier-based bomber designed to have a nuclear strike role, but primarily used in reconnaissance. It was in service between 1961 and 1979.

its air wing. In 1967 three RIM-7 Sea Sparrow launchers were fitted. Later additional defences were mounted, including NSSM Sea Sparrow, three Mk 15 Phalanx CIWS (close-in weapons system) gun mountings, and two 21-cell RIM-116 RAM (rolling airframe missile) launchers, for surface to air defence against anti-ship cruise missiles.

Enterprise was intended to mark a milestone in electronic technology as well as in its propulsion system. The SCANFAR radar system employed two radars, AN/SPS-32 and AN/SPS-33, giving combined search and targeting. Although a pioneer example of a phased array, the most advanced for the time, it had reliability and functional problems and used a huge amount of electric power. It was not fitted to any subsequent carriers and was replaced in 1980. As the first nuclear-powered carrier, the ship inevitably went through a prolonged testing and training period, but it engaged in operational duties from an early stage, including tracking the first American manned orbit of the Earth in February 1962, followed by a deployment to the Sixth Fleet in the Mediterranean. In October 1962 it joined Task Force 135 to enforce the 'quarantine' of Cuba during the missile crisis. After a refit and refuelling of the reactors at Newport News, October 1964 to November 1965, *Enterprise* was directed to the 7th Fleet based at Alameda, California. As flagship of Carrier Division Three it participated in American operations against North Vietnam from December 1965 to 20 June 1967.

Active service

Enterprise was deployed off Korea in January 1968 when North Korea seized the US intelligence-gathering ship *Pueblo*, and flagship of Task Force 71, following a further confrontation with North Korea in April 1969. It then returned to Newport News for a second refitting,

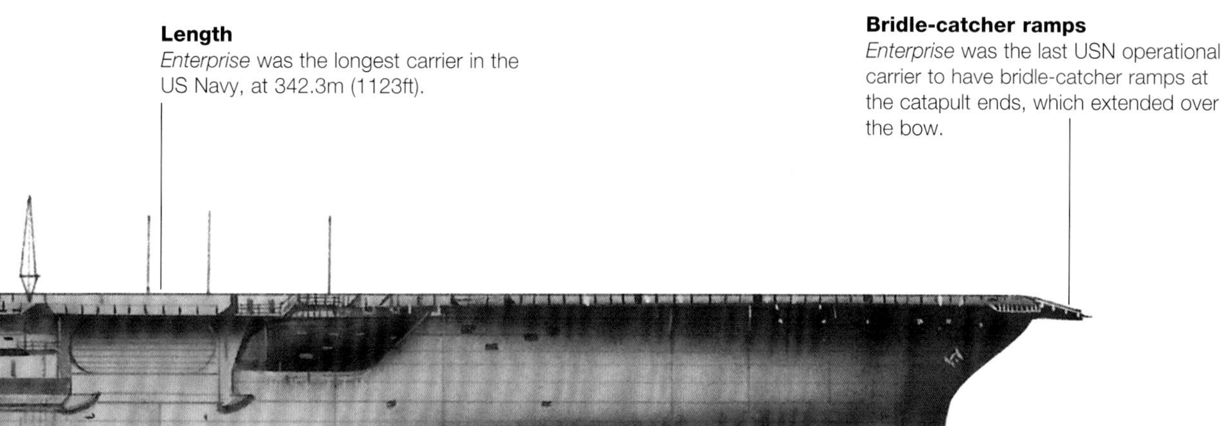

Length
Enterprise was the longest carrier in the US Navy, at 342.3m (1123ft).

Bridle-catcher ramps
Enterprise was the last USN operational carrier to have bridle-catcher ramps at the catapult ends, which extended over the bow.

With such great length and variable surface geometry, a vital part in berthing and anchoring carriers was played by sensors, video links and other internal equipment.

Crewmen man the railings as *Enterprise* leaves Naval Station Norfolk on a scheduled deployment on 2 May 2006.

including new reactor cores that enabled 10 years service without refuelling. The ship was then back in action off the Vietnamese coast, launching strikes against coastal targets, until the ceasefire of January 1973, although a further series of bombing strikes was made over Laos.

Enterprise underwent modification in the winter of 1973–74 to carry the Grumman F-14 Tomcat fighter, operational from 18 March 1974. In April 1975 it joined in the evacuation of US citizens and South Vietnamese civilians from Saigon. After nine deployments in the Western Pacific in the later 1970s, the carrier went through a three-year transformation from January 1979 at the Puget Sound naval yard. The massive SCANFAR radar was removed, the island was rebuilt and the mast was replaced, and additional sponsons were mounted forward on both sides accommodating updated defence systems, with the Mk-29 system for RIM-7 Sea Sparrows replacing the BPDM (basic point defence missile) systems. The dome housing ECM equipment was removed and SPS-48/49 arrays replaced the old SPS-32/33 arrays.

From 1982 to early 1986 it was again deployed in the Pacific, then in April 1986 it transferred to the Mediterranean as part of the US military campaign against Libya and remained in Middle Eastern waters, conducting strikes against Iranian targets in the spring of 1988. After a return to Alameda the carrier made its 14th deployment, circumnavigating the globe to reach its new home port at Norfolk Naval Station and then undergoing a further major overhaul at Newport News from April 1990 to 27 September 1994. From June to December 1966 it was again in European and Middle Eastern waters, enforcing no-fly zones over Bosnia and northern Iraq. From February 1997 to November 1998 the ship was out of action, then a 16th overseas deployment was made to the Persian Gulf, where it was flagship of a battle group in Operation Desert Fox, aimed at the destruction of military targets in Iraq.

After the 11 September 2001 attacks on New York and Washington, *Enterprise*, then in the Persian Gulf area, joined in missile and bombing raids on Al-Qaeda and Taliban targets in Afghanistan before returning to Norfolk. The next combat mission was in support of the invasion of Iraq, September 2003–February 2004, providing continuous air cover for the ground troops and carrying out bombing and missile strikes.

By 2005 *Enterprise* was showing signs of age. The new generation of *Nimitz* super-carriers had been developed with more sophisticated and durable reactors, but in 2006 and 2007 it made six-month tours, including another round-the-world cruise and a stint on duty in the Persian Gulf in June–December 2007. In April 2008 it entered the Newport News shipyard, now part of Northrop Grumman, for an overhaul that turned out to take eight months longer than planned and cost $665 million. This was to be the ship's final refit, and plans were already being formulated for decommissioning. Two further deployments were made in 2011 and 2012, both to the Persian Gulf area, via the Mediterranean; on the final tour its aircraft made

Specification

Dimensions:	Length: 342m (1123ft); Beam: 40.5m (132ft 9in); Draught: 12m (39ft)
Displacement:	84,626 tonnes (76,515 tons)
Propulsion:	8 Westinghouse A2W reactors, 4 steam turbines, 4 shafts; 208,600kW (280,000shp)
Speed:	33.6 knots (62.2km/h; 38.7mph)
Range:	Unlimited
Armament:	2 Sea Sparrow launchers, 2 RIM-116 RAM launchers, 2 20mm Phalanx CIWS
Aircraft:	90
Complement:	5828

Guided missile frigate USS *Taylor*, fast combat support ship USNS *Supply*, and USS *Enterprise* keep station as the supply ship replenishes the carrier's avgas tanks, 2006.

more than 2000 attacks on Taliban targets in Afghanistan. Like all carriers involved in an inherently risky occupation, *Enterprise* had its share of accidents and incidents, mostly relating to plane landings. The huge ship grounded twice, without serious mishap, although on the second occasion, when it struck Bishop's Rock, 161km (100 miles) west of San Diego on 2 November 1985, a 30-m (100-ft) gash was made in the outer hull and one of the propellers was damaged. The most serious accident was at Pearl Harbor on 14 January 1969 when a Mk-32 Zuni rocket loaded on an F-4 Phantom jet accidentally detonated on board the ship, the explosion killing 27 crew members and destroying 15 aircraft. Damage control teams contained the resulting fires, but the whole stern area had to be repaired and rebuilt, a task completed on 1 March 1969.

On 1 December 2012 *Enterprise* was deactivated at Norfolk. The yard that built it, at the time part of Huntington Ingalls Industries, received the contract for defuelling and the ship was towed to Newport News on 4 May 2015. Final dismantling at the Bremerton base in Washington State is a process likely to last into the 2020s.

Service history

In its 51-year service, *Enterprise* covered over 1,000,000 nautical miles (1,852,000km; 1,150,779 miles). In 1964, forming Task Force One with the cruiser *Long Beach* and the guided-missile frigate *Bainbridge*, all nuclear-powered, it made a 56,545-km (30,565-mile) round-the-world voyage, Operation Sea Orbit, to demonstrate the capabilities of nuclear-powered ships. In its second period of operations off Vietnam, March–July 1967, the ship made 13,435 catapult launches and flew 13,392 combat missions in the course of 132 days. A single artefact from the *Enterprise* still goes to sea: one of the ship's 33-tonne anchors has been reused on USS *Abraham Lincoln* (CVN-72) during a refit.

HMS Fearless (1965)

Designed as a highly specialized assault ship capable of operating landing craft and helicopters in any part of the world, *Fearless* played a central part in the Falklands War, and later served as a training ship.

With the run-down of its carrier fleet in the later 1960s, the Royal Navy turned to a type of ship that was smaller, cheaper and more versatile than a carrier, but that still ensured a world-wide operational capacity. HMS *Fearless* was the RN's first purpose-built LPD (landing platform dock) ship. Laid down at Harland & Wolff's Belfast yard on 25 July 1962 and launched on 19 December 1963, it was commissioned on 25 November 1965. A sister ship, HMS *Intrepid*, followed in 1967. An

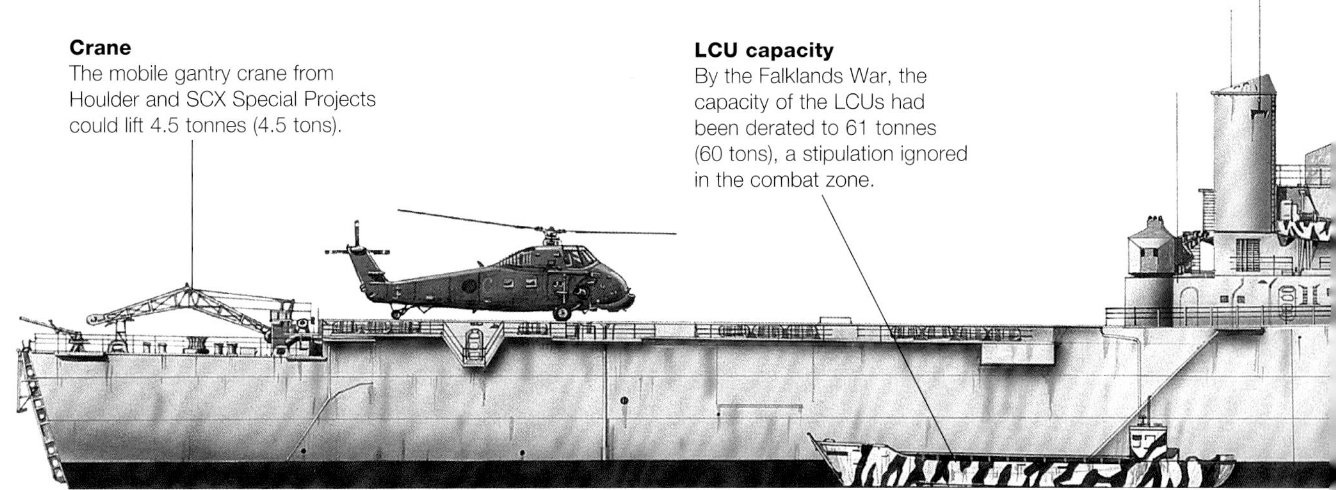

amphibious operations command and control centre for both sea, land and air operations was provided in addition to the ship's own operations room.

Within the hull, forward of the dock was garaging space on two decks, reached by ramps, for tanks or other vehicles. A casualty station with a medical team was also provided. Its most unusual feature was the stern dock, holding four 102-tonne (100-ton) Landing Craft Utility (LCU) boats, which could be released on to the sea surface by admitting 6100 tonnes (6000 tons) of sea water into ballast tanks, lowering the stern by about 3m (11ft). The stern gate was then opened and the landing craft could be floated out. In two separate machinery rooms, two Babcock & Wilcox Y24A boilers drove English Electric turbines, with two shafts. *Fearless* and *Intrepid* were the Royal Navy's last steam-powered surface warships. With a speed of 21 knots (38.8km/h; 24.1mph), they were not fast ships. Four 1000kW (1341hp) Allens turbo alternators generated

It was in the 1960s that the concept of the multi-role assault ship grew up alongside that of the aircraft carrier, with an eye on tactical deployment.

Funnel ducts
Ducts to the funnels were located to port and starboard to maximize interior space – a system developed on car ferries.

electric power, supplemented by four 450kW Paxman diesel generators.

The armament, for defensive purposes, consisted of two 20mm guns and two 20mm Vulcan Phalanx gun mountings. Crew accommodation included provision for 90 Royal Marine commandos of the 4th Assault Squadron, and up to a further 700 personnel could be transported for specific missions. The ship could also transport tanks or armoured cars, or heavy equipment for the Royal Engineers. The LCUs, with a crew of seven, could carry a 57-tonne (56-ton) Chieftain tank or up to 100 troops and had a range of 960km (600 miles). In addition to these, four Landing Craft Vehicle and Personnel boats, mounted on davits, could each carry 25 men or a jeep-size vehicles.

Fearless had no permanently-assigned aircraft but could operate up to four Sea King HC4 assault or multi-role helicopters from two take-off positions on the flight deck. With smaller helicopters such as Gazelles, and allowing for folding rotor blades, six aircraft could be transported. The flight deck, above the dock, was 51 x 23m (165 x 75ft) and could take helicopters up to the size of the RAF Chinook or the US Marine Corps CH53E. The utility Sea King or Wessex could carry an underslung load of up to 2267kg (5000lb). No hangar was provided, meaning that all servicing and maintenance had to be done on the open flight deck, a difficult and dangerous operation in bad weather or Arctic conditions.

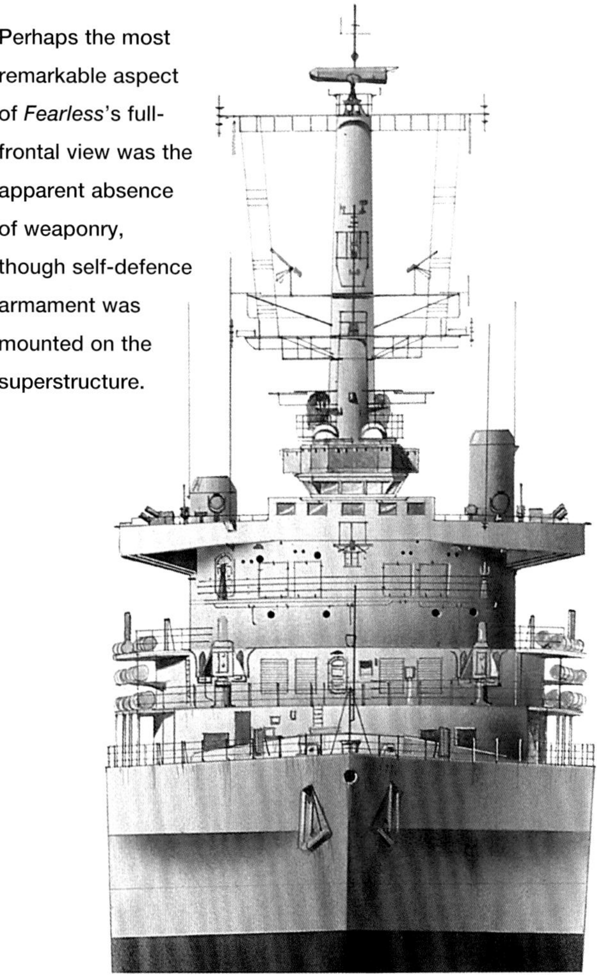

Perhaps the most remarkable aspect of *Fearless*'s full-frontal view was the apparent absence of weaponry, though self-defence armament was mounted on the superstructure.

Specification

Dimensions:	Length: 160m (520ft); Beam: 24m (80ft); Draught: 6.4m (21ft)
Displacement:	12,802 tonnes (12,600 tons); 15,138 tonnes (14,900 tons) full load
Propulsion:	2 B&W Y24A boilers, 2 EE turbines, 2 shafts; 8203kW (11,0000shp)
Speed:	21 knots (39km/h; 24mph)
Range:	10,000nm (18,500km; 11,500 miles)
Armament:	2 BMARC GAM B01 20mm single mounts, 2 20mm Vulcan Phalanx CIWS
Aircraft:	5
Complement:	580

Deployment

The first deployment was made to Aden during anti-terrorist operations before the former colony gained independence in 1966. In 1986 it acted as a floating conference chamber during the British negotiations with Southern Rhodesia (now Zimbabwe) over its unilateral declaration of independence. With the complexity of amphibious operations, the ship was continually involved in a programme of exercises and drills with other RN units and ships of allied navies, as well as giving support to actual British military operations, including the deployment of troops and armoured vehicles to Northern Ireland in Operation Motorman (1972). It also made an appearance in the 1977 James Bond film *The Spy Who Loved Me*.

In the Falklands War, *Fearless* was hurriedly provided with an enhanced satellite communications system – prior

to that it had only a single ship-to-shore VHF link – to enable its use as command ship for the amphibious task force. On this task it spent 100 consecutive days at sea. On 27 May its 20mm Bofors guns downed an Argentinian US-built Douglas A-4B attack plane. In the campaign its flight deck was used at times by Harrier VTOL jets. One of its LCU boats, Foxtrot 4, was sunk by a bomb, killing six Marines, on 8 June. Initial surrender negotiations were held on board the ship. Back in home waters, on 29 September 1983 *Fearless* accidentally rammed the German freighter *Gerhardt* off Portland Bill, and rapid repairs were made before it was deployed to Lebanon in October, where its landing craft delivered equipment to pro-Western groups in the Lebanese civil war.

Amphibious assault squadron

The Navy's first two LPD ships cost between them about £22,500,000, perhaps less than a new fleet carrier. Each carried a Royal Marine amphibious assault squadron, comprising crews for the landing craft, an Amphibious Beach Unit responsible for controlling the beach for the assault force and for landing and retrieval of vehicles, assisted by an armoured recovery vehicle and two tracklaying vehicles. Both ships served in the Falklands conflict. They were succeeded by two new amphibious assault ships, HMS *Bulwark* and *Albion*, of similar capacity but with much-upgraded technology.

***Fearless* off the coast of North Carolina on 9 May 1996, during a NATO Combined Joint Training Field Exercise.**

From 1985 to 1988 *Fearless* was placed on reserve, then underwent a two-year refit at Devonport before return to active duties in 1991, kept effective with parts removed from HMS *Intrepid*, which was laid up in 1991. At this time two BMARC 20mm single mount and two Phalanx CIWS mountings replaced the original AA guns. From 1991 to 1995 the ship was used for sea training of students at the Britannia Royal Naval College, Dartmouth. In November 2000 it was intended to form part of an amphibious Ready Group sent to support UN forces in Sierra Leone, but a fire in the engine room forced it to divert to Malta. In September 2001 after the terrorist attacks on the USA, 200 Marines were embarked on *Fearless* for potential deployment to the Middle East. After a final deployment on amphibious exercises, from 18 March 2002 it was mothballed at Portsmouth and was sold for scrapping in 2007. Two of its 'Foxtrot' landing craft have been preserved.

Veinticinco de Mayo (1969)

Commissioned in the Argentinian Navy in 1969, the carrier already had a long career behind it, with the British and Dutch navies.

The carrier's story begins in World War II, when it was ordered from the Cammell Laird yard in Birkenhead, England, as a '1942 Design Light Fleet Carrier' and laid down on 3 December 1942. It was launched on 30 December 1943 and commissioned on 17 January 1945 as HMS *Venerable*. The first eight of the 1942 Design were known as the *Colossus*-class, and *Venerable* was the fourth to enter service. The design brief was a demanding one: for the ships to be built quickly, at lowest possible cost, and yet be large and robust enough to participate in fleet actions. Considering the compromises involved, it was a remarkably successful design. The hull was unarmoured and built to merchant navy rather than warship specification, but the internal arrangements were different, with a range of bulkheads forming watertight compartments. Mantlet-type protection was fitted to the magazines.

HMS *Venerable*

The ships were driven by Parsons geared turbines, supplied with steam by Admiralty three-drum boilers in two separate engine rooms, the starboard room set forward of the port one. Intended to power cruisers, the system gave the class the moderate (for a carrier) speed of 25 knots (46.2km/h; 28.7mph). Armament was fitted for AA defence at close quarters, originally six four-barrelled 2-pdr gun mountings and 16 Oerlikon 20mm guns, but soon after commissioning these were replaced by 40mm Bofors guns. *Venerable* was capable of carrying up to 52 aircraft, with 24 Supermarine Seafire fighters and 18 Fairey Barracuda torpedo bombers

Here is the *Veinticino de Mayo* as it looked in 1969.

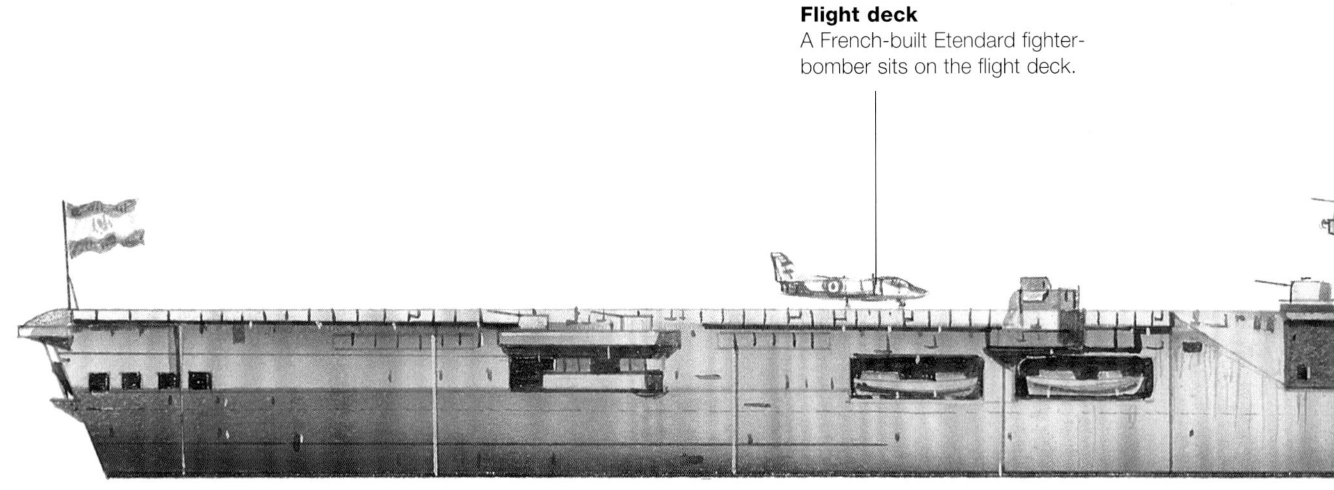

Flight deck
A French-built Etendard fighter-bomber sits on the flight deck.

Veinticinco de Mayo at the time of the Falklands War between Argentina and Great Britain, April–June 1982.

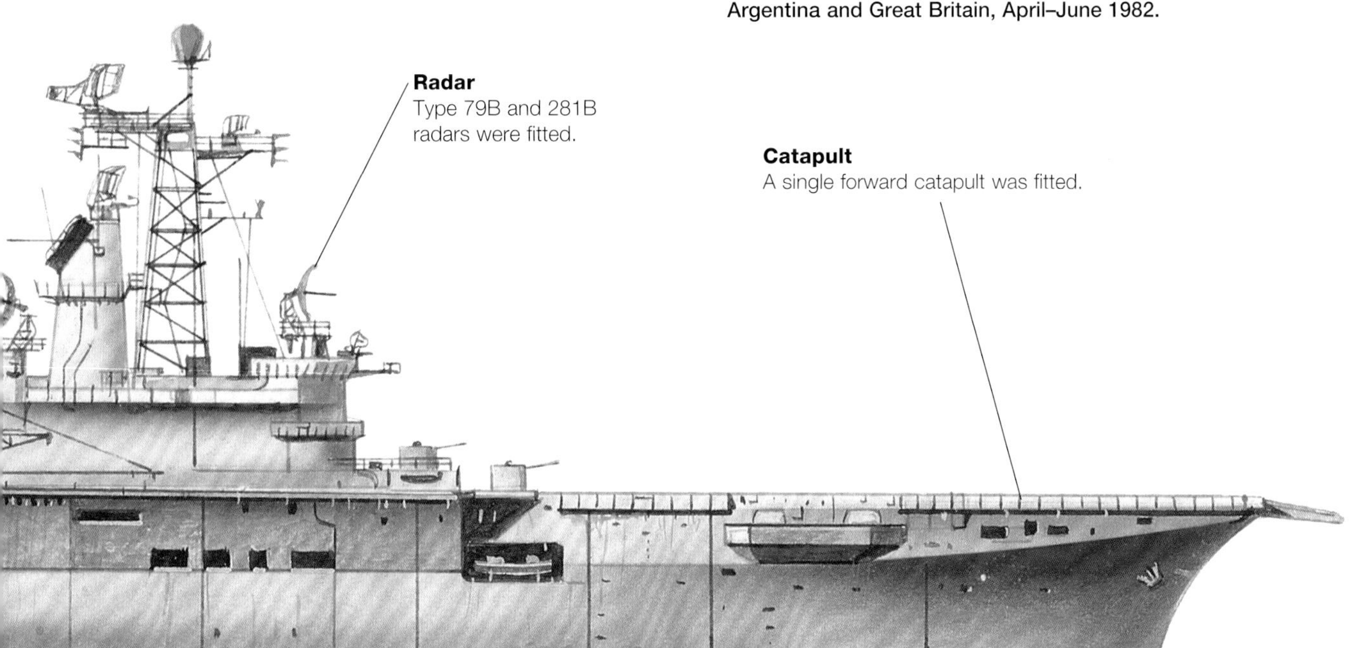

This view of the carrier is from 1982, with Skyhawk A-4Q jets on deck.

Specification

Dimensions:	Length: 192m (585ft 2in); Beam: 24.4m (74ft 4in); Draught: 7.6m (23ft 2in)
Displacement:	16,146 tonnes (15,892 tons); 20,214 tonnes (19,896 tons) full load
Propulsion:	4 Admiralty 3-drum boilers, Parsons geared turbines, 2 shafts; 29,828kW (40,000shp)
Speed:	25 knots (46.25km/h; 28.75mph)
Range:	12,000nm (22,200km; 13,800 miles)
Armament:	12 40mm AA guns
Aircraft:	37
Complement:	1300

being a typical air wing. Hydraulic catapults were fitted as well as two aircraft lifts.

Although designed for wartime use, the war came to an end before any of the class could be engaged in combat, though *Colossus*, *Glory*, *Venerable* and *Vengeance* were formed into the 11th Carrier Squadron in February 1945 and deployed to the Pacific in time to join in the returning of troops and prisoners of war to Britain. They were not intended as permanent additions to the fleet. In 1948 *Venerable* was sold to the Royal Netherlands Navy and recommissioned as *Karel Doorman*: the second Dutch carrier to bear the name, also used on the British carrier conversion HMS *Nairana*, which had been lent to the Dutch Navy between 1945 and 1948.

From 1955 to 1958 it was docked for extensive modernization. The island was rebuilt, the funnel lengthened and its cap tilted back, the masts replaced and fitted with extensive LW-01 and LW-02 radar antennas, a steam catapult was fitted, and the flight deck was reinforced and extended to port by an 8° angled flight deck. These modifications gave it capacity to handle jet aircraft, although only 21 because of the increased size of naval aircraft. In the mid-1960s it underwent further work to become an ASW carrier on NATO duties in the North Atlantic, flying eight Grumman S2F Trackers and six F-28 helicopters. After severe damage from a boiler-room fire on 29 April 1968, much rebuilding was required and the ship was sold to Argentina in October that year to be refitted for the Argentinian Navy, including new Admiralty-type boilers, at Rotterdam's Wilton Fijenoord shipyard as *Veinticinco de Mayo*. It was recommissioned on 12 March 1969 and entered service on 22 August.

Argentinian service

As *Veinticinco de Mayo,* Argentina's only operative carrier from 1970, it shipped first Grumman F9F Panther jets, then A-4Q Skyhawks, Grumman S-2 twin-propeller ASW planes, and Sikorsky SH34 helicopters. Its home port was Puerto Belgrano Naval Base, near Buenos Aires. In the Beagle Sound confrontation over disputed borders with Chile in December 1978, it was deployed to the extreme south as part of Operation Soberania. In the Falklands War of 1982 it was on the opposing side to its original operators, the British Navy. It supported the troop landings on the islands on 1 April, but operational difficulties, including its low speed, now 24 knots (44.4km/h; 27.6mph) at maximum, made it impossible to launch jet strikes from the flight deck and its air wing operated from land bases.

Although targeted by British nuclear submarines, the carrier was recalled after the torpedoing of the cruiser *General Belgrano* by HMS *Conqueror*, and survived the war. In 1983 the BS-34 catapult installed in the mid-50s was improved to make the launch of French Etendard attack planes possible, but the ship, plagued by engine trouble, saw only limited service in the next seven years and was put into reserve in 1990. Various plans and proposals for modernization were put forward, without result. Decommissioning came in 1997 and the hulk was towed to India for scrapping in 2000.

Improvised propulsion

As *Karel Doorman*, the ship had some memorable moments. Dispatched in 1960 to defend the independence of the Dutch ex-colony of West New Guinea against Indonesian claims of sovereignty, it was refused assistance by tug crews to enter Fremantle, Australia, and its crew manoeuvred it into dock using the propulsive power of aircraft chained down on the flight deck to create lateral thrust. The air wing was formed from British Sea Hawk FGA-6 jets and American TBM-35 and 3W Avengers. When it was again deployed to the region in a further confrontation in 1962, a cease-fire agreement saved it from attack by Russian-supplied Tupolev TU-16KS-1 Badger bombers from Indonesia.

A Dutch air force Sea Fury launches from the *Karel Doorman.*

USS Nimitz (1975)

This was the lead ship of a class of ten nuclear-powered super-carriers, considered to be the 'centrepiece' of US naval strength, both in deterrence and attack.

Described as 'floating airfields' or 'movable pieces of sovereign territory', the *Nimitz*-class's great extent is displayed in the plan view of the class leader.

Deck size
Overall deck length is 332.8m (1092ft), and width is 76.7m (251ft 10in). It is covered with an anti-slip coating.

Anti-aircraft missiles
Sea Sparrow launcher.

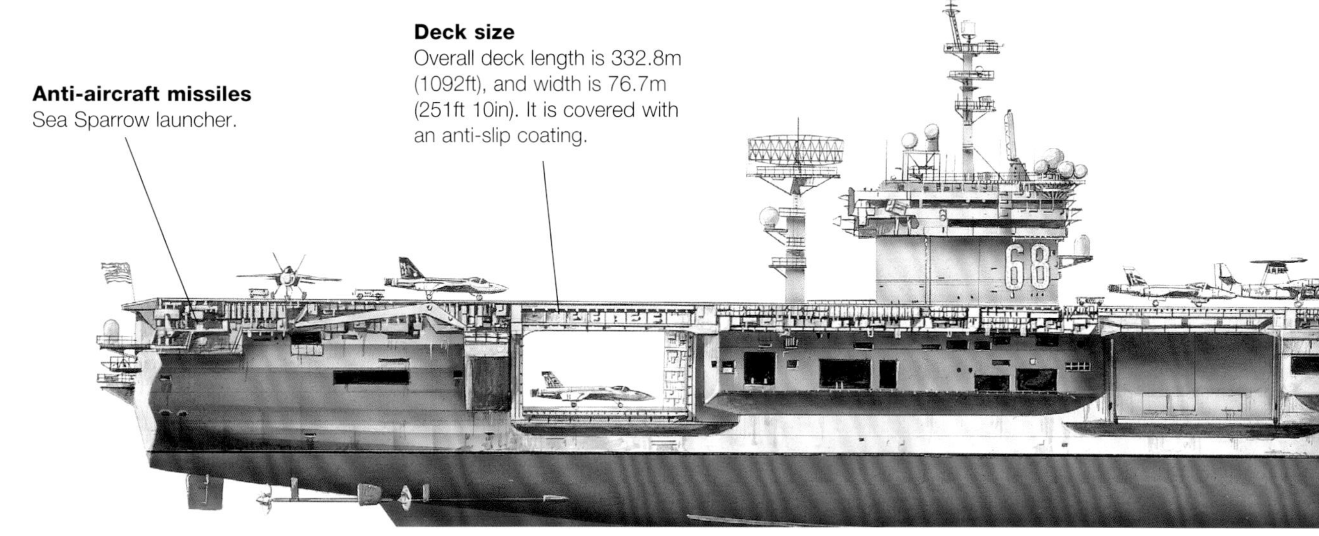

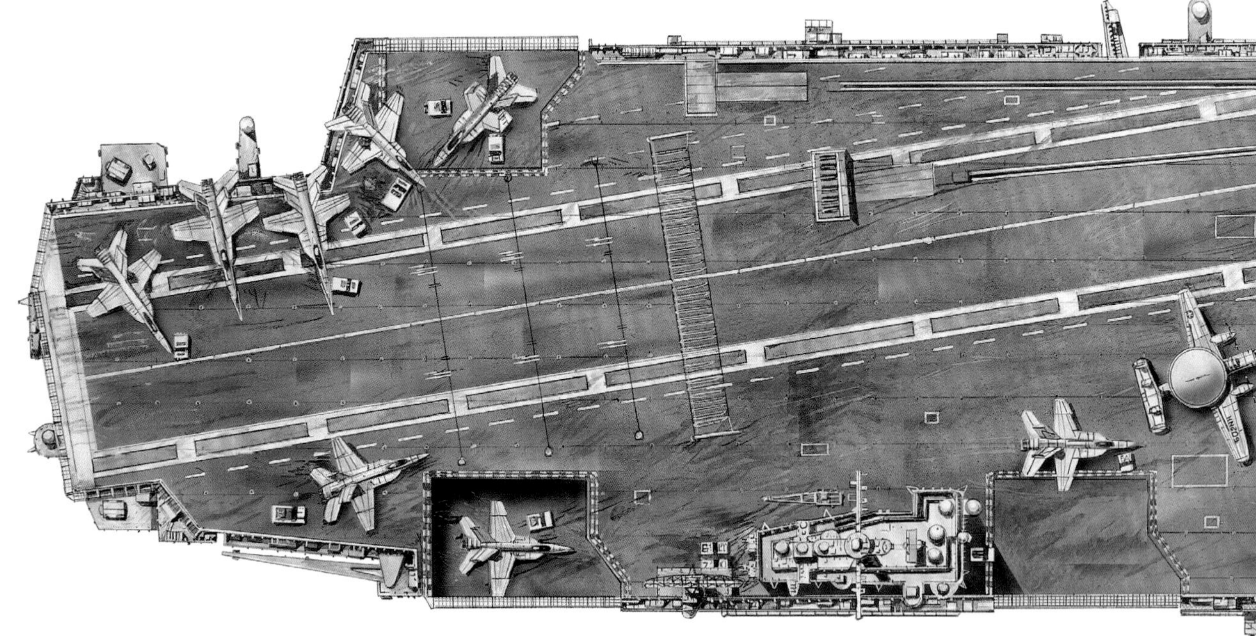

The US Navy's second series of nuclear-powered carriers was planned in the course of the 1960s in order to replace the seven *Forrestal* and *Kitty Hawk*-class ships. Somewhat larger than USS *Enterprise*, although marginally shorter and of similar beam, they shared its unlimited range provided by nuclear power, but had many refinements and improvements. Laid down at Newport News on 22 July 1968, *Nimitz* (CVAN-68) was launched on 13 May 1972 and commissioned on 3 May 1975 as the US Navy's and the world's largest warship. Its cost was around $8.5 billion.

New aspects of hull design included redesigned propellers and a new form of bulbous bow that both gives more buoyancy to the forward parts and a more efficient passage through water. The island is large and rectangular, quite different to the box-shape of USS *Enterprise,* with a high triple-armed mast, constructed of composite materials, rising above. Island and deck edges are rounded off to reduce the ship's radar signature. Kevlar armour 64mm (2.5in) thick is applied to weapons storage and machine spaces. On the 9° angled flight deck a CATOBAR

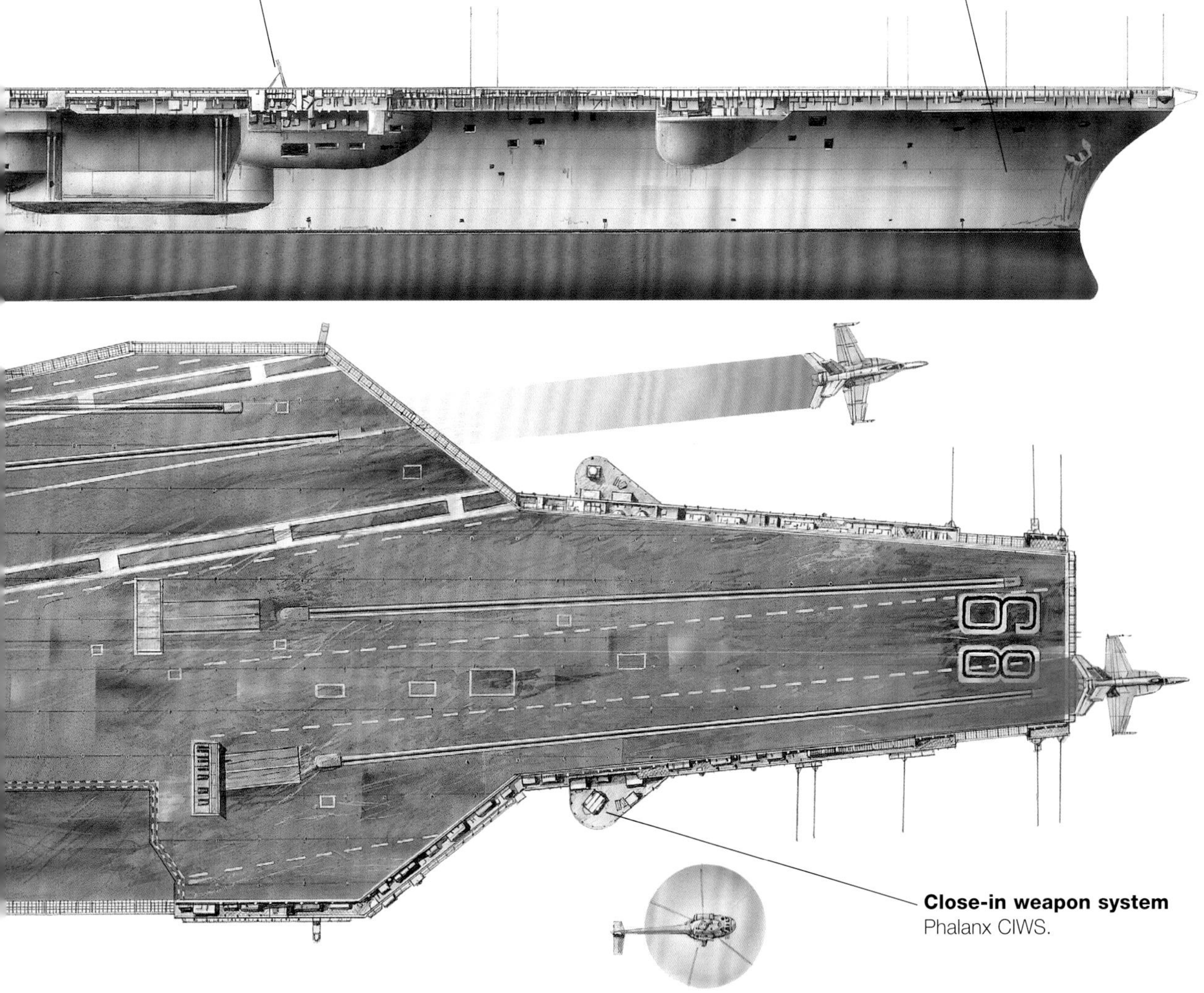

Hull protection
With such a vast hull, anti-corrosion measures are vital and the US Navy Research Laboratory has done much work on the design and protection of CVN hulls, using Impressed Current Cathode Protection rather than zinc sacrificial anodes, to keep the problem to a minimum.

Deflector
Jet blast deflector.

Close-in weapon system
Phalanx CIWS.

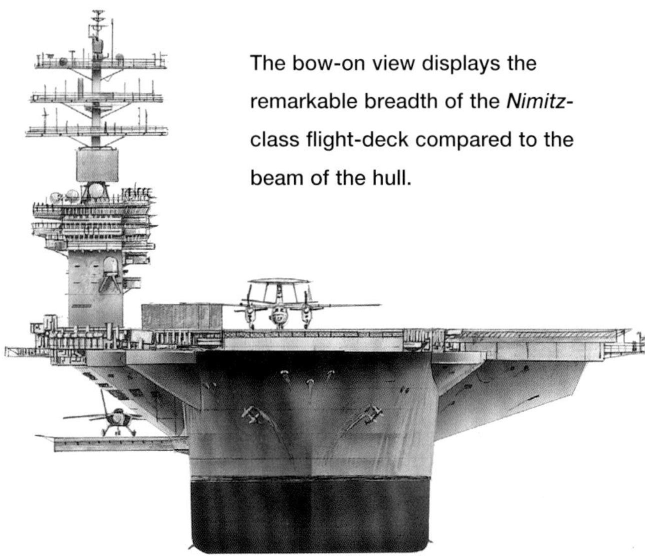

The bow-on view displays the remarkable breadth of the *Nimitz*-class flight-deck compared to the beam of the hull.

arrangement is used with four Mk 7 Mod 3 arrester wires. On the hangar deck, steel fire doors can separate the area into three enclosed spaces. Four steam catapults and four elevators, three to starboard and one to port, are fitted. Two Westinghouse A4W reactors, designed for a single mid-life refuelling in the ship's 50-year activity span, provide power for four steam turbines and four shafts.

Installed armament is two Sea RAM missile launchers and two Mk 29 Sea Sparrow surface-to-air missile launchers. The range of radar and sensor equipment includes AN/SPS-48E3-D and AN/SPS-49(V)5 2-D air search; AN/SPQ-9B target acquisition radar; AN/SPN-46 and AN/SPN-43 air traffic control radar; AN/SPN-41 landing aid radars; and four Mk 91 guidance radars. ECM equipment comprises a SLQ-32A(V)4 countermeasures suite and SLQ-25A Nixie anti-torpedo system. *Nimitz*'s air wing is formed of up to 90 planes. In 1991 it carried 24 Hornets, 24 Tomcats, six Vikings, four Prowlers, four Hawkeyes and 15 Intruders.

Specification

Dimensions:	Length: 317m (1040ft); Beam: 40.8m 1(34ft) ; Draught: 11.3m (37ft)
Displacement:	110,250 tonnes (100,020 tons)
Propulsion:	2 Westinghouse A4W reactors, 4 steam turbines, 4 shafts
Speed:	31.5 knots (58.3km/h; 36.2mph)
Range:	Unlimited
Armament:	2 Sea Sparrow, 2 RIM-116 missile launchers; 2 Phalanx CIWS; 2 .50-cal machine gun mountings
Aircraft:	90
Complement:	5680

New designation

Nimitz arrived at its home port, Norfolk, Virginia, on 12 April 1975. On 1 July 1975 it was redesignated as CVN-68, along with other CVA ships, the new designation intended to reflect a multi-role capability including attack. Its first cruise in foreign waters was to the Mediterranean Sea in July 1976, with Carrier Air Wing 8, and it helped with evacuating US nationals from Lebanon during the civil war there. A further three deployments to the Mediterranean followed in the 1970s. Helicopters from *Nimitz* took part in the disaster-fraught evacuation of US Embassy staff from Teheran in April 1979. On 25 May 1981 a crash-landing EA-6B Prowler started a fire that killed 14 crewmen and destroyed four aircraft, damaging 16 others. Later than year it was in the Mediterranean again and was involved in the Gulf of Sidra stand-off with Libya in August, when two Libyan jets were shot down. On 13 November 2001 it moved home port to San Diego, California.

In March 2003 it supported the US–British invasion of Iraq in Operation Iraqi Freedom as flagship of a Carrier Battle Group that comprised Carrier Air Wing 2, with USS *Constellation* (CV-64), the cruisers *Valley Forge* and *Bunker Hill*, destroyers *Higgins* and *Milius*, frigate *Thach*, fast combat support ship *Rainier* and nuclear submarine *Columbia*. *Nimitz* launched more than 6500 sorties against targets in Iraq during this six-month mission, in which it launched the F/A-18F Super Hornet and E-2C Hawkeye 2000 aircraft on their first combat flights. It was also the first carrier to deploy two Super Hornet squadrons. On return to San Diego it underwent a six-month Planned Incremental Availability overhaul, with a range of work from updated and non-pollutant air-conditioning systems to new steam pipes and reconditioning of the catapults. The carrier made three subsequent deployments to the Persian Gulf area. On 5 February 2008 it was overflown at

A CH-46 Sea Knight of Helicopter Combat Support Squadron Six lifts off from *Nimitz*'s flight deck as the carrier returns from a deployment on Operation Southern Watch in the Persian Gulf, in 1993.

600m (2000ft) by two Russian Tu-95 Bear bombers, but the US Navy played down the significance of this, noting it was in international waters, although not far from the Japanese coast.

Nimitz put into Bremerton naval base on 6 December 2010 for a Drydocking Planned Incremental Availability overhaul, which included the fitting of two new sponsons to support weapons systems or sensor arrays, and on completion transferred home port again to Naval Station Everett, Washington. By that time it was the Navy's oldest carrier, following the retiral of USS *Enterprise* in December 2012, and had passed through several years of intensive duty, building up a backlog of maintenance requirements as a result. Through 2016–17 a combined Planned Incremental Availability and an Extended Planned Incremental Availability were being carried out simultaneously. In 2017 *Nimitz* remains in service with the other nine carriers of its class, with its home port now at Kitsap Naval Base. Its air wing is CVW-11, of nine squadrons comprising both fixed and rotary wing planes: McDonnell Douglas F/A 16C Hornets, Boeing F/A-18-E/F Superhornets, Grumman E-2D Hawkeye, Grumman C-2A Greyhound COD (carrier onboard delivery) and Sikorsky SH-60 Seahawks. It is currently carrying out trials with the new F-35C Lightning II jet.

Fit for purpose

The extremely high efficiency level of US carrier crews is maintained by a meticulously planned set of assessments and tests designed to ensure that the ship is ready to cope with any situation. These tests must be passed for the ship to obtain certification as fit for carrying out its duties. Applying to every aspect of ship management, they include Carrier Assessment Readiness tests, Combat System Ship's Qualification, Tailored Ship's Training Availability and Final Evaluation Problem tests. Each new piece of equipment, such as the arrester wires fitted in 2007, is subjected to test and certified accordingly. These equipment, fitness and readiness tests are specific to the ship and must fit in with the wider programme of drills and exercises conducted with other fleet units.

Flight controllers aboard *Nimitz* stand duty in the island look-out point.

Kiev (1975)

Described as a 'heavy aviation cruiser' *Kiev* was the Soviet Navy's answer to the requirement of multi-role warships in the 1970s, and Russia's first carrier for fixed-wing aircraft.

The Russian Navy had introduced helicopter carriers with the *Moskva*-class in the 1960s. In the later years of that decade it was giving serious consideration to developing a class of very large aircraft carriers, known as Project OREL, to match the United States' construction of the *Kitty Hawk*-class, but finally decided on the *Kiev* class of Project 1143, also known as *Krechyet* (Gyrfalcon) class, a much larger and better-equipped vessel than the Moskvas. The main purpose of the class was to counter US Polaris missile SSBNs and to work in concert with Russian missile submarines. *Kiev* was the first of four, designed by the Nevskoye Planning and Design Bureau, all built at the Nikolayev South, formerly Chernomorsky 444, shipyard at Nikolayev on the Black Sea. Laid down on 21 July 1970, it was launched on 26 December 1972 and commissioned on 28 December 1975.

Design was carrier-style, with a very large island superstructure on the starboard side, including a

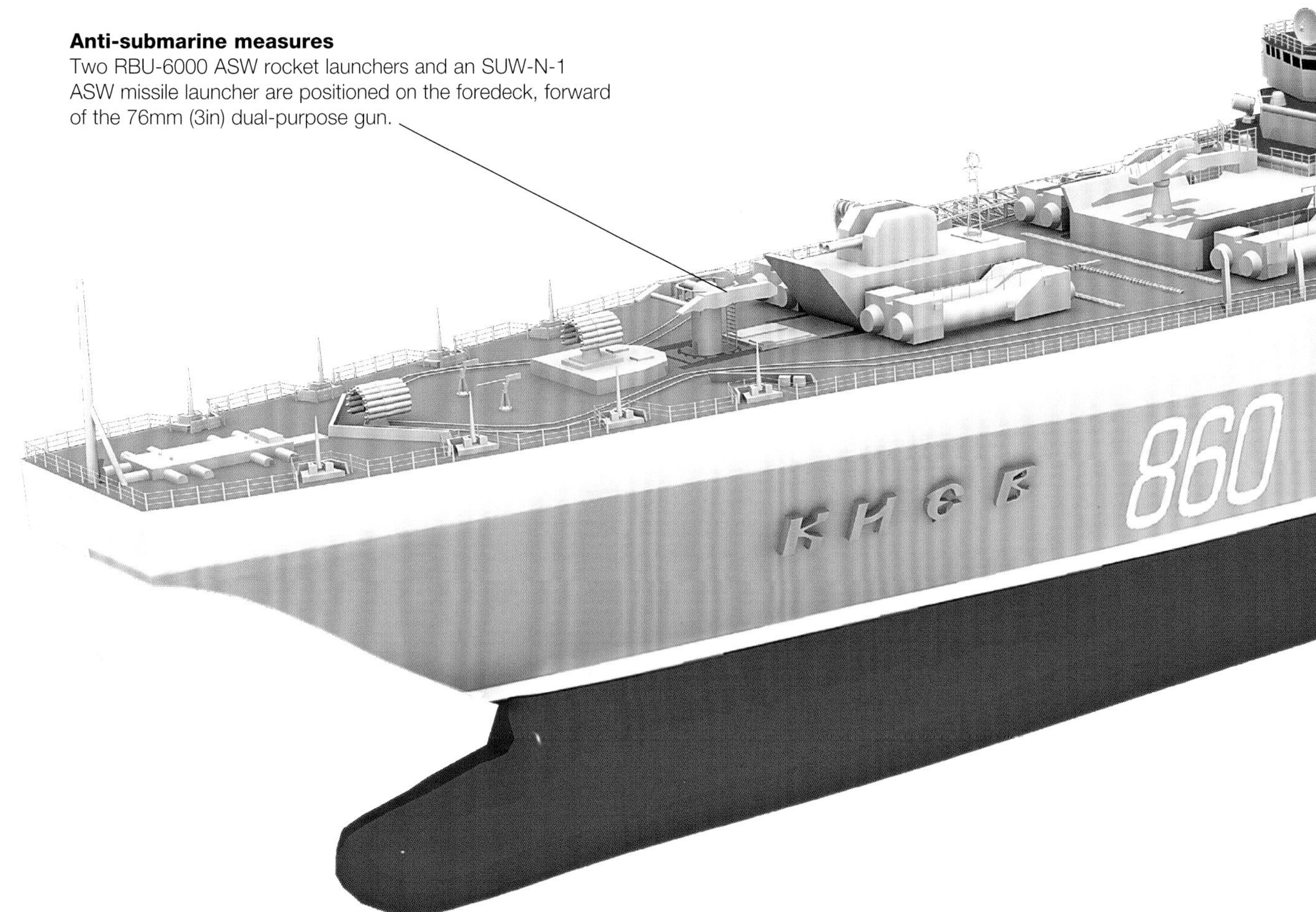

Anti-submarine measures
Two RBU-6000 ASW rocket launchers and an SUW-N-1 ASW missile launcher are positioned on the foredeck, forward of the 76mm (3in) dual-purpose gun.

sternwards-angled funnel, and surmounted by a pylon mast and a great array of radar and sensory equipment. It provided counterbalance to a flight deck 53m (161ft 6in) long, angled out at 4.5° from the port side of the hull, with Tee Plinth optronic landing aids. There was no catapult or arrester gear, restricting on-board aircraft to S/VTOL planes and helicopters. Its power-plant was four TV-12-3 steam turbines, powered by eight turbo-pressurized

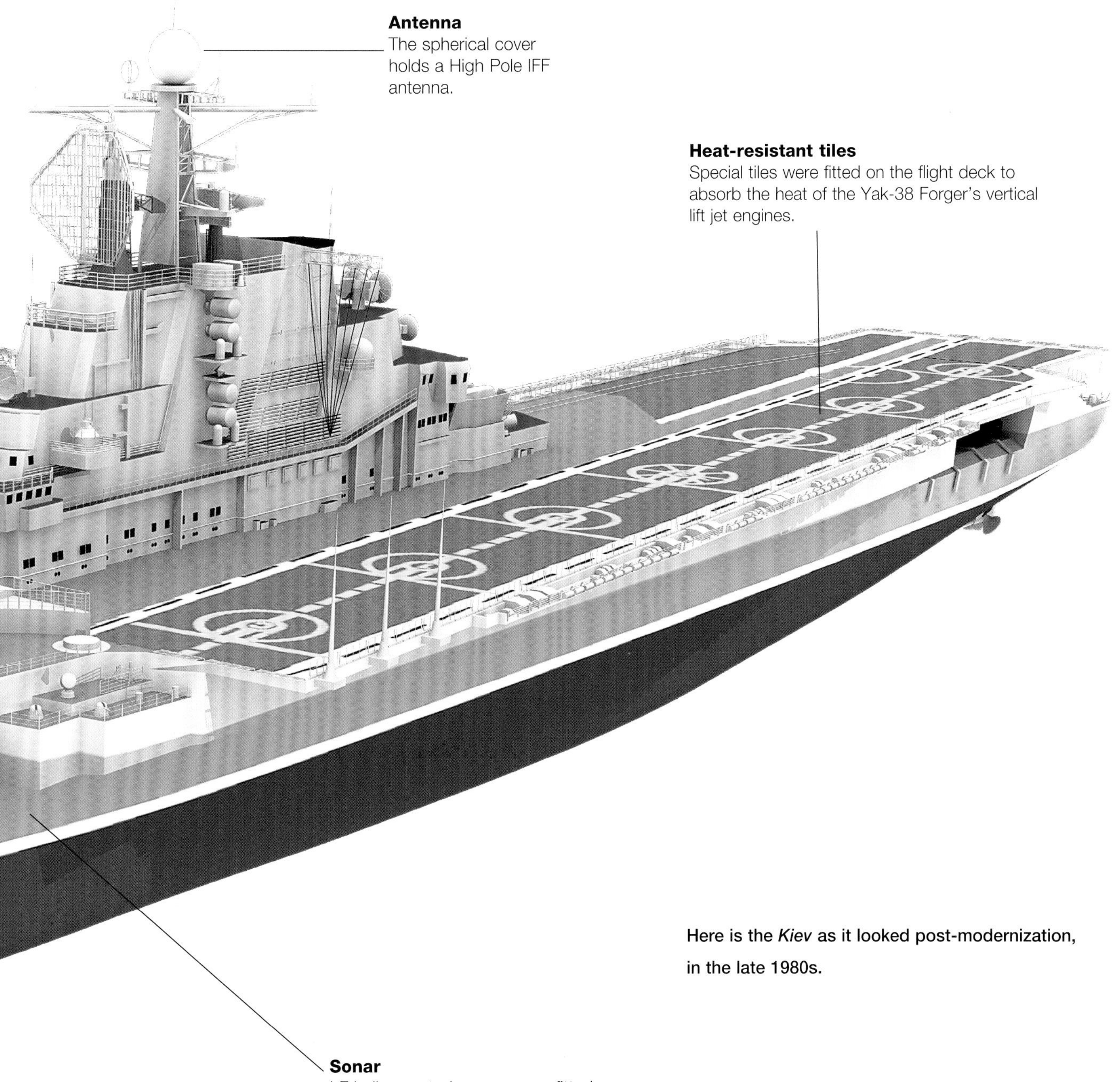

Here is the *Kiev* as it looked post-modernization, in the late 1980s.

Starboard side view of *Kiev*.

boilers, and driving four fixed-pitch propellers. The heavy demand for electric power was met by six 1500kW (2011hp) turbine generators, backed up by four 1500kW diesel generators. A hangar deck with two starboard-side aircraft lifts took up half the ship's length from midships to stern.

On board armament

The ship's hybrid cruiser-carrier appearance was enhanced by the range of armament carried on the foredeck, which also underlined the ship's multi-role purpose. For ASW action there were two 12-barrel RBU-6000 launchers and one twin SUW-N-1 launcher for FRAS 1 missiles; also two twin SA-N-3 and two twin SA-N-4 SAM launchers with 122 missiles; and four twin SS-N-12 SSM launchers with 16 reloads. Twin 76mm cannon were mounted and eight ADMG-630 30mm Gatling mountings with six barrels, providing intensive CIWS fire. In addition these were among the few aircraft carriers to be equipped with torpedo tubes.

The range of sensory and countermeasures equipment was also impressive. Bass Tilt fire control radar was fitted for the CIWS system and Owl Screech for the 76mm guns; Don-Kay and Don 2 navigation radars, Head Light and Pop Group missile control radars for the SA-N-3 and SA-N-4 respectively; Top Sail 3D and Top Steer air surveillance, Vee-Bars and High Pole HF and IFF antennae; and two chaff launchers. Sonar gear was 1 LF bow-mounted, 1 MF hull-mounted and 1 MF variable depth stern-mounted. The air wing combined Yakovlev Yak-38 Forger A attack planes and Forger B trainers, with Ka-25 Hormone A and B helicopters and Ka-27 helicopters. Up to 13 of the S/VTOL planes and 16 helicopters could be carried.

Kiev and its sister ships were widely deployed, as these were the first ships capable of giving air fighter cover to Soviet naval craft, with two assigned to the Northern and two to the Pacific fleet. *Kiev*'s designation as a 'cruiser with aircraft' enabled it to pass through the Bosphorus (forbidden to carriers of any nation) despite protests, and conduct trials in the Mediterranean before making for its home port at Severomorsk in Arctic Russia. While little information was released about the ship's activities, it was observed taking part in fleet and task group exercises

Specification

Dimensions:	Length: 273.1m (896ft); Beam: 31m (102ft); Draught: 8.95m (29ft 5in)
Displacement:	31,018 tonnes (30,530 tons); 42,032 tonnes (41,370 tons) full load
Propulsion:	Four geared steam turbines, 4 shafts; 100,000kW (140,000shp)
Speed:	32 knots (59km/h; 37mph)
Range:	13,500nm (25,000km; 15,500 miles) at 18 knots (33.3km/h; 20.7mph)
Armament:	2 12-barrel RBU-6000 ASW launchers, 1 twin SUW-N-1 launcher for FRAS 1 missiles; 2 twin SA-N-3 and 2 twin SA-N-4 SAM launchers, with 122 missiles; 4 twin SS-N-12 SSM launchers with 16 reloads; 2 twin 76mm cannon, 8 ADMG 630 30mm 6-barrel Gatling CIWS; 10 533mm (21in) torpedo tubes
Aircraft:	32
Complement:	2042

Plan view showing the division of the ship between avionics, with the angled flight deck, and weapons platform, with the missile launchers on the foredeck.

with surface ships and submarines, in line with its multi-role purpose, in different areas of the Atlantic and the Mediterranean and Baltic Seas. From January 1983 to November 1984 it underwent a modernization at the Niolayev Yard, then returned to the Northern Fleet.

Following the collapse of the Soviet Union, *Kiev* was laid up in 1994 and much of its equipment was removed as spares for sister ship *Admiral Gorshkov*. In 1996 it was bought by Chinese interests, and undoubtedly was closely examined by Chinese naval experts, before being put on display from 2004 as a museum ship in a theme park of military and naval interest at Tianjin Binhai. In 2011 the hull was converted to become a luxury hotel. Of its sister ships, *Minsk* was also sold to Chinese buyers in 1995, and from 2000 functioned as a museum ship in 'Minsk World', Guangdong Province, which closed in February 2016. The fourth member of the class, commissioned in 1987 as *Baku* and renamed *Admiral Gorshkov* on 7 November 1990, had sufficient modifications to be regarded as a sub-class on its own, including a much enlarged flight deck. After years of negotiations a deal was made to transfer the ship, its equipment and a number of aircraft and helicopters to India in February 2004. At the FSUE Sevmash yard at Severodvinsk a thorough makeover was carried out, including new machinery and electronics, widened flight deck and a 914-tonne (900-ton) 14° upswept foredeck. Classified as STOBAR (short take-off but arrested recovery), it has been in service since June 2013 as INS *Vikramaditya*.

Nuclear threat

Kiev was understood by NATO intelligence to be armed with cruise missiles, tipped with nuclear warheads, and as such was a new potential threat to coastal locations. In 1977 the British nuclear submarine _Swiftsure_ was deployed in secret to the Barents Sea in order to track the carrier. A large-scale Russian naval exercise was being conducted, with _Kiev_ participating, and the submarine tracked the carrier closely, photographing the hull through its periscope and also obtaining the ship's acoustic signature: the characteristic noise made by its propellers, which is unique to every ship. This was a typical Cold War operation, and a 'game' played by both Soviet and NATO ships and submarines.

A magnified aerial image gives a close-up view of *Kiev*'s substantial armament.

USS Tarawa (1976)

This ship and the others in its class were built in order to transport, land and support US Marine troops on any coastline in the world, as the core of an Amphibious Readiness Group.

Tarawa (LHA-1) was planned as the first of a class of general-purpose amphibious assault ships, able to land Marines and their equipment at virtually any coastal location in the world: in the words of Marine Corps Commandant Robert E. Cushman Jr, 'a versatile amphibious assault ship designed from the keel up with the requirements of the landing forces in mind'. Although nine ships were envisaged, only five were actually built. Laid down on 15 November 1972 at Ingalls Shipbuilding Corp., Pascagoula, Mississippi, it was launched on 1 December 1973 and commissioned at the shipyard on 29 May 1976. In terms of function it was identical to the British HMS *Fearless*; in terms of size it was a substantially bigger ship and capable of landing a larger and more fully equipped force in brigade-

Intense activity on the surface (sea or land), in the air, and on board ship, as *Tarawa* displays its multiple capabilities.

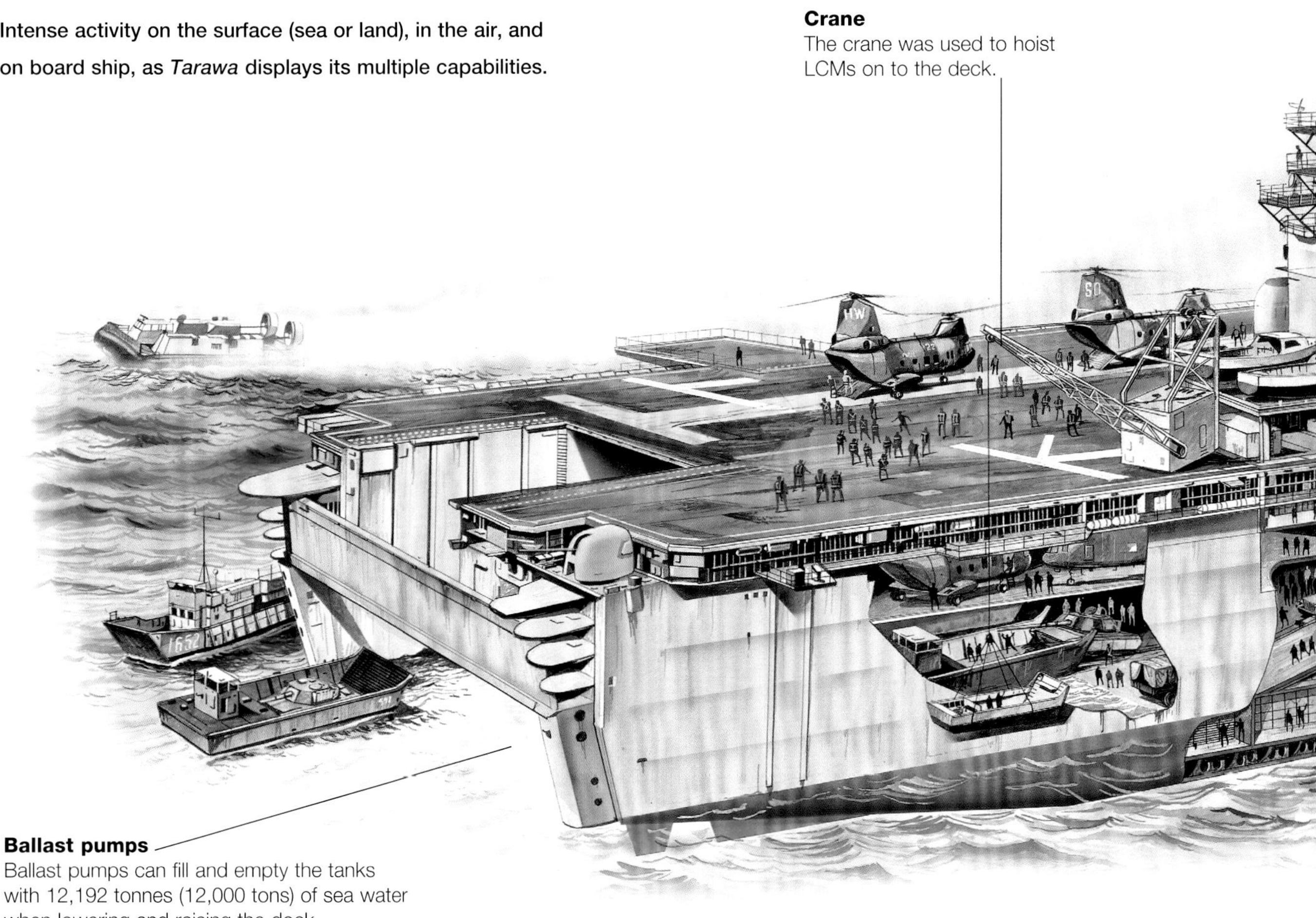

size operations. In effect it combined the features of four previous amphibious ship types: the assault ship (LPH), the dock transport (LPD), the cargo carrier (LKA) and dock landing ship (LSD).

While designed to operate independently, operations rooms and equipment to enable the ship to function as a flagship or multi-vessel command centre were included. These were highly sophisticated systems, needed to keep contact with a range of dispersed ships at sea and personnel on land, and to provide them with information, directions and commands. A tactical amphibious warfare computer system tracked positions both of the ship and hostile units and gave fire control, as well as air and sea-surface traffic control for all ships. An SMQ-11 weather satellite receiver was installed, and communication systems comprised SRR-1, WSC-3 UHF, WSC-6 SHF and USC-38 SHF SATCOM receivers.

Design requirements

Tarawa was constructed on carrier lines, with a full-length flight deck fitted with two deck-edge aircraft lifts, and a long island superstructure set to starboard, with two funnels, and

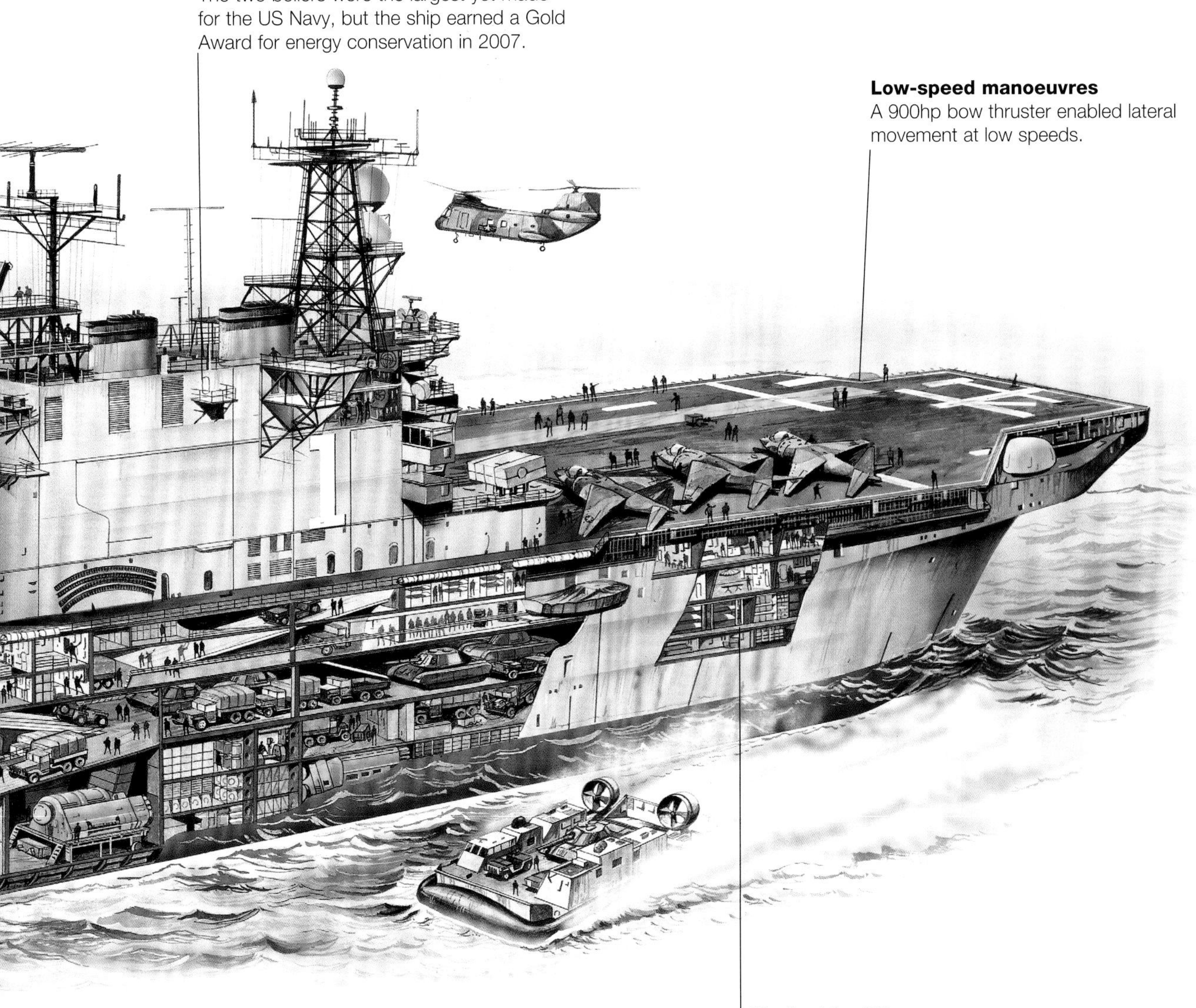

Boilers
The two boilers were the largest yet made for the US Navy, but the ship earned a Gold Award for energy conservation in 2007.

Low-speed manoeuvres
A 900hp bow thruster enabled lateral movement at low speeds.

Medical facilities
A 300-bed hospital was installed, with four operating rooms and three dental surgery rooms.

supporting two masts for the multiplicity of communications and sensor gear carried. The hull sides were vertical for two-thirds of the ship's length towards the stern to hold a well-deck with a stern gate. This allowed for the transport and launching of four LCU 1610 landing craft. Bunk

Specification

Dimensions:	Length: 250m (820ft); beam: 32m (106ft); draught: 7.9m (26ft)
Displacement:	40,030 tonnes (39,400 tons); 40,673 tonnes (40,032 tons) full load
Propulsion:	2 boilers, 2 geared steam turbines, 2 shafts; 57,419kW (77,000shp)
Speed:	24 knots (44.4km/h; 27.6mph)
Range:	10,000nm (19,000km; 12,000 miles) at 20 knots (37km/h; 23mph)
Armament:	2 8-cell Mk 25 Sea Sparrow BPDMS launchers, Mk 49 RAM missile system, 2 Vulcan Phalanx CIWS mountings, 6 25mm automatic cannon.
Aircraft:	43
Complement:	960

***Tarawa* carried up to eight AV-8B Harrier II V/STOL planes in addition to helicopters, on missions to the Persian Gulf and other world trouble spots. The sea-stained hull sides suggest a long deployment is close to ending.**

accommodation had to be provided for 1703 Marines, their vehicles and stores. Most of the interior of the hull was a vast multi-level warehouse, with the elevators set on the centreline, and a system of conveyor belts and monorails to transport items in palletized loads for easy stacking and storing.

Inclined ramps allowed vehicles to access the well deck for loading onto landing craft, or the flight deck for helicopter lifting. The propulsive machinery consisted of two Combustion Engineering boilers operating at 42.2kg/cm^2 (600psi) and two Westinghouse geared turbines, driving two shafts. Two 127mm (5in) guns were tucked to each side of the bow. In its original state, the ship was armed with three 127mm Mk 45 guns, removed during a 1997–98 overhaul, and two 8-cell Mk 25 Sea Sparrow BPDMS launchers. From 1998 it also carried a Mk 49 RAM missile system, two Vulcan Phalanx CIWS mountings and six 25mm automatic cannon.

Four LCU 1610 landing craft were carried, or two LCU (landing craft utility) and two LCM-8 (landing craft mechanized). Depending on the nature of the mission, these might be replaced by 17 LCM-6 or 45 LVT craft. Two LCM (6) and two LCP boats were carried abaft the island. LCAC air-cushion craft could also be carried. Aircraft also were carried for specific missions. *Tarawa* could carry six AV-8 Harrier attack planes, four AH-1W Super Cobra attack helicopter gunships, 12 CH-46 Sea King, nine CH-53 Sea Stallion heavy-lift and four Huey UH-1N general-purpose helicopters, but in the course of varied deployments more Harriers or more helicopters, including ASW helicopters, might be carried.

On 6 August 1976 the ship arrived at its home port of San Diego to join Amphibious Group 3 of the Third Fleet. As a new type, built for the complex operations of amphibious warfare, it had a long training and shakedown period. In March 1979 it made its first cruise to the Western Pacific. For ten years it operated in the Pacific from San Diego, with a short deployment to the eastern Mediterranean in November 1983 and a year out from May 1987 to May 1988 for a complex overhaul. In December 1990 it was flagship of a 13-vessel amphibious task force, in support of Operations Desert Shield and Desert Storm, to liberate Kuwait from Iraqi invasion. After the successful conclusion of Desert Storm it joined in the humanitarian aid effort in typhoon-devastated Bangladesh.

By July 1991 it was back in San Diego. Fresh from another year-long overhaul in February 1998, from 7 February to 7 August *Tarawa*'s three-ship Amphibious Ready Group (ARG), with the 13th Marine Expeditionary Unit, made a rapid deployment across the Pacific to the Arabian Gulf to evacuate US citizens from Eritrea, and was back in the same zone from September 2000–February 2001. All five of the *Tarawa*-class ships were deployed together for the first time, as Task Force 51, in the North Arabian Sea during Operation Iraqi Freedom.

Tarawa was flagship of Expeditionary Strike Group 1 (ESG-1) in the northern Persian Gulf in October–November 2005, and co-ordinated US relief efforts after the earthquake in Pakistan on 8 October, and was again in the Persian Gulf area, on its final deployment, in early 2008 with its Strike Group, deployed to the 5th Fleet; it paid a visit to Hobart, Tasmania on 10–13 May before returning to San Diego. It continued to take part in exercises including the multinational Fuerzes Aliadas PANAMAX in August 2008, with MH-53E Sea Dragon ASW helicopters on board.

Tarawa was decommissioned on 31 March 2009 after almost 33 years of service. It is currently held at the Inactive Ship Maintenance Facility, Pearl Harbor.

Flexible air wing

In the course of its missions *Tarawa* carried a wide range of rotary winged craft, including Bell AH-1W Super Cobra attack helicopters, Boeing Vertol CH-46 Sea Knight (medium lift), Sikorsky Sea Stallion, CH-53E Super Stallion (heavy lift), MH-53E Sea Dragon (mine countermeasures), Bell UH-1N Huey (multi-purpose) and EH-96 Puma. The CH53-E is a three-engined 'flying crane' in production from December 1980. It can carry 55 equipped troops with a 1000-km (621-mile) range, or 13,600kg (30,000lb) internally, plus 16,330kg (36,000lb) slung beneath. A new model of even greater capacity, the jet turbine CH53-K King Stallion, is currently under development.

During a Persian Gulf deployment an AV-8B Harrier II of Marine Medium Helicopter Squadron 166 (Reinforced) takes off from *Tarawa*.

Ivan Rogov (1978)

The Soviet Navy's version of the amphibious assault ship in the 1970s was the four-strong *Ivan Rogov*-class, capable of landing a naval infantry battalion and its equipment.

Naval historians have pondered over the reasons why Soviet Russia did not build a carrier force in competition with the growth of the US Navy's carrier arm from the 1960s and later. The likelihood is that several factors contributed to the decision. Although a carrier design had been worked out in 1937 and again in 1945, it never reached implementation stage. It seems that the naval command had little confidence in the value of carriers, at least in terms of their own strategy, which was primarily concerned with defence of the immensely long coastlines. In the Cold War period, submarine development and production took precedence as the basis of a global naval

The ship's design made it adaptable either to direct beach assaults with land vehicles or to stand-off operations using helicopters and missiles.

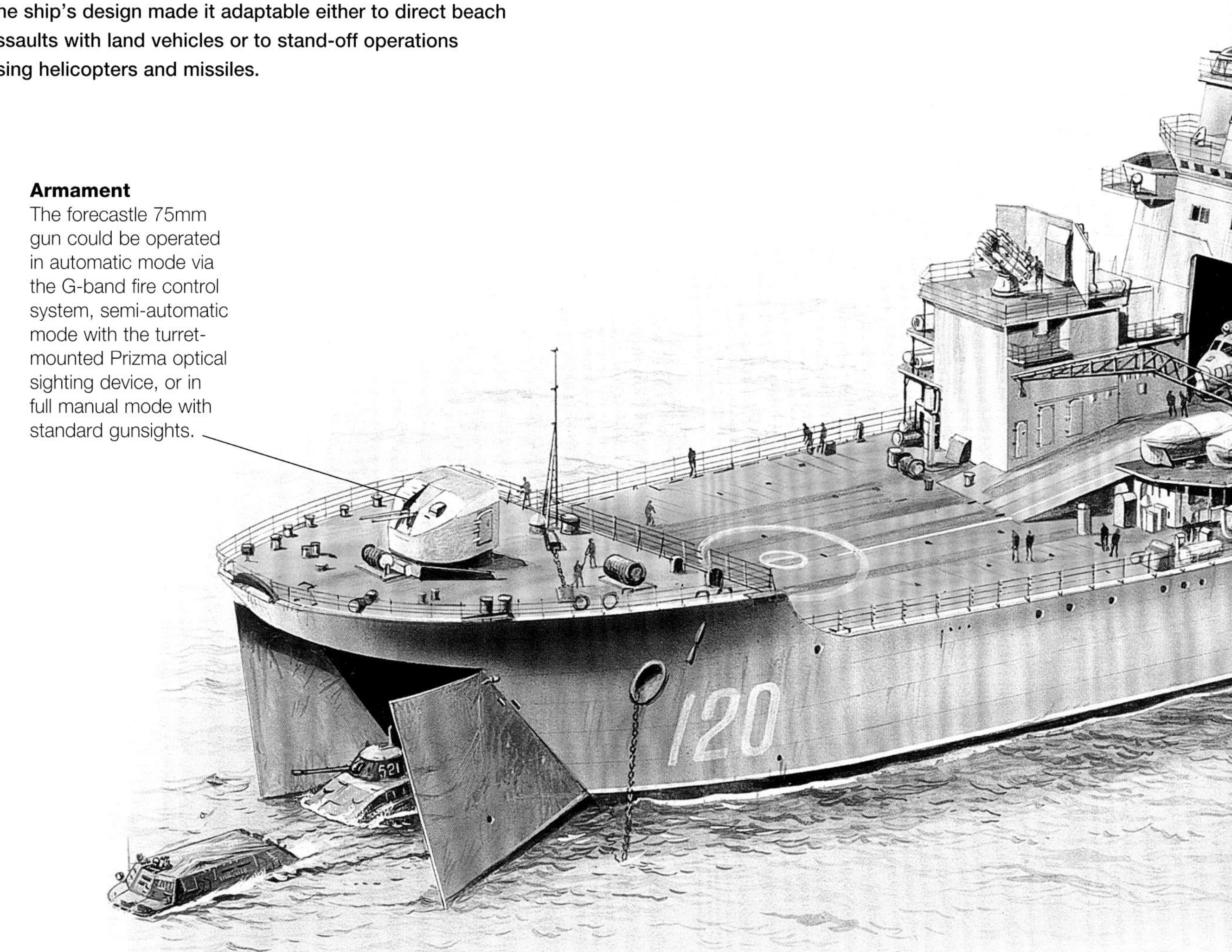

Armament
The forecastle 75mm gun could be operated in automatic mode via the G-band fire control system, semi-automatic mode with the turret-mounted Prizma optical sighting device, or in full manual mode with standard gunsights.

strategy. Also, to proceed at the same time with a carrier fleet would have strained even the Soviet Union's huge resources. Tactical amphibious operations were a different matter. It was in the 1960s that Admiral Sergey Gorshkov, who dominated Russian naval policy in that decade and the 1970s, set about increasing the Soviet Navy's capacity for operations of this kind: linked sea-land-air operations under a single command. It was not an original idea – other countries were already doing the same thing. In Russia this became Project 1174 and the process of planning and design went on quite slowly, following a first technical specification drawn up by the Nevskoe Design Bureau in 1964. However, there was much that was original about the ships themselves.

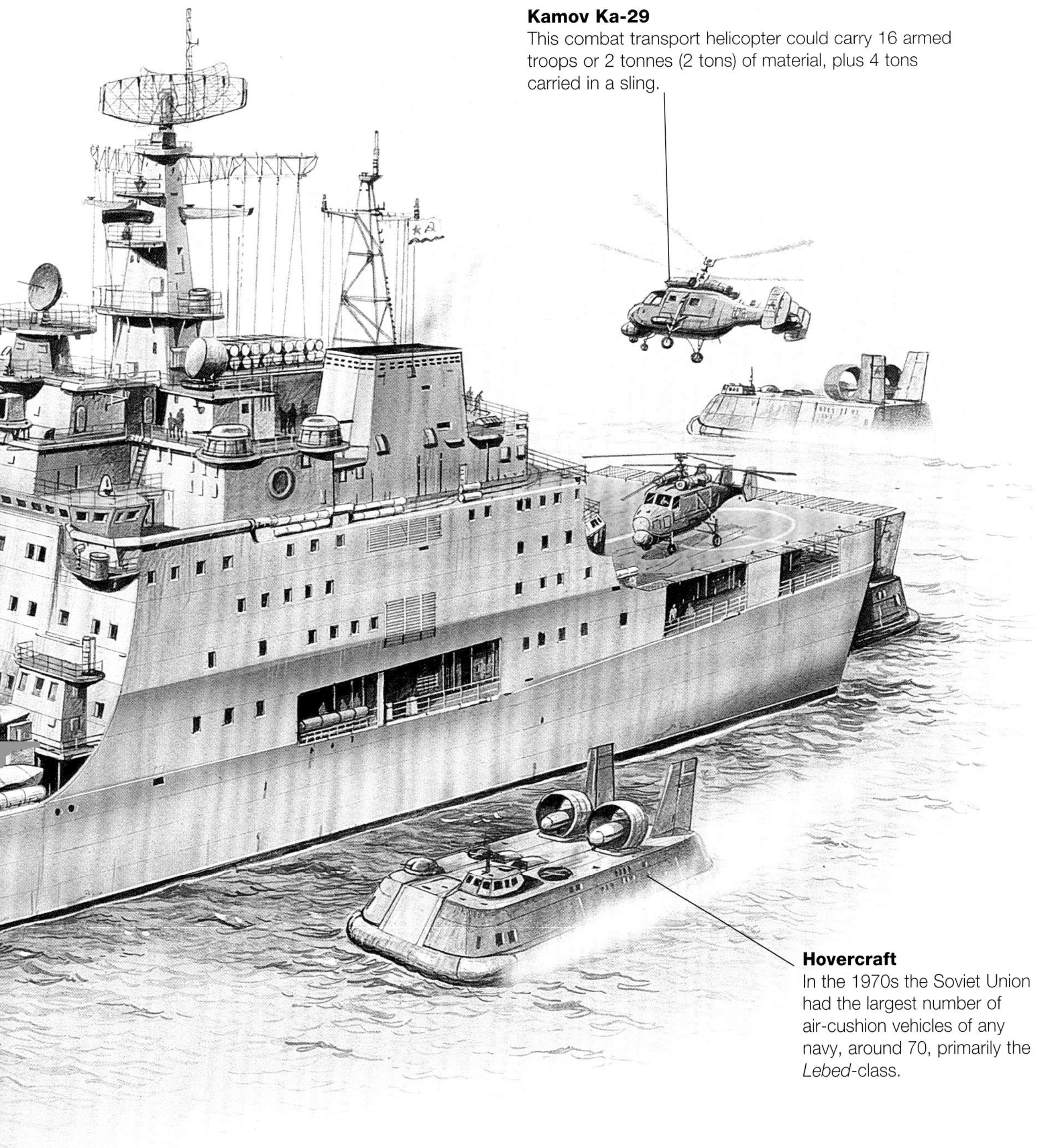

Kamov Ka-29
This combat transport helicopter could carry 16 armed troops or 2 tonnes (2 tons) of material, plus 4 tons carried in a sling.

Hovercraft
In the 1970s the Soviet Union had the largest number of air-cushion vehicles of any navy, around 70, primarily the *Lebed*-class.

Ivan Rogov

The capacities of the *Ivan Rogov*-class substantially improved the Soviet Union's capacity to engage in amphibious warfare.

Named for a former Bolshevik and political commissar of the Navy, *Ivan Rogov* was the first ship of Project 1174, launched at the Yantar Shipyard in Kaliningrad in 1976 and commissioned in 1978 as the Soviet Navy's largest amphibious warfare ship and leader of a class of three. Three times the size of the preceding *Alligator* class landing ships, in size it was closer to the British *Fearless* than the USS *Tarawa*, but its configuration was quite different. A well deck for landing craft and an aircraft hangar were built in. Bow doors were fitted, with an internal ramp leading to the main vehicle parking deck, which could take 25 tanks or a mix of tanks, trucks and support vehicles.

Hydraulic ramps gave access to further vehicle space on the upper deck as well as to the dock. The flooding area was 79m x 13m (240ft 10in x 40ft) wide and the dock could hold two Lebed-class ACVs and a 147-tonne (145-ton) Ondatra-class LCM, or three Gus-class trooper-carrier ACVs. The hangar could hold five Kamov Ka-25 Hormone-C utility helicopters or four Ka-29 combat transports or Ka-27 ASW helicopters. Helicopters could be landed on pads at either end of the superstructure. The ship's working crew was 200, and the large superstructure above the main deck held accommodation for a naval infantry – the Russian equivalent of Marine – battalion of 520 men. The *Ivan Rogov*-class were powered by two gas turbine engines driving two fixed-pitch propellers. In addition, two retractable thrusters were mounted for precise position-keeping and manoeuvring.

Specification

Dimensions:	Length: 158m (518ft 3in); Beam: 24m (78ft 9in); Draught: 8.2m (26ft 11in)
Displacement:	11,176 tonnes (11,000 tons); 13,208 tonnes (13,000 tons) full load
Propulsion:	2 gas turbines, 2 shafts; 37,175kW (50,000shp)
Speed:	23 knots (42.5km/h; 26.5mph)
Range:	12,500nm (23,125km; 14,375 miles) at 14 knots (25.9km/h; 16.1mph)
Armament:	1 twin 76mm (3in) 59-cal gun; 4 30mm ADG6-30 CIWS; 1 SA-N-4 launcher; 1 40-tube 122mm (3in) rocket launchers
Aircraft:	4 helicopters
Complement:	750

Landing and support ship

Radar systems fitted included E-band surveillance radar and two I-band navigation radars. Fire control was on G-band for the forecastle gun, H/I band for the 30mm guns and F/H/I band for the Osa-M missile launcher. The ship was designed not only to deliver and direct a fighting force but to give it active support by use of guns and missiles. Forward of the navigation bridge, on the starboard side was a separate block structure supporting an OSA-M (Gecko in NATO code) missile launcher directable at air, sea or land targets, and at anti-ship missiles. Two close-range portable Strela 3M (Grail) quadruple launchers, using semi-active radar homing, were carried. A twin 75mm dual-purpose gun was placed on the forecastle, with a range of 16km (10 miles) and a firing capacity of 100 rounds a minute. Four 30mm AK-630 air defence guns were also mounted.

The foredeck can be used to hold around 22 trucks or light armoured vehicles, or can be cleared as an additional landing pad.

Ivan Rogov and its sister ships *Aleksandr Nikolayev* and *Mitrofan Moskalenko* marked an advance in the Soviet Union's international power-projection capacity and its ability to intervene in hot-spot situations. Based initially with the Northern Fleet, they were intended to be command and control centres for limited action landings. The bow doors could have been used for beach landings in suitable locations, although in practice they were probably largely used for loading vehicles from a ramp or slipway. In April 1979 *Ivan Rogov*'s presence was noted in the Indian Ocean, along with the cruiser-carrier *Minsk*, on their way to Vladivostok to join the Pacific Fleet. In October 1980 it was again spotted in the Indian Ocean, shadowing American and Australian joint exercises. If it was ever used for actual littoral or offshore military operations, the details have been kept under wraps. A modernization was carried out in 1985, but with the dissolution of the Soviet Union the ship was permanently in dock from late 1991.

As was not unusual with Soviet warships, *Ivan Rogov* carried a variety of pennant numbers during its career. It was decommissioned in 1996 and *Aleksandr Nikolayev* followed in 1997. *Mitrofan Moskalenko* was reported as out of commission in 2012, its usefulness being considered insufficient to justify the cost of modernization, although its fate has not been made public.

Surf class

Russia's Nevskoe Design Bureau is said to be developing a new class of amphibious assault ships, known as the Priboy, 'Surf' class, and intended to enter service in the 2020s. With a displacement greater than the *Ivan Rogov*'s 16,256 tonnes (16,000 tons), they will carry from six to eight large helicopters and a battalion of naval infantry. The ships will have similar vehicle-carrying capacity to the *Rogov*-class. They will be armed with the new 'armoured shield M' type of rocket-artillery complex and have upgraded communications, sensor and control facilities. Intended to begin construction in 2018, the new class is presumably a replacement for the *Mistral*-type ships ordered from France but subsequently sold to Egypt (see *Mistral*).

HMS Invincible (1980)

The development of the VTOL jet fighter transformed this ship from a helicopter carrier to a much more potent and capable warship, underlined by its role in the Falklands War.

Policy for Britain's Royal Navy, scaled down in the 1960s and 70s, left large carriers to its American ally, but in 1970 a class of three light carriers was decided on, capable of carrying large helicopters for use both in anti-submarine warfare and in land assault and support tasks, but with anti-submarine operations as the primary aim. They had the established carrier-form hull but no angled flight deck and no catapult. *Invincible* was launched as a flat-top, but was modified with a 12° swept-up foredeck in order to fly off the new Sea Harrier jet.

Invincible was laid down at the Vickers yard at Barrow-in-Furness on 20 July 1973. It was launched on 3 May 1977, commissioned on 11 July 1980 and assigned to Portsmouth as home port. In design it followed the now-

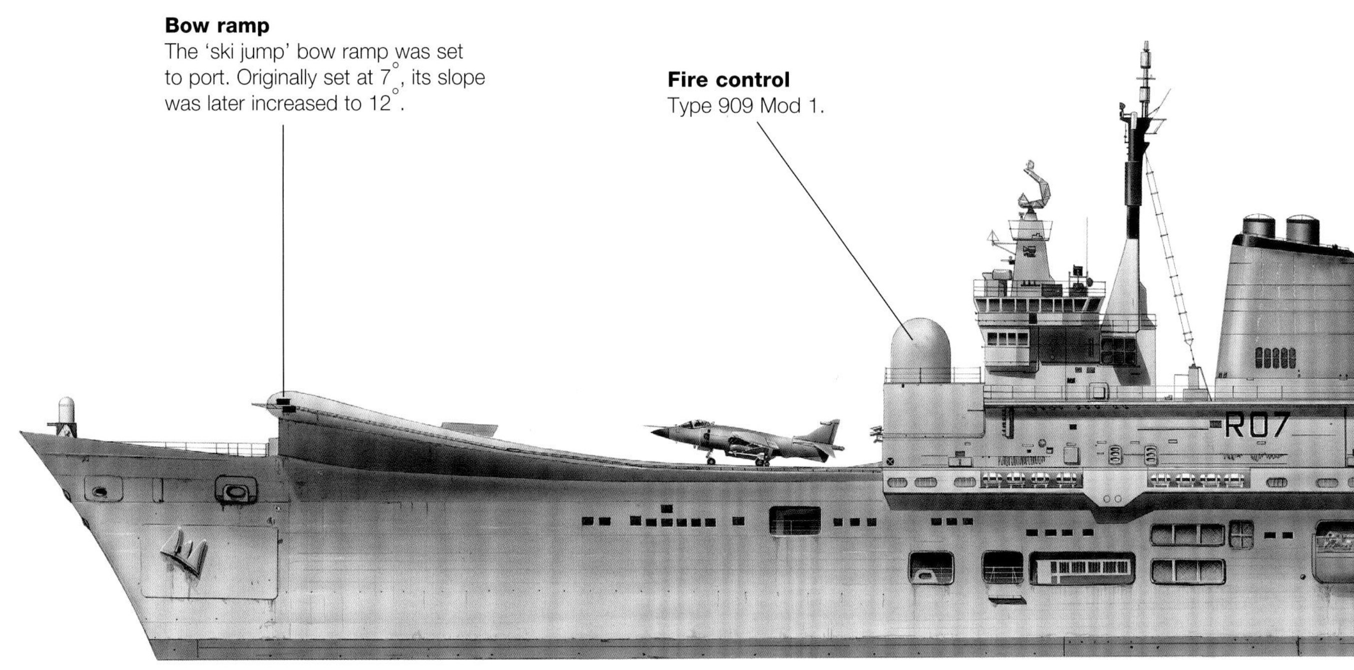

classic carrier configuration with an island to starboard of a full-length flight deck. At first, though, the design was referred to as 'through-deck cruiser.' There were two reasons for this: one was that the RN had newly been deprived of having a 'proper' new aircraft carrier built and did not consider the new class to be the same kind of ship; the other was that the initial role of the ship was that of a cruiser, in hunting down submarines.

Another cruiser-like feature was the island's great length in relation to overall length. For the first time in the British Navy since HMS *Eagle* in 1924 it was a two-funnelled ship, with a fore- and mainmast ahead of each funnel. The class was powered by four Rolls-Royce Olympus TM3B engines and four COGAG (two turbines to a shaft) gas turbines driving twin propellers. Supplementary power came from eight Paxman Valenta YP3 (later RP200) diesel generators.

Anti-air defence

Invincible was armed with a twin Sea Dart missile launcher mounted on the forecastle, but this was removed when the flight deck was extended to give take-off room for RAF Harrier GR.7/9 planes, leaving three Thales Nederland Goalkeeper 30mm CIWS mountings, with a maximum firing rate of 4200 rounds a minute, effective within 1500m (4920ft), and two GAM-BO1 20mm Oerlikon-Contraves/BAE guns. Countermeasures equipment was a Thales Defence Type 675(2) jamming

After post-1990 refits, the all-round capabilities of the *Invincible* class encompassed communication, control and command from ship to ship, ship to air and ship to shore.

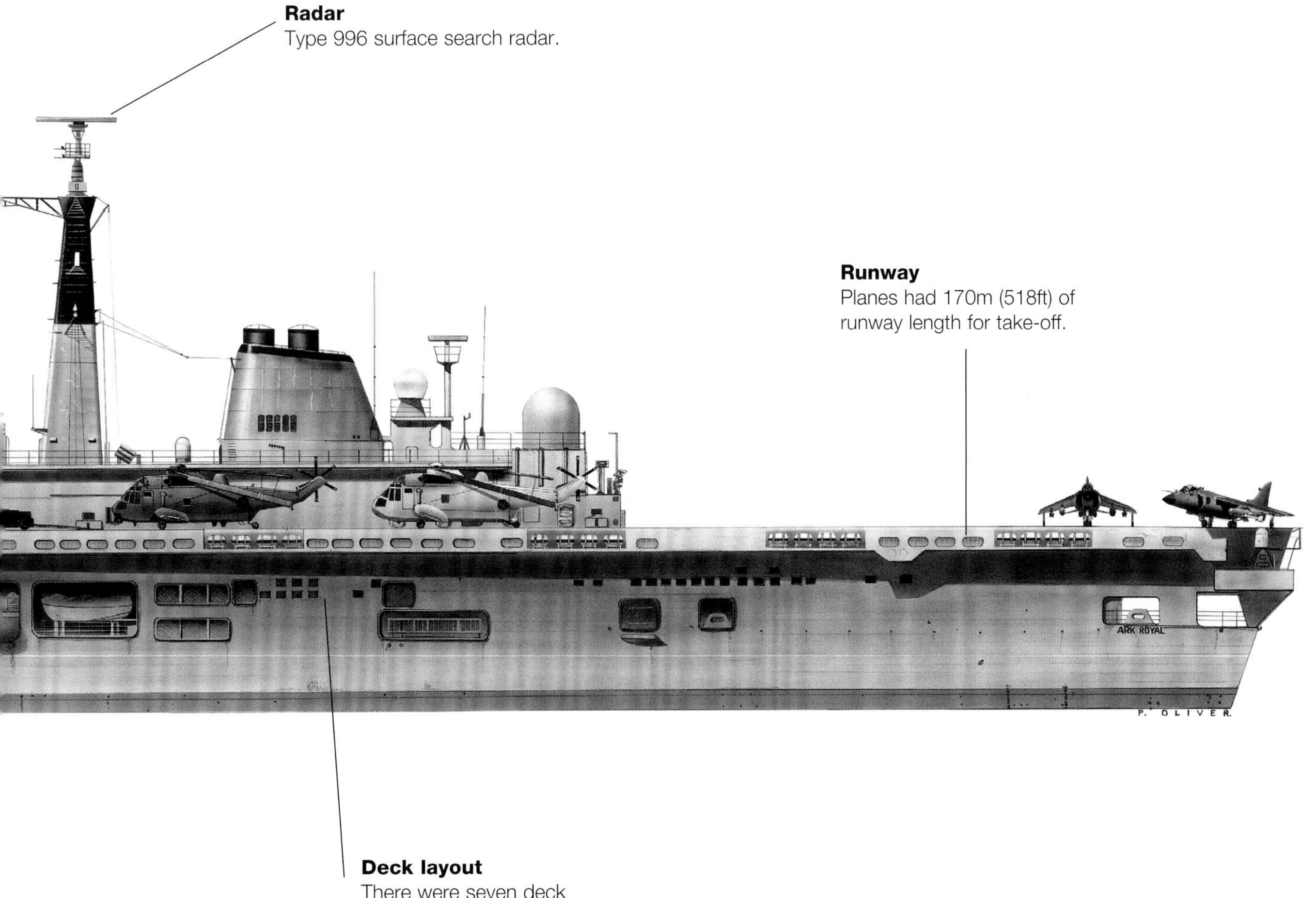

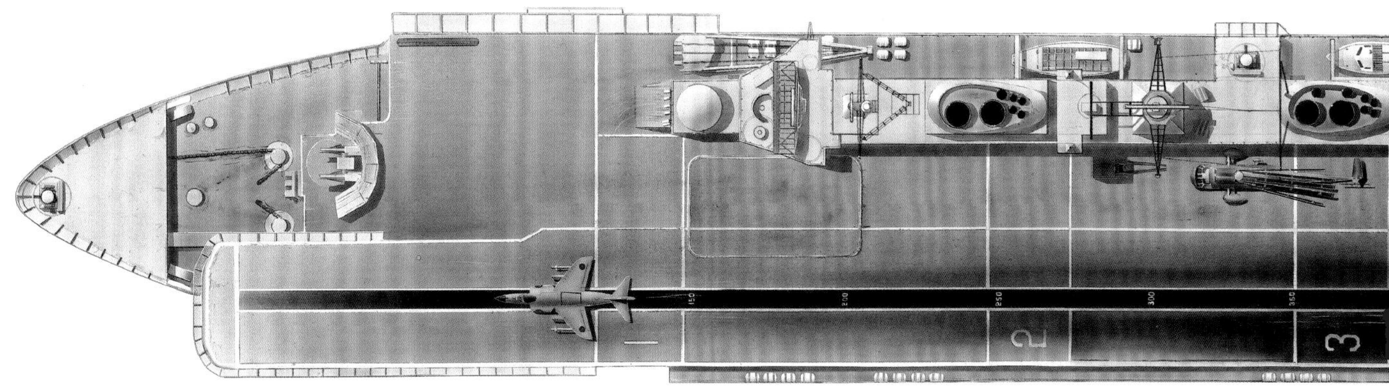

system and UAT (8) ECM from the same maker, along with a RN DLJ Outfit Sea Gnat chaff and infra-red decoy system, from eight 130mm (5in) six-barrel launchers. A BAE Systems ADIMP combat system was installed, with communications links 10, 11 and 14, upgraded in 2002-03 to feature multi-function consoles and flat-panel colour displays. BAE Type 909 G/H band fire control radar was installed while the Sea Darts were carried.

The mainmast carried BAE Type 996 surface search radar, operating at E and F bands, and BAE Type 1022 air search radar at D band. Kelvin Hughes Type 1006 navigation radar was also fitted. The two sister ships, *Ark Royal* and *Illustrious*, also acquired SPN-720 precision approach radar after 2005. Hull-mounted sonar of Type

Specification

Dimensions:	Length: 210m (689ft); Beam: 36m (118ft); Draught: 8.5m (29ft)
Displacement:	16,256 tonnes (16,000 tons); 22,352 tonnes (22,000 tons) full load
Propulsion:	4 R-R Olympus gas turbines, 4 shafts; 84,500kW (112,000shp)
Speed:	28 knots (52km/h; 32mph)
Range:	7000nm (13,000km; 8050 miles) at 18 knots (33.3km/h; 20.7mph)
Armament:	2 GAM-B01 20mm guns; 3 Goalkeeper CIWS
Aircraft:	22
Complement:	1051

An aerial view of *Invincible*. The twin Sea Dart launcher, later removed, can be seen alongside the ramp.

2016 active/passive search was supplied by Thales Underwater Systems.

The air group carried varied according to mission. Up to 24 aircraft could be carried after modification, including nine Harrier GR7 or GR9 planes. Sea King ASaC Mk7 early warning reconnaissance, Merlin HM.1 ASW and Sea King and Chinook general-purpose helicopters were carried. *Invincible* was also understood to have storage facilities for nuclear weapons.

Falklands deployment

The British government was already in discussion with Australia about selling the ship to the Royal Australian Navy, and by September 1981 a sale at a price of A$487 million, inclusive of extensive modifications to design and equipment, was agreed. The crisis caused by the Argentinian occupation of the Falkland Islands from 1 April 1982 abruptly changed *Invincible*'s status from unwanted to vital for the Royal Navy. It joined the somewhat motley fleet assembled to evict the Argentinian forces, and Australia relinquished its purchase. For the South Atlantic the ship embarked eight Sea Harriers and nine Sea Kings, with new arrivals to replace losses in the Falklands War enlarged to ten Harriers and ten helicopters, both Sea Kings and Lynxes. Commanded by Captain J.J. Black, *Invincible* spent 166 days at sea, the longest period known for a conventionally powered carrier.

From the early 1990s, the role of *Invincible* changed from ASW operations to a wider range of action,

described as maritime force projection, working in Task Force groups for strike operations at sea or along coastlines and able to give logistic support as command and control functions to land operations. Between 1993 and 1999 it made numerous deployments to the Adriatic in support of NATO and UN forces seeking to limit the conflicts in the wars following Yugoslavia's collapse. In April 1999 *Invincible* was directed from the Persian Gulf to join NATO forces in the Adriatic as a deterrent to Serbian military activity. From late 2002 until March 2003 the ship went through a refit, with the Sea Dart launcher removed and the flight deck extended. In April 2003 it formed part of the British force that joined with US and other allies in the invasion of Iraq, carrying Merlin HMA1 and Sea King AsaC Mk7 helicopters on their first operational deployment.

Invincible was taken out of commission in 2005, and placed in reserve until 2010 when the decision was taken to scrap the ship and it was offered for sale with engines removed as 'stable for tow' for its scrap value. Its sisters *Ark Royal* and *Illustrious* followed it to the breakers in 2011 and 2016.

Vertical take-off and landing

The potential of a VTOL jet had been much discussed before the Hawker Siddeley company developed a 'jump jet' working prototype in the mid-1960s, with Rolls-Royce Pegasus engines fitted with thrust vectoring nozzles. The Hawker Harrier made its first flight on 28 December 1967. Although it could take off vertically, this seriously limited its payload, and a short take-off run was far preferable, hence the S/VTOL designation. At first wholly land-based, its value as a naval aircraft was obvious, and the Sea Harrier was built to fly from the *Invincible*-class. The Harrier was a high-maintenance plane but an effective one in attack and defence, and McDonnell Douglas and British Aerospace went on to build second-generation Harrier II planes. Russia produced the Yakovlev Yak-38. The existence of this aircraft type had a direct influence on light carrier construction in the 1980s and beyond.

A Sea Harrier launches from the deck ramp of HMS *Invincible*.

USS Carl Vinson (1982)

Popularly known as the 'Gold Eagle', the *Carl Vinson* was the third of the *Nimitz*-class of super-carrier.

Carl Vinson (CVN-70) is the third of the ten *Nimitz*-class carriers. Its keel was laid at Newport News on 11 October 1975, and it was launched on 15 March 1980, the first US Navy ship to be named for a still-living person, the Georgia congressman who led the campaign for naval expansion in 1940. On commissioning, 13 March 1982, its cost was reckoned at $3.8 billion. *Vinson* with *Nimitz* and *Dwight D. Eisenhower* as the first three form a sub-class of their own among the ten super-carriers, although in the course of regular refits many features of the 'improved Nimitzes'

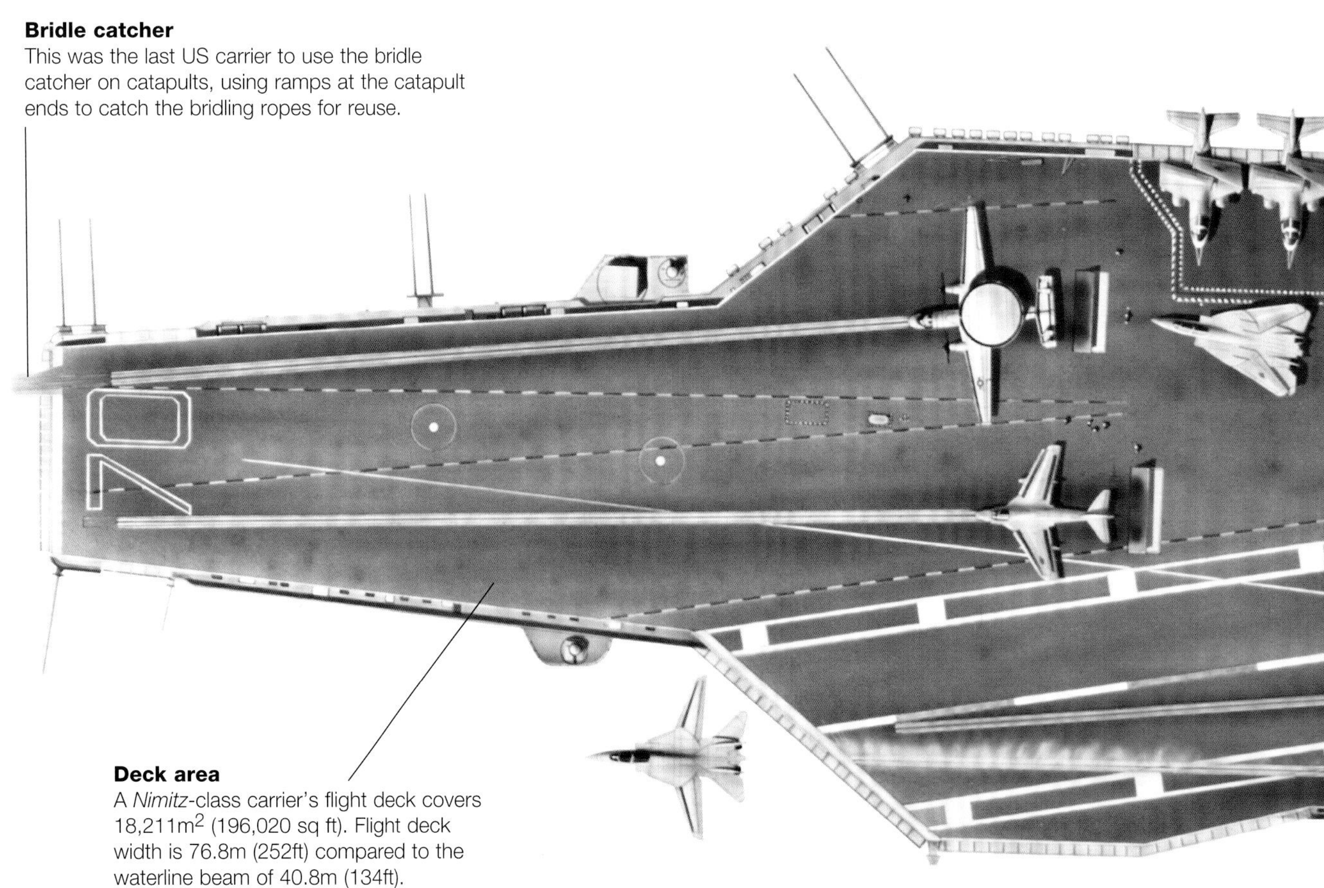

Bridle catcher
This was the last US carrier to use the bridle catcher on catapults, using ramps at the catapult ends to catch the bridling ropes for reuse.

Deck area
A *Nimitz*-class carrier's flight deck covers 18,211m^2 (196,020 sq ft). Flight deck width is 76.8m (252ft) compared to the waterline beam of 40.8m (134ft).

(1986 onwards) have been retrofitted. Standard for all ten are four elevators and four catapults, and the two A4W reactors powering four steam turbines.

Stationed initially at Norfolk, Virginia, for shakedown and trials, the ship transferred to Alameda, California, reaching its new home port on 28 October 1983 after a round-the-world cruise, with Carrier Air Wing 15, which it continued to house until 1994. It carried CVW 14 until 1998, and CVW 11 to 2003. From 2003 to 2005 it carried CVW 9, and from 2010 CVW 17. In 1986–87 it made two cruises in the Bering Sea, between Alaska and Siberia, as well as deployments in the Indian Ocean and off the southern coasts of the Middle East. *Vinson* was the last carrier to launch the A6-E Intruder attack plane in 1997. Its current

From overhead, the vast deck of *Carl Vinson* is marked out to show landing lines, catapults, lifts and parking areas.

Colour coding
Crewmen on deck are distinguished by shirt colour: blue for tractor drivers, plane handlers and elevator operators; red for ordnance handling and crash work; green for catapult and arrester gear operators and cargo handlers; purple for aviation fuel; yellow for plane directors; white for medical team; and brown for Air Wing plane captain and Leading Petty Officers.

Elevator
The deck edge elevators are vulnerable to occasional exceptional waves. Seven men were swept overboard from No.1 elevator, positioned at hangar deck level 8m (25ft) above the waterline, on 16 August 1986. All were rescued.

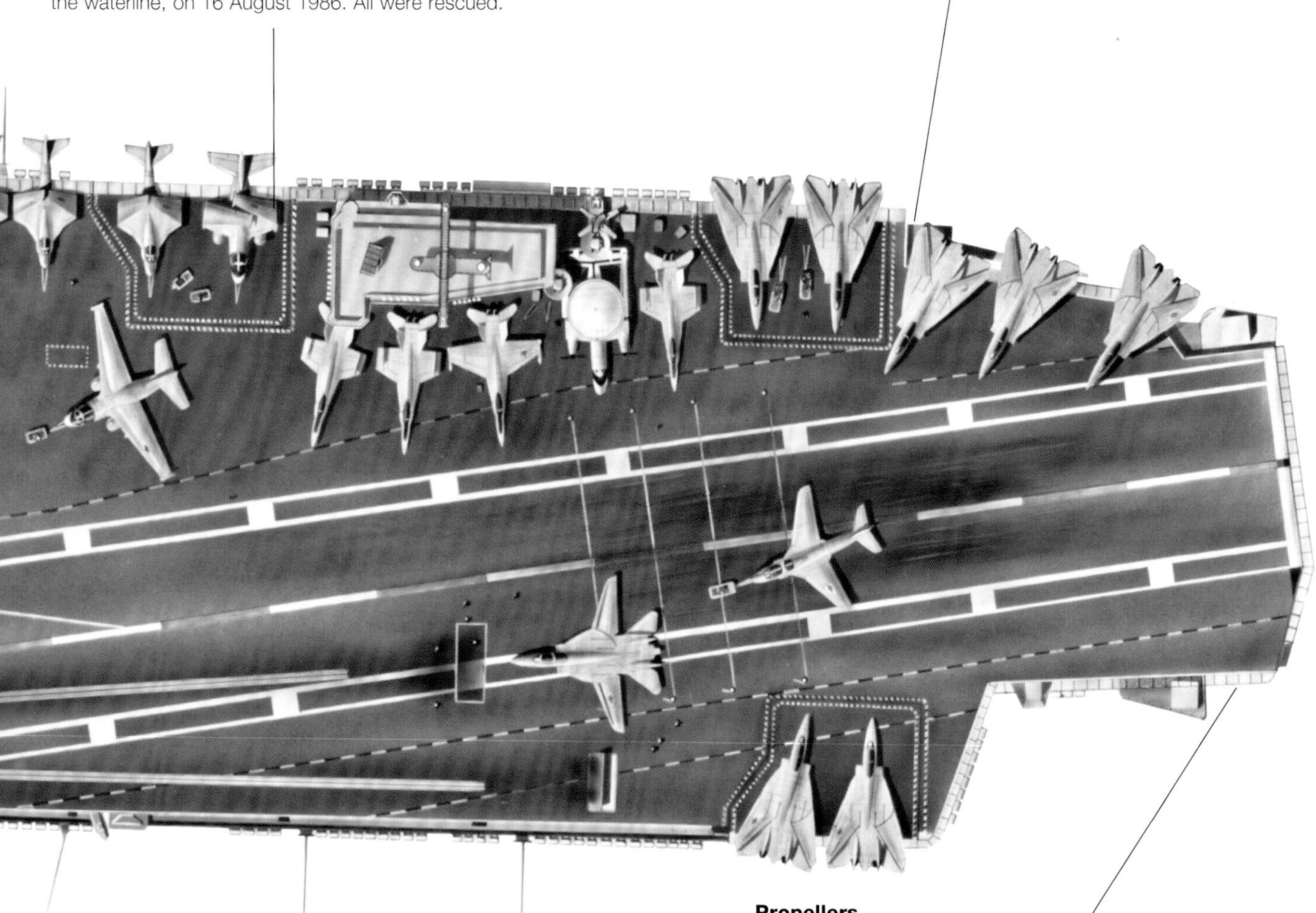

Propellers
Vinson had frequent problems with its propellers. The new design fitted in 2007, of 6.9m (21ft) diameter and weighing about 36.5 tonnes (36 tons) each, are also intended to be used on the *Gerald R. Ford* class carriers.

Carl Vinson on 'routine patrol' in the South China Sea.

Specification

Dimensions:	Length: 317m (1040ft); Beam: 40.8m (134ft); Draught: 11.5m (37ft 10in)
Displacement:	113,500 tonnes (101,300 tons)
Propulsion:	2 A4W reactors, 4 steam turbines, 4 shafts; 193,700kW (260,000shp)
Speed:	30 knots (56km/h; 35mph)
Range:	Unlimited
Armament:	2 RIM-116 RAM launchers; 2 Sea Sparrow Mk 57 Mod 3 SAM launchers; 3 Phalanx 20mm CIWS
Aircraft:	90
Complement:	5680

complement includes Helicopter Sea Combat Squadron 4, the 'Black Knights', formed of Sikorsky MH-60S Seahawks.

In a Drydock Selected Restricted Availability (DSRA) from March to August 1987 all four propellers were removed and reconditioned at Hunter's Point Naval Base. Kevlar armour 64mm (2.5in) thick was fitted around weapons storage spaces in 1989. From August 1999 to June 2000 a ten-month Drydocked Planned Incremental Availability was conducted at Puget Sound Naval Shipyard, a $230 million upgrade that included a new local area network (LAN) and a range of accommodation improvements. Three-level bunks are standard, with separate berthing for male and female crew members.

Stealth attack

During RIMPAC exercises in August 1998 the potential vulnerability of even a super-carrier was demonstrated when the Australian submarine *Onslow* approached *Vinson* without being detected and 'sank' it from a range of 300m (984ft), prompting urgent attention to countermeasures against stealth attacks. Further improvements were made

in January–May 2002 when the flight deck fittings and catapults were completely renovated and the Smart Carrier System installed, an automated technology that monitors damage control, aviation fuel and list control. On 31 July 2005 *Carl Vinson* transferred home port to the Atlantic coast at Norfolk, Virginia, and began a lengthy overhaul and refuelling process lasting until July 2009 and costing $1.94 billion, intended to keep it in action for a further 25 years. Propellers of a new design, designed to reduce erosion and minimize detectability, were fitted, the two upper decks of the island were replaced, a new mast was fitted to carry the updated communication and sensor systems, and the three CIWS mountings were replaced by two RAM launchers. Since 2010 it has been based at San Diego, pausing on 12 January en route to its new base to lend humanitarian assistance to Haiti following the destructive earthquake.

On 2 May 2011 the body of the Al-Qaeda leader Osama Bin Laden, shot by a SEAL team raid in Pakistan, was buried at sea at an undisclosed location from the deck of *Carl Vinson*. On the 22nd of the same month it was the first US nuclear carrier to visit the People's Republic of China, calling at Hong Kong before returning to San Diego.

Vinson **currently embarks Carrier Air Wing 2, with F/A Super Hornet, E-2C Hawkeye, EA-18G Growler and MH-60S Seahawk types among its 80-plus aircraft.**

Reconstruction programmes

Nimitz**-class carriers were built for a 50-year service life. This period is divided by four Drydocking Planned Incremental Availabilities (DPIAs) and 12 shorter Planned Incremental Availabilities, which would not normally involve dry-docking. In addition, a Refuelling and Complex Overhaul is scheduled in mid-life, a three-year spell out of action during which the nuclear reactors are refuelled and every aspect of the ship's systems is checked, overhauled, or if necessary, replaced by more modern versions. In the case of *Carl Vinson*, its RCOH from 2005 to 2009 included reconstruction of the two upper levels of the island, new antenna mast and radar tower, new communication and navigation systems, refurbished radar, new ship defence missiles, new oxygen and nitrogen generation equipment, catapult control mechanisms, environment oil pollution control system and enhancements to the aircraft landing and recovery systems.**

Between the periodic PIA (planned incremental availability) dockings, the *Carl Vinson*, like its nine classmates, maintains a heavy operational schedule of exercises, patrols and readiness for potential combat action. A *Nimitz*-class carrier may remain at sea for six months at a time, during which many replenishments are made.

In a move that indicates an important aspect of the future for aircraft carriers, a UAV command centre was installed on *Carl Vinson* in April 2016. Among other current drone uses, drone targets are used for testing the RIM 116 rolling airframe and Phalanx CIWS systems, but plans in development include the MQ-XX programme for an unmanned aerial tanker to refuel naval jets. From January 2017 *Carl Vinson* was deployed with its 3rd Carrier Strike Group to add a third carrier to the force patrolling the South China Sea. The group includes the cruiser *Lake Champlain* and two guided missile destroyers.

Giuseppi Garibaldi (1985)

Italy's first through-deck carrier, *Giuseppi Garibaldi*, was at first denied the right to carry fixed-wing aircraft.

Italy had two carrier conversions on the stocks in the course of World War II but neither ever reached completion. A law of 1937 precluded the Navy from operating fixed-wing aircraft, with the intention of keeping all air operations under control of the Air Force, as with the Luftwaffe in Germany. In the post-war years the Marina Militare focused its attention on helicopters, carried at first on frigates. Although in the 1960s successful test flights of British Sea Harrier vertical take-off jets were made on the cruiser *Andrea Doria*, *Giuseppe Garibaldi* was first planned as a helicopter carrier. However, final plans incorporated a bow ramp.

Laid down at the Fincantieri shipyard at Monfalcone on 26 March 1981, it was launched on 11 June 1983 and commissioned on 30 September 1985. Designated C551 and based at Taranto, it was regarded as the flagship of

Giuseppe Garibaldi was a test case for Italian naval design and construction, as Italy had never before built an aircraft carrier.

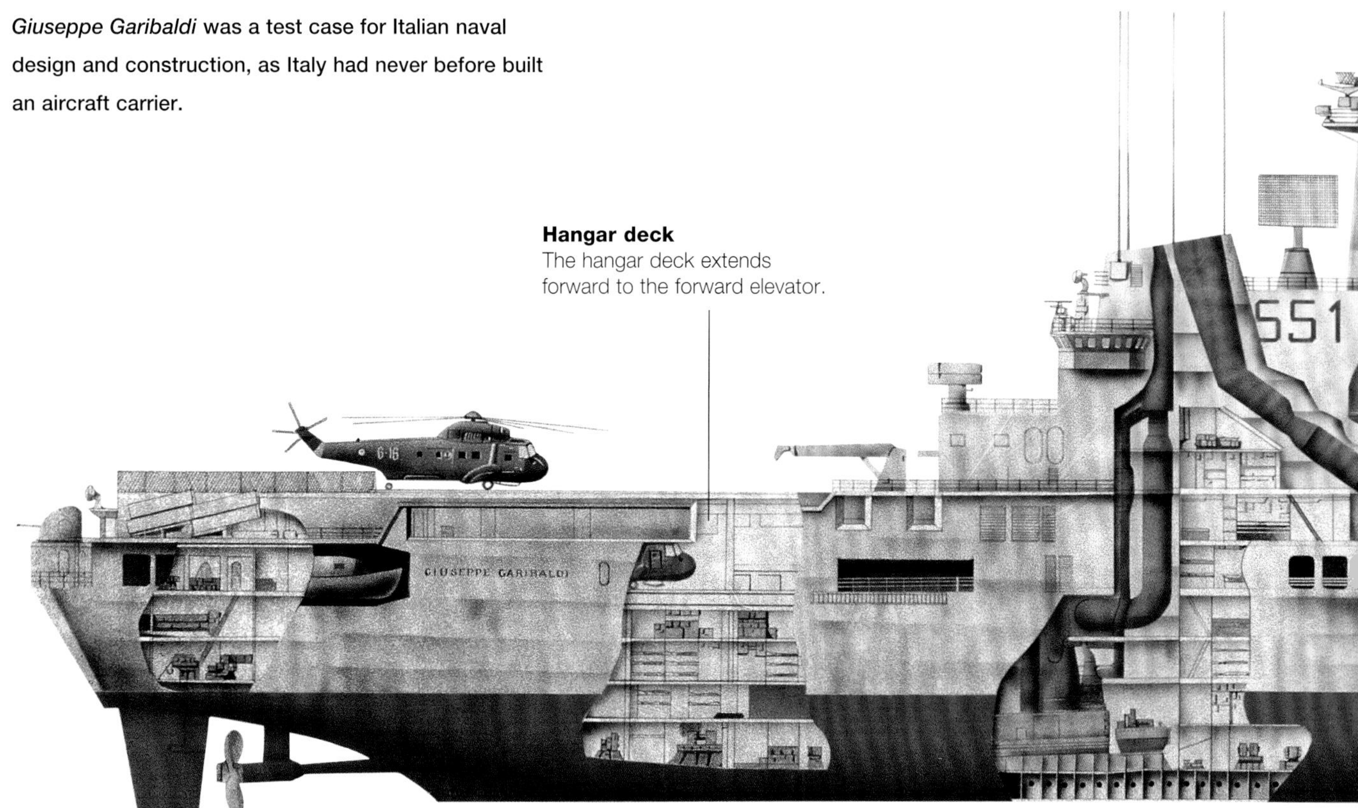

the Marina Militare until the completion of the larger carrier *Cavour* in 2009.

It was built on traditional carrier lines, with an island supporting two masts mounted forward of a short boxy funnel, placed to starboard of the flush deck, which was axial in form but with a slightly canted flight strip. Six helicopter landing spots are marked out, but the 6.5° bow ramp also provided for STOL aircraft. Within the hull six deck levels are parted by 13 watertight bulkheads to provide strength and survivability. Apart from the ship's own operations room, command and control rooms are provided for directing a task force. The hangar deck, 105m (320ft) long, 15m (45ft 9in) wide, and 6m (18ft 4in) high, can be rapidly partitioned into three sections in the event of a fire. It occupies the rear two-thirds of the vessel, below the flight deck, which is accessed by two lifts. The ship is powered by four GE COGAG gas turbines, built under licence by Fiat, and driving two propeller shafts. Six Grandi Motori Triesti diesel generators are also installed.

Anti-submarine operations were seen as *Giuseppe Garibaldi*'s main function, primarily to be carried out by helicopters, although two ILAS triple tube torpedo launchers were mounted, capable of firing 324mm (12.75in) MU-90 torpedoes. Four AOSM Otomat Mk2 surface-to-surface missile systems mounted at the stern were taken out in 2003, leaving two eight-cell launchers

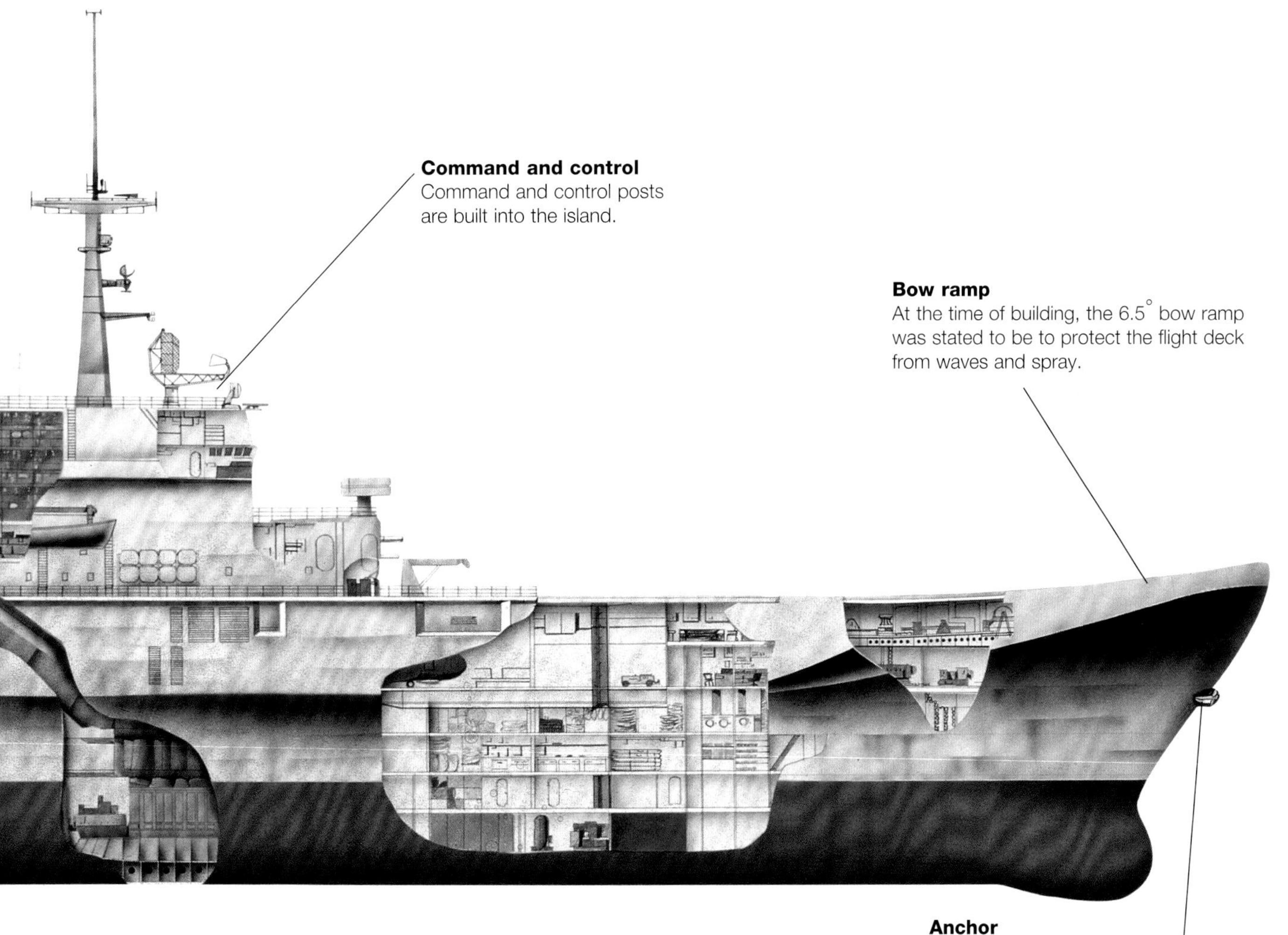

Command and control
Command and control posts are built into the island.

Bow ramp
At the time of building, the 6.5° bow ramp was stated to be to protect the flight deck from waves and spray.

Anchor
Mooring deck. The ship has a single bow-mounted anchor.

The flight control station, communications, sensory and defensive (Albatross SAM launcher) systems are all apparent, as well as the telescopic-armed hydraulic crane.

Specification

Dimensions:	Length: 180.2m (591ft); Beam: 33.4m (110ft); Draught: 8.2m (27ft)
Displacement:	10,100 tonnes (9940 tons); 13,850 tonnes (13,631 tons) full load
Propulsion:	4 GE-Avio gas turbines; 2 shafts; 60,400kW (81,000shp)
Speed:	30 knots (56km/h; 35mph)
Range:	7000nm (13,000km; 8100 miles) at 20 knots (37km/h; 23mph)
Armament:	4 AOSM Otomat Mk2 (removed 2003); 2 eight-cell launchers for SARH Aspide missiles; 3 OTO Melara Twin 40L70 DARDO CIWS; 2 surface-to air-Albatross launchers
Aircraft:	18
Complement:	830

for SARH Aspide missiles, and three CIWS mountings for OTO Melara Twin 40L70 DARDO guns. Two surface-to-air Albatross launchers (48 missiles) are mounted on the superstructure. Countermeasures equipment was two SCLAR 20-barrel launchers for chaff, decoys and jammers, and an SQL-25 Nixie towed torpedo decoy. From 2001 the French-Italian SLAT torpedo detection and evaluation system was installed. Long-range SPS-768, surface scanning SPS-702, 3-D search SPS-52C, combined-watch SPS-774 and navigational SPN-749 radar systems were all carried on the ship in 2009, together with fire-control SPG-74 for the 40mm (1.57in) guns and SPG-75 for the Albatross launchers. DMS 2000 hull sonar is also fitted. SADOC 2 combat control assures effective liaison with other vessels in international forces, run from a central operations room.

An AN SH-3D/H Sea King helicopter stands on the flight deck, during a visit to Baltimore, USA, in 1994.

Harriers and helicopters

The original air wing was 18 helicopters, Agusta-Bell AB-212ASW and 212NLA, for anti-submarine and transport respectively, and the ship also carried Agusta Westland EH101 110 ASW and 112-AEW for ASW and ASuW (anti-surface warfare) and airborne early warning, as well as 410-ASH/413-TTH transport helicopters. The original 212s have been replaced by Italian-built NH90 NFH and TTH maritime and transport helicopters. When in 1989 the Marina Militare was finally authorized to operate fixed-wing planes, *Giuseppe Garibaldi* was immediately adapted to embark S/VTOL craft, piloted by naval personnel. It could carry up to 11 AV-8B Sea Harriers plus two search-and-rescue helicopters, or a mix of Harriers and helicopters. The Harriers were armed with Maverick air-sea and AMRAAM AIM-120 air-to-air missiles.

Giuseppe Garibaldi was deployed in Operation Restore Hope off the coast of Somalia in February–April 1994 and again in 1995. The ship's first combat mission was in May–June 1999, when its Harriers carried out air strikes with Mk 2 GBU-16 bombs and AGM-65 Maverick missiles against targets in the Kosovo War, just across the Adriatic. In November 2001 it was flagship of an Italian naval group sent to the Indian Ocean and Persian Gulf in support of Operation Enduring Freedom. After a major modernization in 2003–04, the ship was redesignated as a multi-purpose command ship, with accommodation for a 100-strong landing force. Aircraft from *Garibaldi* joined in the NATO strikes made on Libya in 2011, with eight AV-8B Harriers dropping a total of 160 guided bombs. A further modernization at Taranto was completed in November 2014. Intended to extend the carrier's active life by several years, this included replacement of the propulsion and electricity generation systems, renewal of the flight deck, aircraft lifts and handling equipment, and updating of the sensor systems, with the aim of improving its usability as an amphibious assault ship. Despite this extensive modernization its principal limitation remains its small size, and it is likely to go into reserve, leaving *Cavour* as the Marina Militare's only operational carrier. *Cavour* has been adapted to carry the Lockheed-Martin F-35C Lightning S/TOVL fighter.

MU 90 torpedo

This is a French-Italian project for anti-submarine warfare. Weighing 304kg (670lb), 2.85m (9ft 6in) long and with a diameter of 324mm (12.75in), it can also be launched from fast-moving aircraft. A pump jet motor makes it virtually undetectable at low speed, with a range of 23km (14.3 miles), or 10km (6.25 miles) at its maximum speed of 50 knots (93km/h; 58mph). Equipped for active/passive acoustic homing, it is claimed to be capable of locating and destroying immobile vehicles on the seabed. An anti-torpedo version, MU-90 Hard Kill, has also been developed. As a weapon, the MU 90 compares with the American Mk 4, the British Sting Ray, the Chinese Yu-7 and the Russian APR-3E torpedoes.

Principe de Asturias (1988)

Its name going back in naval history to the Spanish Armada in 1588, this STOVL carrier was the Spanish Navy's flagship from 1988 to 2013.

The Spanish Navy's first fixed-wing carrier was *Dedalo,* ex-USS *Cabot* (CVL-28), acquired on loan from the USA in August 1967 and formally purchased in 1972. Used originally for ASW helicopter duties, it was converted to carry Harrier jump jets in 1972 but was never really suitable for jet aircraft, and was retired in 1989 after *Principe de Asturias* came into service. The new carrier, originally to be named *Almirante Carrero Blanco* after a close associate of the Spanish dictator Francisco Franco, instead received a name celebrating Spanish naval tradition and royalty. It was based on an American design, from Gibbs & Cox of New York, as a modified version of the 'Sea Control Ship'

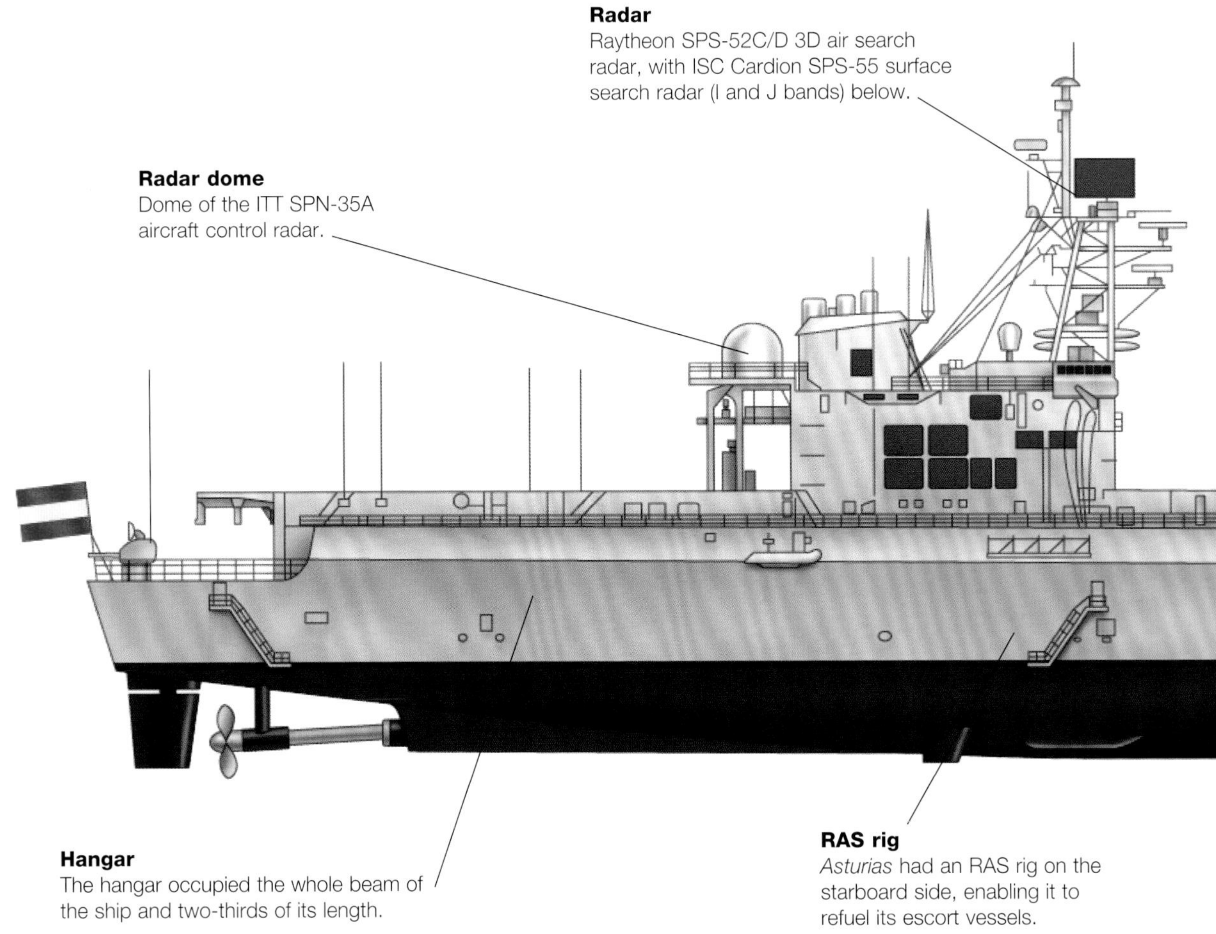

proposed for an escort/ASW carrier, which was never implemented by the US Navy but was taken up by some other fleets. In fact the same yard built the similar but smaller *Chakri Nabuet* for the Thai Navy in 1997.

Laid down at the Izar (now Navantia) shipyard at Ferrol on 8 October 1979, and launched on 22 May 1982, the new carrier underwent six years of fitting out, modifications and testing before being commissioned on 30 May 1988, when it was designated flagship of the Spanish Navy. Its final cost, reckoned at 200 million pesetas, was over six times the original estimate. In form it followed the standard carrier pattern, with a block-like island partially sponsoned out to starboard, set aft of amidships. The mast, a complex pylon structure heavily arrayed with communication and sensor equipment, was mounted directly on top of the navigation bridge. The flight deck was axial with take-off and landing on the port side, and two lifts, one forward on the island, with a retractable crane, the other at the stern. The ship had no catapult, but a 12° bow ramp helped get the planes into the air. A four-flue funnel was placed between the mast and a radar dome on a rearward extension platform. Two sets of computer-controlled

***Principe de Asturias* was planned not only to add power to the Spanish Navy but also as a model compact carrier that might be sold to other navies.**

Deck area
Restricted space on the flat deck kept the crew constantly moving aircraft about and delayed take-offs. This is one reason why the ship normally carried less than its potential aircraft wing.

Specification

Dimensions:	Length: 196m (643ft); Beam: 24.3m (80ft); Draught: 9.4m (31ft)
Displacement:	16,166 tonnes (15,912 tons); 16,967 tonnes (16,700 tons) full load
Propulsion:	2 COGAG turbines, single shaft; 34,568kW (46,400shp)
Speed:	26 knots (48km/h; 30mph)
Range:	6500nm (12,000km; 7500 miles) at 20 knots (37km/h; 23mph)
Armament:	4 FABA Meroka Mod 2B CIWS systems with 12-barrelled Oerlikon L120 20mm guns
Aircraft:	29
Complement:	830

Principe de Asturias **joined in Exercise Dynamic Mix in late 1995, in the Mediterranean Sea, with the Italian carrier** ***Giuseppe Garibaldi*** **and the British HMS** ***Invincible*****.**

stabilizers were fitted to minimize rolling when launching and landing in seas up to 4m (12ft) high.

Gas turbine propulsion was favoured at the time for light carriers, and the ship was equipped with a COGAG system, two Bazan-GE gas turbines connected to individual reduction gear boxes driving a single propeller shaft. The hydraulically controlled five-blade propeller was one of the largest in the world when installed, with a diameter of 6.1m (18ft 7in). A single or both turbines could be used depending on the speed required. In addition, two retractable electrically powered auxiliary azimuth-rotation propulsion units were fitted, both for emergency drive and for precision manoeuvring. A digital Tritan command and control system was installed with Link 11 and Link

14 Naval Tactical Display data terminals for reception and transmission. The armament was four FABA Meroka Mod 2B CIWS systems, with FABA SPG-M2B tracking radar and Indra thermal imaging, firing 12-barrelled Oerlikon L120 20mm (.78in) guns. Two were mounted on the stern deck and one each to port and starboard of the flight deck. For countermeasures the ship carried a Lockheed Martin Sippican Super RBOC (rapid-bloom offboard countermeasures) system, firing chaff and flares from multi-barrel launchers over a 4-km (2.5-mile) range. Radar interception and jamming was done with a Nettunel ECM unit. An Elettronica Argon ST AN/SLQ-25 Nixie towed torpedo decoy could be deployed.

Air wing

For the original air wing on *Dedalo*, eight AV-8B (VA.2) Harrier II V/STOL multi-purpose attack planes were ordered, with a further four in 1980 and 12 additions delivered for *Principe de Asturias* between 1987 and 1988. They carried AIM-9L Sidewinder and AIM-120 AMRAAM air-to-air missiles and AGN-65E Maverick air-to-ground missiles. SH-60B Seahawk ASW helicopters were also part of the air wing. The Spanish Harriers were known as Matadors, although the second batch of four supplied in 1980 were unofficially referred to as Cobras. In 1996 a further eight AV-8B+ jets joined the squadron. Normal aircraft complement was 24, although often fewer were carried. With deck parking another 13 could be carried, although it was rare, if ever, that the ship embarked so many. Later the normal mix was formed of up to 12 AV-B planes, two SH-60B, up to four Agusta Bell 212 ASW (at least one always carried in order to mount search and rescue missions) and 10 SH-3H Sea King helicopters.

The carrier was based at Rota Naval Station, also HQ of 9 Escuadrilla of Spanish Naval Aviation, on the southern coast. Considered as primarily suitable for ASW operations, as well as limited strike action, it was not extensively used but took part in numerous NATO exercises in the Atlantic and the Mediterranean, including one in 1996 when it, with the British *Invincible* and Italian *Giuseppe Garibaldi,* formed a light carrier squadron in mock combat with American and French units. It was estimated to cost around €100 million a year to maintain *Asturias* in service with its air wing. It was decommissioned in February 2013, but has not been disposed of, and reports have occasionally been made of interest from other navies, including those of Indonesia and the Philippines and even Angola.

Design principles

The Sea Control Ship (SCS) design on which *Principe de Asturias* was based was a 1970s concept of the US Navy. Proposed by Admiral Elmo Zumwalt, then Chief of Naval Operations, it envisaged a relatively small ship that could be built at low cost and be used for a variety of purposes, including convoy control and escort duties, protection of fleet replenishment craft and some combat situations, where its limited avionics capacity would still be strong enough to be effective. Eight could be built for the cost of one large fleet carrier. In the end, however, the concept, although much debated, was not pursued by the United States. Instead, the programme of large carriers was complemented by the building of tactical amphibious assault ships.

Principe de Asturias at Pinto Wharf, Grand Harbour, Malta on 16 March 2007, with a mix of fixed-wing and rotary aircraft on board.

Admiral Kuznetsov (1995)

Flagship of Russia's fleet, the ship's original purpose was to provide support for submarines against air attack, but it is now also used on power-projection missions.

Project 1143.5, run by the Nevskoye Planning & Design Bureau, was the programme that would produce the Soviet Union's first carrier. Described as an 'aviation cruiser' to indicate a wider range of capabilities than an aircraft carrier, although the designation also enables it to pass through the Bosphorus (a route not permitted to aircraft carriers exceeding 15,240 tonnes; 15,000 tons by international agreement), this ship is the first of a class of two. One, *Varyag*, was sold by Ukraine to China, where it was refurbished and rearmed as *Liaoning*. A third, of

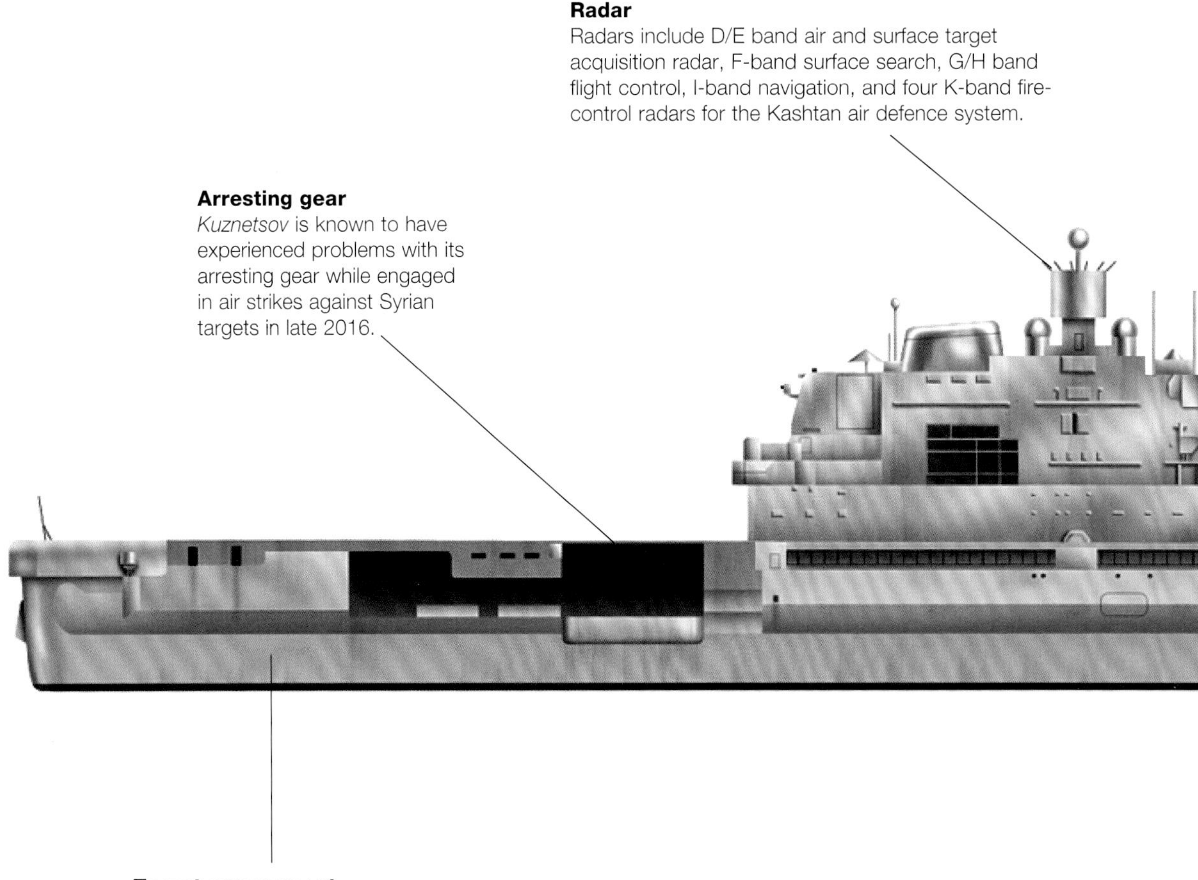

markedly greater size and different design, including nuclear propulsion, *Ulyanovsk*, was scrapped on the stocks in 1992. Essentially, the purpose of *Admiral Kuznetsov* was to provide supporting cover for Russian missile submarines against air attack, although also capable of action against surface and sub-surface craft.

Northern Fleet

The design passed through successive stages of enlargement before the ship was built at the Nikolayev South Yard in Ukraine (then part of the Soviet Union). Laid down on 22 February 1983, it was launched on 5 December 1985 and its carrier's first outing in service was in October 1989. Its name was finally confirmed on 4 December 1989 after several previous names including *Riga* and *Leonid Brezhnev*, and it was commissioned on 21 January 1991. However, it does not appear to have become a fully operational part of the Northern Fleet until 1995.

The hull design is an enlarged version of the *Kiev*-class. It has a through deck with starboard island and a distinctly angled landing deck with arrester gear. There is a 12° bow ramp but no catapult is fitted, giving a STOBAR configuration. Total flight deck area is 14,700m^2 (158,229sq ft). Two lifts are fitted, both to starboard. Mechanically it is a traditional ship, with eight turbo-pressurized boilers feeding steam to four turbines, each driving a fixed-pitch propeller.

Radar gear comprises I-band navigation, D/E band air and surface targeting, F-band surface search, and

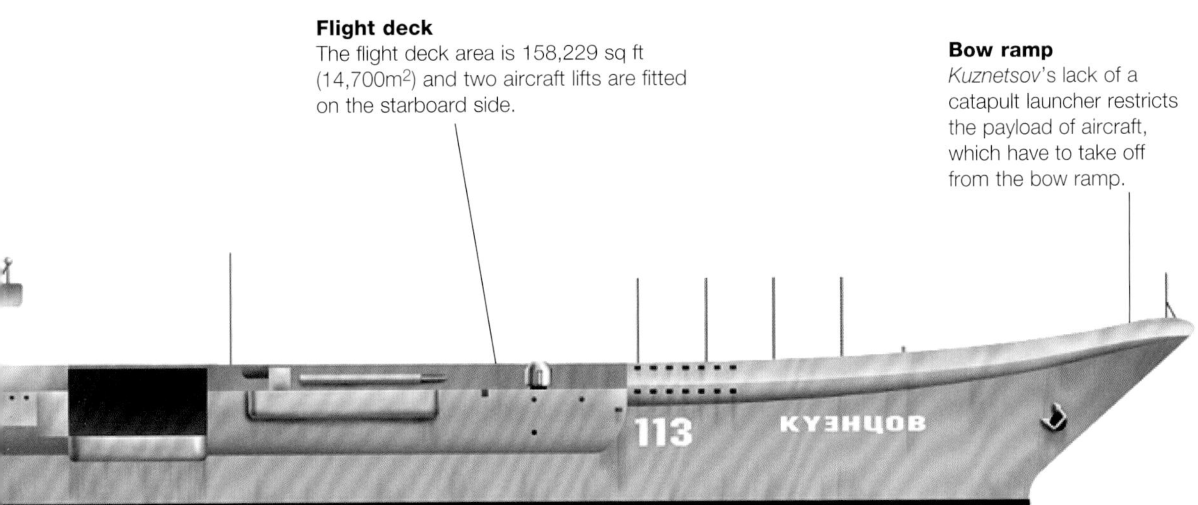

Like some other warships dating back to the Cold War period, *Admiral Kuznetsov* has been adapted for the requirements of twenty-first century naval policy and practice.

Admiral Kuznetsov

The Sukhoi Su-33 is a naval version of the land-based Su-27: a single-seat multi-role aircraft. It has been in service since 1994. Its home base is with the 279th Shipborne Fighter Aviation Regiment (KIAP) at Severomorsk.

G/H band flight control. For a time Skywatch 3D radar was fitted. The ASW defence/offence arm is a UDAV-1 system intended to divert and destroy torpedoes as well as to depth-charge submarines and UVs with 111SG projectiles within a range of 3000m (9,840ft) and to a depth of 600m (1830ft). It can also launch mines (Type 111SZ) and 111SO diverter missiles. Hull-mounted search and attack sonars, operating at medium and low frequency, assist. A 12-launcher Granit anti-ship missile system is installed, firing SS-N-19 missiles coded Shipwreck by NATO, as well as a Klinok air defence system with 24 vertically mounted launchers controlled by a multi-channel, autonomously steered phased array radar. Its Kashtan air-sea defence system, controlled by four radars, is a multi-functional CIWS intended to combat air and low-level incoming missiles or planes at short range, up to 8km (5 miles) with either rapid-fire 30mm (1.18in) twin gun or laser-controlled missiles. In addition, the ship carries six AK630 AD 30mm AA guns. Unlike Western carriers, *Kuznetsov* thus has a strong self-defence capacity.

Specification

Dimensions:	Length: 305m (1001ft); Beam: 72m (236ft); Draught: 11m (36ft)
Displacement:	53,848 tonnes (53,000 tons); 59,537 tonnes (58,600 tons) full load
Propulsion:	8 boilers, 4 turbines, 4 shafts; 149,000kW (200,000shp)
Speed:	29 knots (54km/h; 33mph)
Range:	8000nm (14,800km; 9200 miles)
Armament:	12-launcher Granit anti-ship SS-N-19 missiles; 24 vertically mounted Klinok launchers; Kashtan multi-functional CIWS; 6 AK630 AD 30mm AA guns
Aircraft:	50
Complement:	2100

Short take-off and vertical landing

The first aircraft carried were Sukhoi Su-27K, MiG 29K and Yakovlev Yak-41M. Later these were replaced by Yak-43 and Su-33. The Sukhoi Su-33 naval aircraft (Flanker-D in NATO code) has short, broad wings and reinforced undercarriage specifically for STOVL launches and landing. It carries a 30mm cannon and six R-27 and 4 R-73 air-to-air missiles, plus other bombs and rockets according to mission. Helicopters may include Ka-31 airborne early warning craft, Ka-27-Ld Helix, Ka-27 PLO and Ka-27-S. The Ka-27 ASW helicopters are equipped with surface search radar, dipping sonar, sonobuoys and magnetic anomaly detectors.

In 1991 during the break-up of the Soviet Union, the ship was removed from the Ukrainian Black Sea port of Feodosia to steam around the coasts of Europe and join the Northern Fleet at Severomorsk, which remains its home port, in the same region as Russia's main submarine bases. In August 2000 it took part in the unsuccessful rescue operation of the damaged nuclear submarine *Kursk*. An overhaul was done in 2015 to update its capabilities. It was not a stranger to the

A port beam view of *Admiral Kuznetsov* in the Mediterranean south of Italy, making its way back to the Northern Fleet base at Severomorsk.

Russian resurgence

The deployment of *Admiral Kuznetsov* to assist the Assad Syrian government forces in late 2016 raised international speculation on Russia's future use of carriers, as it reasserts its status as a global power. Modernization of the *Kiev*-class *Admiral Gorshkov* for the Indian Navy has sharpened Russian experience in up-to-date carrier design. The Krylovsky State Research Centre at St Petersburg has embarked on a super-carrier design, Project 23000E Shtorm, which would be of 101,604-tonne (100,000-ton) displacement and field 90 aircraft, comparable to the US *Nimitz*-class. Whether it would have nuclear or other propulsion is not clear. Such a project, if put into construction, would also require a major extension of docking and maintenance facilities. Any such ship would not be in active service before the late 2020s.

Mediterranean Sea, having made several cruises to it since 1995, and its first combat mission was in mid-October 2016 when, trailed by NATO ships and planes, it sailed to the eastern Mediterranean with a task force of other warships including the nuclear-powered missile cruiser *Pyotr Velikiy* and the ASW ship *Severomorsk*, plus several support ships, to assist the Syrian government in the siege of Aleppo.

After launching 420 air strikes during November and December 2016, its aircraft operating from land bases as well as the ship, the carrier returned to Russia in January 2017. Two aircraft were lost on the mission due to problems with the arrester gear. The deployment was said to have given valuable pointers to the design of a successor class of carrier.

Plans are also in hand to make a substantial modernization of *Admiral Kuznetsov*, likely to include a new propulsion system and new arrester gear, and also the ability to support Ka-52K Katran reconnaissance and combat helicopters, originally designed for French *Mistral*-class amphibious assault ships, and that carry air-to-air and air-to-ground missiles. These upgrades will keep the ship active until 2025.

HMS Ocean (1998)

The Royal Navy's only Landing Platform Helicopter is equipped for giving air support to littoral operations and for ASW warfare.

Landing Platform Helicopter designates a ship equipped for amphibious warfare by operating as a launch and recovery platform for helicopters and other VTOL craft. *Ocean* was laid down at the Kvaerner Govan Yard on the River Clyde on 30 May 1994, and launched on 11 October 1995. It proceeded under its own power to Vickers (VSEL) at Barrow-in-Furness for military fitting out, and the ship was commissioned on 30 September 1998. At that point it was the largest ship

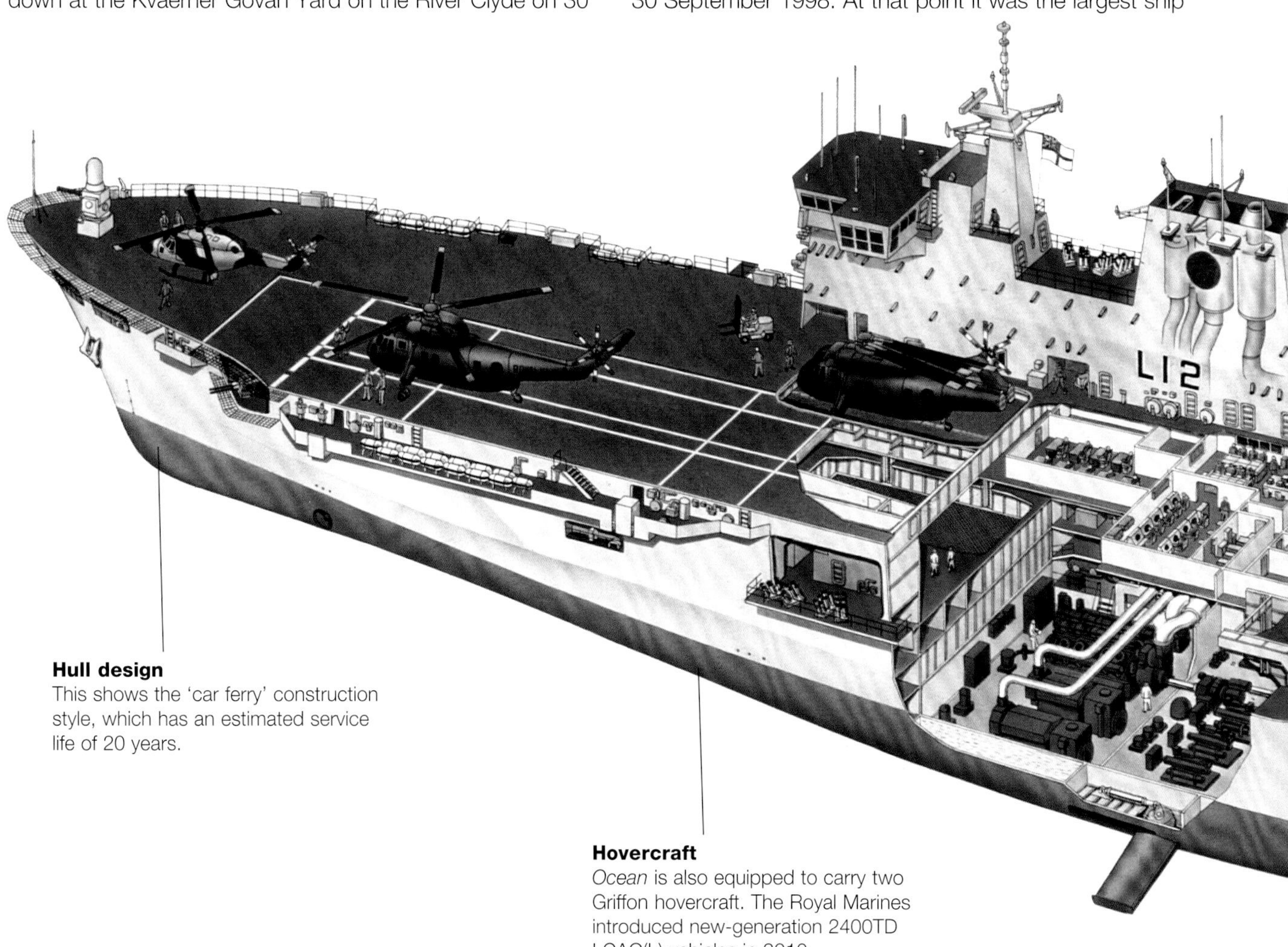

Hull design
This shows the 'car ferry' construction style, which has an estimated service life of 20 years.

Hovercraft
Ocean is also equipped to carry two Griffon hovercraft. The Royal Marines introduced new-generation 2400TD LCAC(L) vehicles in 2010.

By 1998 HMS *Ocean* was a third-generation Royal Navy approach to the design and operation of a multi-role amphibious warfare command ship.

in the Royal Navy. However, budgetary constraints had a big influence on the ship's design – construction cost was around £170 million, exclusive of aircraft.

The hull form is essentially that of a merchant vessel, with 'bolt on' features to give it some of the essential capabilities of a naval ship. These include such aspects as strengthening and fireproofing interior walls and coverings to withstand both heavy seas and battle conditions. The traditional approach to warship design is to maximize the ship's survivability so that it will continue to fight even when damaged. In the case of *Ocean*-type design, the survivability emphasis is on saving the crew. The rectangular island is surmounted by the bridge deck, and two tower masts separated by a tapering rectangular funnel around the diesel exhausts. *Ocean* is driven by two Crossley Pielstick V12 diesel engines with two propellers. A single 450kW (603hp) Kamewa bow thruster was also fitted but later removed.

Helicopter carrier

The flight deck, 170 x 33 metres (557ft x 108ft) has six landing and six parking spots. *Ocean* has carried Sea King HC4/Merlin troop lift and Lynx or WAH-64 Apache attack helicopters. It has also flown Agusta Westland AW 159 Wildcats, Boeing Chinooks and Blackhawks. Currently it has full facilities for 12 EH101 Merlin and six Lynx helicopters and can also land and refuel Chinooks. Although it has been used for transporting fixed-wing aircraft, it cannot launch them as it has neither a catapult nor a ski-jump deck. The ship is primarily a helicopter carrier but it also carries four LCVP (Landing Craft Vehicle Personnel),

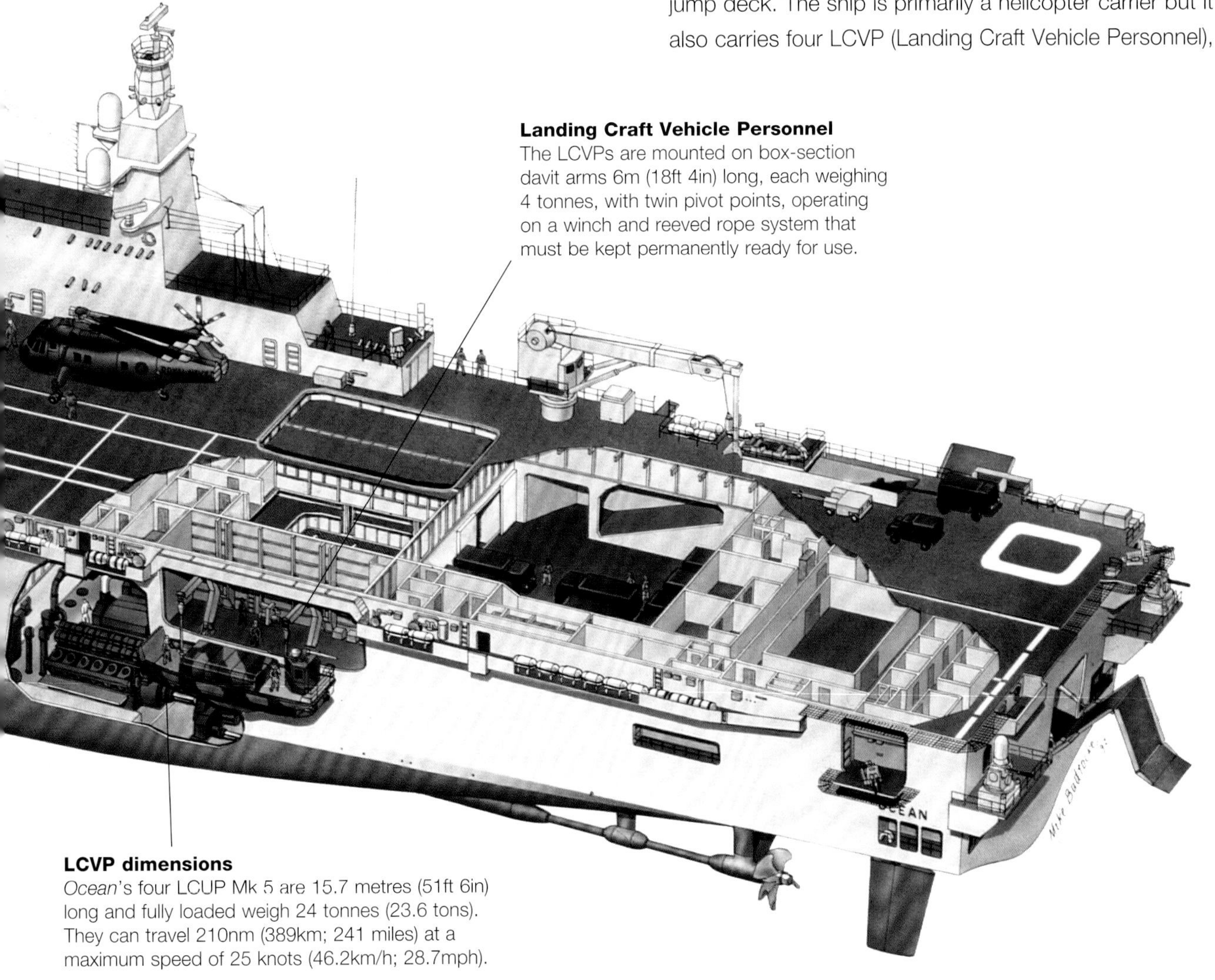

Landing Craft Vehicle Personnel
The LCVPs are mounted on box-section davit arms 6m (18ft 4in) long, each weighing 4 tonnes, with twin pivot points, operating on a winch and reeved rope system that must be kept permanently ready for use.

LCVP dimensions
Ocean's four LCUP Mk 5 are 15.7 metres (51ft 6in) long and fully loaded weigh 24 tonnes (23.6 tons). They can travel 210nm (389km; 241 miles) at a maximum speed of 25 knots (46.2km/h; 28.7mph).

HMS Ocean

High blank sides and a reduction of extraneous detail mark modern warship design in an era in which 'stealth' is at a premium and protection against radiation has to be allowed for.

with two slung on each side, and has garage space for around 40 vehicles. An above-the-waterline folding ramp and pontoon arrangement at the stern allow for loading vehicles and personnel onto landing craft. A roll-on/off vehicle ramp is also mounted on the port side for use in harbour.

Other craft on board include Mk 3 Rigid Raider craft, 8m (24ft 4in) long, powered by a 540bhp inboard engine and able to travel for 120nm (222km; 138 miles) at a speed of 30 knots (55.5km/h; 34.5mph); also the smaller 'Zodiac' type, 5m (15ft 3in) long and able to carry five troops with a range of 40nm (74km; 46 miles) and a speed of 20 knots (55.5km/h; 34.5 miles). An embarked military force of around 500 can be carried, rising to 800 if packed in tightly. Secondary roles include at-sea training in simulated combat environments and use as a command centre in tactical operations against terrorist groups where the emphasis is on raids or action within a limited theatre.

A BAE Systems ADAWS 2000 combat data system, Link 11, 14 and 16 communications, an Astrium SATCOM 1D satellite communications system and a Merlin computer link are all fitted. Weapons on board include three Vulcan Phalanx Mk 15 CIWS and eight Oerlikon/BMARC GAM-BO3 20mm guns in four twin mountings. It carries Type 997 Artisan 3D radar, Type 1008 navigational radar and two Kelvin Hughes Type 1007 aircraft control radars. It has 'Outfit DLH' countermeasures. ECM and decoy fittings include UAT electronic support measures, DLH decoy launchers and surface ship torpedo defence (SSTD).

Despite its construction to less than naval standards, *Ocean* has proved to be a versatile and effective ship with a record of constant activity. From its home port in Devonport, its first mission was to help with relief operations in Honduras after Hurricane Mitch in October–November 1998. In 1999 it was deployed to the Mediterranean for UN support operations in the Kosovo War. In the next year it was at Sierra Leone as flagship of the Navy's Amphibious Ready Group, mounting action as part of Operation Palliser, a UN response to rebel forces. On that occasion it was carrying 42 Commando of the Royal Marines, two Mk 7 Lynxes and two Gazelles of the Royal Marine Air Squadron, and two RAF CH-47 Chinooks.

In 2003 it was part of the naval force dispatched to the Persian Gulf as part of the British involvement in the Iraq War along with the carrier *Ark Royal*, three destroyers, a nuclear submarine and support ships. During the Iraq War, problems in the hydraulic and salt-water cooling systems were found with *Ocean*'s Mk5A landing craft. They were replaced with Mk 5B by March 2004. Also in 2004, between March and May *Ocean* was the first ship to test the Apache AH Mk1 helicopter at sea. A major refit was undertaken at Devonport in 2007. This included the installation of a single-

Specification

Dimensions:	Length: 203.4m (667ft); Beam: 35m (115ft); Draught: 6.5m (21ft)
Displacement:	21,500 tonnes (21,200 tons)
Propulsion:	2 Crossley Pielstick 16 PC2.6 V 200 diesels, 2 shafts; 17,557kW (23,904bhp)
Speed:	18 knots (33.3km/h; 20.7mph)
Range:	7000nm (13,000km; 8000 miles)
Armament:	3 Vulcan Phalanx Mk 15 CIWS and 8 Oerlikon/BMARC GAM-BO3 20mm guns in 4 twin mountings
Aircraft:	18
Complement:	365

Pilot training in the course of an Arabian Gulf deployment in December 2012. A UH-60 Black Hawk from the 111th Aviation Regiment gets landing guidance from a Leading Aircraftman.

chamber pyrolosis unit, compaction screw and gasifier for the treatment and disposal of 'domestic' waste. Between 2008 and 2011 the ship was engaged in a regular series of exercises with allied navies, mostly concerned with providing rapid response to emergency situations by means of a multi-function task group.

Hull repairs

Ocean's electronic equipment was brought up to date by mid-2015. Its original Selex Sensors and Airborne Systems Type 996 air and surface search radar has been replaced by the Royal Navy's new generation maritime medium range radar (MRR). Perhaps the least satisfactory aspect of the ship is the state of the hull, which was intended only for a 20-year lifespan. While the RN has two amphibious assault ships in HMS _Bulwark_ and HMS _Albion_, successors to the _Fearless_ class, they have very limited helicopter capacity. Withdrawal of HMS _Ocean_ would seem to leave a gap in the Royal Navy's capacity to provide a multi-function task group.

Royal Navy flagship

In 2011 *Ocean* spent four months on station off the coast of Libya. In 2012 the ship was berthed at Greenwich, London, as part of the security arrangements for the Olympic Games.

In 2014–15 it underwent a scheduled maintenance period at Devonport costing £65 million. It was officially named as flagship of the Royal Navy in June 2015. In June 2016 it took part in Exercise Baltops in the Baltic Sea, then in July 2016, despite having only a limited anti-submarine warfare capability, it was command ship in the international ASW exercise Deep Blue II in the Mediterranean.

On 20 September 2016 *Ocean* left Plymouth along with the LPD ship HMS *Bulwark* and support vessels on a six-month deployment to Mediterranean and Middle Eastern waters as part of the inaugural Joint Expeditionary Force (Maritime) Task Group, with a Marine commando company and helicopters from 845 Naval Air Squadron, 662 Army Air Corps Squadron and RAF 27 Squadron.

Ocean is currently planned for decommissioning at the end of March 2018, with no provision for an equivalent replacement. The new carrier *Prince of Wales* is to be fitted with equipment to support Royal Marine operations. Some expert commentators have argued for extension of the ship's commission or for its replacement by a purpose-built amphibious warfare vessel of lesser size and specification than *Prince of Wales*.

Charles de Gaulle (2001)

Flagship of the Marine Nationale, Charles de Gaulle is the only non-American nuclear-powered aircraft carrier and the only nuclear-powered surface ship in a European navy.

Nuclear-powered and nuclear-armed, the *Charles de Gaulle* is seen as fundamental to maintaining France's place among the nations and its ability to participate in high-level international diplomacy. Its keel was laid on 24 November 1987 at the DCNS shipyard in Brest, launch was 7 May 1994 and sea trials began in 1999. Commissioning was on 18 May 2001. Funding difficulties for the €3 billion project put the commissioning five years behind the original schedule. It is the largest warship of any European navy, although the British *Queen Elizabeth*-class will exceed it.

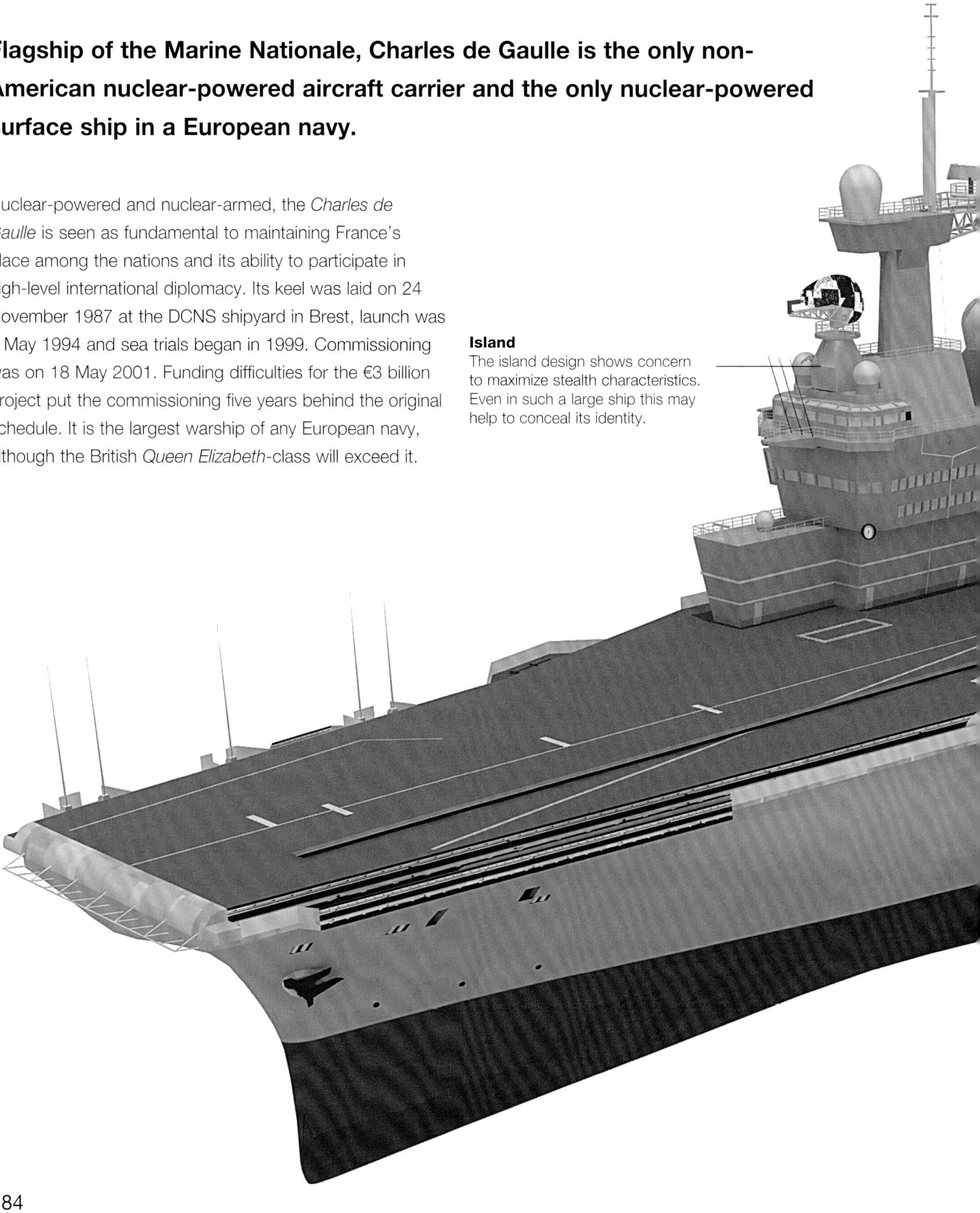

Island
The island design shows concern to maximize stealth characteristics. Even in such a large ship this may help to conceal its identity.

With no need to incorporate a funnel to vent the engines, the island is placed well forward and is notably high, containing the bulk of the ship's detection and communication systems. The tip of the mast is 75m (228ft 6in) above the waterline. Up to 800 commando troops can be accommodated, with 500 tonnes (492 tons) of ammunition. Around 15 per cent of the crew are women. The two side lifts, at the stern, can carry two planes at a time, up to 36 tonnes (35 tons), and can bring two planes to the flight deck every two minutes. The flight deck is angled at 8° and measures 203m by 20m (618ft 9in by 61ft). Two American Type C 13-3 catapults, 75m (228ft 6in) long can launch a 25-tonne aircraft at 270km/h (167mph) every two seconds. Three Mk7 Mod3 arrester wires are fitted for landings. Two French-designed AREVA K15 pressurized water reactors and two Alstom steam turbines produce propulsive power through two shafts. On-board electric power of 21,400kW (28,697hp) is provided by four turbo-alternators each of 4000kW (5364hp), four diesel-alternators of 1100kW (1475hp), and four 250kW (535hp) gas-turbine alternators.

The sophisticated electronic equipment includes two Racal-Decca DRBN-34 radars, also three-dimensional DRBJ-11 B, DRBV-26 D and DRBV-15 C low-level

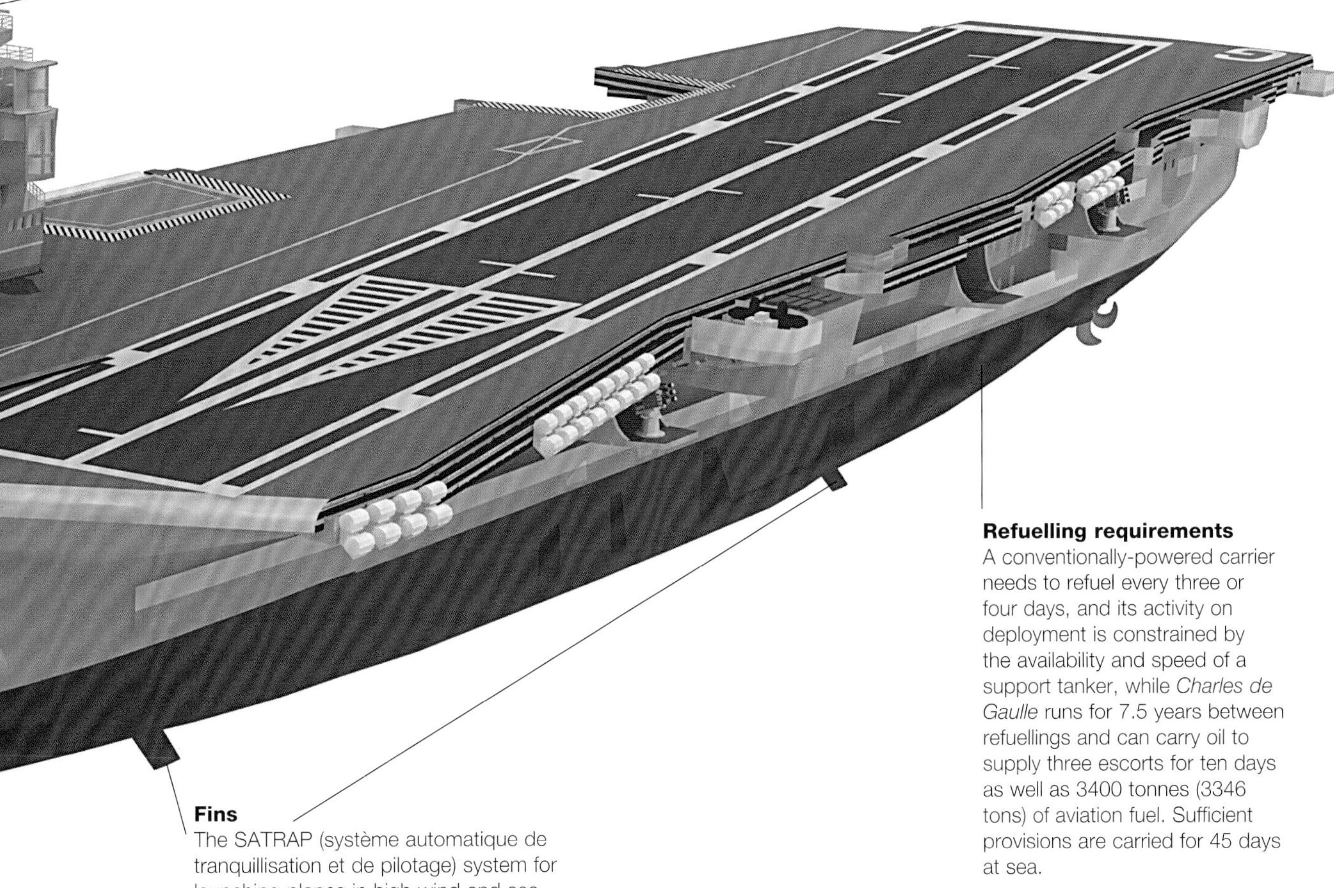

Pressure vents
Although no funnel is needed, the island incorporates steam safety-valve vents to release excessive pressure in the turbine and catapult systems.

Refuelling requirements
A conventionally-powered carrier needs to refuel every three or four days, and its activity on deployment is constrained by the availability and speed of a support tanker, while *Charles de Gaulle* runs for 7.5 years between refuellings and can carry oil to supply three escorts for ten days as well as 3400 tonnes (3346 tons) of aviation fuel. Sufficient provisions are carried for 45 days at sea.

Fins
The SATRAP (système automatique de tranquillisation et de pilotage) system for launching planes in high wind and sea conditions combines lateral stabilization with two sets of retractable fins with the movement of 12 22-tonne rolling weights mounted on rails below the flight deck, whose movement can compensate for weight adjustment of take-offs.

In some respects the most modern carrier in design terms until the US Navy's *Gerald R. Ford* in 2017, *Charles de Gaulle*'s modest displacement keeps it out of the 'super-carrier' league.

Charles de Gaulle

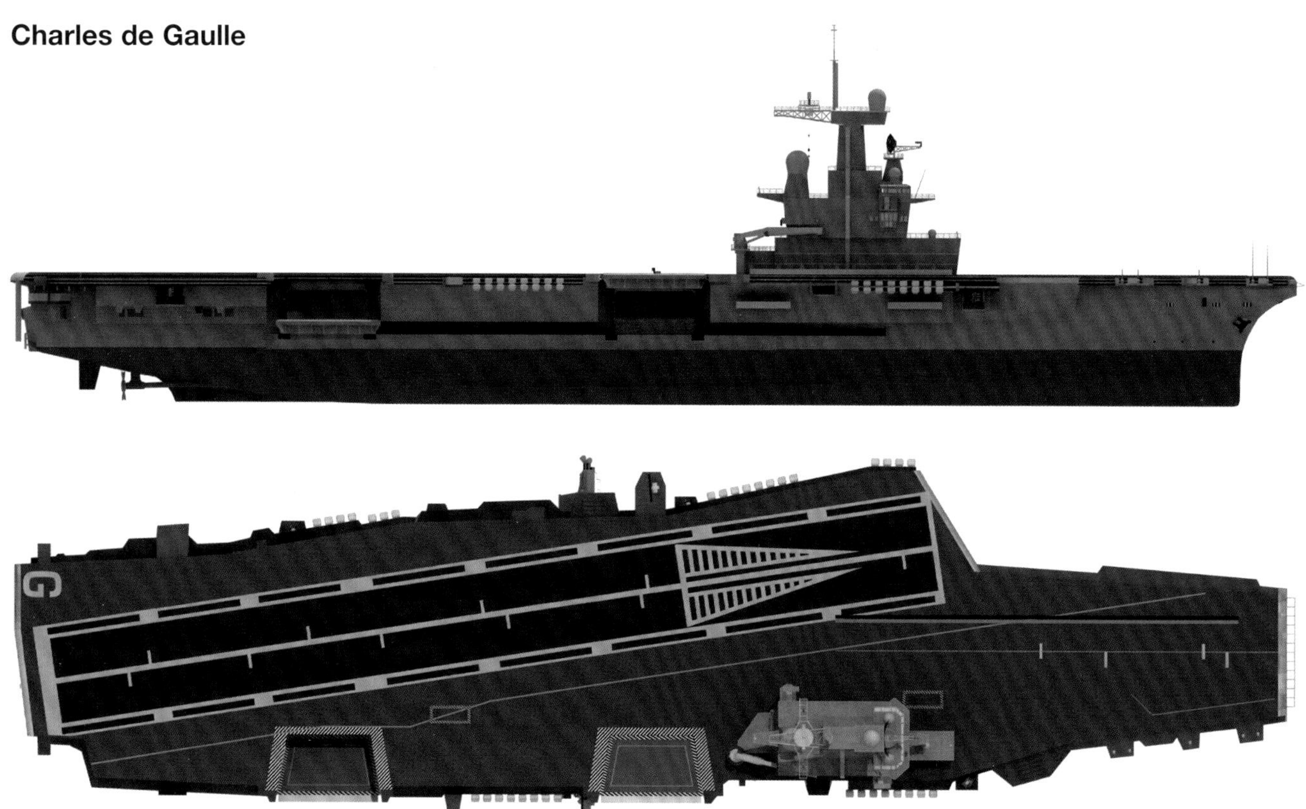

Charles de Gaulle in outline. Compared to American carriers, the island is set relatively far forward.

air search, and ARABEL target acquisition radar. Countermeasures are an ARBR-21 detector, two ARBB-33 jammers, four Sagaie decoy launchers, a SLAT anti-torpedo decoy system and ARBG-2 MAIGRET interceptor system, with TACAN NRBP-20A. A SENIT 8/05 with Links 11 and 16 provides combat information and direction. Two optronic DIBC-2A (Vigy 105) fire control systems are fitted, along with infrared VMB DIBV-2A surveillance radar. Syracuse, Fleetsatcom and Inmarsat telecommunications systems are installed. Armament consists of two eight-cell Sylver launchers for MBDA Aster 15 SAMs, two six-cell Sadral launchers for Mistral short-range missiles and eight Giat 20F2 20mm cannon.

De Gaulle's original air wing was formed of 16 Super-Etendard combat planes, one E-2C Hawkeye reconnaissance plane, two Dassault Rafale M twin-engine multi-role jets and several helicopters. Its current air wing consists of up to 40 Rafale M planes and three E-2C Hawkeye reconnaissance planes. It can also support the AS 565 Panther and Dauphin helicopters.

Specification

Dimensions:	Length: 261.5m (858ft); Beam: 64.3m (211ft 3in); Draught: 9.4m (30ft 11in)
Displacement:	37,085 tonnes (33,530 tons); 42,500 tonnes (41,830 tons) full load
Propulsion:	2 K15 reactors, 2 Alstom steam turbines, 2 shafts; 61,000kW (83,000shp)
Speed:	27 knots (50km/h; 31mph)
Range:	Unlimited
Armament:	2 eight-cell Sylver launchers for MBDA Aster 15 SAMs, 2 six-cell Sadral launchers for Mistral missiles and eight Giat 20F2 20mm cannon
Aircraft:	40
Complement:	1950

Refit

De Gaulle's home port is Toulon in the south of France. The ship has been involved in numerous missions to world troublespots, including its first deployment in November 2001 to support the US-led Operation Enduring Freedom

Charles de Gaulle moored at the naval base, Toulon, while undergoing a technical refit, December 2012.

against the Taliban regime in Afghanistan. A further four missions to South-West Asia and the Indian Ocean followed into 2007. A 15-month refit began in September 2007, which included refuelling of the nuclear reactors and the fitting of new propellers. Defects in the original propellers had forced the ship to use the spare propellers of the smaller *Foch* and *Clemenceau* carriers, limiting its speed to 24 knots (44.4km/h; 27.6mph).

Anglo–French collaboration

The French government originally planned to maintain a two-carrier fleet, with the aim of at least one being deployable at any time. The proposal for PA (porte-avions) 2 did not envisage an updated *Charles de Gaulle* design but, from 2003, the possibility emerged of sharing the design of the British *Queen Elizabeth*-class carrier, through collaboration between the Thales and DCNS builders. The design would have been modified to allow for the French ship to be a catapult-fitted CATOBAR carrier, and possibly to have nuclear propulsion. Although initial agreements were signed in January 2006, political, financial and strategic considerations, particularly the volatile price of oil, led the French government to abandon the plan for a second large carrier in 2013.

In October 2010 the carrier was flagship of French Navy Task Force 473 during a four-month deployment that took them to the Mediterranean and Red Seas, the Persian Gulf and Indian Ocean, working in concert with US Carrier Strike Groups 9 and 10, and with British naval units.

Charles de Gaulle is recognized as the largest and most sophisticated of non-American carriers and is the only carrier and aircraft group fully interoperable with US *Nimitz*-class carriers, able to support the F/A-18E/F Super Hornet and C-2 Greyhound supply aircraft. Exercises with Indian Navy ships began in 2011 before a return to the Mediterranean to participate in enforcing the UN-ordered no-fly zone over Libya. French pride in the possession of a nuclear-powered carrier has resulted in a flow of comparisons between the performance of *Charles de Gaulle* and its predecessors: in the Bosnian conflict, between 1993 and 1996, *Clemenceau* and *Foch* were deployed there for most of the time, with 35 planes launching 1500 sorties, almost all in daytime. Off Libya, with 18 fighters and a Hawkeye reconnaissance plane, *de Gaulle* launched 1573 sorties, day and night, in a little over five months.

Although *de Gaulle* is slower than *Clemenceau*, it can attain a speed of 20 knots (37km/h; 23mph) from zero in four minutes, full speed within seven minutes and maintain its maximum 27 knots (50km/h; 31mph) indefinitely. From 2015 the carrier has made three deployments to conduct operations against Islamic State (ISIS or Daesh) targets in response to terrorist attacks both in mainland France and in the Middle East. With scheduled refits, it is expected to have a working life of 40 years.

USS Ronald R. Reagan (2003)

Flagship of the world's largest navy, this huge carrier displays a number of alterations and additions to the earlier ships of the *Nimitz*-class.

Ninth ship of the Nimitz-class, *Ronald R. Reagan* (CVN-76) was laid down on 12 February 1998 at the Northrop Grumman yard, Newport News, Virginia, launched on 4 March 2001 and commissioned on 12 July 2003. In the course of building the super-carriers, the Navy and the yard were able to incorporate a variety of new techniques designed to save costs and to enhance effectiveness. The island, mounted as a single pre-constructed 660-tonne unit, had many modifications, including a new design of mainmast and rearranged antennae. *Reagan*'s island has one deck less than the preceding Nimitzes, but greater internal height makes it the same height as

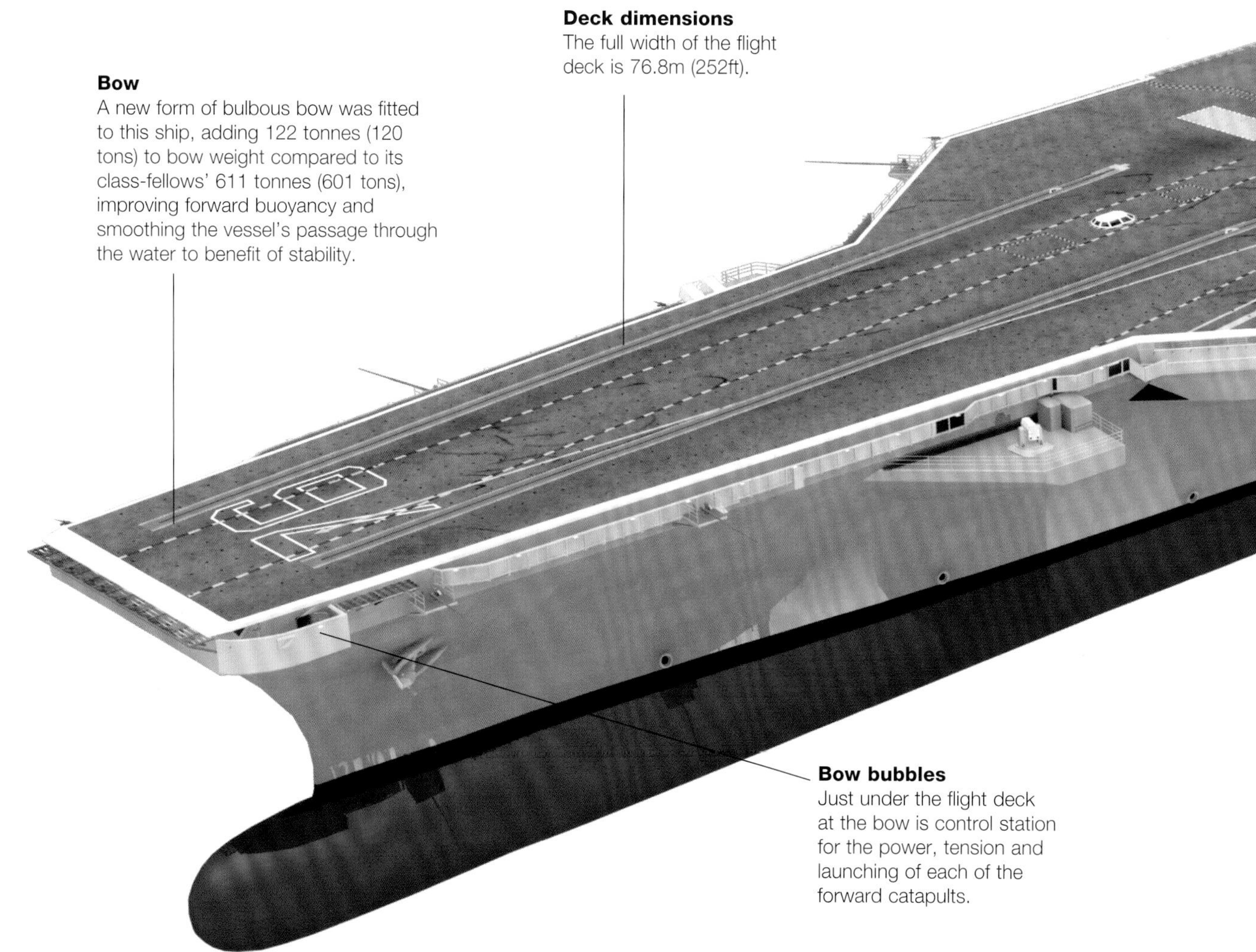

Deck dimensions
The full width of the flight deck is 76.8m (252ft).

Bow
A new form of bulbous bow was fitted to this ship, adding 122 tonnes (120 tons) to bow weight compared to its class-fellows' 611 tonnes (601 tons), improving forward buoyancy and smoothing the vessel's passage through the water to benefit of stability.

Bow bubbles
Just under the flight deck at the bow is control station for the power, tension and launching of each of the forward catapults.

the others. The flight deck has the usual four elevators and four steam catapults. Hangar areas are designed so that outbreaks of fire can be contained and quickly dealt with. A countermeasure washdown system includes a sprinkler system throughout the ship to cope with fire, biological, chemical and radiological attacks. As with the others in the *Nimitz*-class, the power derives from two Westinghouse AS4W reactors, coupled to four steam

Masts
Instead of a separate mast abaft the island, the second mast is incorporated in the island structure.

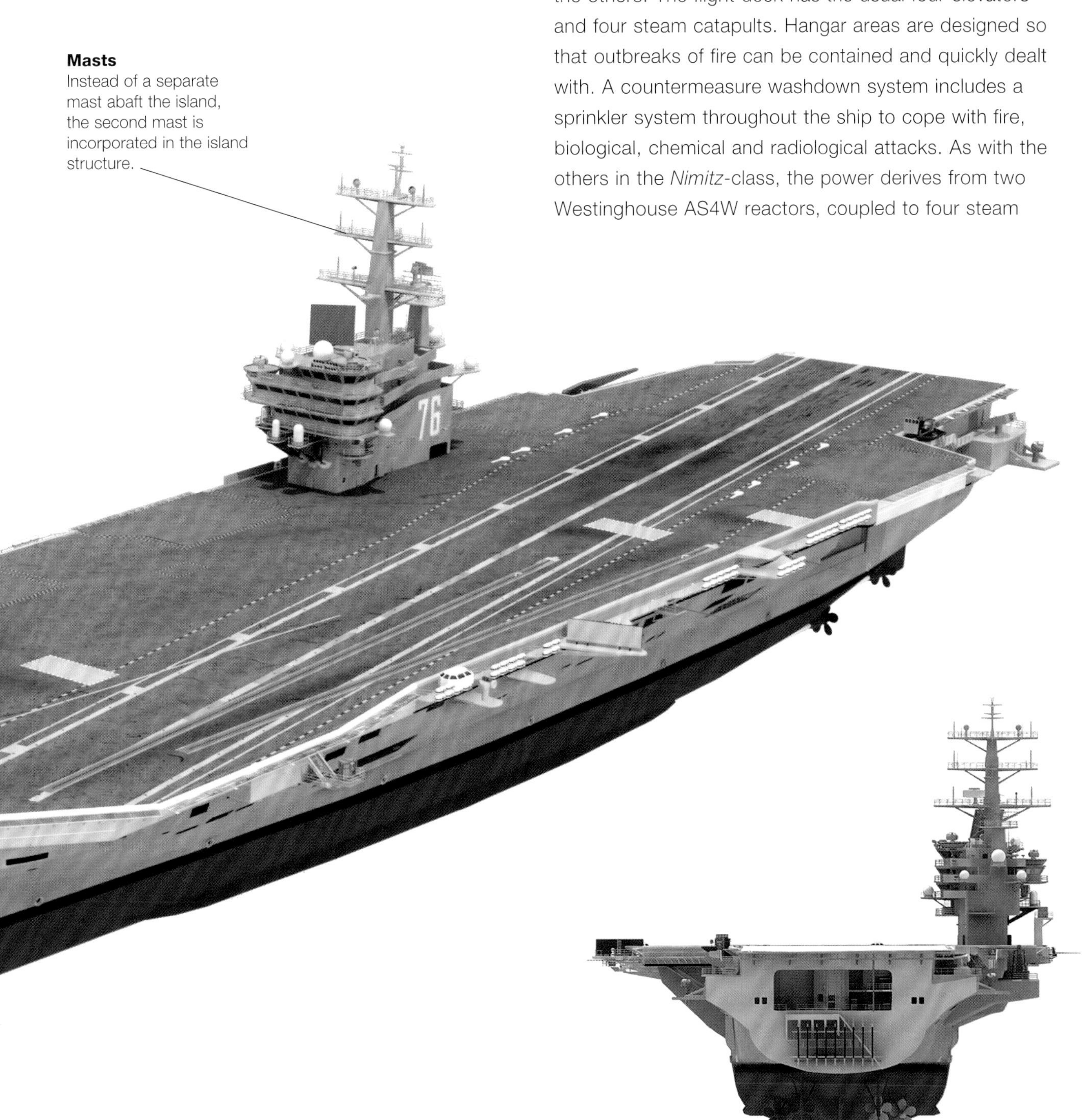

The convention of naming super-carriers after US presidents began with *John F. Kennedy* (CV-67) in 1968. It has been criticised by some, especially for selecting recent incumbents. When Congress laid down rules for the naming of warships in 1862, aircraft carriers were scarcely dreamt of.

USS Ronald R. Reagan

In traditional style, crewmen line the railings as *Reagan* arrives in Pearl Harbor on 31 July 2010 to participate in the biennial RIMPAC, the world's largest multinational maritime exercise.

Specification

Dimensions:	Length: 332.8m (1092ft); Beam: 40.8m (134ft); Draught: 11.3m (37ft)
Displacement:	113,600 tonnes (101,400 tons)
Propulsion:	2 A4W nuclear reactors, 4 steam turbines, 4 shafts; 194,000kW (260,000shp)
Speed:	30 knots (56km/h; 35mph)
Range:	Unlimited
Armament:	2 RIM-162 Evolved Sea Sparrow eight-cell MK 29 SAM medium range launchers, 2 RIM-116 21-cell RAM short range missile surface-to-air launchers, CIWS
Aircraft:	90
Complement:	5680

turbines, driving four shafts. While the stated speed is 30 knots (55.5km/h; 34.5mph), it is likely that the ship can exceed this. Although consuming no oil fuel itself, it has bunkers enabling it to refuel escort vessels as well as to store jet fuel for the air wing. As well as conducting RAS, the ship is capable of at-sea loading and offloading of ordnance and other supplies, even in bad weather conditions.

Installed armament comprises two RIM-162 Evolved Sea Sparrow eight-cell MK 29 SAM medium-range launchers, and two RIM-116 21-cell RAM short-range missile surface-to-air launchers. The ship supports up to 90 aircraft, fixed or rotary wing.

In June 2004, *Reagan* was the first nuclear-powered carrier to pass through the Straits of Magellan en route to its designated home port based at Naval Air Station (NAS) North Island Coronado, California. On the way it shared exercises with the Brazilian carrier *São Paulo* and with Argentinian naval aircraft in an 11-nation set of manoeuvres. At the start of 2006 it made its first deployment, until 6 July, described as performing maritime security operations in the Persian Gulf region in support of the global war against terrorism, and taking part in Exercise Valiant Shield in 2006, testing naval proficiency in detecting, tracking and engaging with suspect operations on sea and land, in the air and in cyberspace. In 2007 it led Carrier Strike Group 7 in joint exercises with the South Korean navy. In June 2008 it joined in humanitarian relief following the ravages of Typhoon Fengshen on the coast of the Philippines, then on 28 August it launched its first combat sorties in operation Enduring Freedom, supporting ground forces in southern Afghanistan.

Radioactive scrubdown

A six-month Planned Incremental Availability (PIA) was undertaken at NAS North Island, Coronado, California. It was again involved in disaster relief after the devastating tsunami of 11 March 2011 off the northeast coast of Tokyo, serving as a floating platform off the Japanese coast of Honshu for refuelling Japanese helicopters and naval ships. Its proximity to the damaged and radioactive Fukushima nuclear plant necessitated a thorough scrubdown and other counter-radiation measures. *Reagan* entered a docking PIA period for upgrades and repairs at Puget Sound Naval Shipyard on 6 January 2012, emerging on 12 March 2013 after the US$210 million refit. A further PIA was carried out at Coronado, California, between September 2014 and 17 April 2015.

From 31 August 2015 the carrier changed home port from San Diego to the US Navy forward base at Yokosuka, Japan, embarking Carrier Air Wing Five. As the keystone ship of Carrier Strike Group Five it makes regular patrols in the seas around Japan and Korea and participates in exercises with allied units. These are potentially hostile waters, with many islands in dispute between different countries.

Strike group

A Carrier Strike Group is currently formed with a *Nimitz*-class carrier at the centre. A nuclear submarine of the *Los Angeles*- or *Virginia*-classes is also part of the group. Typically it might include two guided missile cruisers of the *Ticonderoga*-class, with two destroyers of the *Arleigh Burke*- or *Spruance*-classes, armed primarily with anti-air missiles, and two frigates of the *Oliver Hazard Perry*-class, armed primarily for anti-submarine warfare, flanking the group.

USS *Enterprise* (CVN-65) leads its strike group in the Atlantic Ocean on 7 May 2006. Other ships are guided missile frigate USS *Nicholas*, guided missile cruiser USS *Leyte Gulf*, guided missile destroyer USS *McFaul*, and fast combat support ship *Supply*. The group has a 'surge deployment' addition in the guided missile destroyer *James E. Williams*.

The group can be refuelled or rearmed by a replenishment ship, which might be one of the USN's *Supply*-class fast combat support ships, 49,600-tonne (48,800-ton) ships carrying fuel, ordnance and all kinds of supplies to keep warships at sea, and capable of a speed of 25 knots (46.2km/h; 28.7mph). While based at its home port, the group remains on the alert for a Surge Deployment that might dispatch it anywhere on the globe.

Mistral (2006)

This amphibious assault vessel was the first all-electric large warship, and the first to be driven by pod thrusters.

Officially known as *bâtiments de projection et de commandement* (BPC), or power projection and command ships, the French Navy has three ships of the *Mistral*-class. Work on the design began in 1997, with the aim of strengthening the Marine Nationale's capacity in amphibious operations. The intention required a ship capable of supporting an air wing and of carrying and landing military vehicles and armed troops sufficient for landing and supporting four combat companies and 280 vehicles within a 100-km (62-mile) deep sector for up to ten days. The design was to be of modular type in the interest of selling it to other fleets, keeping costs down and for effecting easy updating of electronic equipment. Much revision, addition and deletion went on before a firm plan was reached and approval given for the construction of the first two ships, *Mistral* and *Tonnerre*, in December 2000.

The prime contractor was DCN of Brest, sharing the task with Chantiers de l'Atlantique of St-Nazaire. Numerous component parts were constructed at the Stocznia Remontowa yard in Gdansk, Poland, and transported to France. These are the first large French warships to be built

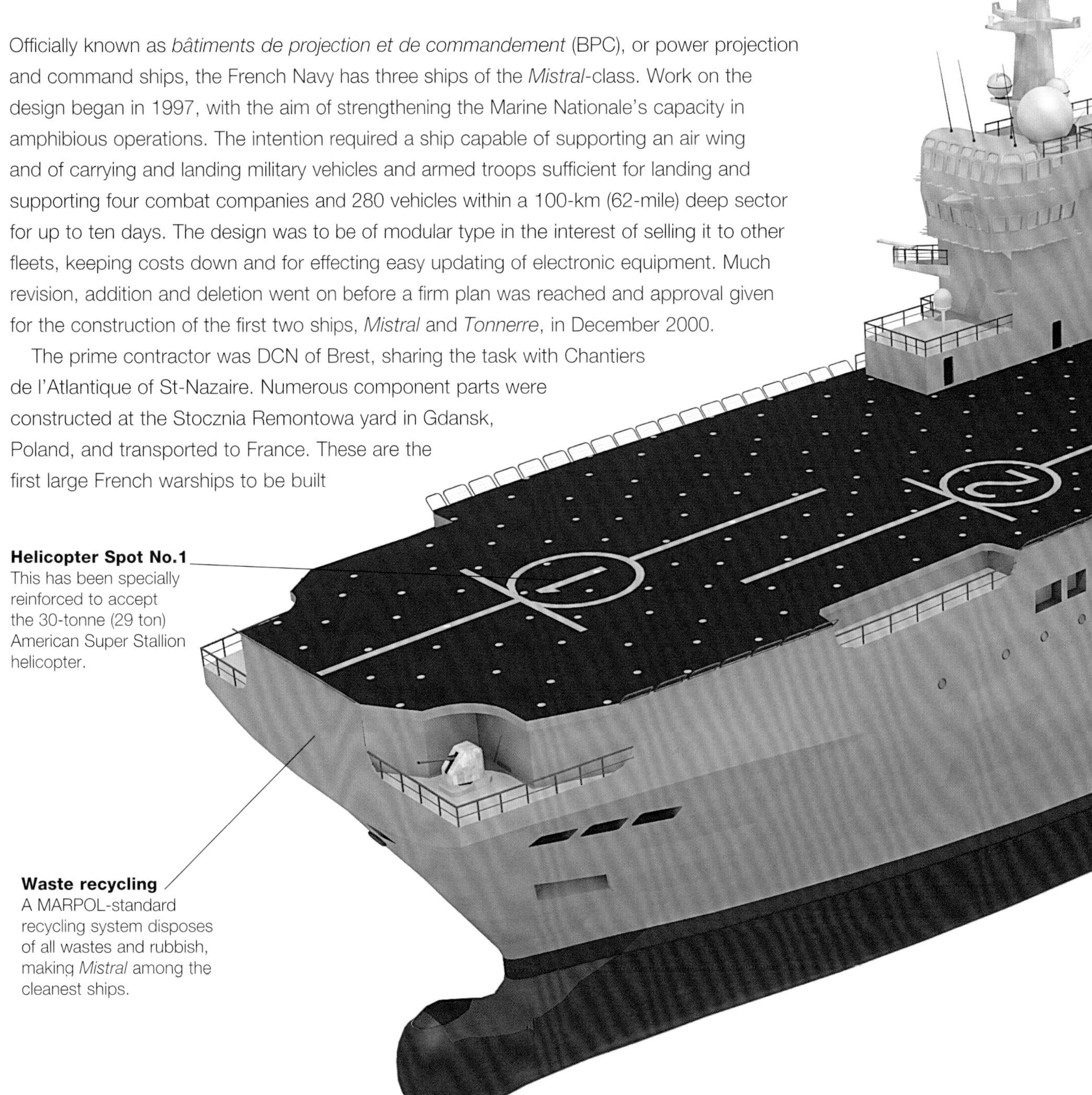

Helicopter Spot No.1
This has been specially reinforced to accept the 30-tonne (29 ton) American Super Stallion helicopter.

Waste recycling
A MARPOL-standard recycling system disposes of all wastes and rubbish, making *Mistral* among the cleanest ships.

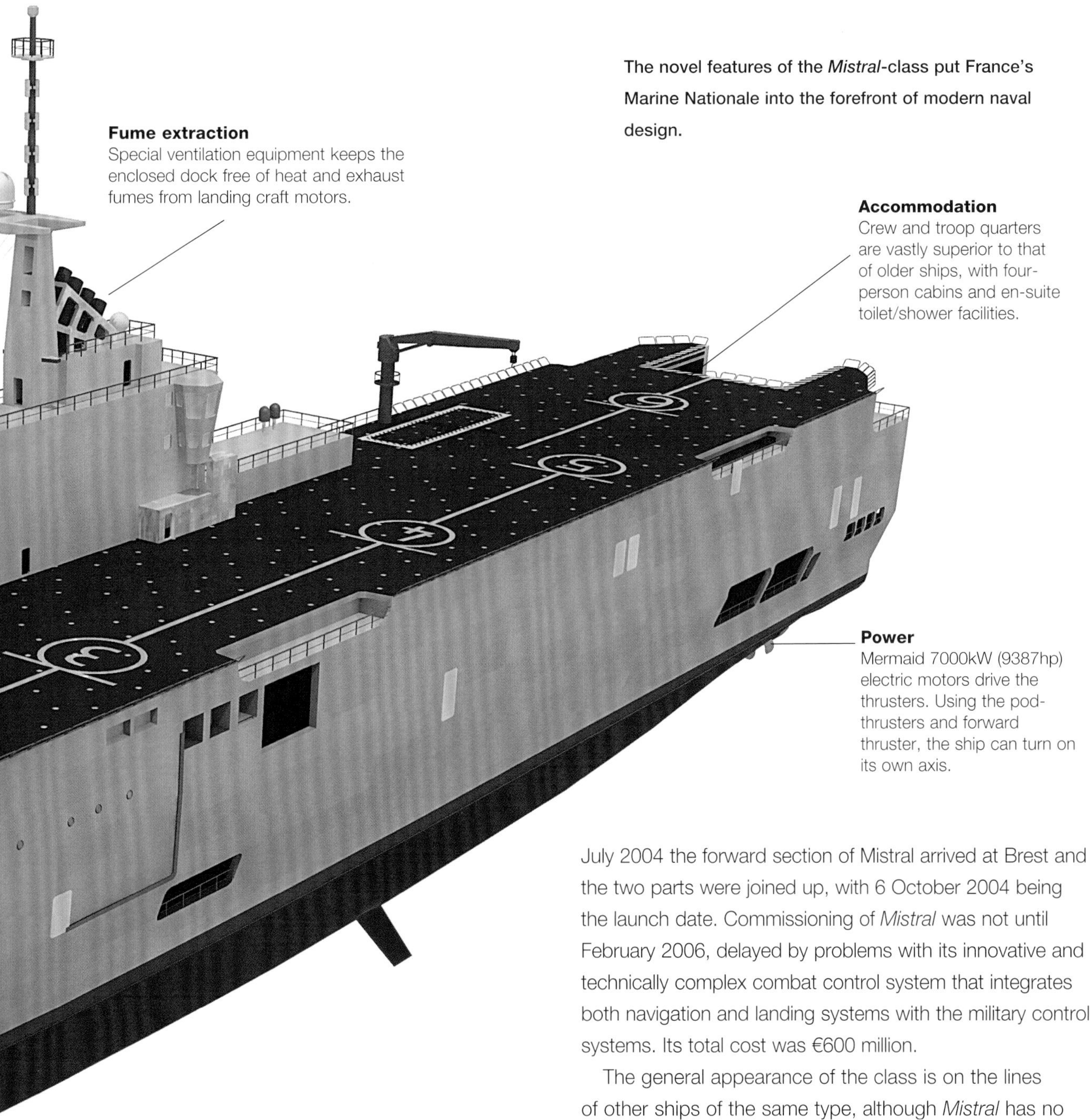

The novel features of the *Mistral*-class put France's Marine Nationale into the forefront of modern naval design.

in 'merchant navy' fashion rather than to previous warship survivability standards. The forward sections were built at St-Nazaire and floated to Brest, where the aft sections were built and the entire ship was assembled. Keel laying was thus done twice for each ship, with *Mistral*'s after section laid down on 9 July 2002 and the forward part on 13 December. This form of distributed construction was becoming more widely used in European naval building (it was also applied to the new British *Queen Elizabeth*-class carriers). On 19 July 2004 the forward section of Mistral arrived at Brest and the two parts were joined up, with 6 October 2004 being the launch date. Commissioning of *Mistral* was not until February 2006, delayed by problems with its innovative and technically complex combat control system that integrates both navigation and landing systems with the military control systems. Its total cost was €600 million.

The general appearance of the class is on the lines of other ships of the same type, although *Mistral* has no bow ramp or catapult. A short mast above the navigation bridge is forward of the mainmast, part of an integrated structure that also incorporates four stern-canted exhaust flues. The nerve centre of the ship is the command room, on the second deck below the flight deck, with an area of 850m^2 (9444sq ft) and 150 work stations. From here communication and information can be exchanged with landed units, other ships, aircraft and submarines. One lift is aft of the island, with a 17-tonne crane adjacent, and

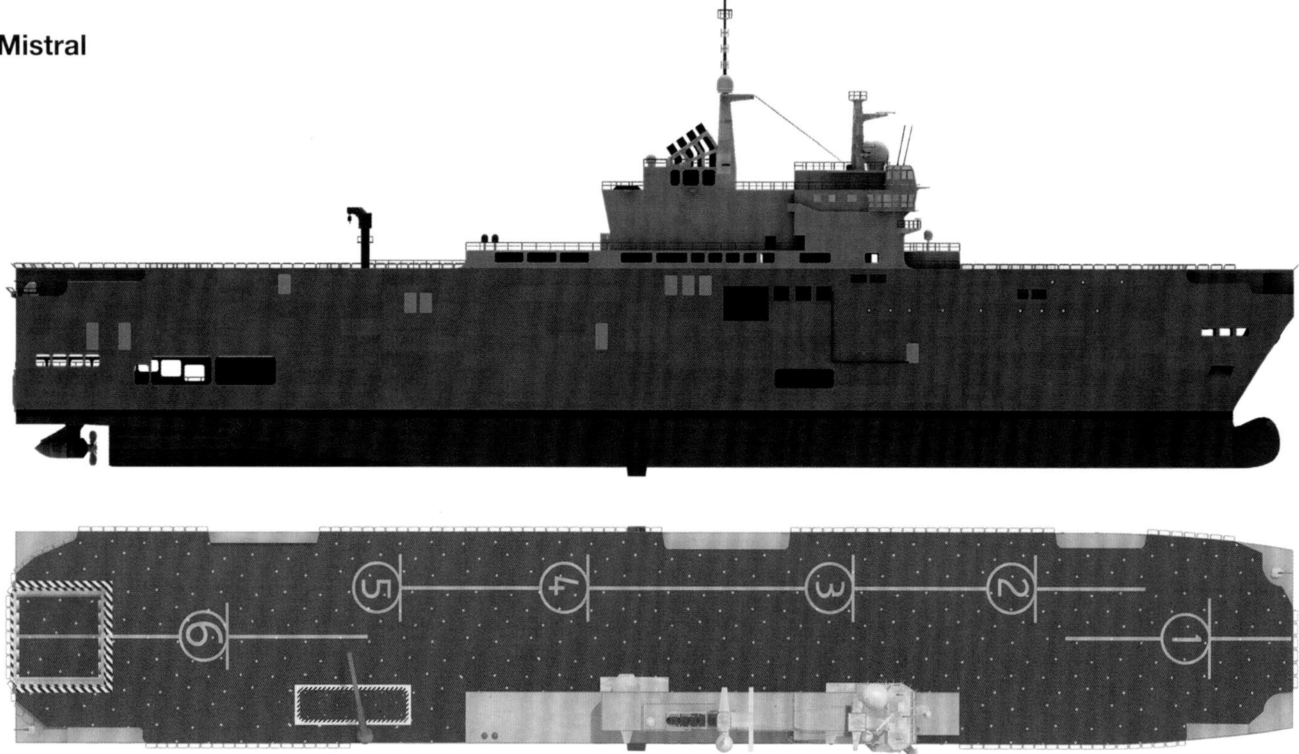

the other is mounted at the stern. The stern dock, 60m (183ft) long and 15.4m (47ft) wide, can hold four landing craft capable of holding medium tanks, or two large LCAC hovercraft, or two French EDA-R rapid landing amphibious craft. Internal ramps lead to dock and deck levels. A lateral loading ramp is fitted to starboard.

Specification

Dimensions:	Length: 199m (653ft); Beam: 32m (105ft); Draught: 6.2m (20ft 6in)
Displacement:	16,500 tonnes (14,918 tons); 21,300 tonnes (19,258 tons) full load
Propulsion:	2 Alstom Mermaid thruster pods; 14,000kW (18,774hp)
Speed:	18.8 knots (35km/h; 21.6mph)
Range:	5800nm (10,000km; 6670 miles) at 18 knots (33.3km/h; 20.7mph)
Armament:	2 Simbad sea-air missile launchers; twin 30mm Breda-Mauser cannon; 4 Browning 12.7mm M2-Hb guns
Aircraft:	16 (large) or 32 (light) helicopters
Complement:	310

The *Mistral* class is intended to operate helicopters only, and has no need for a bow ramp, catapult, or arrester wires.

Amphibious assault ship

Essentially the ships are helicopter carriers and amphibious assault platforms, with command ship abilities. Occasional use as training ships is also part of the official specification and support facilities also include hospital accommodation of 69 beds (extendable by another 50) plus two operating theatres, with its own elevator to deck level. Here, too, modular design is standard, and additional medical equipment can be stored in modules in the aircraft hangar.

Retractable fin stabiliszers are also fitted. The propulsion system was unique for this type of warship, from two electric-powered manoeuvrable azimuth pods, originally developed for cruise liners, and a bow thruster. Provision of the necessary electrical power is assured by three main Wärtsilä 16V 32 diesel alternators generating 4850kW (6503hp), an auxiliary Wärtsilä 3000kW (4025hp) alternator and an emergency 800kW (1072hp) generator. In total 450 fully-equipped troops can be embarked for a six-month campaign, and this number can be almost doubled for short periods. The hangar occupies 1800m^2 (19,355sq ft), and can hold 16 helicopters. Two 13-tonne lifts access the flight deck, which has an area of 5200m^2 (55,944sq ft). Garage space amounts to 2560m^2 (27,527sq ft), enough

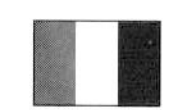

Mistral leaving Valetta, Malta, on 20 August 2011, after a break from international operations against Libya.

for up to 60 vehicles, depending on size and weight: 60 armoured cars, or 46 13 AMX-56 Leclerc medium tanks.

Armament includes a bow-mounted Simbad missile launcher, a Breda-Mauser 30mm (1.18in) gun at the stern and four M2-HB Browning 12.7mm (.5in) machine guns. Two SIGMA 40 inertial navigation centres using Ring Laser Gyro (RLG) technology provide an integrated navigation system that, with the SENIN mapping system, ensures high-precision positioning. The communications system server can handle eight megabytes per second and all actions are managed in real time. The SENIT 9 combat direction system is a development of the format used on the carrier *Charles de Gaulle*. It collates information from the sensors and detectors and assembles it into a form to assist with action decisions.

With its home port at Toulon, the ships are designed for sea-basing, away from their home port for months on end, with Replenishment at Sea (RAS) supplementing their own large stocks of materials from food to ordnance and oil. Video games, satellite TV and a gymnasium help the crew to relax and keep fit. A key factor in the design was to cut down on the prolonged periods of maintenance periodically required by warships. Much of the internal work is carried out at sea while on patrol, and *Mistral* can be at sea for 350 days if necessary.

Two *Mistral*-class carriers were ordered by Russia in 2009. With the ships on the verge of completion the Ukrainian crisis broke out, when Russia annexed a substantial amount of Ukrainian territory along the Black Sea coast. By late 2014 there were suggestions that France would withhold the ships, and in August 2015, at a very late stage, with much Russian-designed equipment already installed, the French government cancelled the sale and returned around €900 million to Moscow. It was left with two ships that its Marine Nationale did not need or want. Eventually a sale of both to Egypt was concluded in 2016. In the Egyptian Navy they are *Gamal Abdel Nasser* and *Anwar El Sadat*, currently outfitting with assistance from Russia.

Sister ships

Mistral's sister ships are *Tonnerre* (commissioned 2007) and *Dixmude* (2012), both of very similar design and equipment. They are genuine multi-role vessels with the ability to carry four LCM landing craft or two 95-tonne LCAC. *Dixmude* as the most recent (commissioned January 2012) may have some newer control equipment, but basically all share the same technology. *Dixmude* has participated in anti-pirate operations off the East African coast and also in a number of French interventions and evacuation missions from African states and Yemen. *Tonnerre* has taken part in many exercises with NATO ships, joining with *Mistral* and HMS *Ocean* in attacks on Libyan targets in 2011, and in anti-drug trade operations off West Africa. A fourth ship of the class was planned but appears to have been cancelled.

Liaoning (2012)

Originally an aircraft-carrying cruiser of the Soviet Navy, this ship was transformed into China's first carrier and the prototype for a new class of carriers.

The history of China's first carrier goes back to the Soviet Union in the 1980s and Project 1143.5, developed by the Nevskoye Planning & Design Bureau, for an 'aviation cruiser' for the Soviet Navy. Two ships resulted, *Admiral Kuznetsov* and *Varyag*. When *Varyag*'s keel was laid in December 1985 at the Nikolayev South shipyard on the Black Sea, the plan was to name it *Riga*, and it was launched in December 1988. The name was changed to *Varyag* in late 1990. With the dissolution of the Soviet Union in 1991, ownership rights of the still unfinished ship were passed to Ukraine. No further work was done, however, and the ship remained at Nikolayev until 1998. Unwanted by Ukraine, it was sold by auction to a Chinese travel company, which proposed to convert it into a floating casino. Just how it came to be transferred to the People's Liberation Army Navy (PLAN) has never been officially disclosed, but the purchase apparently included all plans and blueprints.

In November 2001–February 2002 the ship was towed by way of Gibraltar and the Cape of Good Hope to the state-owned Dalian Shipyard in Liaoning Province. In June 2005 it was dry-docked at Dalian and work began to transform it into a new ship, classed as an aircraft carrier. On 25 September 2012 it was commissioned and named after Liaoning Province. By then it had undergone sea trials but much had still to be done, including installation of flight control, fire control, radar and weapons systems.

Little is known outside the PLAN about key features of the ship, other than those that are apparent to external view. Even the nature of propulsion is unclear, be it the original Project 1143.5 steam turbines or a subsequent replacement. Some reports suggest that steam turbines remain, working at reduced pressure, although many observers believe that marine gas turbine engines based on Ukrainian designs are now installed. Turbo-generators (perhaps nine) and six diesel generators are certain to be installed for electrical and back-up power.

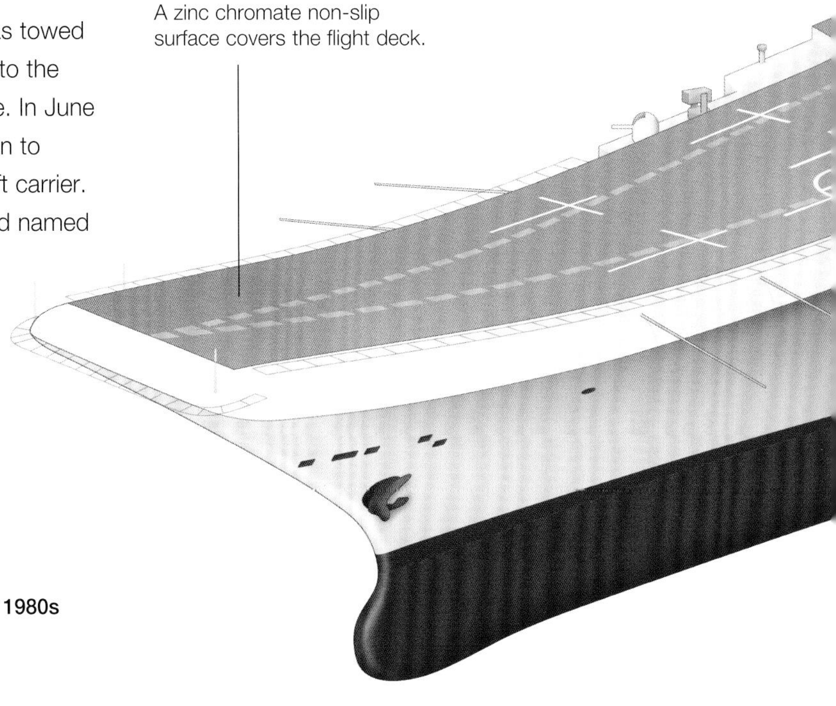

Non-slip grip
A zinc chromate non-slip surface covers the flight deck.

***Liaoning*'s streamlined structures give little hint of its 1980s origins as a Soviet Navy 'aviation cruiser'.**

The ship follows the *Kuznetsov* form, with a 12° 'ski-jump' bow ramp to assist take-off, and arrester wires for landing, but no catapult, putting it in the STOBAR category. Two aircraft elevators are mounted to starboard, fore and aft of the island. Its air wing consists of 24 Shenyang J-15 multi-role fighters, which are Chinese-built and modified versions of Russia's Sukhoi-33. These planes have digital flight avionics and advanced radars and include the two-seater training model J-15S. On 23 November 2012 J-15 fighters first landed on the ship. A range of helicopters has also been observed on *Liaoning*, including Changhe Z-18 transport, Z-18J AEW, Z-18F ASW and Harbin Z-9D SAR helicopters, also Kamov Ka-31 Helix AEW helicopters.

Launching of HQ-10 controlled Type 1130 close-in air defence missiles from four 18-cell launchers has been demonstrated. They fire 30mm shells at missiles and aircraft. *Liaoning* also has four 18-cell launchers for FL-3000N missiles, also known as HongQi (Red Flag) 10,

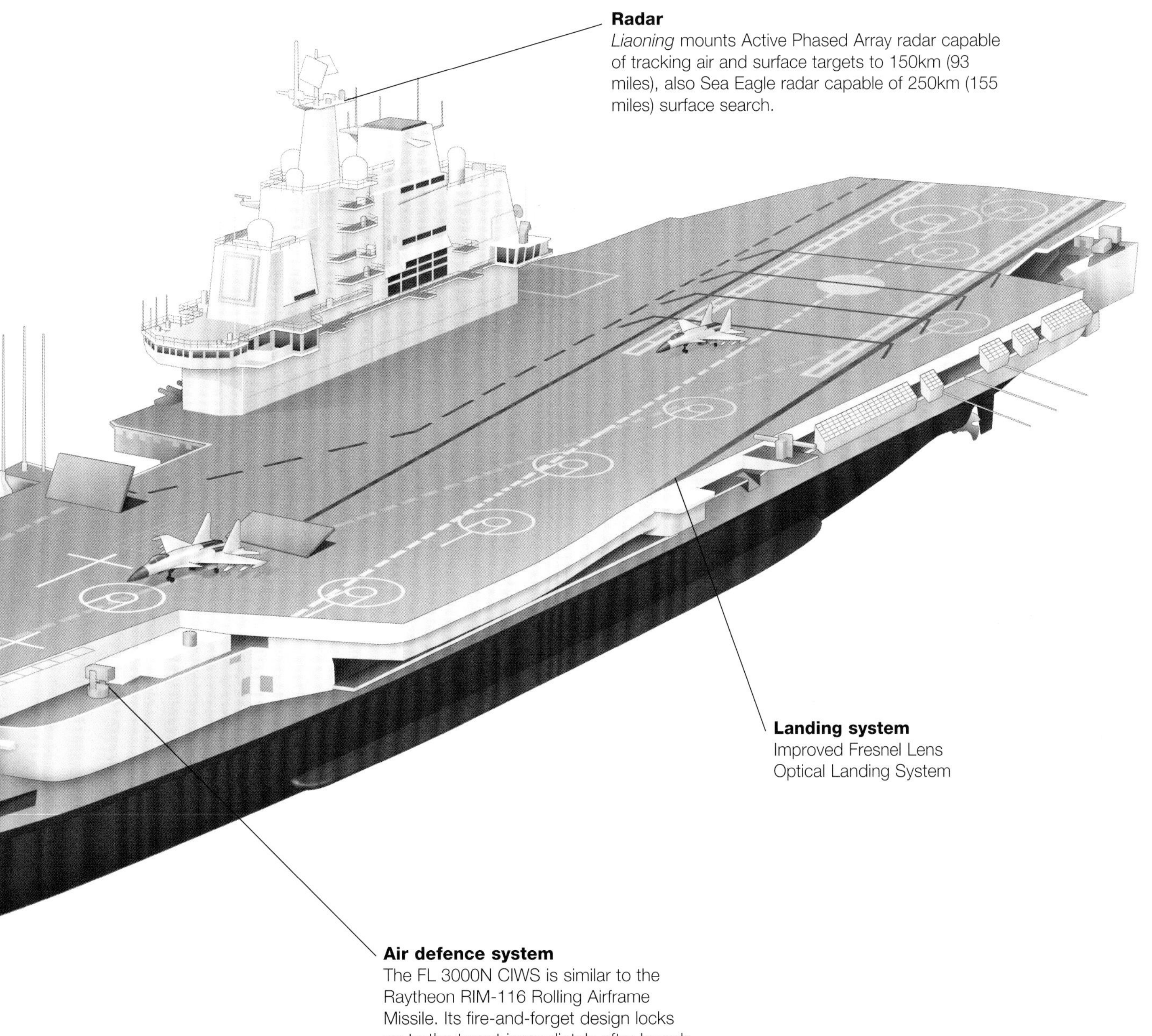

A Chinese Navy J-15 fighter takes off from *Liaoning* during training exercises in the South China Sea, 2 January 2017.

120mm (4.72in) in diameter and about 2m (6ft) long, with a dual passive radar/infra-red homing seeker and a maximum range of 9000m (29,530ft). Chaff/decoy launchers are fitted on the island and at the stern.

The range of sensors has been noted as including Type 382 Sea Eagle S/C air search radar, mounted on the mast-top, Type 346 air search radar with four ASEA panels on the bridge, HQ-10 SAM fire-control radar, air surveillance and sea search radar, navigation radar and antennas for datalink and satellite communication. *Liaoning* has many automated functions and computerized systems. The ship's crew numbers 1960, plus 626 air group personnel. Movement of crew among the 3600 rooms is controlled by their personal ID cards that need to be swiped at access doors, restricting access to authorized personnel only: a feature of most modern carriers. LED screens in mess halls give news reports as well as duty announcements.

Specification (as *Liaoning*)

Dimensions:	Length: 304.5m (1000ft); Beam: 73/15m (240ft); Draught: 10.97m (36ft)
Displacement:	approx 53,050 tonnes (52,215 tons); 59,100 tonnes (58,169 tons) full load
Propulsion:	gas turbine, unconfirmed; 4 shafts
Speed:	not known
Range:	not known
Armament:	3 Type 1130 SAM; 2 H/PJ11 CIWS
Aircraft:	36
Complement:	2586

Integrated operations

Information from Chinese sources indicates that *Liaoning* is seen as a multi-purpose ship, with ability to take part in integrated operations with land forces, although it is not equipped as an assault ship. It is plain that it is a test and training ship, in anticipation of further carriers to be constructed for the PLAN. In 2015 a second carrier was laid down at Dalian Shipbuilding, to be built from the keel up as a new ship. From external appearances this vessel, known as Type 001A, is of similar size to *Liaoning*, and is also equipped with a bow ramp, and is not nuclear-driven. It will be the largest naval ship yet built in China. By October 2016

Liaoning at Dalian shipyard in its home province, on 25 September 2012, the day it was commissioned into the People's Liberation Army Navy, confirming China's big step towards air superiority in the southwest Pacific region.

Global carrier forces

The Chinese carrier-building programme has kept naval strategists busy in comparing and computing relative naval air strengths in the seas around Southeast Asia. India has one STOBAR carrier, *Vikramaditya*, in service and *Vikrant* approaching completion. Thailand has the V/STOL *Chakri Naruebet*, commissioned in 1997 and currently in very limited use; Japan has four 'helicopter destroyers'; South Korea has one amphibious helicopter-carrying assault ship and plans for two more, and Australia has two bow-ramp-fitted amphibious assault ships. Apart from the regional powers, there is also a forward-based US *Nimitz*-class carrier, currently *Ronald R. Reagan*, at Yokosuka, Japan, and the possibility of other US carrier strike forces to be deployed.

the island had been put in place, lifted on it in two sections. Unlike *Liaoning*, it will have Type 346A radar and may be fitted with a catapult.

Even this ship is likely to be a stepping-stone towards larger carriers, part of a training and development programme to give the Chinese fleet a corps of experienced carrier crewmen who are masters not merely of running a large ship but of maintaining the aviation systems at a high degree of functionality and readiness. In the next few years, a combination of training and tactical missions is likely, as China uses its new carrier capacity to support territorial claims, participate in HADR missions and assert diplomatic clout in the region.

HMAS Canberra (2014)

Australia's largest warship is a state-of-the-art amphibious warfare vessel, capable of playing a variety of roles, particularly enhancing the Australian Navy's off-shore capabilities.

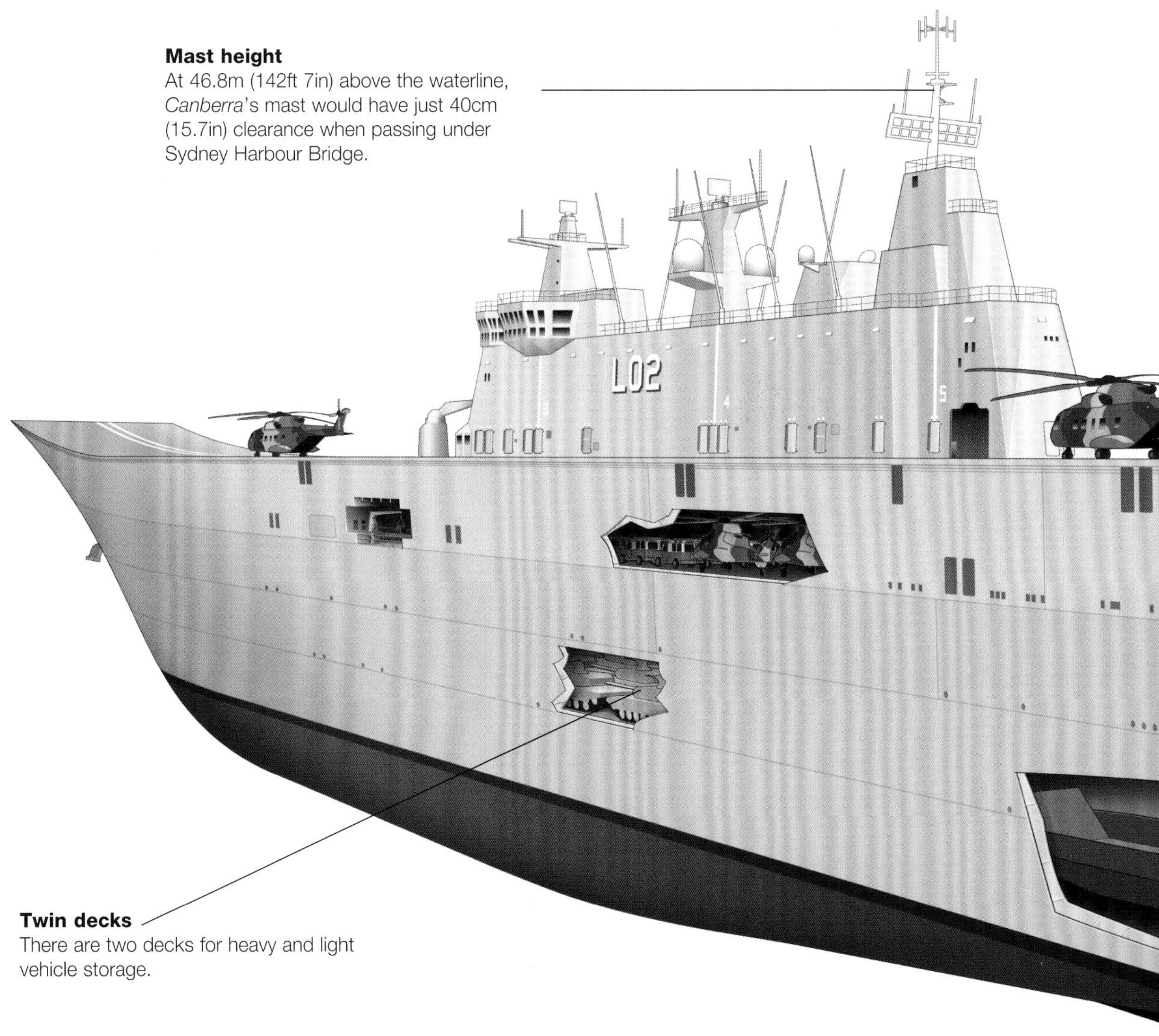

Mast height
At 46.8m (142ft 7in) above the waterline, *Canberra*'s mast would have just 40cm (15.7in) clearance when passing under Sydney Harbour Bridge.

Twin decks
There are two decks for heavy and light vehicle storage.

Australia's latest warships are, after much discussion, based on a Spanish design, built in Spain, and finally assembled in Australia.

Changing circumstances both in strategic and tactical requirements in Australia's part of the globe were underlined by the difficulties in managing the logistics of the UN peacekeeping force in East Timor in 1999–2000. This led to an Australian government plan to improve the country's amphibious warfare ability, centred on two large Landing Helicopter Dock (LHD) vessels. In the mid-2000s tenders were received for the French *Mistral* design and a Spanish design based on the Spanish Navy's LHD *Juan Carlos I*, commissioned in 2010. The Spanish version was chosen, and with numerous adaptations specified by the Royal Australian Navy, it forms the two-ship *Canberra*-class. The builder was Navantia, of Ferro. The keel of *Canberra* was laid there on 23 September 2009 and it was launched on 17 February 2011.

Construction was modular, with the ship assembled in three separate parts, although in the same yard, then joined together. By 17 October 2012 the hull, without island, was transferred by heavy lift ship to Williamstown Shipyard, Victoria, for completion and fitting out by BAE Systems Australia. *Canberra*, although lead ship and first to be commissioned on 28 November 2014, carries pennant No.L02 while the other class member, *Adelaide*, is L01. *Adelaide* was commissioned on 4 December 2015. The two LHDs substantially expand Australia's capacity to influence events and operate in the Indian and Pacific Oceans, with their numerous hot-spots of diplomatic and military tension.

Construction

Construction cost was A$1.5 billion. The ships share the major features of European naval LHDs, with a long triple-masted island set to starboard and an axial flight deck area 202.3m (616ft 6in) long and 32m (97ft 6in) wide. Intended as a helicopter carrier, it has no provision for catapult or arrester gear. However, a bow ramp set to the port side is fitted to enable it to launch V/STOL planes, although none are carried at present, and six landing spots allow for simultaneous take-offs and landings by six helicopters of NRH90 or Blackhawk size, or four Chinooks.

There are three main decks below the flight deck: the hangar deck with storage also for light vehicles and cargo; the main accommodation deck and the well dock, 69.3m

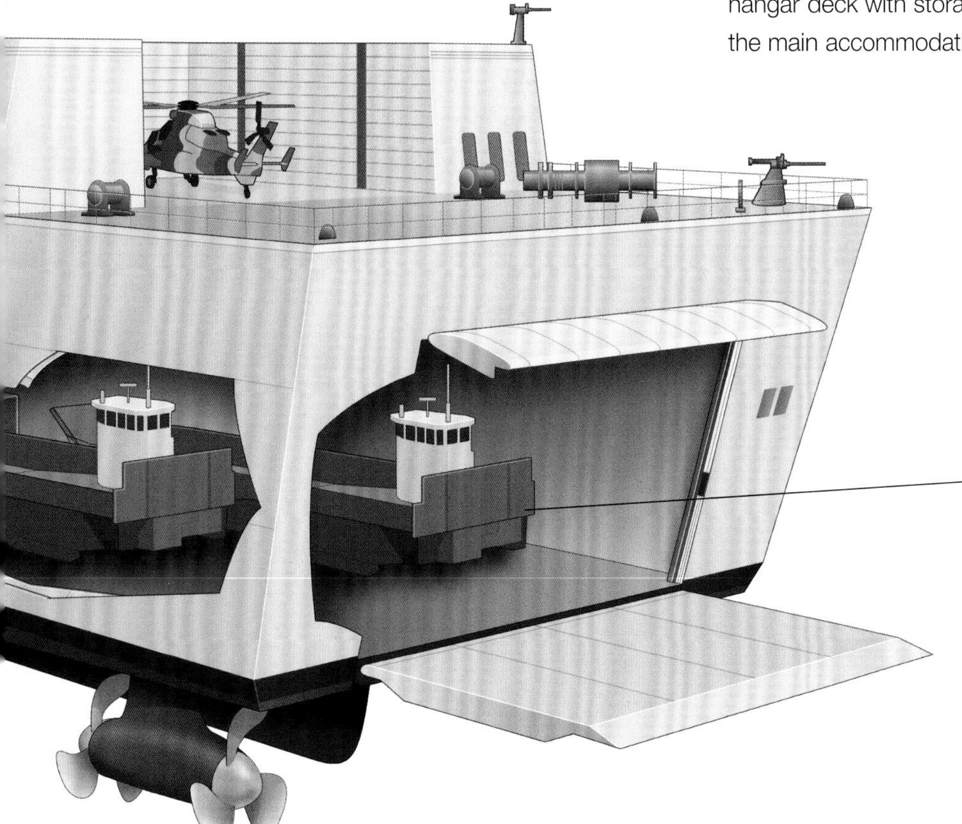

Landing craft
The four LCM 1E landing craft have an endurance of 190nm (389km; 242 miles). They can 'comfortably' hold 120 personnel with full combat load, but this can be stretched to 170.

Propeller
Thruster propellers are 4.5m (15ft) in diameter.

Canberra **moored at Fleet Base East, Sydney Harbour, in June 2015.**

by 16.8m (211ft 3in by 51ft) that occupies the stern part of the ship, with heavy vehicle accommodation forward of it. The dock normally holds four LCM 1E landing craft, but is fitted for other types, including US and British variants, both conventionally engined craft and air-cushion LCAC vessels. The lower deck can hold armoured vehicles of up to 65 tonnes (64 tons), which allows for the 60-tonne (59-ton) Abrams battle tank. Internal ramps as well as the two aircraft lifts and a 16-tonne cargo lift give access between decks, and lateral doors are fitted to port and starboard. In all, up to 110 vehicles can be carried. The stern door also has a ramp attachment for landing vehicles directly on to a beach. Its 7m (23ft 2in) draught allows it to come close in for littoral operations and to enter the many shallow bays and lagoons of the Australian coast and Pacific islands. To fulfil its various functions, the ship is jointly crewed by naval, army and air force personnel. Apart from its crew the ship can hold an embarked force of 1000 personnel and their equipment.

Propulsion is by electric drive. A single General Electric LM2500 gas turbine generator of 19,160kW (25,693hp) and two MAN 16V32/40 diesel generators each of 7448kW (9987hp) are backed up by a Progener-Mitsubishi S16MPTA emergency diesel generator able to generate 1350kW (1810hp). Two Siemens azimuth POD units, each fitted with two propellers of 4.5m (14ft 9in) diameter, mounted at the stern, develop 11MW each, and two bow thrusters of 1500kW (2011hp) give the ship exceptional manoeuvrability. The maximum speed is 19 knots (35.1km/h; 21.8mph) with the ship fully loaded. A Saab 9LV Mk 4 combat management system incorporates

Specification

Dimensions:	Length: 230.8m (757ft 4in); Beam: 32m (105ft); Draught: 7m (23ft 2in)
Displacement:	27,940 tonnes (27,500 tons); 27,534 tonnes (27,100 tons) full load
Propulsion:	1 GE LM2500 gas turbine; 2 MAN 16V32/40 diesel generators, 2 Siemens azimuth thrusters; 22,000kW (29,502hp)
Speed:	19 knots (35km/h; 22mph)
Range:	9000nm (17,000km; 10,000 miles) at 15 knots (27.7km/h; 17.2mph)
Armament:	4 Rafael Typhoon RWS, 6 12.7mm machine guns
Aircraft:	18
Complement:	358

a Sea Giraffe 3D surveillance radar and Vampir NG IR search and track system. Four Israeli-made Rafael Typhoon 25mm remote weapons stations are fitted at the flight deck edges to bow and stern. Countermeasure systems are a towed AN/SLQ-25 Nixie torpedo decoy and an Australian-designed Nulka hover-type missile decoy (also used by US warships).

Canberra can embark 18 mission-ready helicopters of the Australian Defence Force (ADF), although in routine patrols the number is closer to eight. Available aircraft include MRH90, CH-47 Chinook, Blackhawk, S-70B-2 Seahawk and Romeo Seahawk helicopters, giving a range of capacities depending on the mission, from troop and cargo carrying to reconnaissance, ASW operations and ASuW strikes. It is anticipated that *Canberra* and *Adelaide* could carry the new Lockheed-Martin F-35B V/STOL fighter when it is in production if the Australian government is willing to buy it.

Cyclone preparedness

Canberra's home port is Fleet Base East, Sydney. Land-based simulator training prepared the crew for handling the new ship before its first outing under its own power on 3 March 2014, and a further year was spent on sea training and general shaking down to ensure that the vessel was fully capable in all likely situations. Navies owning LHDs and similar assault ships place a high emphasis on their potential role in humanitarian aid and disaster relief (HADR), and while this may be good for public relations at home and abroad, it is also borne out by events. *Canberra* is to be stationed at Townsville, Queensland, during the cyclone season. In February–March 2016 *Canberra* brought relief personnel, equipment and stores to Fiji in the wake of Cyclone Winston. In June 2016 it participated in the joint RIMPAC exercise off Hawaii, flying American Sikorsky CH-53E Super Stallion and Bell Boeing V-22 Osprey helicopters as well as its own aircraft in its first international deployment.

Adaptation designs

The fitting of a bow ramp to both *Canberra* and *Adelaide* has provoked debate about the possibility of their use as carriers of fixed-wing V/STOL aircraft. It appears that this was an early option for the Australian planners, especially as the adopted *Juan Carlos I* design incorporated a ramp, and it has been suggested that when the idea of carrying fixed-wing aircraft was dropped, it was cheaper to retain the ramp design rather than to reconfigure the entire front end. In 2015 the Australian defence ministry investigated the costs of purchase of the naval version of the Lockheed-Martin F-35B, with the necessary adaptation of the LDH ships to embark F-35B squadrons, but rejected the idea because of excessive cost. The debate continues as to whether this would enhance the ships' multi-role capacity, or render them unsuitable as amphibious warfare vessels.

A close-up view of HMAS *Adelaide*'s bow section contrasts the sculptured appearance of the ship's bow with the straight-sided boxy hull, in effect a floating dock plus garage.

Izumo (2015)

Classed as 'helicopter destroyers' to avoid contravention of Japan's constitution, the two ships of the *Izumo*-class are fast and powerful multi-role warships.

Japan had one of the largest carrier fleets in the world until virtually all its carriers, old and new, were destroyed between 1942 and 1945. The post-war Japanese Maritime Self Defence Force, set up in 1954, consisted of relatively small ships, and later also submarines, intended for the self-defence of home waters. Later in the twentieth century,

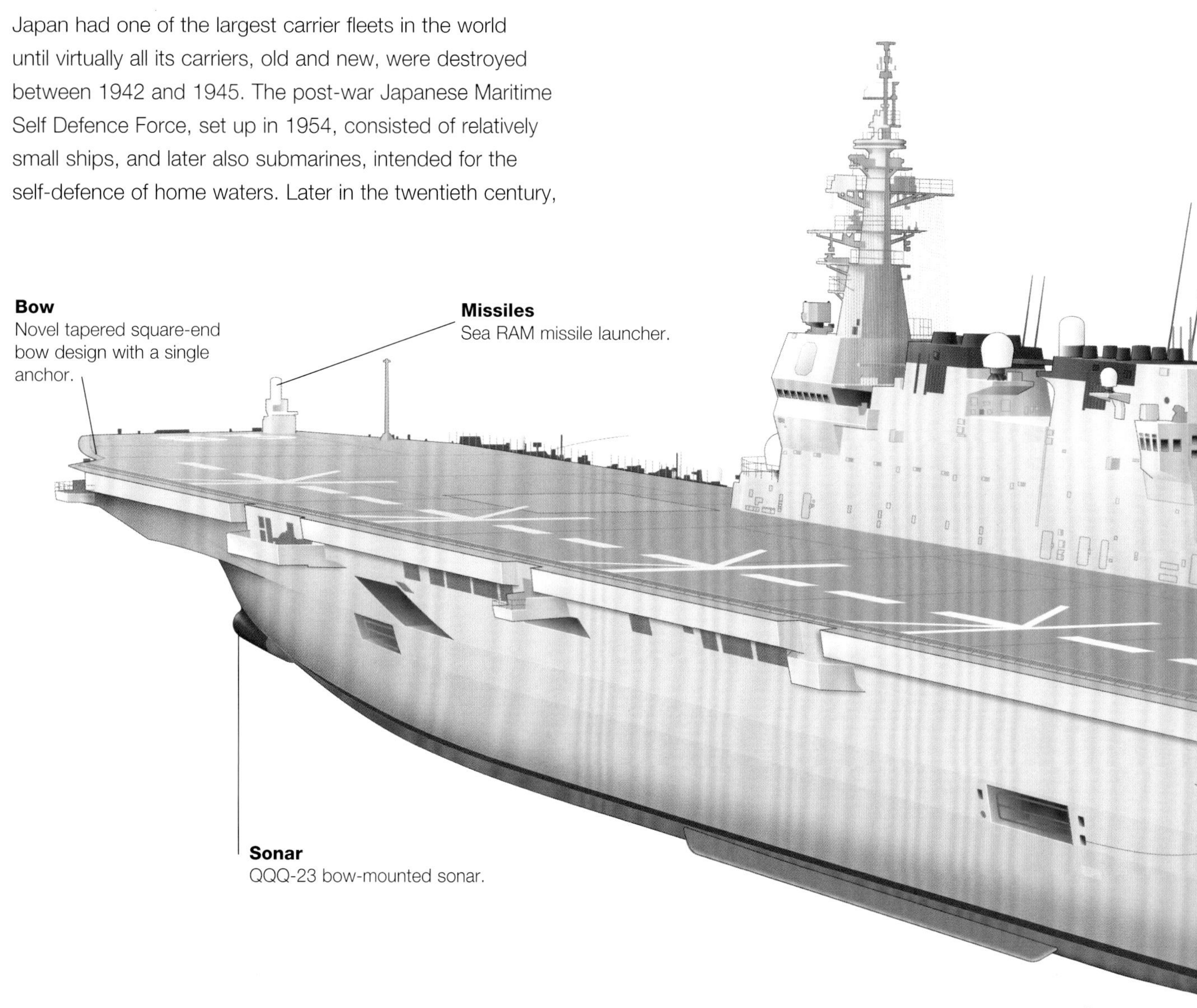

The two *Izumo*-class ships are the largest vessels yet built for the Japanese Maritime Self-Defence Force.

the aggressive stance of North Korea, the growing naval power of China and the numerous regional tensions around the world, including claims on Japanese-held islands, prompted the Japanese government to take a wider view of the situation. This led to the construction of the large *Shirane*-class destroyers, built from 1977 to 1981, which carried three ASW helicopters, with hangar and flight pad at the stern. Due for withdrawal, their replacement began in 2009–11 with *Hyuga* and *Ise*, larger still, with a full-length flight decks and capacity for up to 18 helicopters.

Like the *Shiranes*, they were classed as helicopter destroyers. This official designation, unique to the Japanese Navy, is necessary because Japan's constitution bars the construction of weapons beyond those essential for national defence. A destroyer comes into this category while an aircraft carrier, with its obvious offensive potential, does not. However, the resemblance of the *Hyūga*-class to the ships being built for various navies as helicopter platforms, with or without a docking facility as well, was clear, and although ASW was still noted as the main purpose, they were also equipped to act as flagships for command and control in tactical situations, making them in effect as suitable for tactical operations as the British, French and Italian and Spanish helicopter carriers.

In one respect at least they were superior, with a speed in excess of 30 knots (55.5km/h; 34.5mph). The *Izumo*-class, while sharing the helicopter destroyer designation, represents a further step. They are the largest warships built in Japan since World War II. *Kaga* is the second ship in the class; its name, that of an original province, was also borne

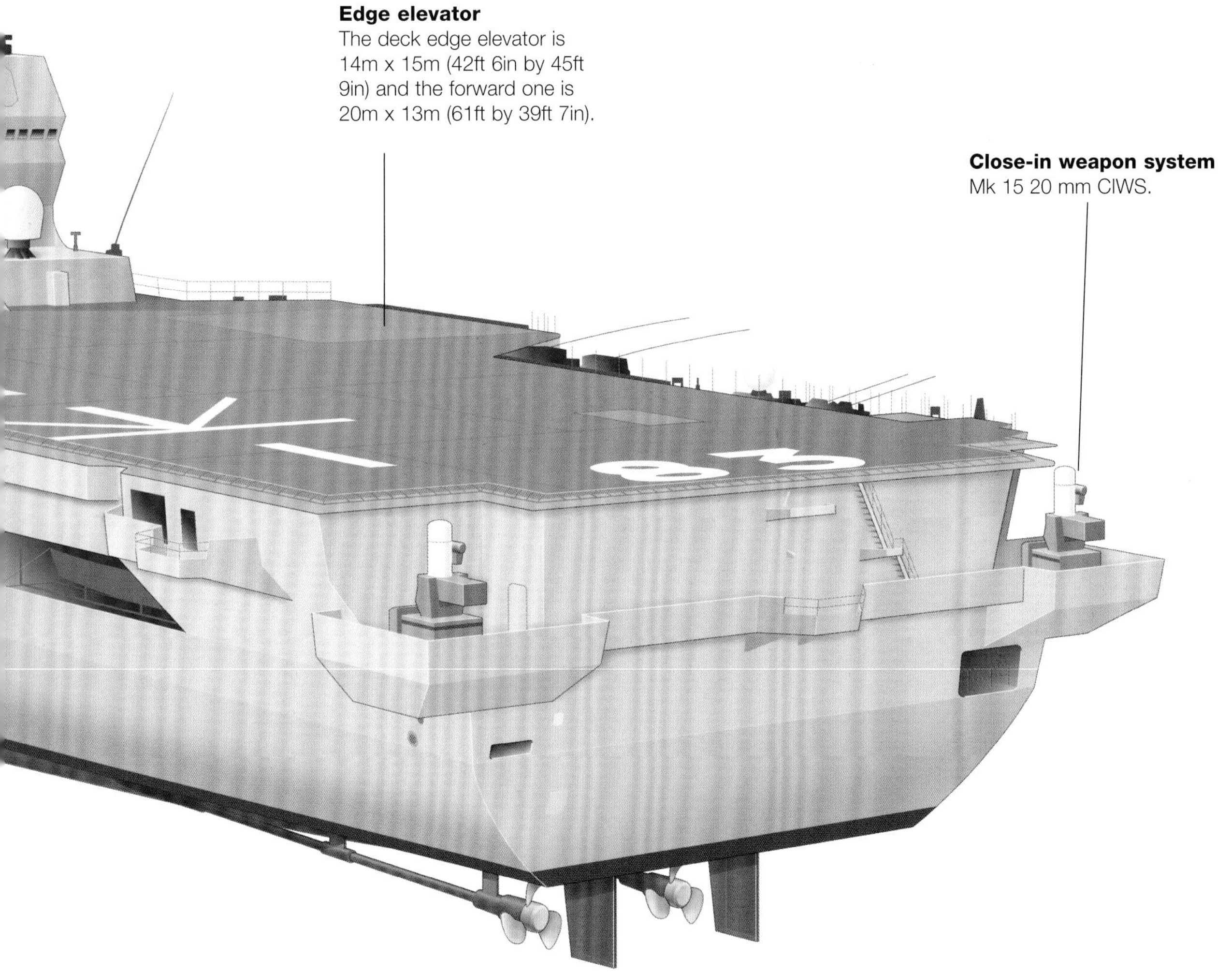

Izumo at sea. Unlike US ships, the Japanese carriers are rarely depicted with aircraft parked on the flight deck.

Specification

Dimensions:	Length: 248m (814ft); Beam: 38m (125ft); Draught: 7.5m (25ft)
Displacement:	19,800 tonnes (19,500 tons); 27,432 tonnes (27,000 tons) full load
Propulsion:	COGAG system, 4 LM2500IEC gas turbines, 2 shafts
Speed:	30 knots (55.5km/h; 34.5mph)
Range:	Not disclosed
Armament:	2 Phalanx CIWS; 2 SeaRAM missile launchers
Aircraft:	28
Complement:	470

by the World War II carrier involved in the attack on Pearl Harbor in 1941 before Japan declared war on the USA. *Kaga* was laid down at the Japan Marine United yard at Yokohama on 7 October 2013 and launched on 27 August 2015, with commissioning anticipated for March 2017. *Izumo* was commissioned on 25 March 2015, at a cost of 114 billion yen.

The island is 70m (213ft) long, five levels high, midships-situated and virtually windowless except for the navigation bridge and flight control point. It carries a high pole mast, tilted slightly sternwards and with double bracketed yardarms to support the multiplicity of antennas and aerials. A squat, square-format funnel takes up exhaust gases. The flight deck has five landing spots and can engage in simultaneous take-off and landing action. Two lifts are fitted, one on the centreline by the island and the other abaft the island on the starboard deck edge. The ships have the ability to embark up to 400 troops plus equipment and around 50 3.5-tonne (3.5-ton) military vehicles, admitted via ramp on the starboard side. Each vessel also houses a 35-bed hospital with a surgical suite.

ASW function

The steady build-up of China's submarine strength has kept the JMSDF's submarine detection skills both challenged and well-honed, and ASW is the prime function of the *Izumo*-class, although HADR relief operation is also emphasized. Defensive armament comprises two 20mm Phalanx CIWS mountings and two Mk 31 RIM-116 Sea-RAM missile launchers. The forward CIWS is set on the starboard side of the flight deck and all other weapons are mounted on sponsons or on the island. Apart from the capacities of their own helicopters, the ships will normally be deployed with an escort force of both surface ships and submarines to ensure further defensive power.

While up to 28 helicopters can be carried with deck parking, the normal number carried is around 14, and the basic peacetime complement is said to be seven SH-60K ASW helicopters built by Mitsubishi, or seven Agusta-Westland MCM 101 mine countermeasure helicopters. *Kaga* and *Izumo* can carry many other types, including the Bell-Boeing V-22 Osprey tilt-rotor plane, which has been ordered by the Japanese defence ministry, and has a span with rotors turning of 25.78m (84ft 6in) and a maximum gross take-off weight of 23,859kg (52,600lb). Five landing spots are marked out on the flight deck. It has been noted that the flight deck is arranged in such a way that adaptation for V/STOL aircraft operation would be readily possible. Despite their lack of catapult launchers, the ships may also be used for launching certain types of UAV, but nothing is known about whether such capacity is envisaged.

Izumo and *Kaga* are both driven by a COGAG system with four GE/IHI LM2500IEC integrated electronic control gas turbines turning two shafts. Four LM500 turbines generate each ship's electric power. A top speed in excess of 30 knots (55.5km/h; 34.5mph) makes the Japanese ships faster than most amphibious warfare ships and enables them to keep up with an American nuclear carrer strike force – Japan's Maritime Self Defence Force collaborates closely with the US Seventh Fleet – as well as making it easier to launch STOVL planes.

With its two smaller *Hyuga*-class helicopter destroyers, Japan now has four such ships. Eastern Asia is often described as the world's most rapidly militarizing region, and the increasing size and capacity of the JMSDF is backed by the strategic aim of maintaining a defensive power to protect what the Japanese government sees as the nation's vital interests.

Stern view of *Izumo*. Japan's helicopter destroyers can accommodate large aircraft like the MV-22 Osprey of the US Marine Corps.

Future planning

The next step for the expansion of the JMSDF is for a larger ship that will be an air-capable landing dock ship, with a full length flight deck. Such a ship, perhaps based on the USS *Wasp* type, successors to *Tarawa*, would be capable of defending outlying islands with a full range of amphibious action. Although it could be capable of launching V/STOL planes it would fall short of being a strike weapon, and it does not seem likely that Japan would currently contemplate the construction of a carrier whose prime purpose would be a capacity for attack. The Japanese government places strong reliance on its military treaties with the USA and the presence of the US Seventh Fleet in preserving stability in its region.

HMS Queen Elizabeth (2017)

The two ships of the *Queen Elizabeth* class will be the largest carriers and largest warships built for the Royal Navy.

As is not unusual in present-day shipbuilding, several shipyards participated in construction, with BAE Systems as preferred prime contractor and Thales UK as key equipment supplier. All contractors are enrolled in the Aircraft Carrier Alliance to ensure effective co-ordination of supply and assembly from multiple sources. The combined cost of both ships is currently £6.2 billion. CAD modelling enabled all contractors to follow the structure as it grew.

Queen Elizabeth is assembled from nine main blocks, with construction beginning on 7 July 2009, although design work had already been in hand for ten years. Final assembly was done at Rosyth Naval Dockyard in Scotland. The ship was named at Rosyth on 4 July 2014 and floated out of dry dock on 17 July. Fitting out was then put in hand.

Sea trials are expected to start in March 2017, with commissioning intended for May 2017. However, the ship

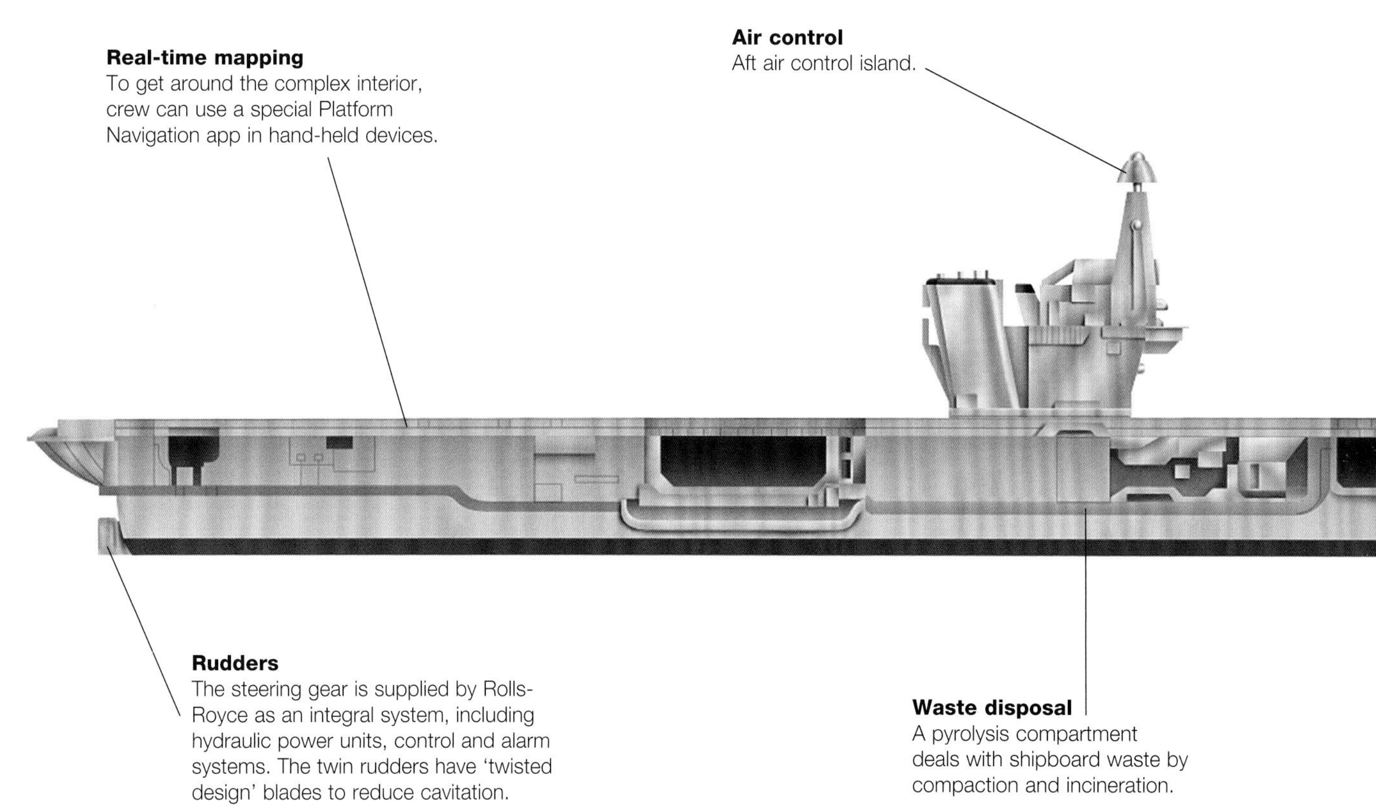

The Royal Navy has little to learn from the Chinese Navy about how to keep silent about what it does not wish to be known, but basic details of the QE-class, including the two islands, are entirely apparent.

is unlikely to be fully operational until 2020. The design is novel, with two island units to starboard, separated by a deck-edge lift. The forward island, for ship control, is topped by a long-range radar antenna and the rear one, for flight control, carries the mainmast (which can be lowered for passage under bridges) and Artisan 3D radar. This configuration is also claimed to reduce air turbulence over the flight deck. Each island supports uptakes from the forward and after gas turbine power-plants.

Fifty-year life

The nine-deck hull design, containing over 3000 compartments, has been planned for a 50-year service life. It does not have side armour or armoured bulkheads. The flight deck is axial with a maximum width of 73m

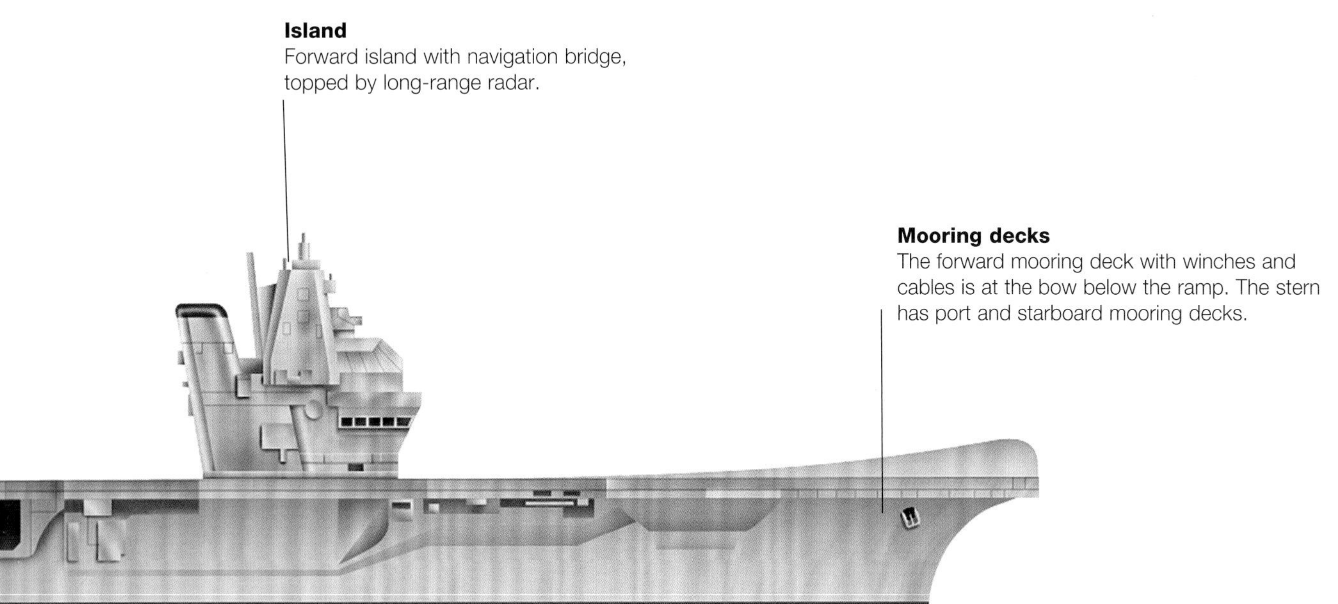

Both ships are STOVL type carriers, intended to embark the Lockheed-Martin F-35C multi-role jet, itself still completing development as the carriers near completion.

Queen Elizabeth fitting out at Rosyth Dockyard, sometime in 2016.

(222ft) narrowing to a 13° take-off ramp 6m (18ft 4in) high. Its total area is 19,000m² (204,514sq ft) with some sections, approximately 2000m² (21,500sq ft) given a specially-developed thermal coating of aluminium and titanium alloy capable of withstanding a temperature of 1500°C (2730°F) in order to support the F-35B Lightning II jet fighter. There are 12 deck positions that can service either fixed or rotary wing aircraft. In general the design has incorporated the likelihood of retrofitting or installing of new technology over the next five decades.

Lean-manning is an essential feature of these carriers. A crew of 679, no greater than that of the much smaller *Invincible*-class, can operate the ship due to extensive automation and the use of bulk handling, palletized loads, specialist mechanical equipment and computerized inventory controls. The 'highly mechanized weapons handling system' is based on commercial warehouse picking and conveying systems, controlled from one central point.

Actions are greatly speeded up, with the ship capable of taking on full provisions with 12 operators within an eight-hour shift, a task that formerly took days, if not weeks, for much larger numbers. Crew cabins are six-berth but can be adapted to eight-berth if troop-carrying is necessary. Four galleys provide food, and a cinema and fitness suites are also installed. Reverse osmosis desalination equipment provides 500 tonnes (492 tons) of fresh water daily and a pyrolysis chamber disposes of waste.

Specification

Dimensions:	Length: 284m (932ft); Beam: 72.97m (239ft 5in); Draught: 10.97m (36ft)
Displacement:	71,730 tonnes (70,600 tons)
Propulsion:	2 RR Marine Trent MT30 gas turbines, 2 shafts; 71,520kW (96,000shp)
Speed:	27 knots (50km/h; 31mph)
Range:	10,000nm (18,500km; 11,500 miles)
Armament:	3 Phalanx CIWS
Aircraft:	40
Complement:	1450

Powerplant

The integrated electric propulsion system is provided by Rolls-Royce MT30 gas turbines, said to be the most powerful in service in the world, and first used on the littoral combat ship USS *Freedom* in 2008. Alternators are supplied by GE, formerly Converteam. Two independent sets are mounted beneath each island, with two tandem 20MW advanced induction electric propulsion motors driving two fixed-pitch bronze propellers. Four Wärtsilä 38 diesels, two 12-cylinder and two 16-cylinder providing around 40MW, are also installed. A low-voltage electrical power system is distributed via 13 main switchboards and there is an emergency switchboard and 34 electrical distribution centres. The ship carries approximately 8600 tonnes (8464 tons) of fuel for its own engines and the air wing. Advanced technologies on board include the fixed fire-fighting system that discharges a mix of aqueous film forming foam and sea water in a pressure spray.

Despite its substantial size, bigger than the French *Charles de Gaulle*, *Queen Elizabeth* is not equipped with catapult launchers or arrester wires, and can only accommodate V/STOL aircraft. The air wing will consist of approximately 40 aircraft, and the designated planes are American Lockheed-Martin F-35Bs. A deployment is likely to involve anything between 12 and 24 F-35Bs and a mixture of helicopters, including Merlins, Chinooks, Apaches and Wildcats. It is also possible that one or both ships will be adapted to carry landing craft for vehicles and personnel (LCVP) in their boat bays.

The functional aspects of Command, Information, Communication and Air Management and Protection are combined in a fully integrated system. CCTV throughout the ship uses 220 cameras, monitored at 24 work-stations. Internal communication is effected by self-powered telephones, 2000 broadcast and alarms speakers, and 'Leaky Feeder' wireless system. Air Group Management Application software is under development to assist in planning complex flying programmes, organize deck movement of various aircraft types and programme weapons, aircraft and aircrew for round-the-clock action.

The primary role of the ships, of which only one will be in service at any time, except in emergency, is defined as 'carrier-enabled power projection' and as a 'rapidly deployable sovereign base to deliver expeditionary air operations.' In 2004 this was described by Britain's naval head as an air wing of 36 fighters, with a rate of 75 sorties per flying day. By 2016 it was quoted as 110 sorties. The concept of versatility is often mentioned but not explained in any detail, although 'soft power', as in disaster relief, is regularly cited.

The role of armour

One of the most striking aspects of carrier design in the later twentieth and twenty-first centuries is the virtual elimination of what was once considered an essential aspect: the provision of armoured protection. Care is taken in such aspects as fire-proofing and damage control, with far more powerful systems than existed on World War II carriers, and internal materials are selected for fire resistance, but hulls and decks are relatively thin. Many carriers are built to merchant ship hull standards, much less robust than traditional warship practice. The reasons for this change include the huge cost of an armoured ship of 100,000 tonne-plus, the propulsive power needed to drive it at carrier speeds, and the deep draught it would have. But modern armament and countermeasures also play a part. Weapons now have vastly more destructive force than the shells and torpedoes of 70 years ago, and to armour a ship against direct hits would be impossible. Instead the carrier must rely on the firepower of its escort vessels, and on the effectiveness of its own anti-missile defences to stop any attack before it strikes home.

The bulk of the *Queen Elizabeth* overhangs the sides of the dry dock in which its parts were assembled.

USS Gerald R. Ford (2017)

The first of a new generation of nuclear-powered super-carriers, this ship is intended to maintain and extend the US Navy's preponderance for decades to come.

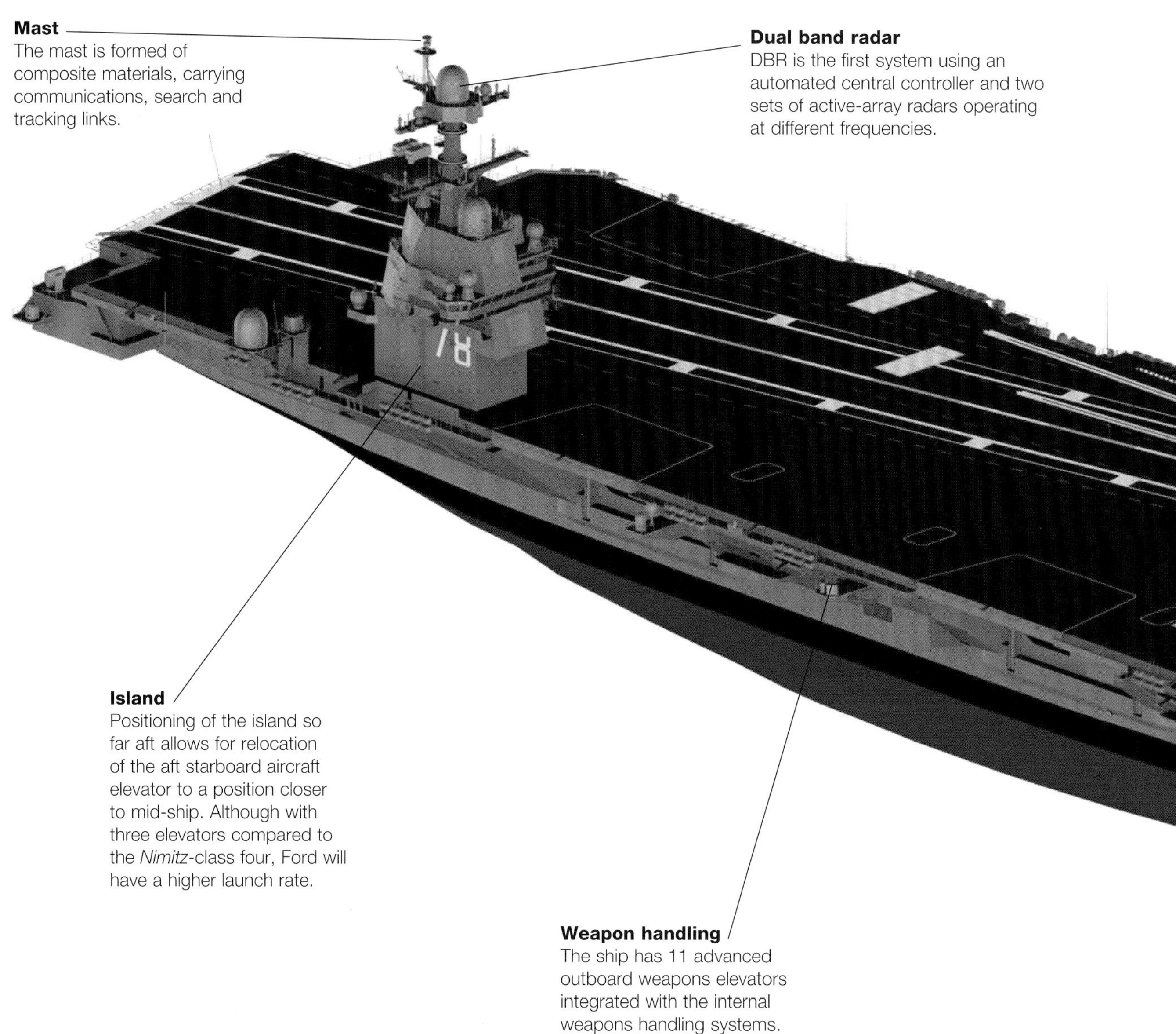

As of early 2017, the multi-billion-dollar *Ford* is known as a 'pre-commissioning unit' (PCU). The island is set notably far towards the stern.

The USA's ten *Nimitz*-class super-carriers form by far the largest 'power projection' capacity of any country. Yet with the ships requiring periods out of action for appraisals, inspections, overhauls and modifications, the number available for service can barely fulfil the required schedule of duties, which includes the stationing of at least one in the Pacific and another in the Middle East, with maximum deployments lasting six or seven months. The *Gerald R. Ford*-class, initially of three ships, is planned to supplement the Nimitzes, enabling requirements to be met with more flexibility and anticipating the retirement of the oldest ships.

Ford (CVN-78) was ordered on 10 September 2008, laid down at Newport News on 13 November 2009 and launched on 9 November 2013. Modular construction techniques were used, with almost 500 sections built in different parts of the shipyard, or elsewhere, assembled in a vast dry-dock with the assistance of a 1050-tonne (1033-ton) gantry crane, and welded together. The ship's crew moved on board in August 2015 to begin the process of bringing the vast assemblage into a cohesive and effective warship. With a construction cost topping $13 billion it is the most expensive warship yet built. Over a 50-year operational life, the ship is said to save $4 billion in 'total ownership cost' through its designed ability to need a smaller crew (almost 700 fewer than on a *Nimitz*) and air wing personnel (400 fewer) due to the use of smart-system automated techniques and modular equipment, with very extensive use of software. Future installation of new or updated systems, including direct energy weapons, is provided for in the basic design. *Ford* is the first super-carrier to have all-electric power for its machinery and to need no high-maintenance steam pipes. More than 3 million metres (9.8 million feet) of electric cable and 1.22 million metres (3.9 million feet) of fibre optic cable thread the vessel.

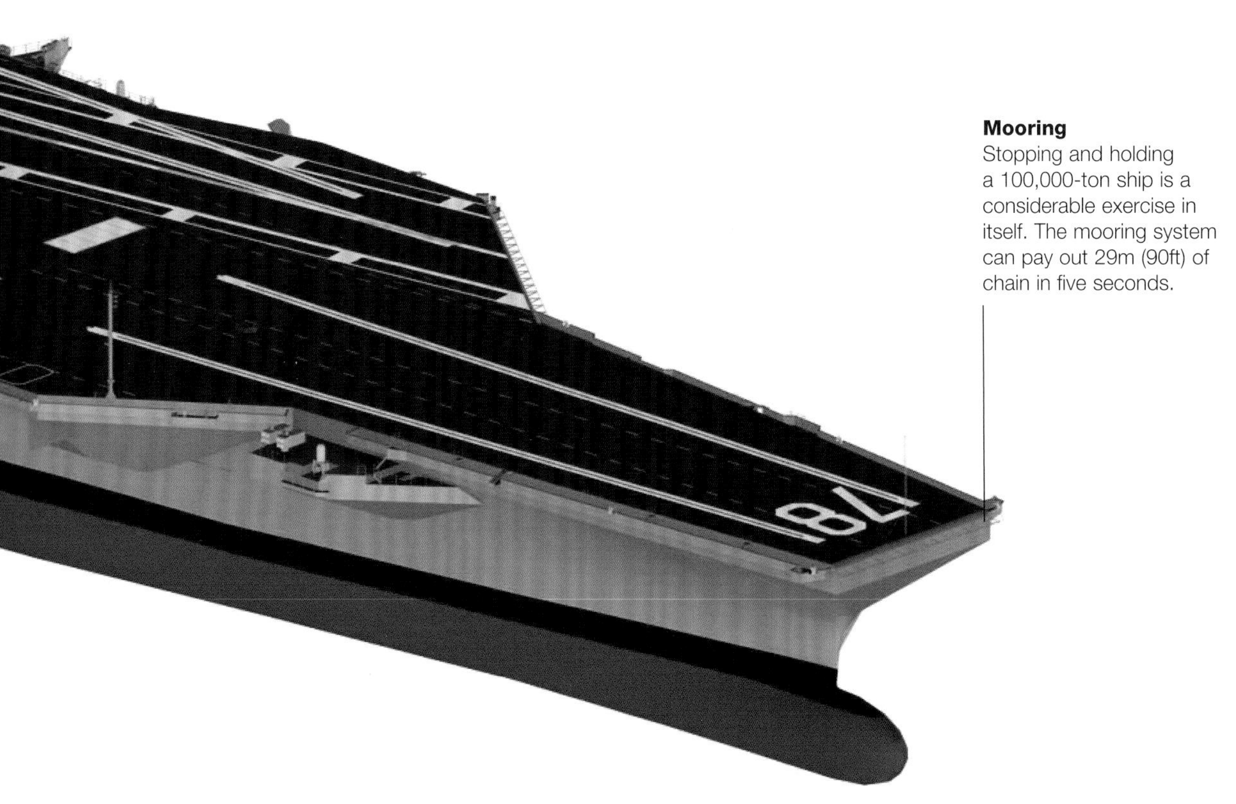

Mooring
Stopping and holding a 100,000-ton ship is a considerable exercise in itself. The mooring system can pay out 29m (90ft) of chain in five seconds.

Gerald R. Ford in the James River, the anchorage for the National Defense Reserve Fleet, 11 June 2016.

The island is smaller than on the Nimitzes, although 6m (20ft) higher than on *Ronald Reagan*, positioned well aft and canted outwards. Each crew berthing area will hold 86 personnel, compared to 200 on *Nimitz*-class carriers, and will have adjacent washroom facilities. Recreation areas, fitness suites and full air-conditioning of crew spaces are all provided, with an eye on six-month deployments that might be spent wholly at sea. *Ford* is powered by two new-generation A1B reactors (their total power output undisclosed) built by Bechtel Marine Propulsion Corp., driving four propellers. The reactors will require refuelling only once after approximately 25 years. The four main turbine generators built by Northrop Grumman Marine Systems form a power-plant said to provide more than three times the electrical power of previous carriers, although *Ford*'s new operating and weapons systems will require it all.

Specification

Dimensions:	Length: 337m (1106ft); Beam: 41m (134ft); Draught: 12m (39ft)
Displacement:	approx 101,600 tonnes (100,000 tons)
Propulsion:	Two A1B nuclear reactors, 4 steam turbines
Speed:	30 knots (56km/h; 35mph)
Range:	Unlimited
Armament:	2 RIM-162 ESSM; 2 RIM-116 RAM; 3 Phalanx CIWS
Aircraft:	75
Complement:	4317

EMALS catapults

The flight deck area is 20,234m^2 (217,796sq ft) with four launch positions, two at the bow and two amidships, as with the *Nimitz*-class. In combat operations the ship can simultaneously launch at least two aircraft while landing a third. A key feature is the four linear-drive electromagnetic launch system (EMALS) catapults fitted instead of the steam catapults used on previous carriers, whose design, although much enhanced, goes back to the 1950s. While promising great improvements in reliability and efficiency, development has had to overcome many problems. The precision aircraft landing system (PALS) already in use on the *Nimitz*-class has been upgraded. Advanced Arresting Gear incorporating water-twister components is installed. The aim is to achieve an increase of 33 per cent in the sortie generation rate of strike aircraft over the *Nimitz*-class.

COTS (commercial off-the-shelf) computers and components are extensively used in *Ford*'s range of electronic systems. It possesses a new integrated warfare system and equally new dual band radar (DBR) combining AN/SPY-3 X band multi-function and AN/SPY-4 S band volume search radar. On-board defence systems comprise two improved RIM-162 Evolved Sea Sparrow surface-

On 26 January 2013, the giant Newport News crane lowers the carrier's 555-tonne (546-ton) island precisely into place.

to-air missile launchers, two RIM-116 RAM missile suites and three Phalanx CIWS. Beyond this, further potential armament includes free-electron laser (FEL) guns capable against airborne missiles and surface swarm-boat attacks.

The ship will carry around 75 aircraft, including both fighters and strike planes, as well as transport, reconnaissance and other specialist craft, including unmanned aerial vehicles (UAV). The basis of the air wing will be the F-35C carrier variant (fitted for CATOBAR) of the Lightning II Fighter, with stealth characteristics and hacking/jamming ability in addition to a formidable weaponry including AIM-120 AMRAAM air-to-air and air-to-surface guided missiles, two GBU-31 JDAM guided bombs, eight GBU-38 bombs and a 35mm GAU-22A series cannon. Its total payload is 8160kg (17,993lb) and its operational radius is 1100km (440 miles).

At the time of *Ford*'s planning, the Defence Department had introduced the strategic theme of 'transformation' to drive forward the incorporation of the most advanced technology in defence procurement. Extensive use of cutting-edge and innovative technology, undergoing test and trial even as the ship was under construction and requiring reassessments and modifications, has delayed the carrier's commissioning date. By January 2017 the ship was officially reported as 99 per cent overall complete. Planned initial deployment is in 2021. A second ship, USS *John F. Kennedy*, intended to replace USS *Nimitz* (CVN-68), is under construction, and a third – USS *Enterprise* – is currently programmed. It would seem that while construction of *Kennedy* goes ahead, installation of its electrical system will be held back, perhaps in order to ensure that the new and untried all-electrically-worked systems of *Gerald R. Ford* are fully tested in actual operating conditions. This is, after all, a warship class whose later ships are expected to last until 2105 or beyond.

Linear-drive electromagnetic launch system

The EMALS linear motor drive catapult system has been intensively tested at land bases, but its effectiveness on a carrier in service will be proved on *Gerald R. Ford*. Its advantages are numerous, including less strain on the ship's structure, a more compact structure in itself, a higher degree of efficiency and responsiveness to control and ability to launch lightweight aircraft including unmanned aerial vehicles, as well as the heaviest naval planes. Giving smoother, although extremely swift, acceleration puts much less stress on an aircraft frame than a steam catapult does. EMALS's demands on the ship's electric power supply, combined with those of sensor, handling and control systems, place it beyond the power of the *Nimitz*-class, and require the much greater power output of *Ford*'s reactors.

INS Vikrant (2018)

India's first home-built aircraft carrier is helping to expand and develop the country's military technology, but also suffering delays in commissioning.

A concept design for a 38,100-tonne (37,500-ton) carrier to be built in India was created by DCN of France in 1990 but has gone through a vast number of revisions. Design and construction of the ship was approved by the Indian government in January 2003. Variously known through the years of its planning as an Air Defence Ship and as Indigenous Aircraft Carrier, at least 4270 alterations to its General Arrangement drawings and over 1150 modifications to the hull structure were made prior to launching. The plans continue to be adapted and modified during the fitting-out process.

Vikrant was laid down at Cochin Shipyard, Kochi, on 28 February 2009 and launched on 12 August 2013. Operationally it is a STOBAR carrier, fitted with a bow ramp to assist short take-off planes and with three arrester wires to allow them to land. Two deck-edge lifts are mounted to starboard. The hull and flight deck are constructed from Indian-forged steel: DMR 249 Grade A for the hull and DMR 249 Grade B, which has greater elasticity, for the flight deck. Other special steels are used in the engine room and magazine areas. Construction is of modular type, formed from around 870 blocks, to a well-established standard carrier plan with an angled landing deck and a large island on the starboard side.

Vikrant's power source is non-nuclear, with four GE LM2500+ G4 aeroderivative gas turbines driving two propeller shafts, with a speed of 28 knots (51.8km/h; 32.2mph). Diesel alternators will prove 24MW of electric power for the ship's requirements. A high proportion of the technological equipment, which includes much in the way of automated systems, is Indian-made, including the main switchboard, the steering gear, the air-conditioning and refrigeration systems, the main gear boxes, the pumps and the integrated platform management systems.

There is capacity for 36 aircraft, although hangar space for only 17. The aircraft complement will be formed from multi-role Mikoyan MiG 29K folding-wing STOL planes and Ka-31 AEW and Ka-28 ASW helicopters, as well as HAL-Dhruv general utility helicopters. Indian-built Hindustan Aeronautics Ltd (HAL) Tejas planes have reportedly been turned down for use on *Vikrant* as too heavy, although they may be deployed on the second ship of the class, which is likely to be a larger vessel fitted with catapults. Russia is supplying the aviation facilities, comprising aviation armament, stationary and mobile systems and all

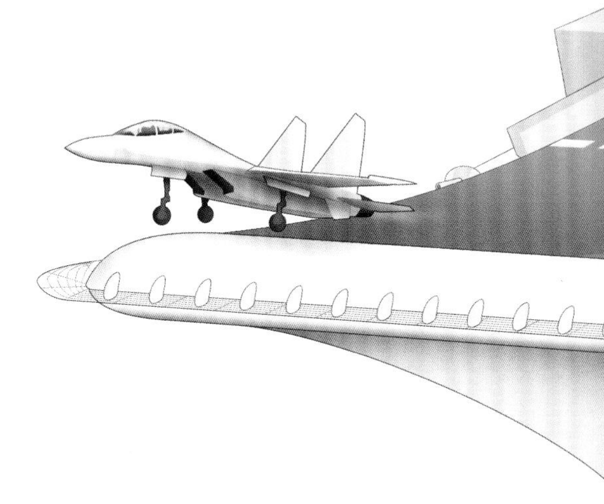

Vikrant **is a STOBAR carrier, capable of handling short take-off aircraft, but without a catapult.**

equipment relating to onboard servicing. The MiG 29K is likely to be the carrier's prime weapon. Introduced in 2010 and described as a fourth-generation ++ aircraft, this plane is the successor of the long-serving Sukhoi Su-33. Military co-operation agreements have also been signed between India and the USA. These are unlikely to impact on the completion of *Vikrant* but may have greater influence on the successor vessel, *Vishal*, currently under construction.

Sensory and directional equipment will consist of C/D band early warning radar, V/UHF tactical air navigational and direction finding systems and carrier control approach radar. Selex Sistemi of Italy are supplying RAN-40L three-

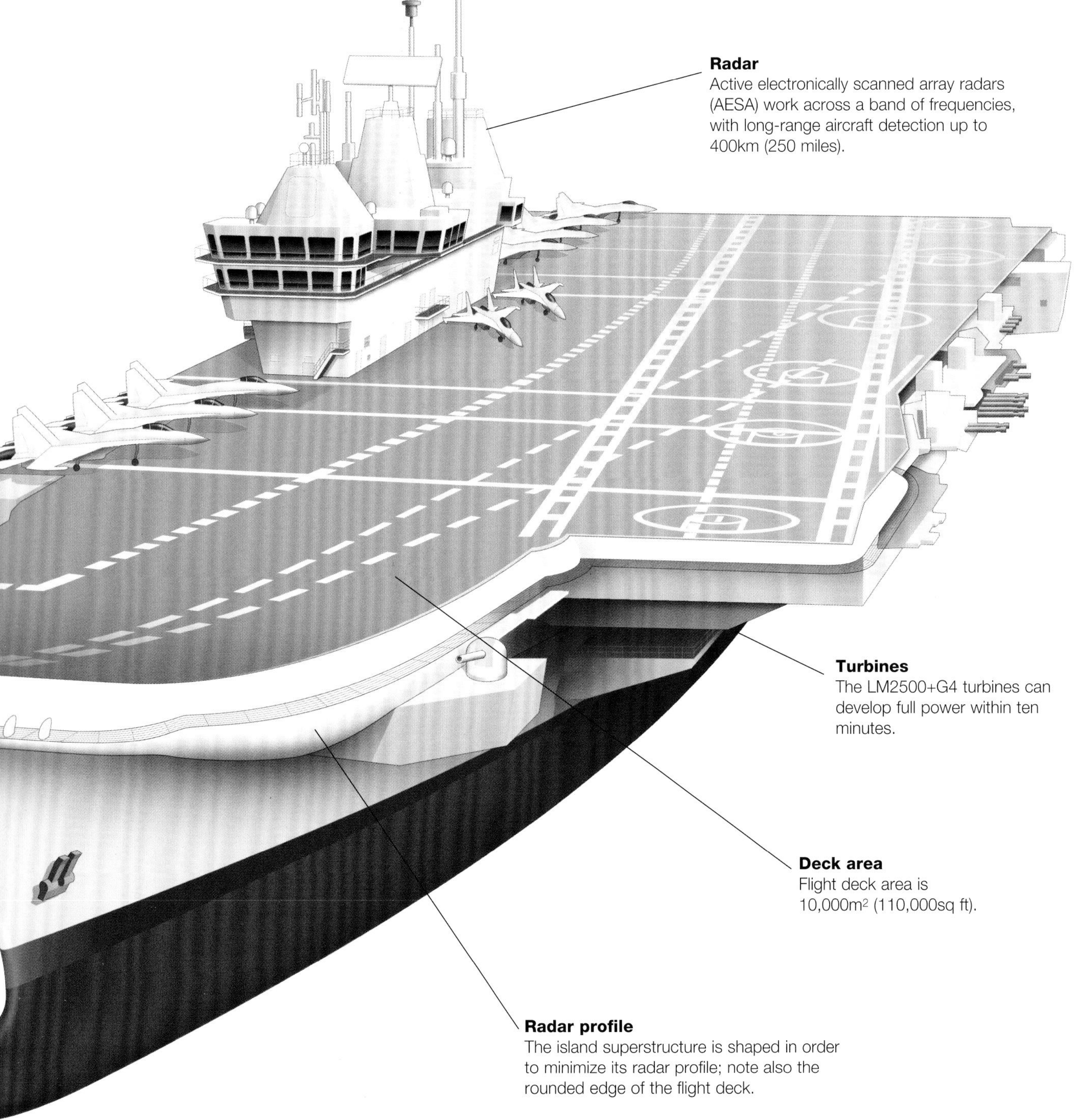

Radar
Active electronically scanned array radars (AESA) work across a band of frequencies, with long-range aircraft detection up to 400km (250 miles).

Turbines
The LM2500+G4 turbines can develop full power within ten minutes.

Deck area
Flight deck area is 10,000m^2 (110,000sq ft).

Radar profile
The island superstructure is shaped in order to minimize its radar profile; note also the rounded edge of the flight deck.

The newly-launched hull of *Vikrant* is towed away to its fitting-out berth, 12 August 2013.

dimensional L Band surveillance radar for long-range early warning. An Israeli EL/M-2248 MF-STAR (multi-function surveillance, track and guidance radar) is also being installed. An Indian-manufactured Combat Management System will integrate the ship's defences.Two Israeli-built Barak air defence missiles are to be installed, with 16-cell vertical launch systems and long-range guidance system with multi-function radar. For closer-range air defence Russian AK-630 CIWS will be provided. In adddition, four Italian OTO Melara 76mm (3in) Super Rapid guns, firing 120 rounds a minute at a range of 300km (186 miles), will be mounted.

Specification

Dimensions:	Length: 259m (850ft); Beam: 58m (190ft) ; Draught: 8.4m (28ft)
Displacement:	38,100 tonnes (37,500 tons); 40,640 tonnes (40,000 tons) full load
Propulsion:	4 GE LM2500+ gas turbines, 2 shafts; 80,000kW (107,281hp)
Speed:	28 knots (52km/h; 32mph)
Range:	7500 nm (13,875km; 8625 miles) at 18 knots (33.3km/h; 20.7mph)
Armament:	4 OTO Melara 3 in (76mm) DP guns, Barak 1 and Barak 8 SAM launchers, AK-630 CIWS
Aircraft:	36
Complement:	1560

Revised timetable

India's stated aim is to eliminate dependence on outside sources for its own defence, and *Vikrant* certainly marks a significant step forward in this. Another aim is to have at least two carriers in the fleet, for each of the country's two coastlines, an ambition that will not be realized for some time, as to maintain two ships in constant availability requires a third, to allow for periods of maintenance and refit. As of 2017, the *Vikrant* project has fallen substantially behind its original and revised timetables, and there are conflicting forecasts of service entry date. India's Comptroller and Auditor General (CAG) published a report in July 2016 listing a range of delays because of design amendments, problems with the supply of equipment and failure to keep the procurement process on time. The slow progress demonstrates the problems of building a carrier for the first time, with the difficulty of co-ordinating

The carrier's hull is decorated for the launch, and Cochin Shipyard workers gather to watch, on 12 August 2013.

Project 23000E

The Indian Navy is said to be planning a fourth carrier of equivalent size to the US *Nimitz*-class. While India appears determined to press on with its aim for self-sufficiency in military matters, it has also held discussions with both Russia and the United States about co-operation in future carrier development. The USA is already building the new-generation *Gerald R. Ford*-class CVN, and the Russians have unveiled a plan for Project 23000E 'Shtorm', a 101,600-tonne (100,000-ton) super-carrier that could have either nuclear or conventional propulsion. Russia is said to be more willing than the USA, France or Britain, which is also building two carriers, to pass on its latest technological advances.

a multiplicity of sub-contracts and the difficulties of liaison with international suppliers. If a handover to the Indian Navy is made in early 2019, the ship is likely to be still without most of its avionics and able to go through basic sea trials only, not at full load displacement. The cost has also escalated to 2,551,000,000 rupees ($3.6 billion).

India's actual plans for deployment and use of aircraft carriers have been widely speculated on. It has been pointed out that *Vikrant* and *Vishal* will carry only from 12 to 16 fighters, and even if operating in concert would have less strike power than the French *Charles de Gaulle* and much less than the USN *Nimitz*-class. Strategic experts consider this too modest for sustained 'power projection' on-shore. *Vikrant*'s at-sea endurance is reckoned at 45 days.

Ship Index

Page numbers in *italics* refer to illustration captions.

General Index

Index

Index